W9-AYM-975

Building Thinking Skills®

LEVEL 1

Critical Thinking Skills for Reading · Writing · Math · Science

Building Thinking Skills® Series
📖 Beginning 📖 Primary 📖 Level 1
📖 Level 2 📖 Level 3 Verbal 📖 Level 3 Figural

Written by
Sandra Parks
Howard Black

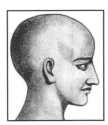

© 2006, 1997, 1984
THE CRITICAL THINKING CO.™
www.CriticalThinking.com
Phone: 800-458-4849 • Fax: 831-393-3277
P.O. Box 1610 • Seaside • CA 93955-1610
ISBN 978-1-60144-149-2

MIX
Paper from
responsible sources
FSC® C011935

Table of Contents

CHAPTER FOUR—FIGURAL CLASSIFICATIONS

CHAPTER FIVE—FIGURAL ANALOGIES

CHAPTER SIX—DESCRIBING THINGS

DESCRIBING SHAPES—SELECT

DIRECTIONS: Circle one word on each line to describe the shape.

EXAMPLE: This shape is

(tall)   short

(narrow)   and   wide

A-1   This shape is

tall   short

narrow   and   wide

A-2   This shape is

tall   short

narrow   and   wide

A-3   This shape is

tall   short

narrow   and   wide

A-4   This shape is

tall   short

and

narrow   wide

DESCRIBING SHAPES—SELECT

DIRECTIONS: Look at each shape. Say or write the number of square corners each shape has. Use the numbers in the choice box.

CHOICE BOX: 0, 1, 2, 3, 4, 5, 6

EXAMPLE: This is a square corner. ⌐

A-5

This shape has __**4**__ square corners.

A-6

This shape has____square corner.

A-7

This shape has____square corners.

A-8

This shape has____square corners.

A-9

This shape has____square corners.

DESCRIBING SHAPES—SELECT

DIRECTIONS: Say or write the number of corners each shape has. Say or write how many are square corners. Use the words in the choice box.

CHOICE BOX: all, none, one, two, three, four, five, six

EXAMPLE: This shape has ___three___ corners, and ___one___ is a square corner.

A-10

This shape has _____corners, and _____are square corners.

A-11

This shape has _____corners, and _____are square corners.

A-12

This shape has _____corners, and _____are square corners.

A-13

This shape has _____corners, and _____are square corners.

DESCRIBING SHAPES—SELECT

DIRECTIONS: Count how many sides each shape has. Circle the correct number. Say or write how many sides are the same length. Use the words and numbers in the choice box.

CHOICE BOX: all, none, 1, 2, 3, 4, 5, 6

A-14 EXAMPLE:

2   ③   5   6   sides

_____**2**_____ are the same length.

A-15

1   3   4   6   sides

_____ are the same length.

A-16

3   4   5   6   sides

_____ are the same length.

A-17

2   3   4   6   sides

_____ are the same length.

A-18

1   2   3   4   sides

_____ are the same length.

DESCRIBING SHAPES—SELECT

DIRECTIONS: Say or write how many sides each shape has. Then say or write how many sides are the same length. Use the words in the choice box.

CHOICE BOX: all, none, one, two, three, four, five, six

A-19

This shape has _____sides

and _____ are the same length.

A-20

This shape has _____sides

and _____ are the same length.

A-21

This shape has _____sides

and _____ are the same length.

A-22

This shape has _____sides

and _____ are the same length.

A-23

This shape has _____sides

and _____ are the same length.

DESCRIBING SHAPES—SELECT

DIRECTIONS: Say or write how many sides and corners each shape has. Say or write the name of each shape. Use the words in the choice box.

CHOICE BOX: hexagon, octagon, pentagon, rectangle, triangle, trapezoid

A-24

_____ sides　　　　_____ corners

This shape is named _____ .

A-25

_____ sides　　　　_____ corners

This shape is named _____ .

A-26

_____ sides　　　　_____ corners

This shape is named _____ .

A-27

_____ sides　　　　_____ corners

This shape is named _____ .

DESCRIBING SHAPES—EXPLAIN

DIRECTIONS: Describe each shape. Use complete sentences to say or write the description.

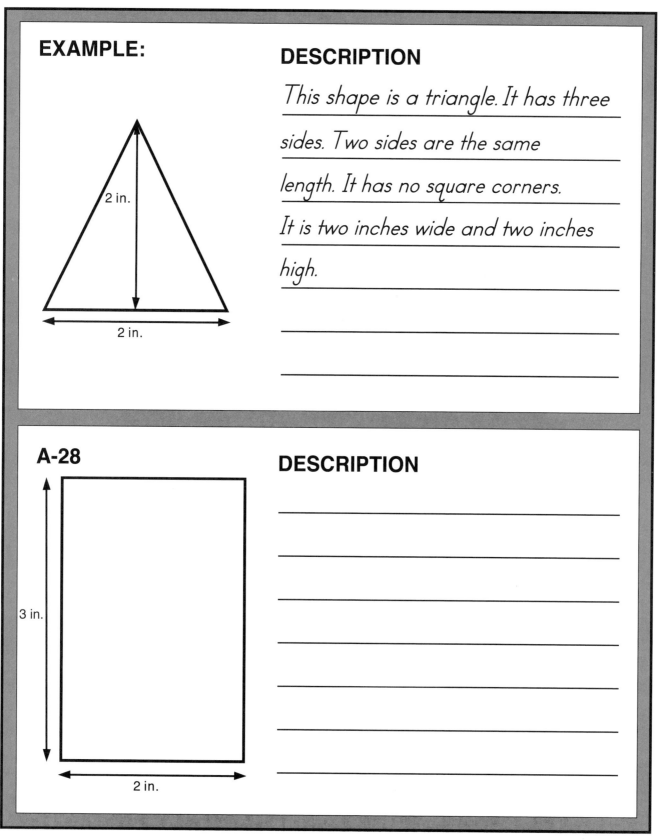

EXAMPLE:

2 in.

2 in.

DESCRIPTION

This shape is a triangle. It has three sides. Two sides are the same length. It has no square corners. It is two inches wide and two inches high.

A-28

3 in.

2 in.

DESCRIPTION

DESCRIBING SHAPES—EXPLAIN

DIRECTIONS: Describe each shape. Use complete sentences to say or write the description.

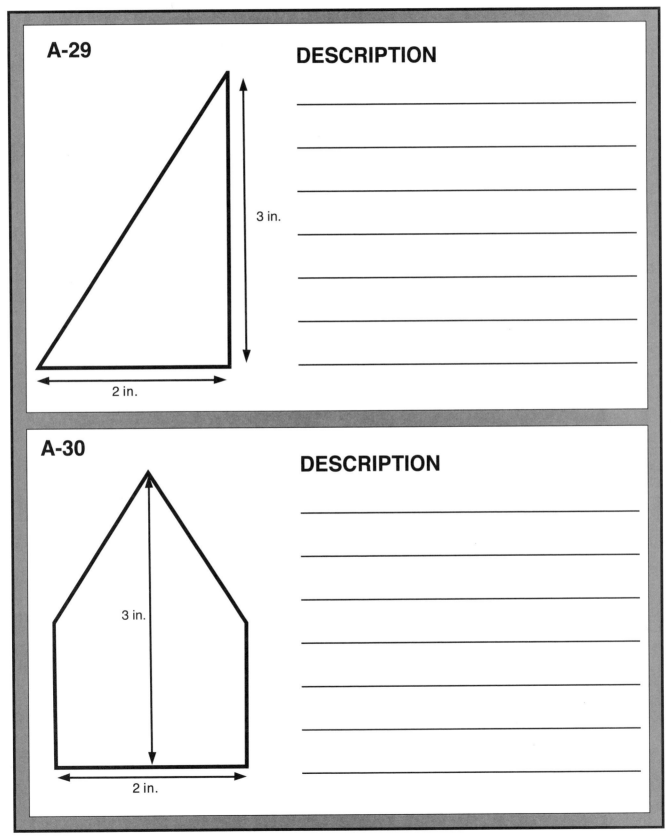

A-29

DESCRIPTION

3 in.

2 in.

A-30

DESCRIPTION

3 in.

2 in.

DESCRIBING SHAPES—EXPLAIN

DIRECTIONS: Say or write a description of the shape in the picture at the left. Use complete sentences.

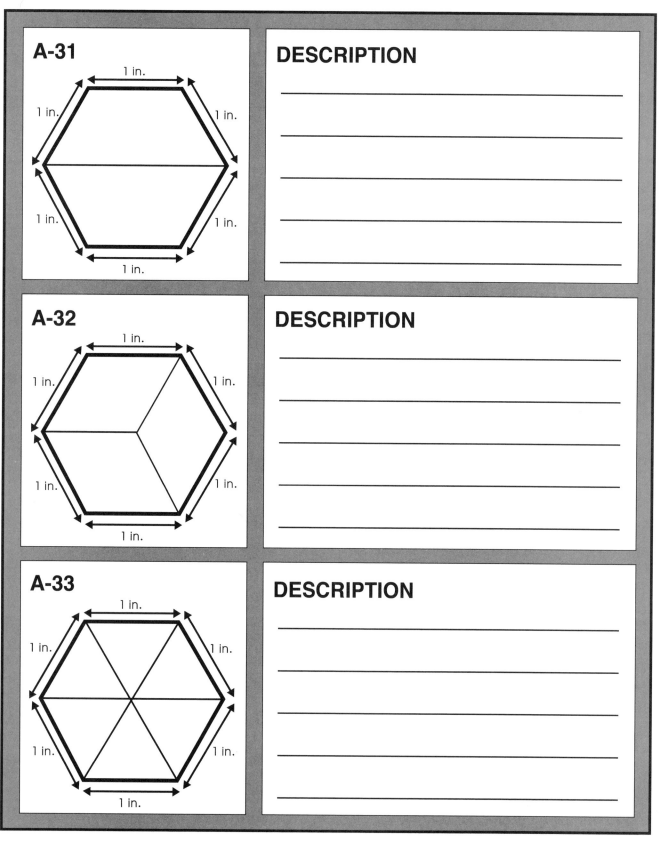

A-31

1 in.
1 in.   1 in.
1 in.   1 in.
1 in.

DESCRIPTION

_____

_____

_____

_____

_____

A-32

1 in.
1 in.   1 in.
1 in.   1 in.
1 in.

DESCRIPTION

_____

_____

_____

_____

A-33

1 in.
1 in.   1 in.
1 in.   1 in.
1 in.

DESCRIPTION

_____

_____

_____

_____

FOLLOWING DIRECTIONS

DIRECTIONS: Mark the shapes according to the directions.

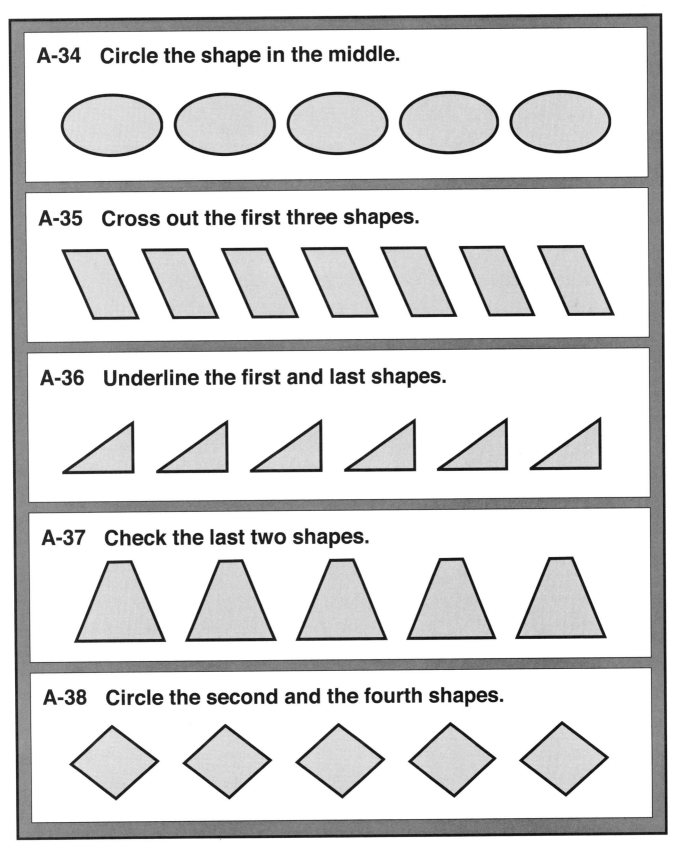

A-34   Circle the shape in the middle.

A-35   Cross out the first three shapes.

A-36   Underline the first and last shapes.

A-37   Check the last two shapes.

A-38   Circle the second and the fourth shapes.

FOLLOWING DIRECTIONS

DIRECTIONS: Mark the shapes according to the directions.

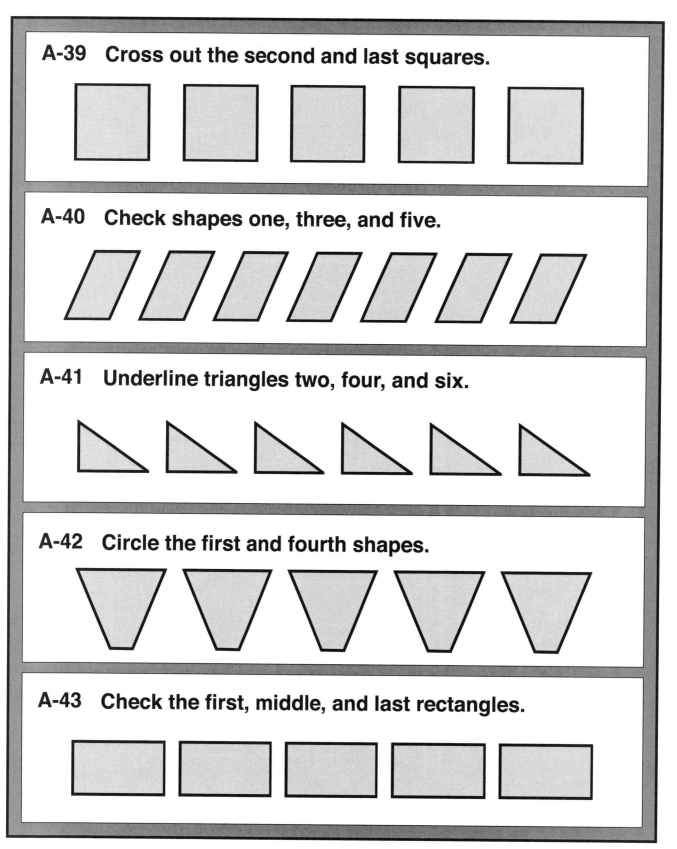

A-39 Cross out the second and last squares.

A-40 Check shapes one, three, and five.

A-41 Underline triangles two, four, and six.

A-42 Circle the first and fourth shapes.

A-43 Check the first, middle, and last rectangles.

GIVING DIRECTIONS

DIRECTIONS: Look at the shapes that are marked. Ask yourself, "How would I tell someone to mark the shapes this way?" Say or write the directions you would give.

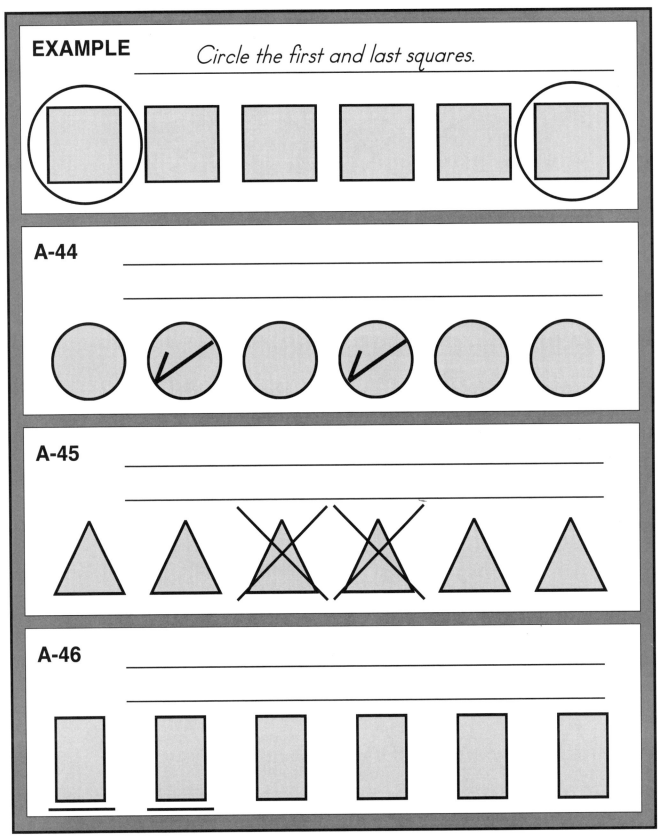

EXAMPLE   *Circle the first and last squares.*

A-44 _____

A-45 _____

A-46 _____

13

GIVING DIRECTIONS

DIRECTIONS: Look at the shapes that are marked. Ask yourself, "How would I tell someone to mark the shapes this way?" Say or write the directions you would give.

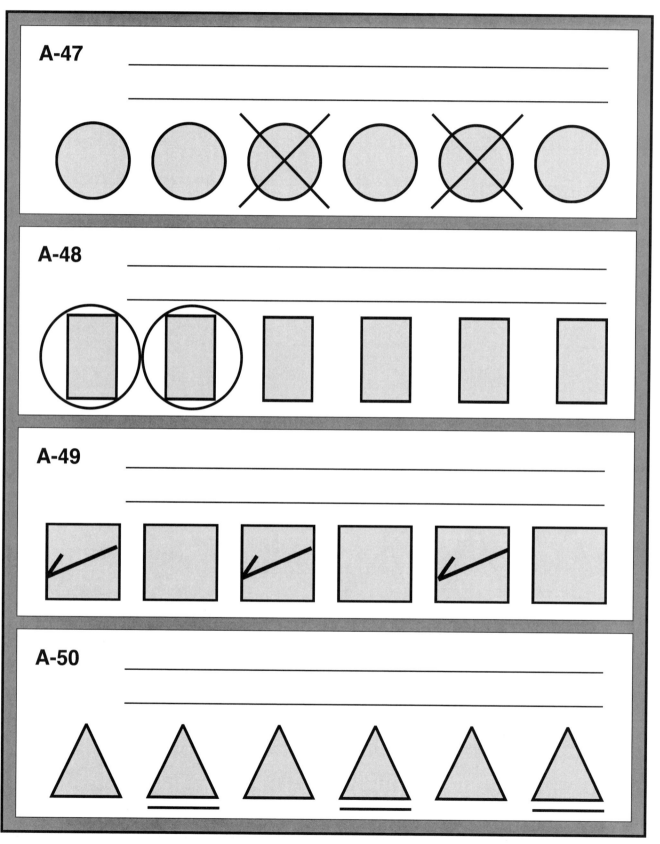

GIVING DIRECTIONS

DIRECTIONS: Decide how you want to mark the shapes. Say or write directions for marking them. (Exchange papers with a classmate and see if you can follow each other's directions.)

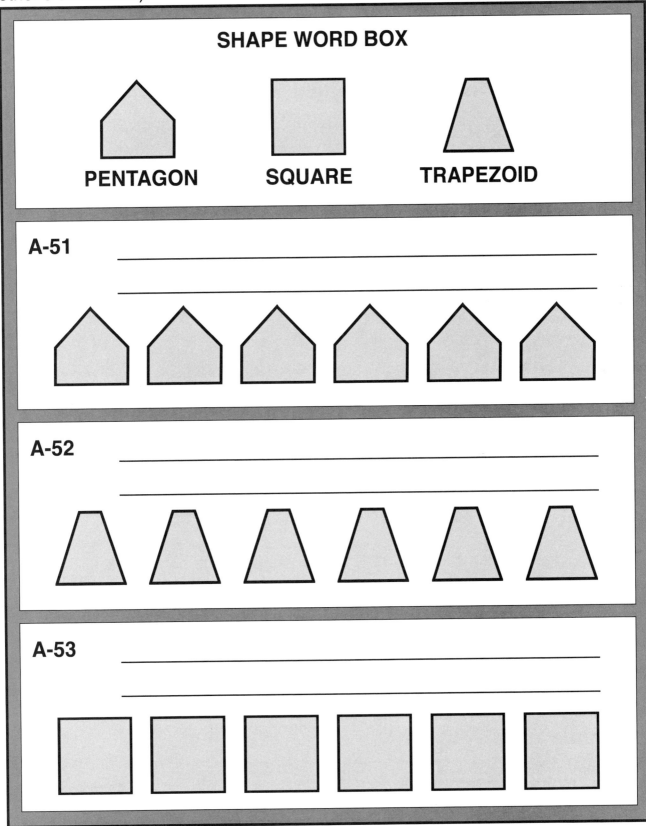

SHAPE WORD BOX

PENTAGON   SQUARE   TRAPEZOID

A-51 _____

A-52 _____

A-53 _____

DESCRIBING POSITION—A

INSTRUCTIONS: Complete the sentences with the correct words from the choice box. Say or write your answers. Draw a figure as directed.

CHOICE BOX

center   circle   left   right   square   triangle

A-54

The shape near the upper _____ corner is a circle. Near the lower right corner is a _____ .

Draw a white triangle near the upper right corner.

A-55

The shape in the center is a _____. Near the lower _____corner is a square.

Draw a white triangle near the upper right corner.

DESCRIBING POSITION—A

INSTRUCTIONS: Complete the sentences with the correct words from the choice box. Say or write your answers. Draw a figure as directed.

CHOICE BOX

center   circle   left   right   square   triangle

A-56

The shape near the upper _____ corner is a black square. Near the lower _____ corner is a white _____ .

Draw a black circle near the lower left corner.

A-57

The black rectangle is near the upper _____ corner. The white _____ is near the lower _____ corner.

Draw a black triangle near the upper left corner.

DESCRIBING POSITION—B

DIRECTIONS: Write a description of each set of blocks.

EXAMPLE

The gray block is above the white block. The black block is below the white block.

A-58

DESCRIBING POSITION—B

DIRECTIONS: Write a description of each set of blocks.

A-59

_____

_____

_____

_____

_____

A-60

_____

_____

_____

_____

CHARACTERISTICS OF A SHAPE

DIRECTIONS: Look at the triangle in the center of the diagram. Say or write four characteristics of the triangle. Use these characteristics to describe the triangle. Say your description or write it in the description box.

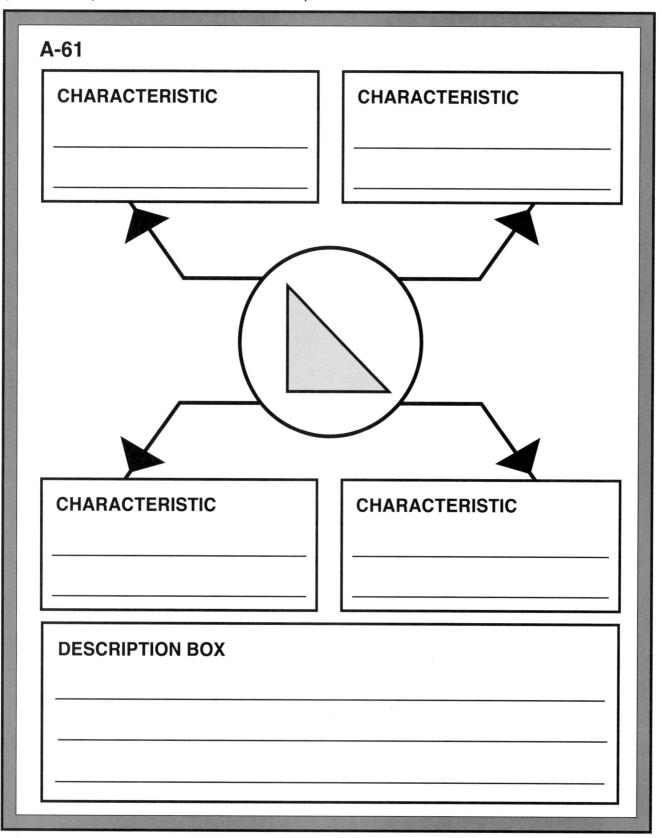

A-61

CHARACTERISTIC

_____

_____

CHARACTERISTIC

_____

_____

CHARACTERISTIC

_____

_____

CHARACTERISTIC

_____

_____

DESCRIPTION BOX

_____

_____

_____

CHARACTERISTICS OF A SHAPE

DIRECTIONS: Look at the trapezoid in the center of the diagram. Say or write four characteristics of the trapezoid. Use these characteristics to describe the trapezoid. Say your description or write it in the description box.

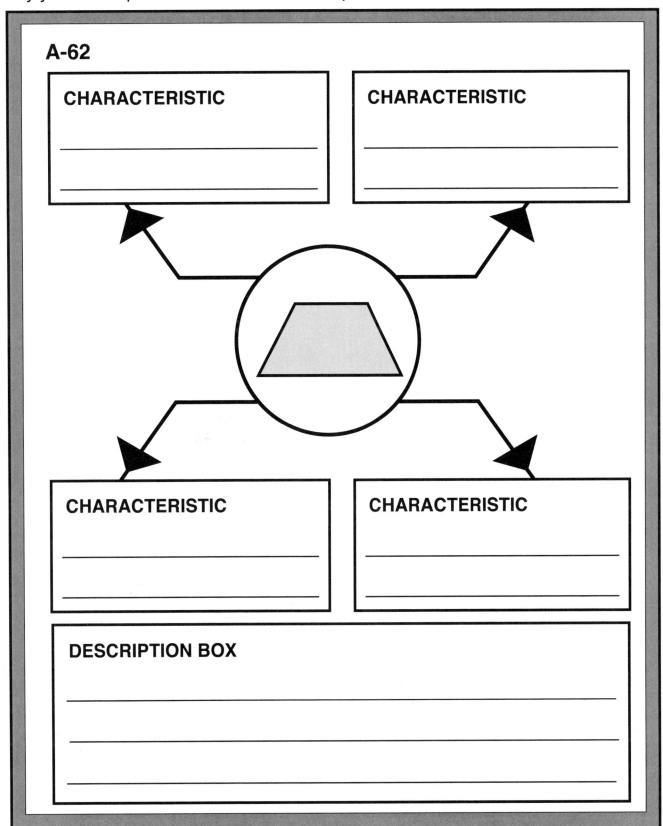

A-62

CHARACTERISTIC

CHARACTERISTIC

CHARACTERISTIC

CHARACTERISTIC

DESCRIPTION BOX

CHAPTER TWO

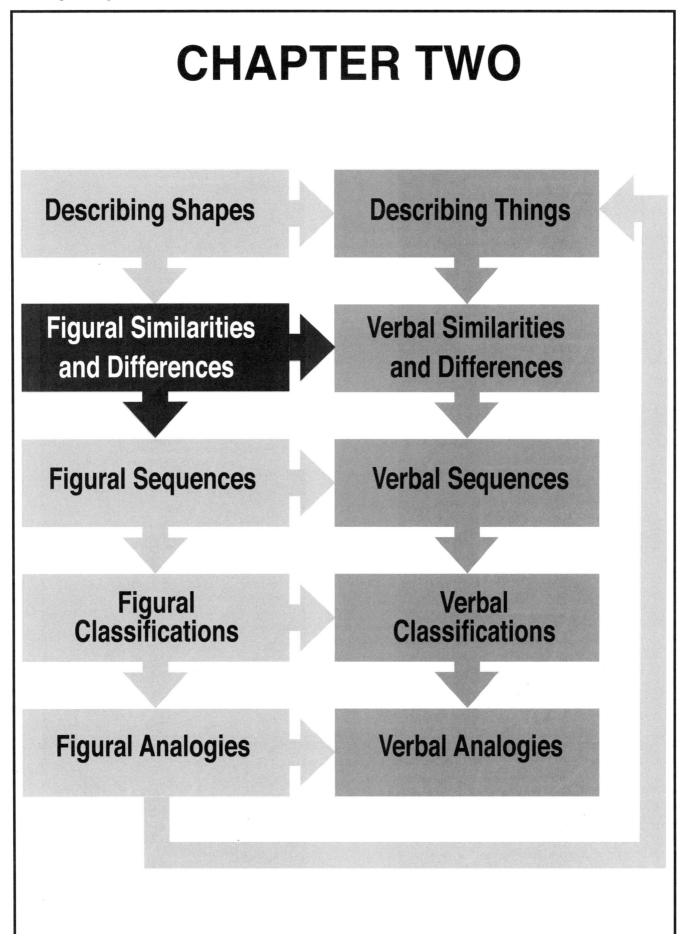

MATCHING SHAPES

DIRECTIONS: In each row, circle the shape that matches the one at the left.

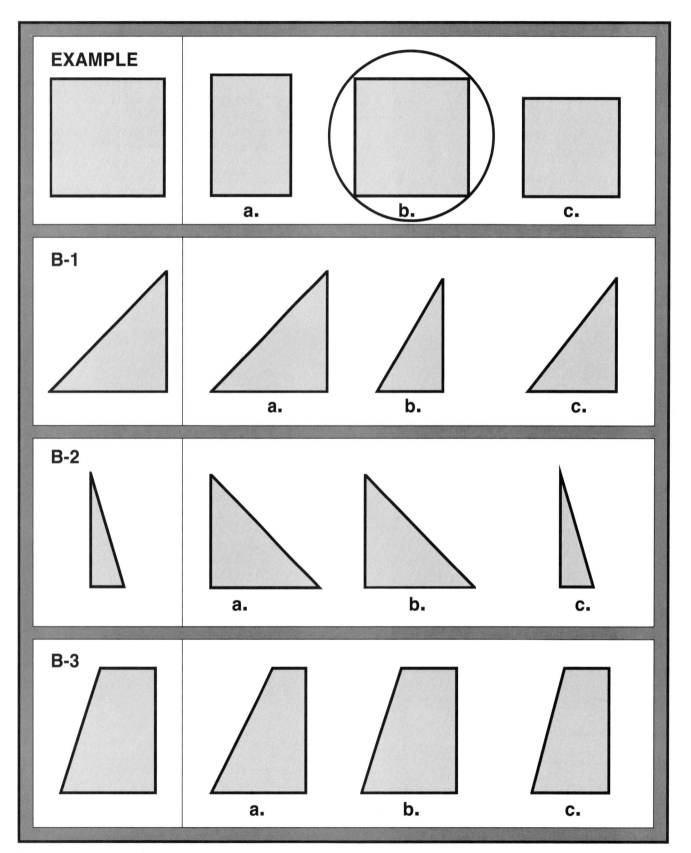

EXAMPLE

a.   b.   c.

B-1

a.   b.   c.

B-2

a.   b.   c.

B-3

a.   b.   c.

MATCHING SHAPES

DIRECTIONS: In each row, circle the shape that matches the one at the left.

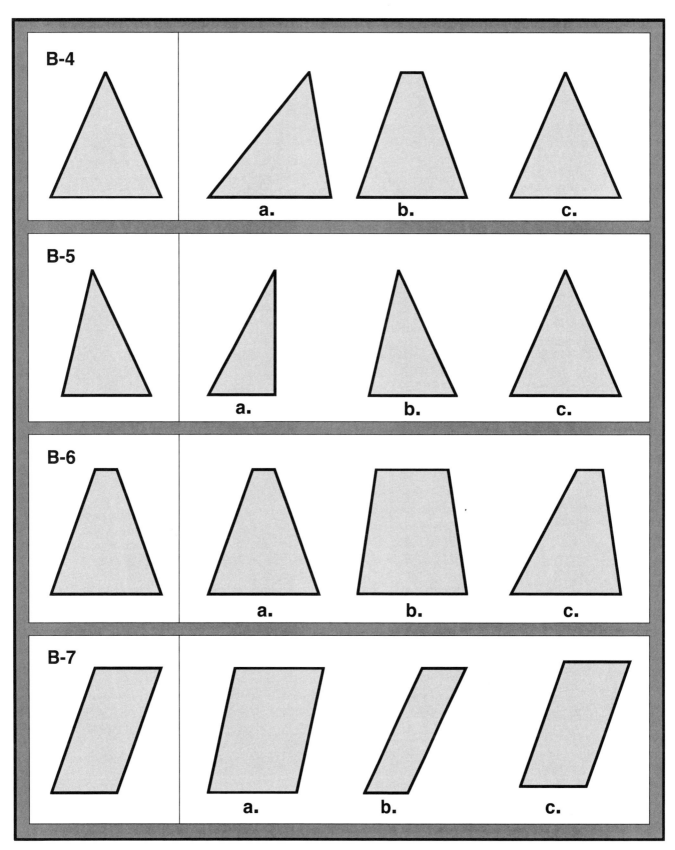

MATCHING SHAPES

DIRECTIONS: In each row, circle the shapes that are the same.

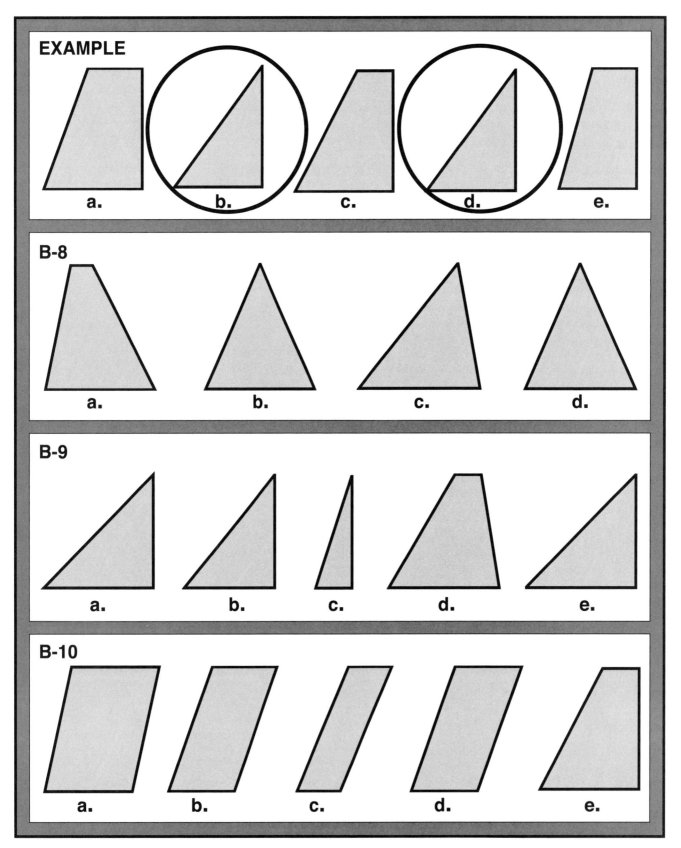

EXAMPLE

a.　　b.　　c.　　d.　　e.

B-8

a.　　b.　　c.　　d.

B-9

a.　　b.　　c.　　d.　　e.

B-10

a.　　b.　　c.　　d.　　e.

MATCHING SHAPES

DIRECTIONS: In each row, circle the shapes that are the same.

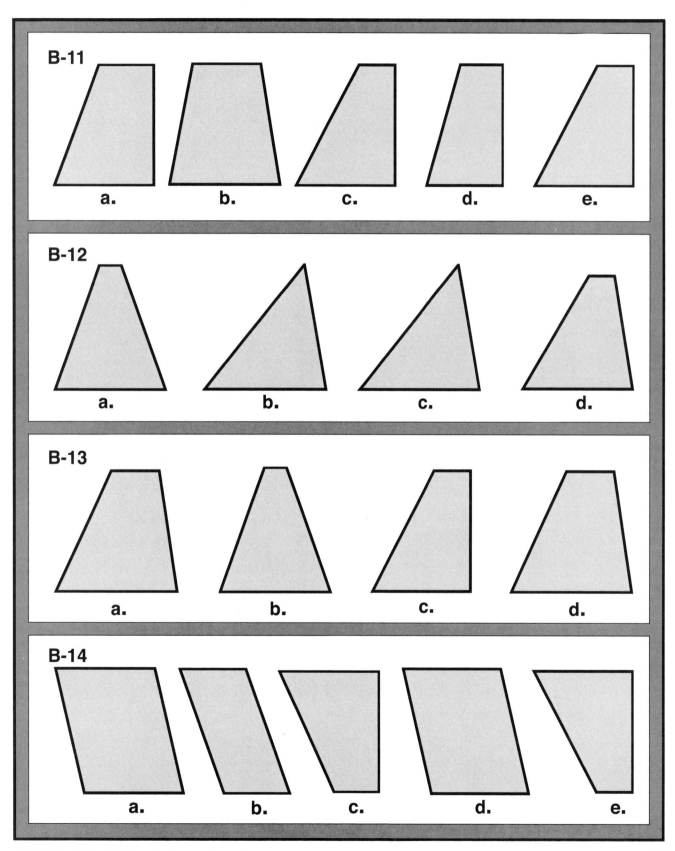

MATCHING SHAPES

DIRECTIONS: Draw a line from each shape in the left column to its twin in the right column. (A twin is the same shape and size as the original.)

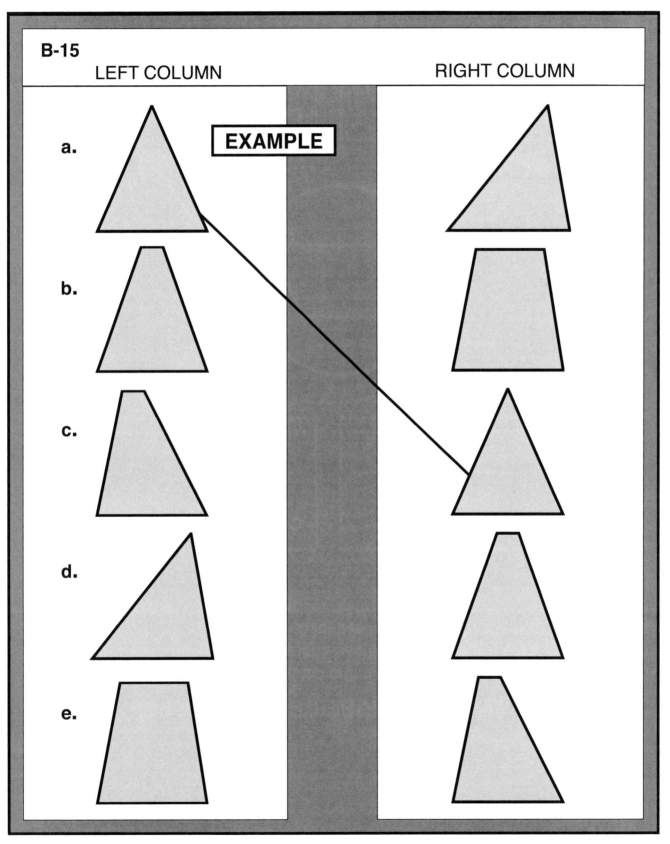

MATCHING SHAPES

DIRECTIONS: Draw a line from the shape in the left column to its twin in the right column.

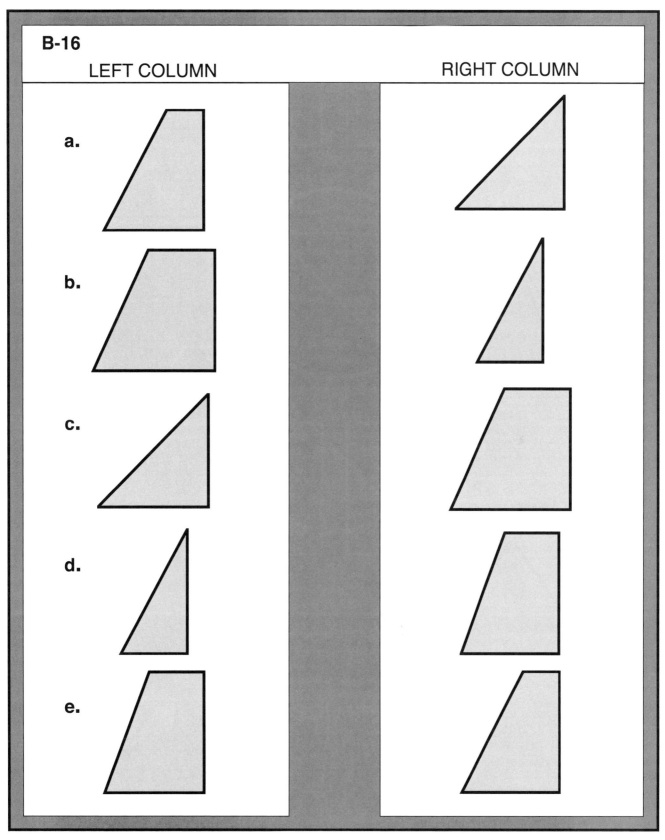

MATCHING SHAPES

DIRECTIONS: Draw a line from the figure in the left column to its twin in the right column.

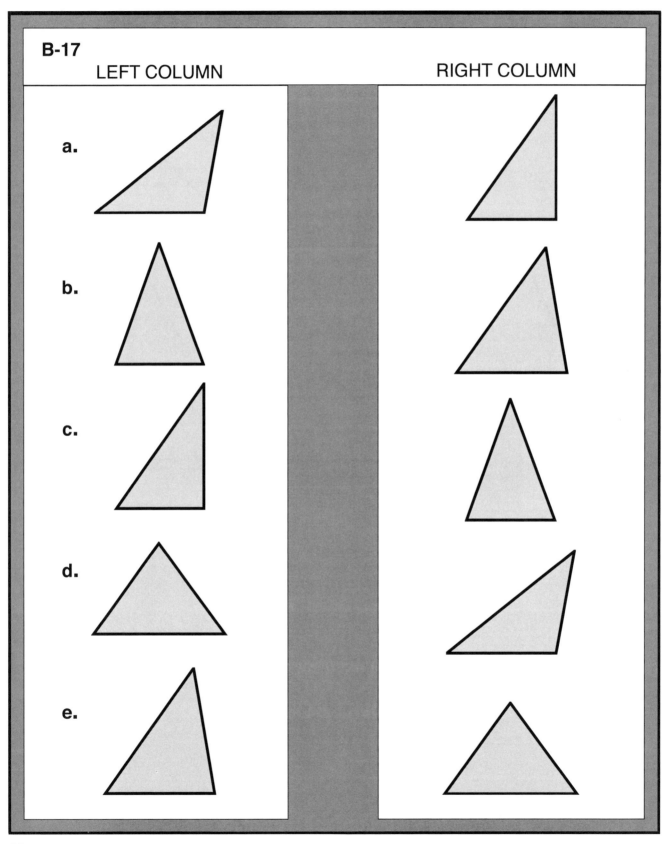

B-17

LEFT COLUMN　　　　　　　　　　RIGHT COLUMN

a.

b.

c.

d.

e.

WHICH SHAPE DOES NOT MATCH?

DIRECTIONS: Cross out the shape in each row that does <u>not</u> match the one at the left. The matching shapes must all face the same direction.

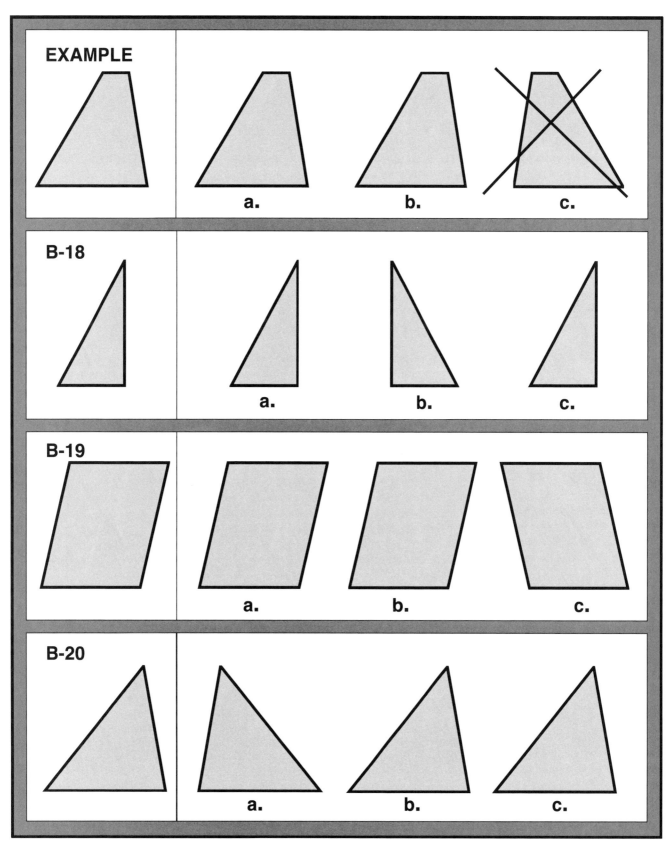

EXAMPLE

a.

b.

c.

B-18

a.

b.

c.

B-19

a.

b.

c.

B-20

a.

b.

c.

WHICH SHAPE DOES NOT MATCH?

DIRECTIONS: Cross out the shape in each row that does <u>not</u> match the one at the left. The matching shapes must all face the same direction.

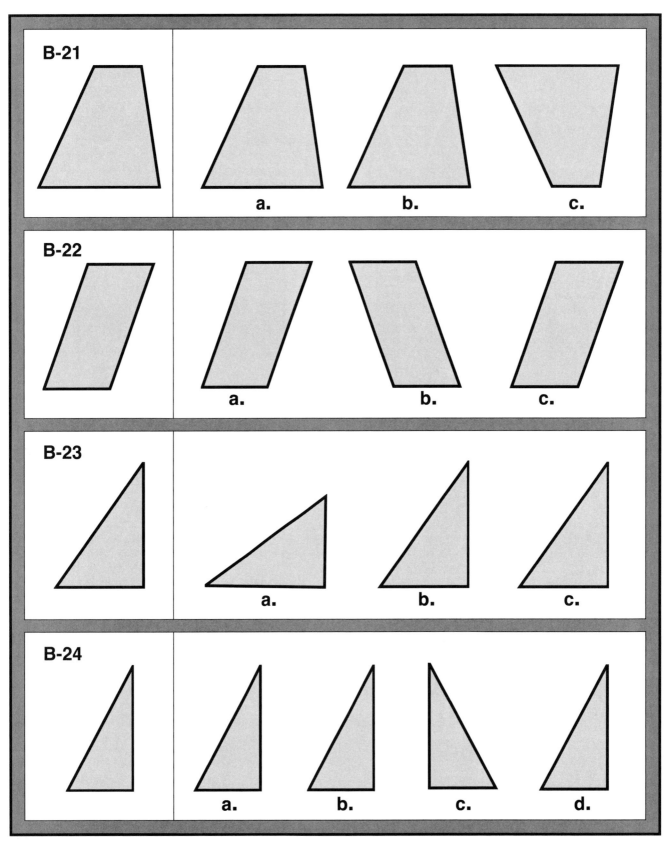

MATCHING SHAPES THAT HAVE BEEN TURNED

DIRECTIONS: "Twins" are figures having the same shape and size even if they face a different direction. Draw a line from the figure in the left column to its twin in the right column. BE CAREFUL—THE SHAPES HAVE BEEN TURNED!

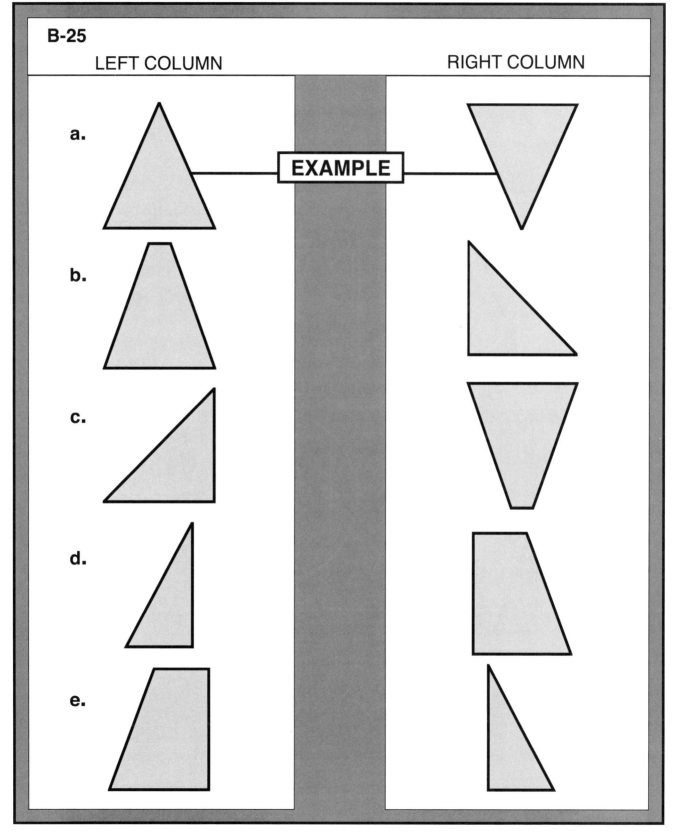

MATCHING SHAPES THAT HAVE BEEN TURNED

DIRECTIONS: Figures having the same shape and size are "twins" even if they face a different direction. Draw a line from the figure in the left column to its twin in the right column. BE CAREFUL—THE SHAPES HAVE BEEN TURNED!

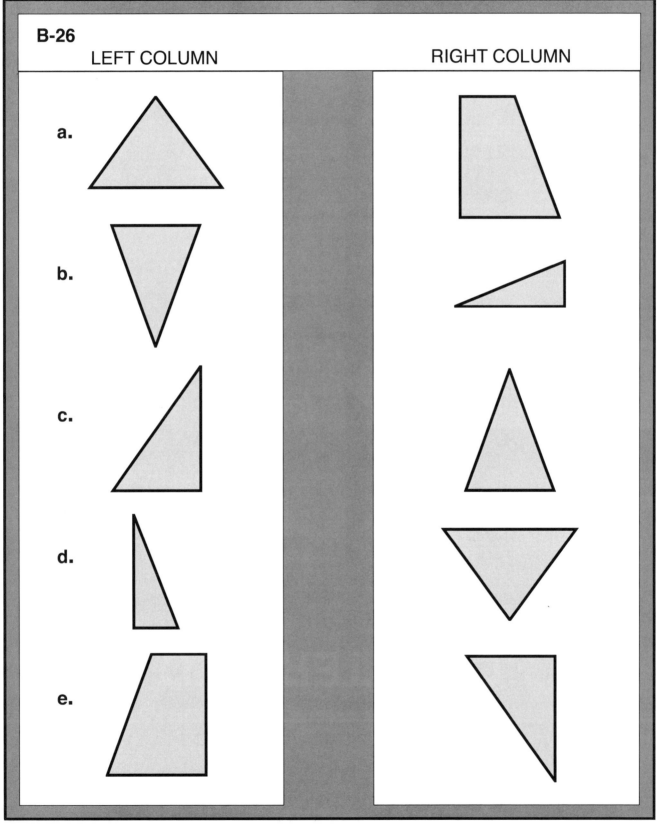

B-26

LEFT COLUMN   RIGHT COLUMN

a.

b.

c.

d.

e.

FINDING SHAPES

DIRECTIONS: In the box at the right, circle any shape that matches exactly one of the shapes in the box at the left.

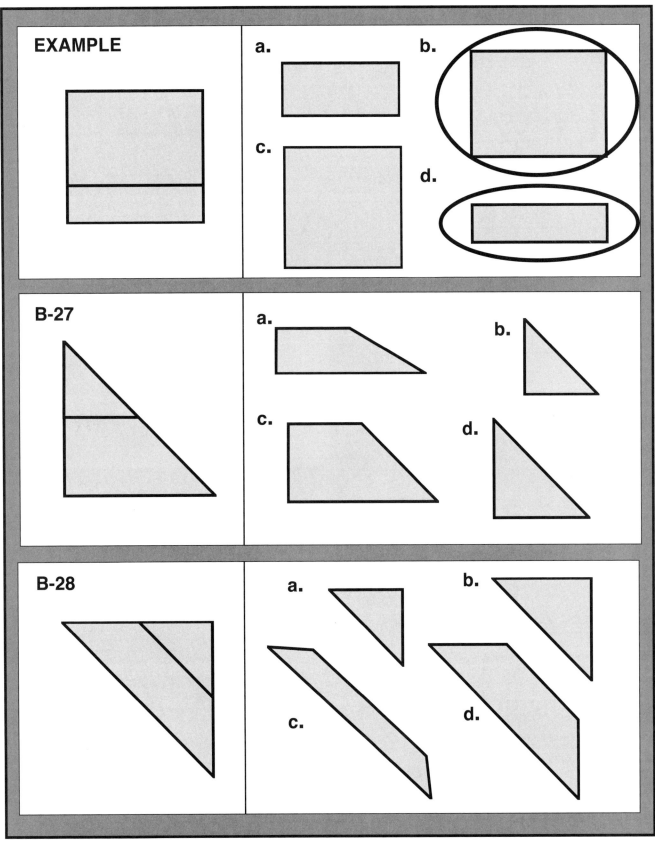

FINDING SHAPES

DIRECTIONS: In the box at the right, circle any shape that matches exactly one of the shapes in the box at the left.

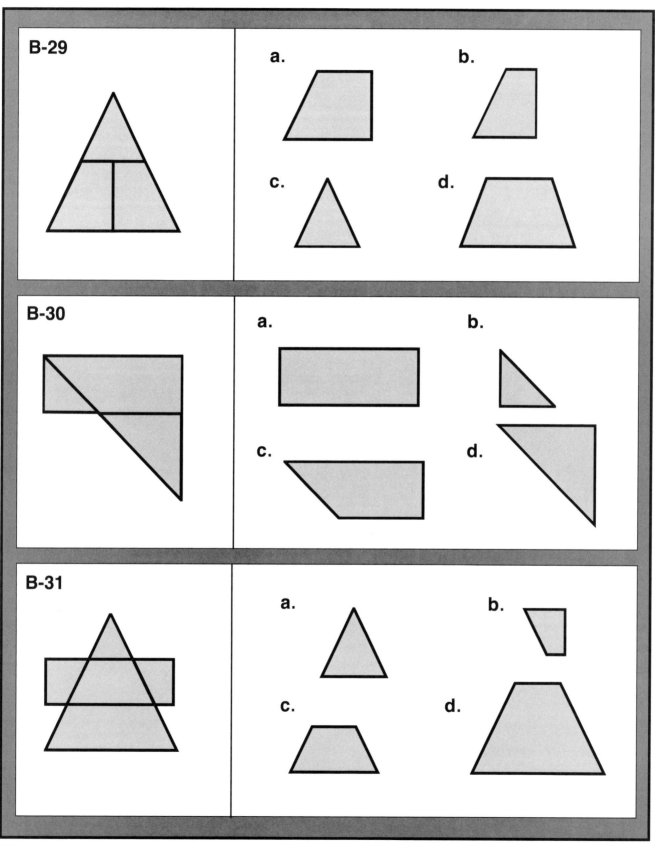

FINDING SHAPES

DIRECTIONS: In the box at the right, circle any shape that matches exactly one of the shapes in the box at the left.

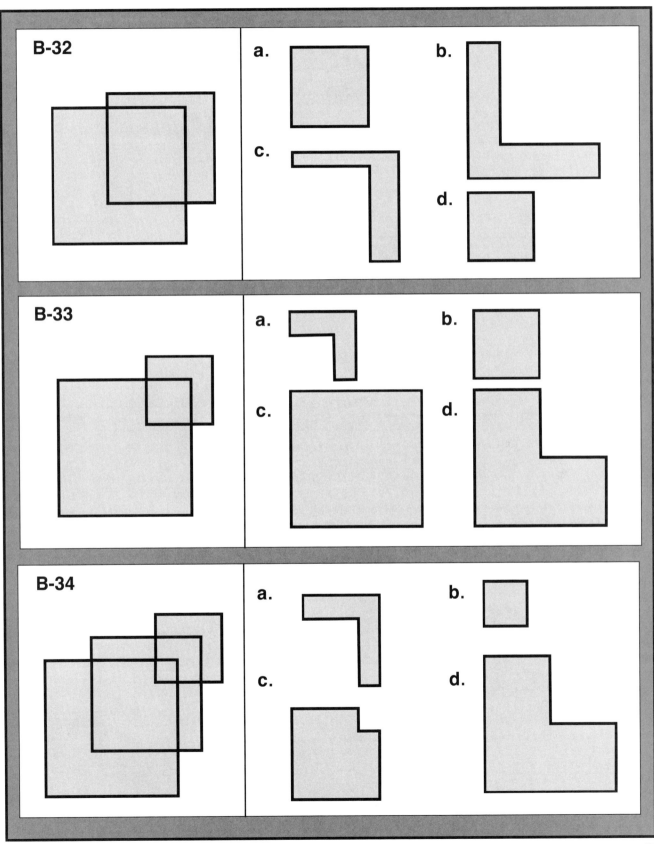

COMBINING CUBES

DIRECTIONS: Circle the shapes on the right that can be formed with the cubes at the left.

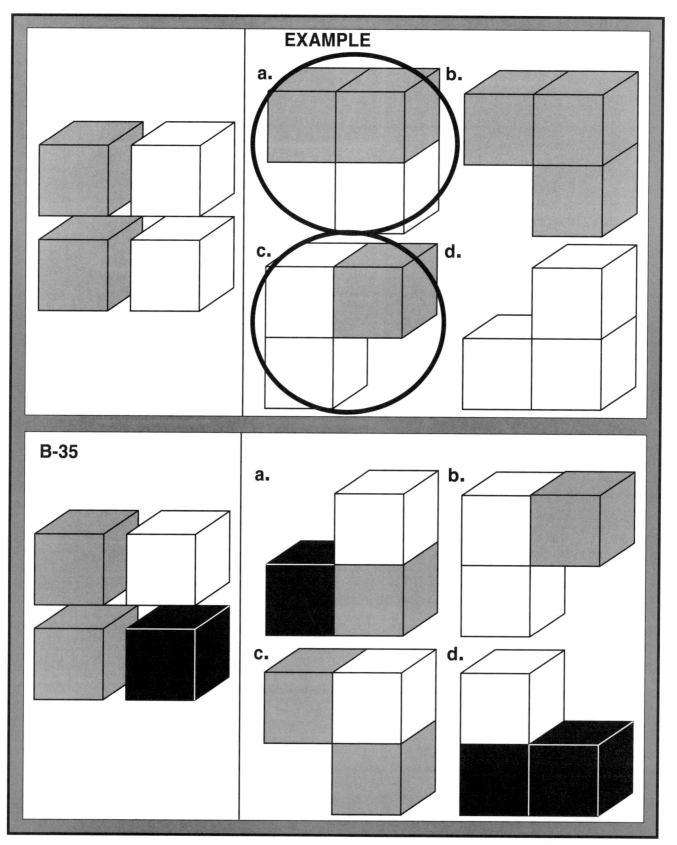

COMBINING CUBES

DIRECTIONS: Circle the shapes on the right that can be formed with the cubes at the left.

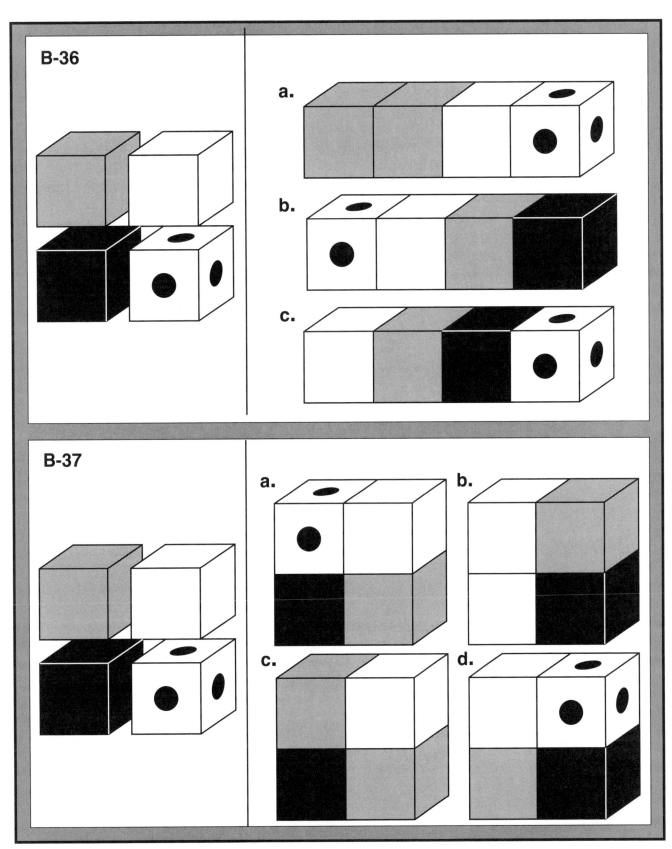

COMBINING CUBES

DIRECTIONS: Circle the shapes on the right that can be formed with the cubes at the left.

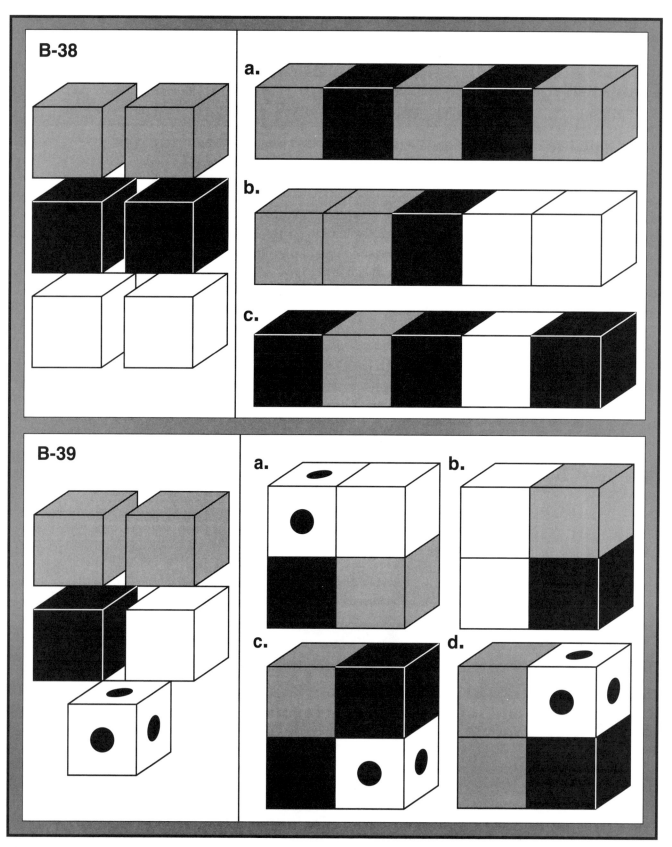

COMBINING SHAPES

DIRECTIONS: Circle the figures that can be formed by joining the two shapes in the box.

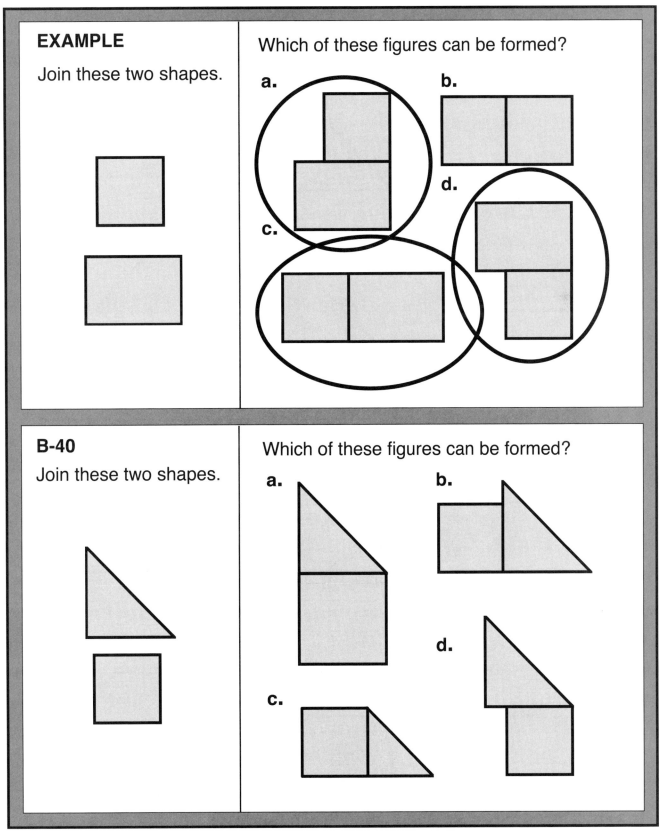

EXAMPLE

Join these two shapes.

Which of these figures can be formed?

a.　b.

c.　d.

B-40

Join these two shapes.

Which of these figures can be formed?

a.　b.

c.　d.

COMBINING SHAPES

DIRECTIONS: Circle the shapes that can be formed by joining the shapes in the box.

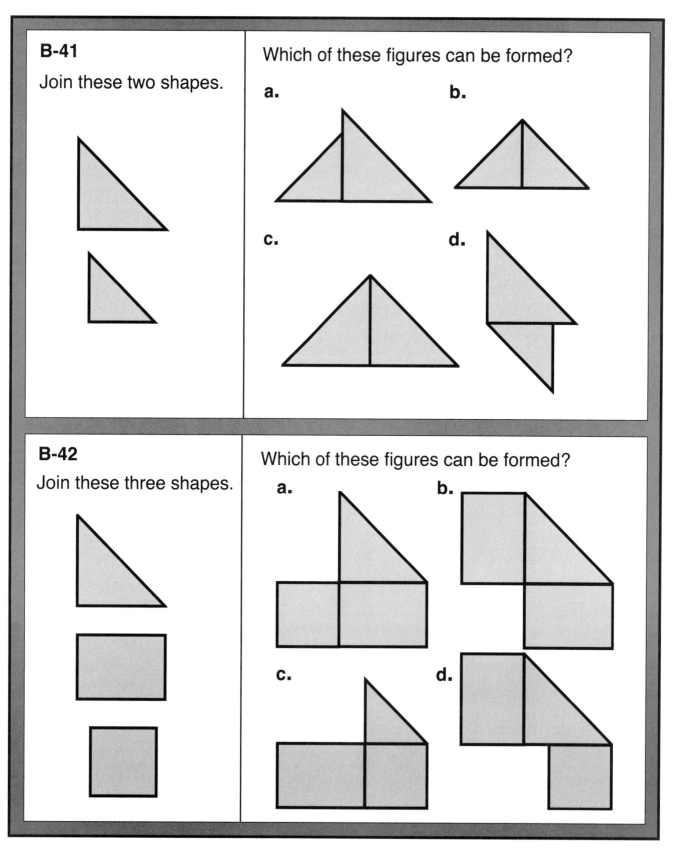

B-41

Join these two shapes.

Which of these figures can be formed?

a.

b.

c.

d.

B-42

Join these three shapes.

Which of these figures can be formed?

a.

b.

c.

d.

FINDING AND TRACING PATTERNS

DIRECTIONS: Circle any figure that contains the shape on the left. The shape must be in the same position but may have extra lines. Trace over the matching shape to make sure you are right.

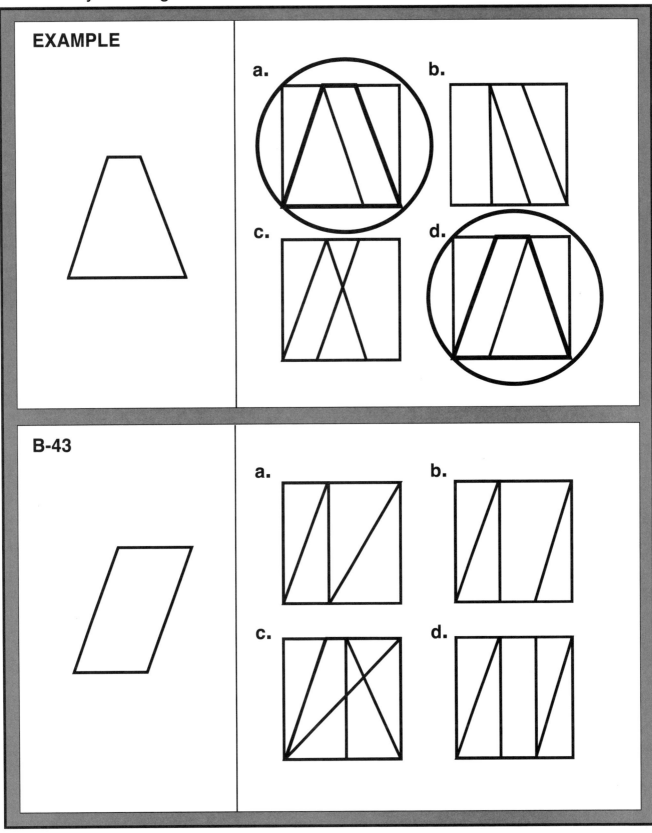

FINDING AND TRACING PATTERNS

DIRECTIONS: Circle any figure that contains the shape on the left. The shape must be in the same position but may have extra lines. Trace over the matching shape to make sure you are right.

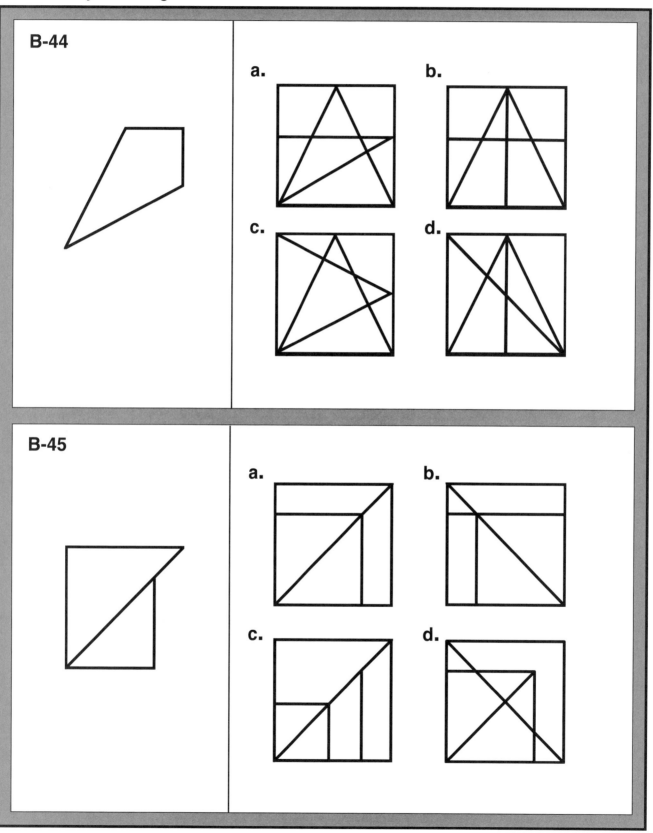

FINDING AND TRACING PATTERNS

DIRECTIONS: Circle any figure that contains the shape on the left. The shape must be in the same position but may have extra lines. Trace over the matching shape to make sure you are right.

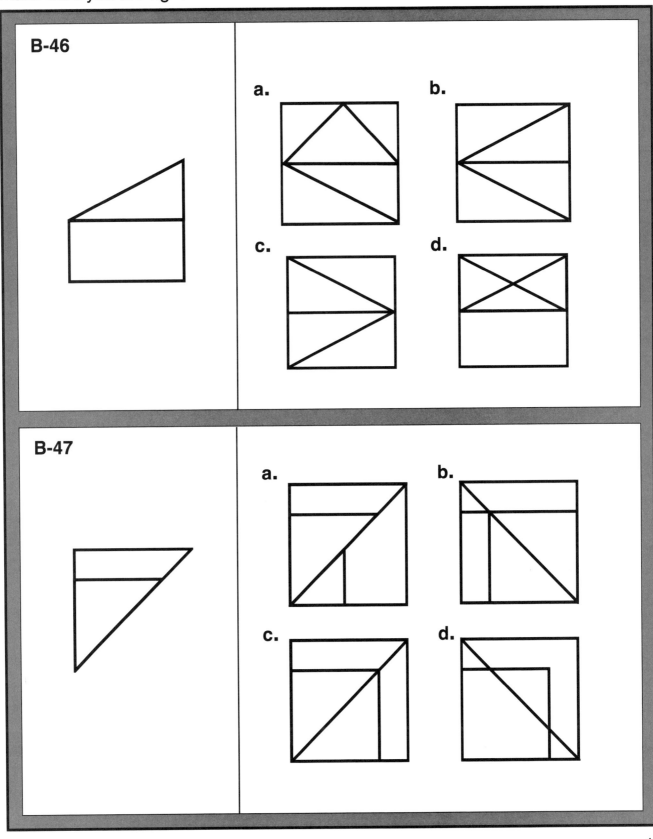

DIVIDING SHAPES INTO EQUAL PARTS—A

DIRECTIONS: Use a pencil or crayon to color half of each set of squares. No two drawings can look the same.

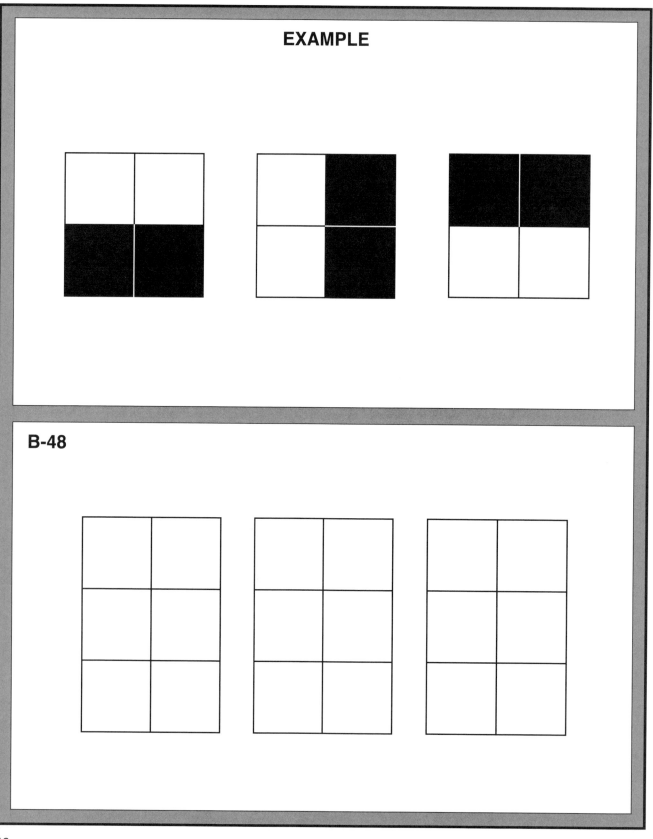

DIVIDING SHAPES INTO EQUAL PARTS—A

DIRECTIONS: Use a pencil or crayon to color half of each set of squares. No two drawings can look the same.

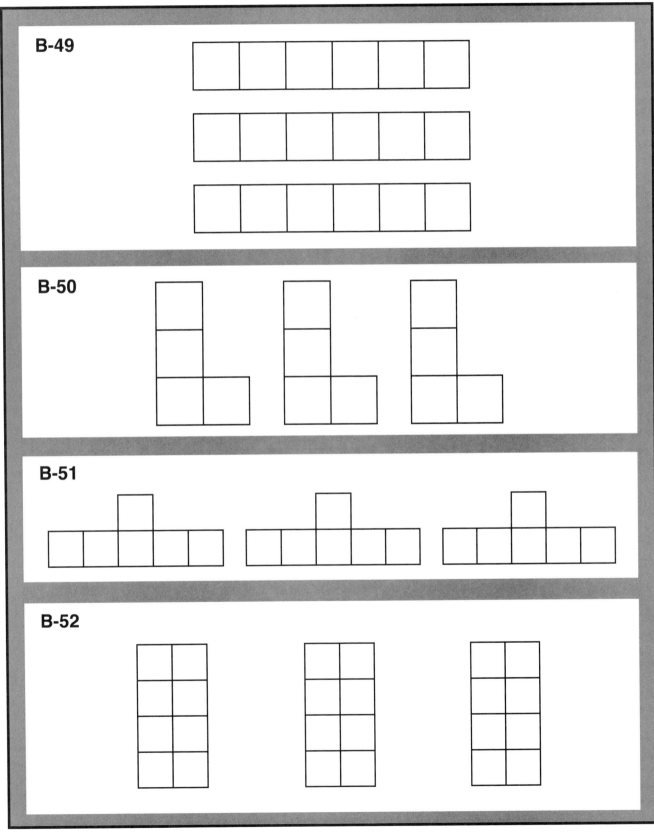

DIVIDING SHAPES INTO EQUAL PARTS—B

DIRECTIONS: Look at the two parts of the shape. Answer the question, "Are the parts exactly alike?" Write *yes* or *no* in the blank below each question.

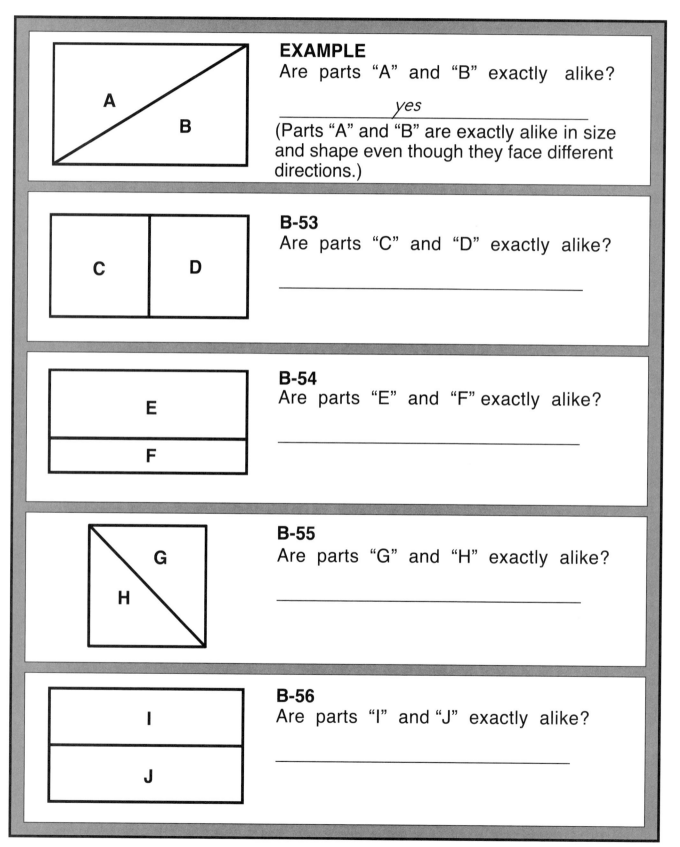

EXAMPLE
Are parts "A" and "B" exactly alike?

_____*yes*_____

(Parts "A" and "B" are exactly alike in size and shape even though they face different directions.)

B-53
Are parts "C" and "D" exactly alike?

_____

B-54
Are parts "E" and "F" exactly alike?

_____

B-55
Are parts "G" and "H" exactly alike?

_____

B-56
Are parts "I" and "J" exactly alike?

_____

DIVIDING SHAPES INTO EQUAL PARTS—B

DIRECTIONS: Look at the two parts of the shape. Answer the question, "Are the parts exactly alike?" Write *yes* or *no* in the blank below each question.

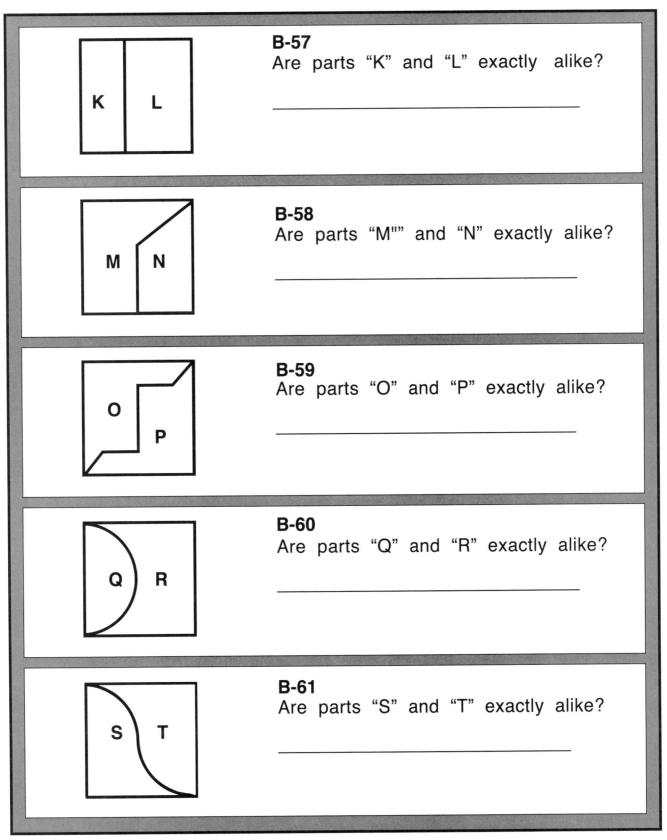

B-57
Are parts "K" and "L" exactly alike?

_____

B-58
Are parts "M"" and "N" exactly alike?

_____

B-59
Are parts "O" and "P" exactly alike?

_____

B-60
Are parts "Q" and "R" exactly alike?

_____

B-61
Are parts "S" and "T" exactly alike?

_____

DIVIDING SHAPES INTO EQUAL PARTS—C

DIRECTIONS: Here are four rectangles. Divide each into two shapes that are exactly alike. Use one straight line each time. The divided shapes do not have to face in the same direction.

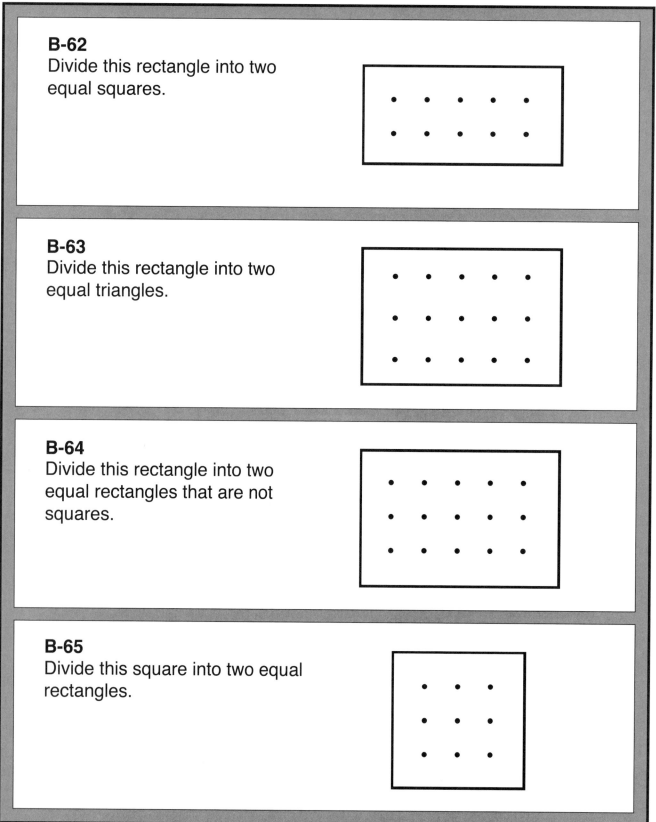

B-62
Divide this rectangle into two equal squares.

B-63
Divide this rectangle into two equal triangles.

B-64
Divide this rectangle into two equal rectangles that are not squares.

B-65
Divide this square into two equal rectangles.

DIVIDING SHAPES INTO EQUAL PARTS—C

DIRECTIONS: Here are five triangles. Divide each of them into two equal triangles that are exactly alike. The divided shapes do not have to face in the same direction.

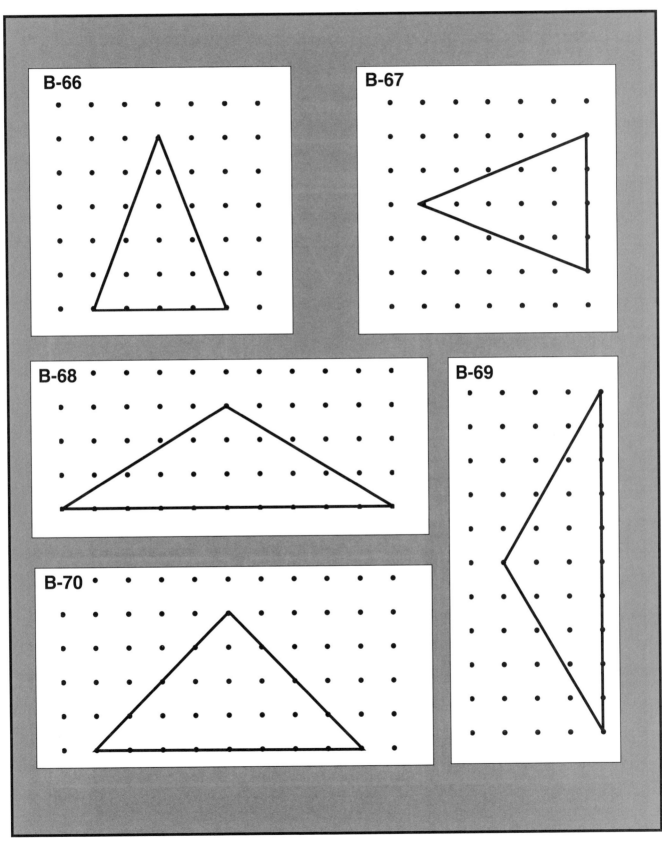

DIVIDING SHAPES INTO EQUAL PARTS—C

DIRECTIONS: Here are several four-sided shapes called parallelograms (opposite sides are parallel). Divide each parallelogram into two equal shapes, as directed below. The divided shapes do not have to face in the same direction.

B-71 Divide each shape into two equal triangles that are exactly alike.

B-72 Divide each shape into two equal parallelograms that are exactly alike.

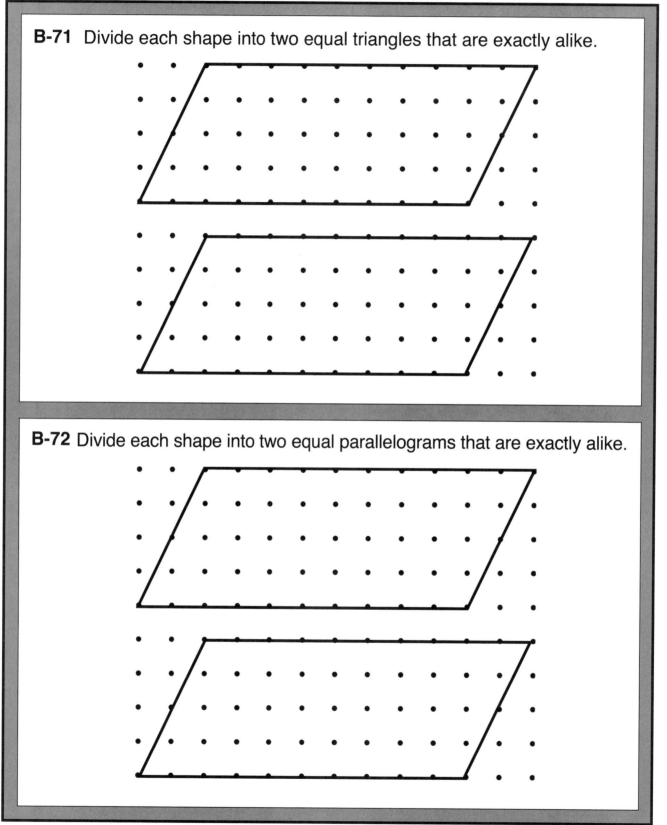

WHICH SHAPE COMPLETES THE SQUARE?

DIRECTIONS: Circle the shape that completes the big square.

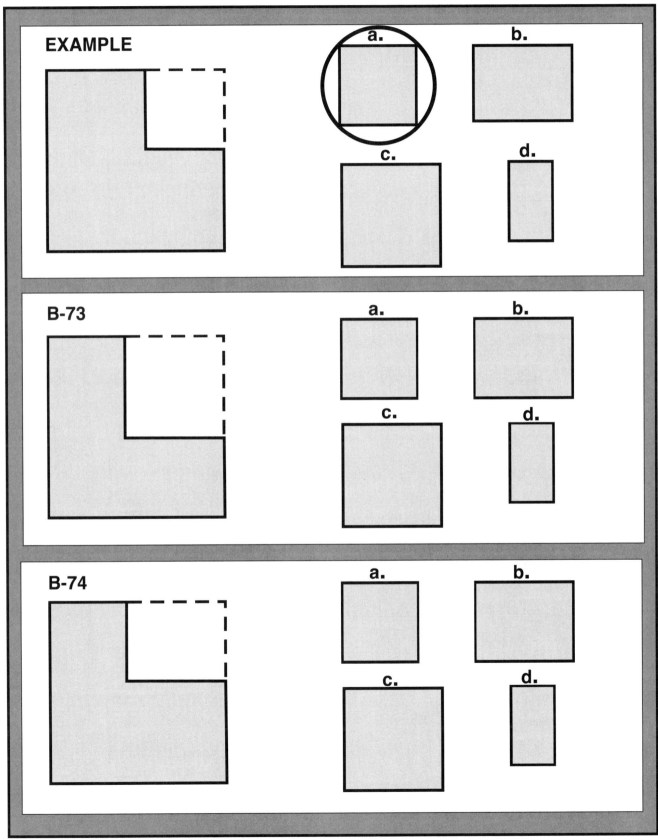

WHICH SHAPE COMPLETES THE SQUARE?

DIRECTIONS: Circle the shape that completes the big square.

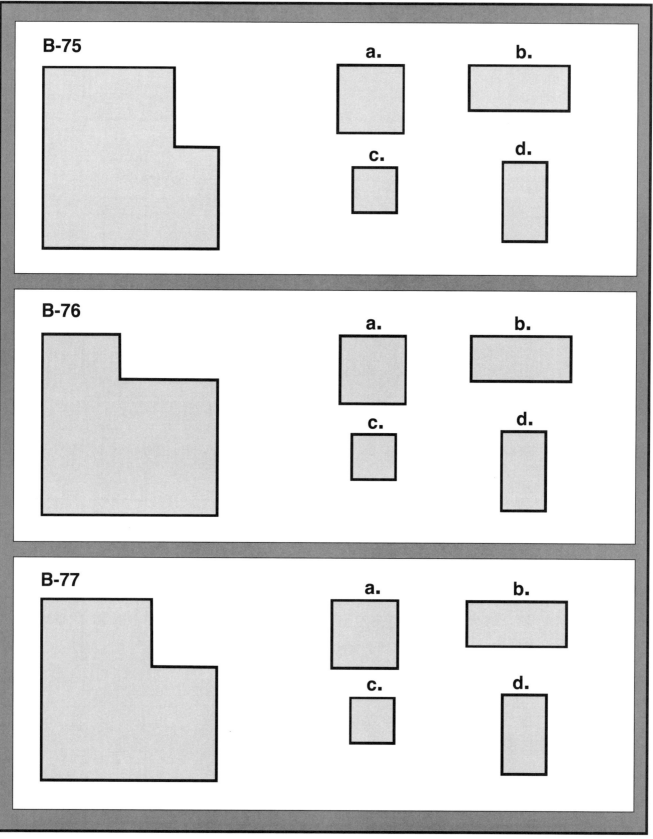

B-75
a.
b.
c.
d.

B-76
a.
b.
c.
d.

B-77
a.
b.
c.
d.

WHICH SHAPE COMPLETES THE SQUARE?

DIRECTIONS: Circle the shape that completes the big square.

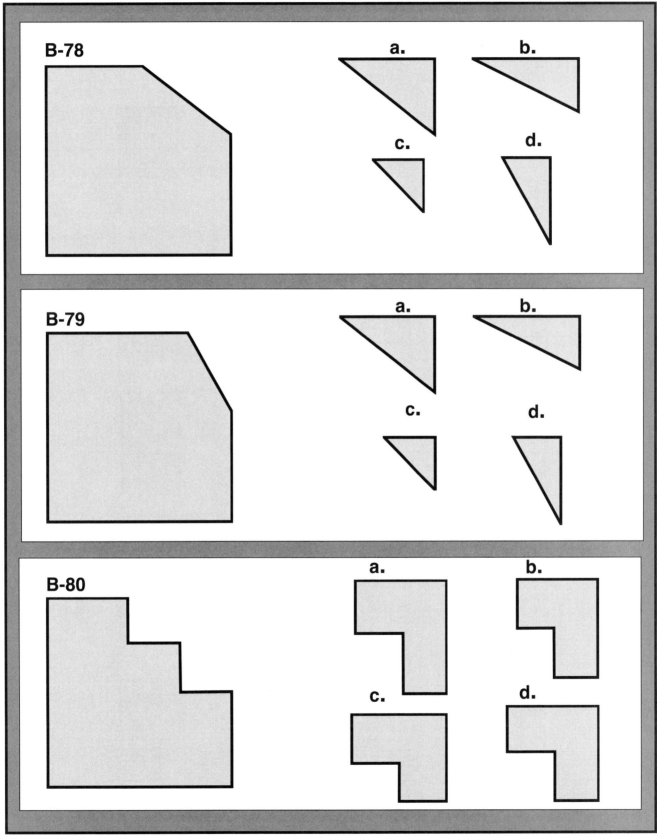

WHICH SHAPES MAKE SQUARES?

DIRECTIONS: Draw a line from a shape in the left column to the shape in the right column that completes the square.

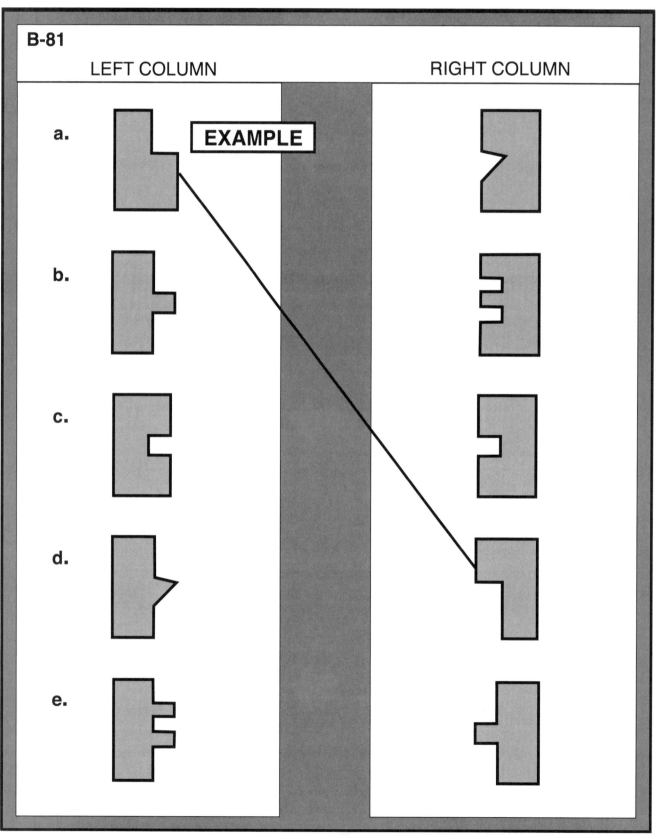

WHICH SHAPES MAKE SQUARES?

DIRECTIONS: Draw a line from a shape in the left column to the shape in the right column that completes the square.

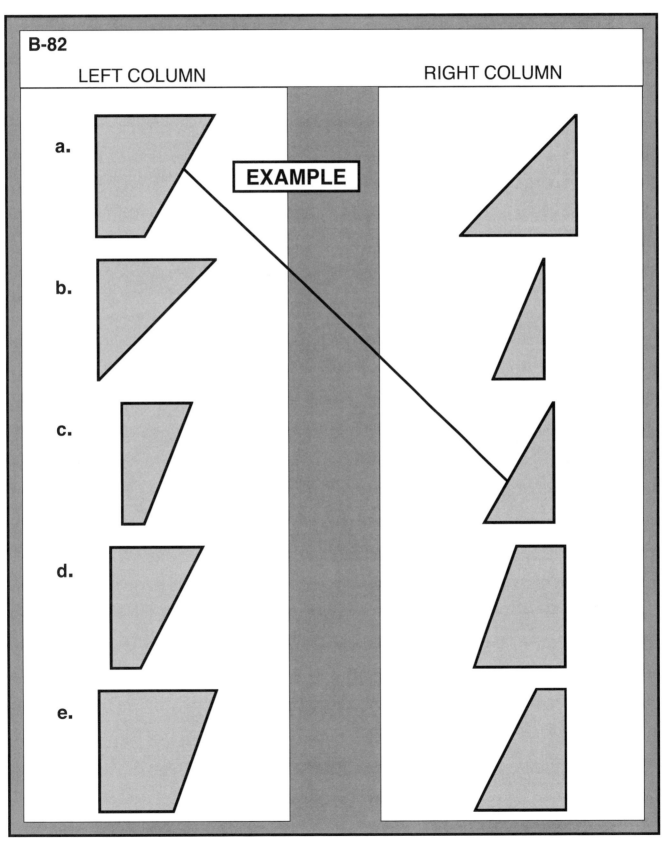

WHICH SHAPES MAKE SQUARES?

DIRECTIONS: Draw a line from a shape in the left column to the shape in the right column that completes the square.

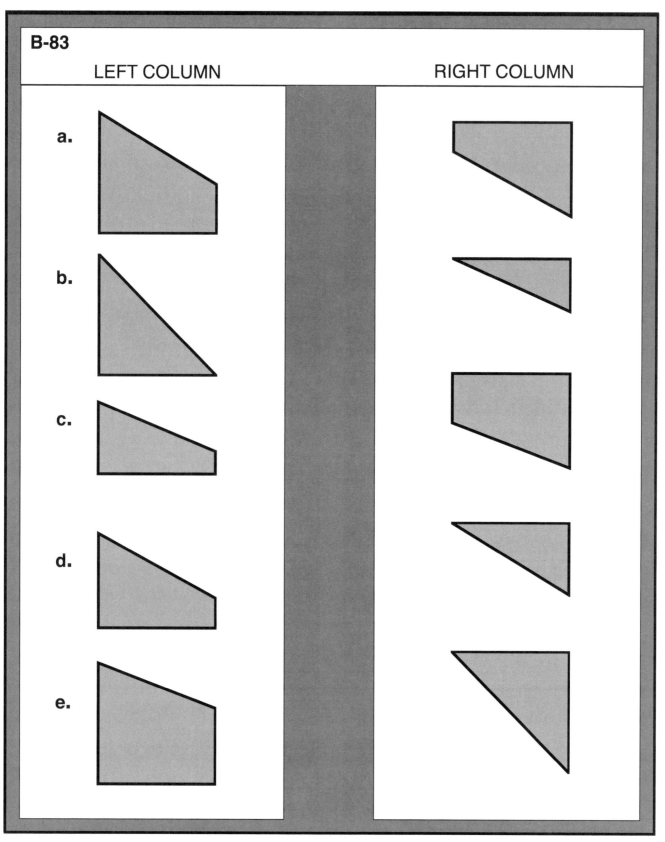

COPYING A FIGURE

DIRECTIONS: Use a pencil and the grid to copy each of the figures.

B-84   **EXAMPLE**

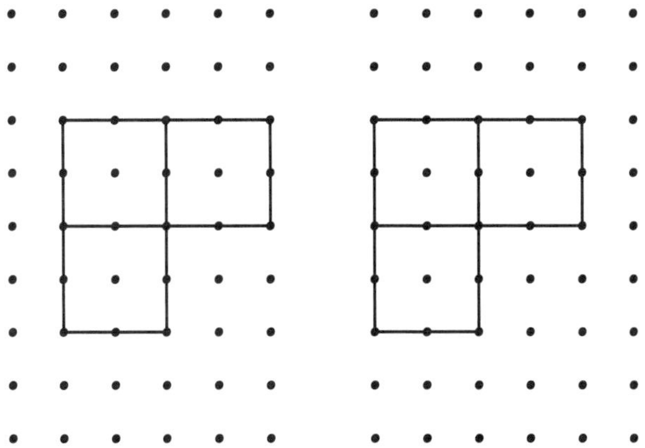

B-85

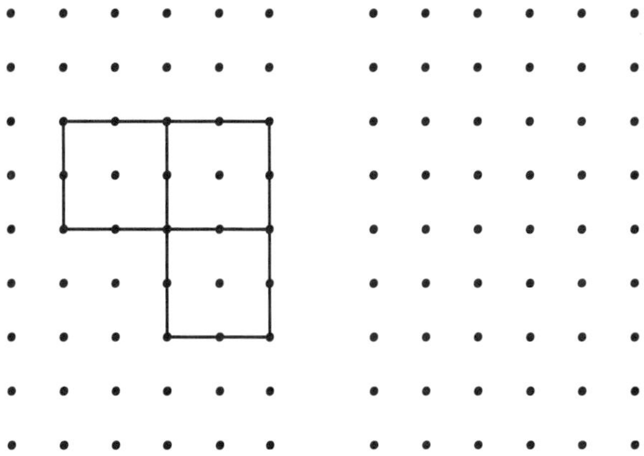

B-86

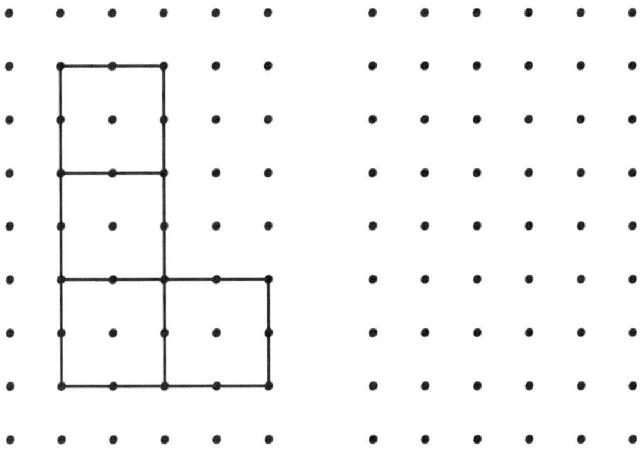

B-87

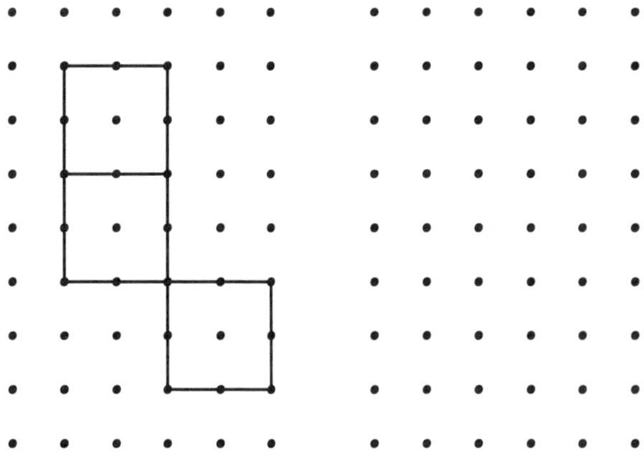

B-88

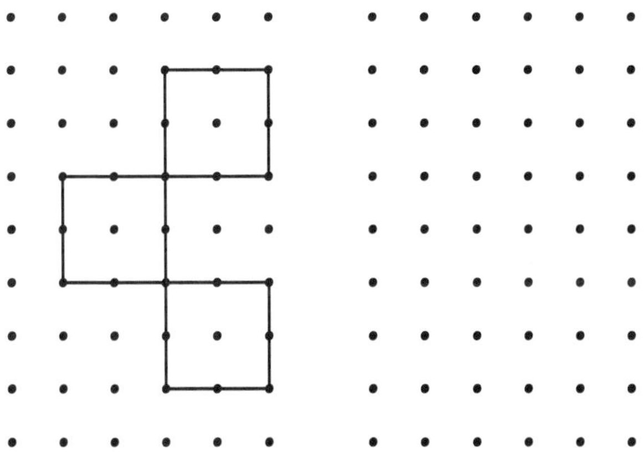

B-89

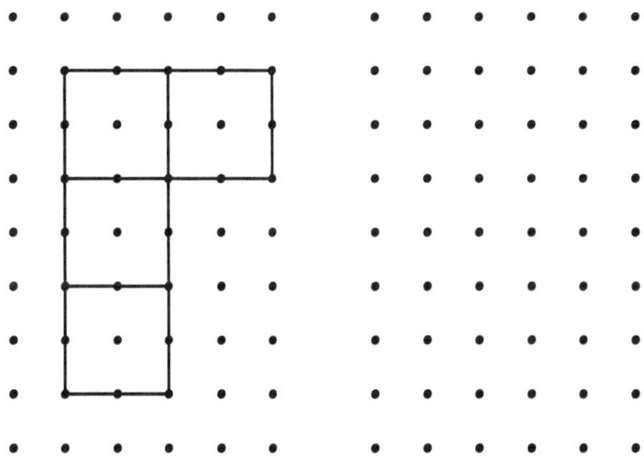

COPYING A FIGURE

DIRECTIONS: Use a pencil and the grid to copy each of the figures.

B-90

B-91

B-92

DRAWING IDENTICAL SHAPES

DIRECTIONS: Use the grid to draw a shape identical to the shape on the left. Note that identical means exactly the same size and shape. Color your drawing.

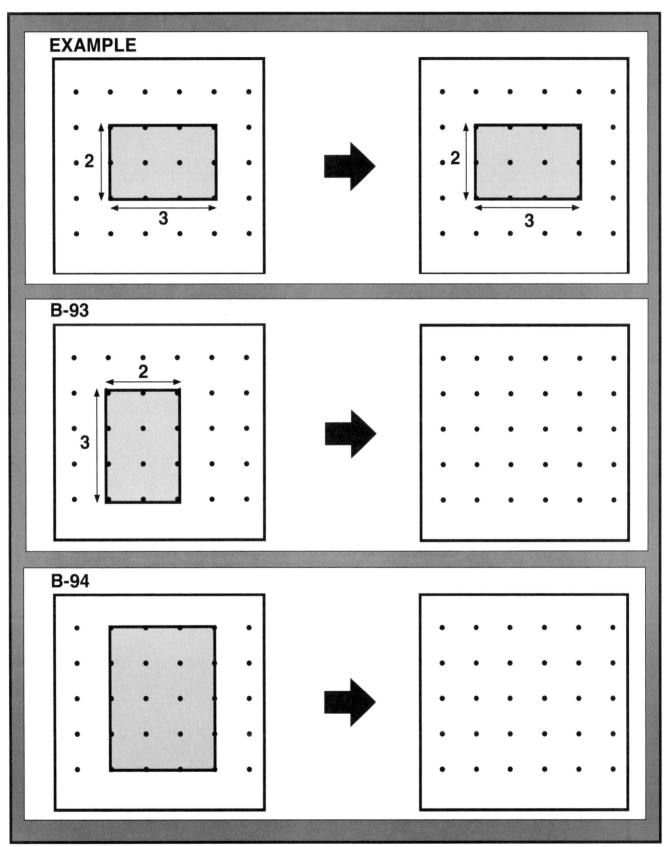

EXAMPLE

B-93

B-94

DRAWING IDENTICAL SHAPES

DIRECTIONS: Use the grid on the right to draw a shape identical to the shape on the left. Note that identical means exactly the same size and shape. Color your drawing.

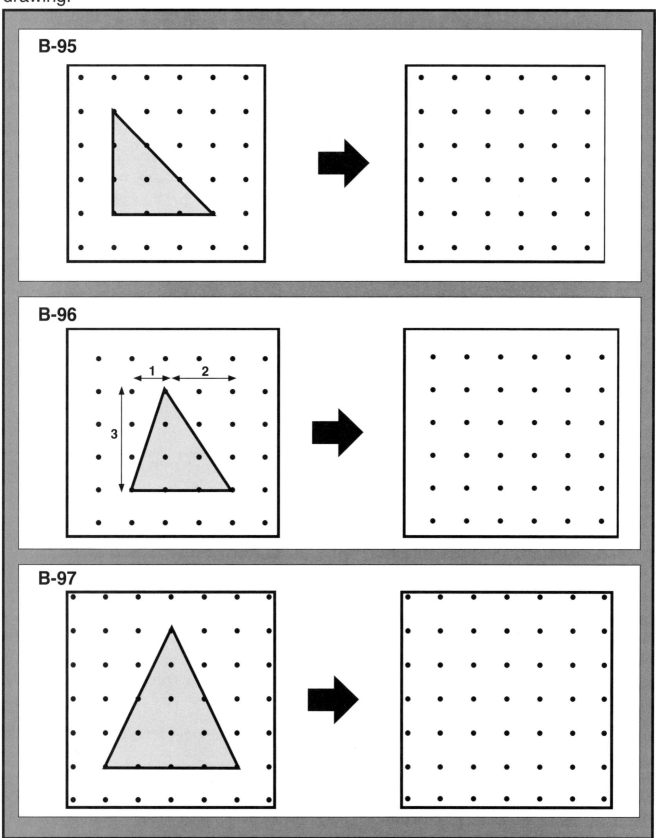

B-95

B-96

B-97

DRAWING IDENTICAL SHAPES

DIRECTIONS: Use the grid on the right to draw a shape identical to the shape on the left. Note that identical means exactly the same size and shape. Color your drawing.

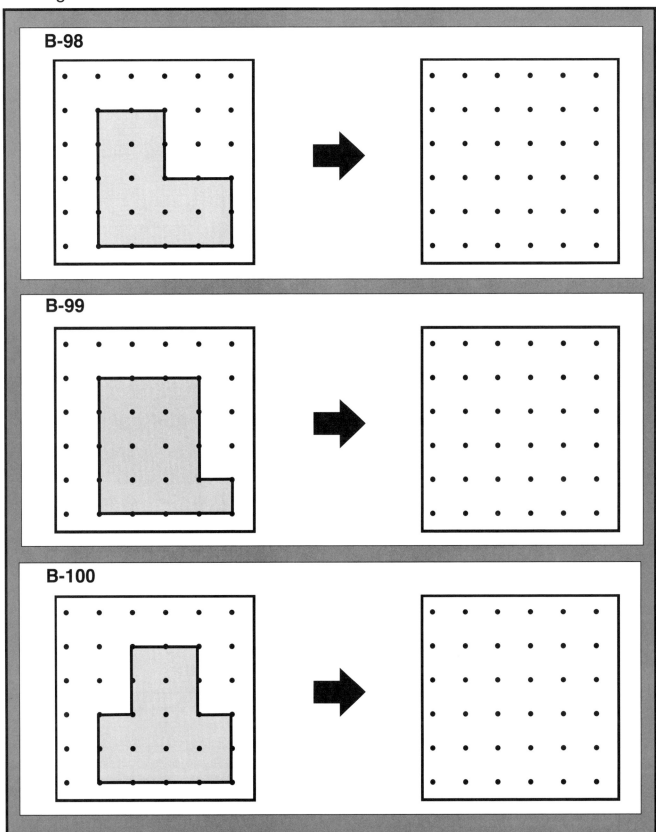

B-98

B-99

B-100

COMPARING SHAPES—SELECT

DIRECTIONS: Under the three pictures, two shapes are described. Read each description and decide which of the pictures it describes. Write the letter of the correct picture on the line.

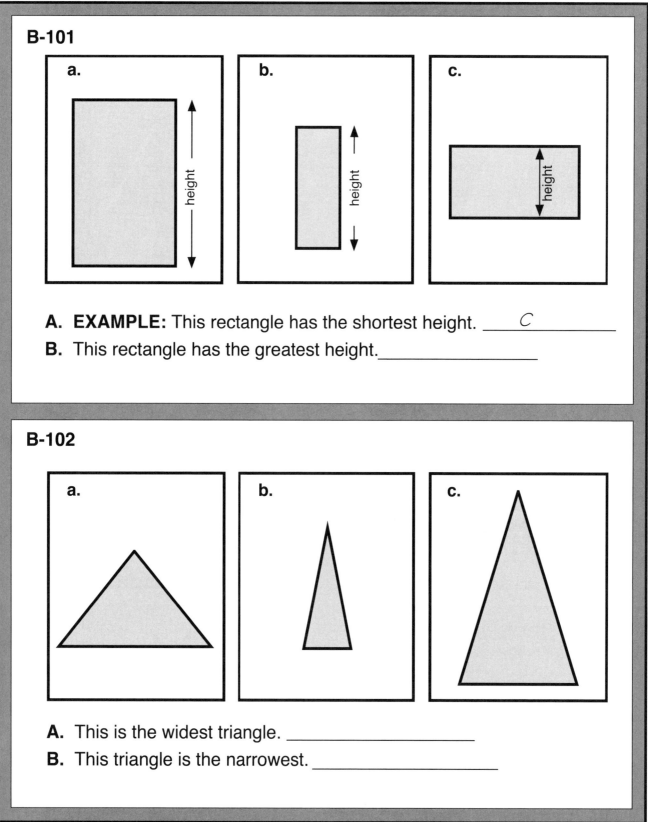

B-101

a.

b.

c.

height

height

height

A. EXAMPLE: This rectangle has the shortest height. _____C_____

B. This rectangle has the greatest height._____

B-102

a.

b.

c.

A. This is the widest triangle. _____

B. This triangle is the narrowest. _____

COMPARING SHAPES—SELECT

DIRECTIONS: Under the three pictures, two shapes are described. Read each description and decide which of the pictures it describes. Write the letter of the correct picture on the line.

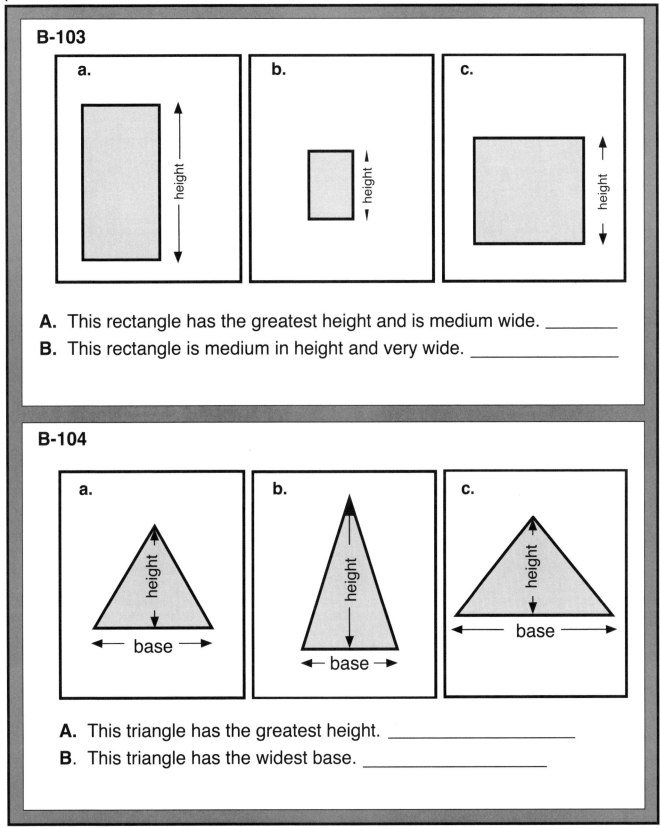

B-103

a.

b.

c.

A. This rectangle has the greatest height and is medium wide. _____

B. This rectangle is medium in height and very wide. _____

B-104

a.

b.

c.

A. This triangle has the greatest height. _____

B. This triangle has the widest base. _____

COMPARING SHAPES—SELECT

DIRECTIONS: Under the three pictures, two shapes are described. Read each description and decide which of the pictures it describes. Write the letter of the correct picture on the line.

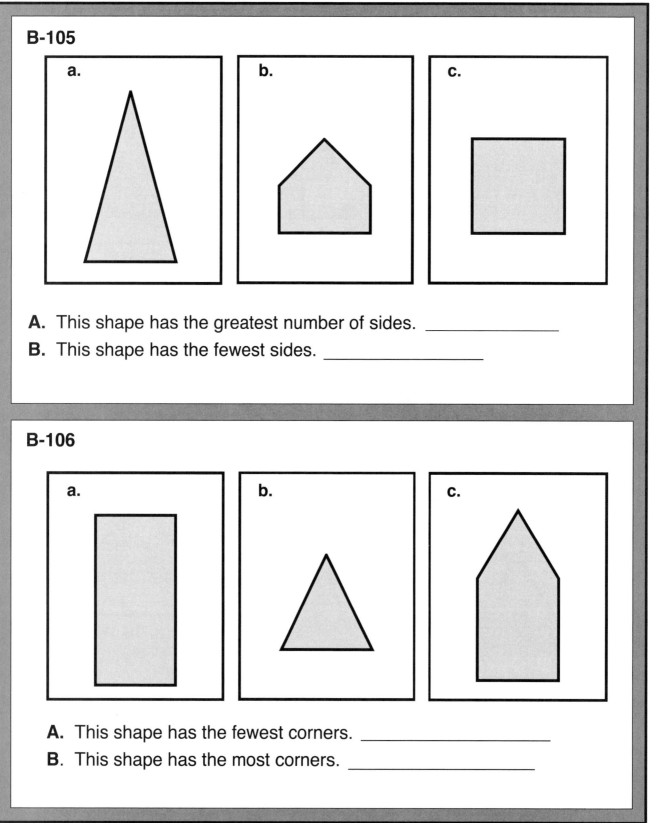

B-105

a.

b.

c.

A. This shape has the greatest number of sides. _____

B. This shape has the fewest sides. _____

B-106

a.

b.

c.

A. This shape has the fewest corners. _____

B. This shape has the most corners. _____

COMPARING SHAPES—EXPLAIN

DIRECTIONS: Compare the shapes in each box. Describe them, using complete sentences.

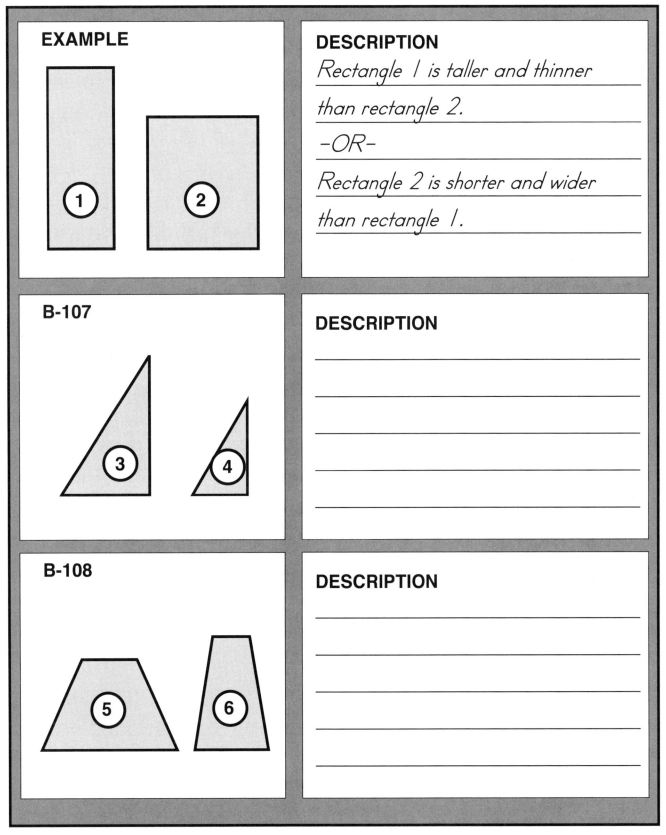

EXAMPLE

DESCRIPTION

Rectangle 1 is taller and thinner than rectangle 2.

–OR–

Rectangle 2 is shorter and wider than rectangle 1.

B-107

DESCRIPTION

B-108

DESCRIPTION

COMPARING SHAPES—EXPLAIN

DIRECTIONS: Compare the shapes in each box. Describe them, using complete sentences.

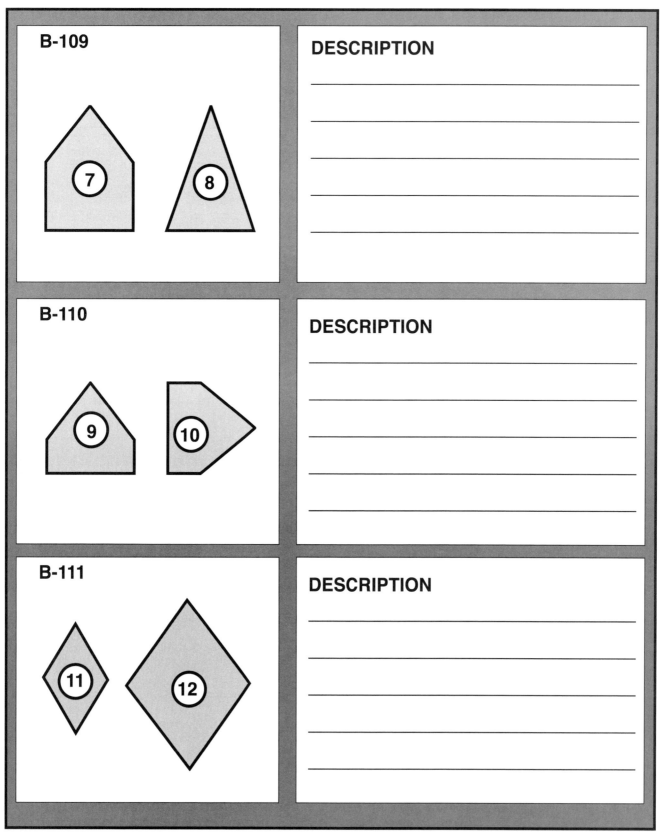

B-109

DESCRIPTION

B-110

DESCRIPTION

B-111

DESCRIPTION

COMPARING SHAPES—EXPLAIN

DIRECTIONS: Use this diagram to organize your thinking about how the triangle and rectangle are alike and how they are different.

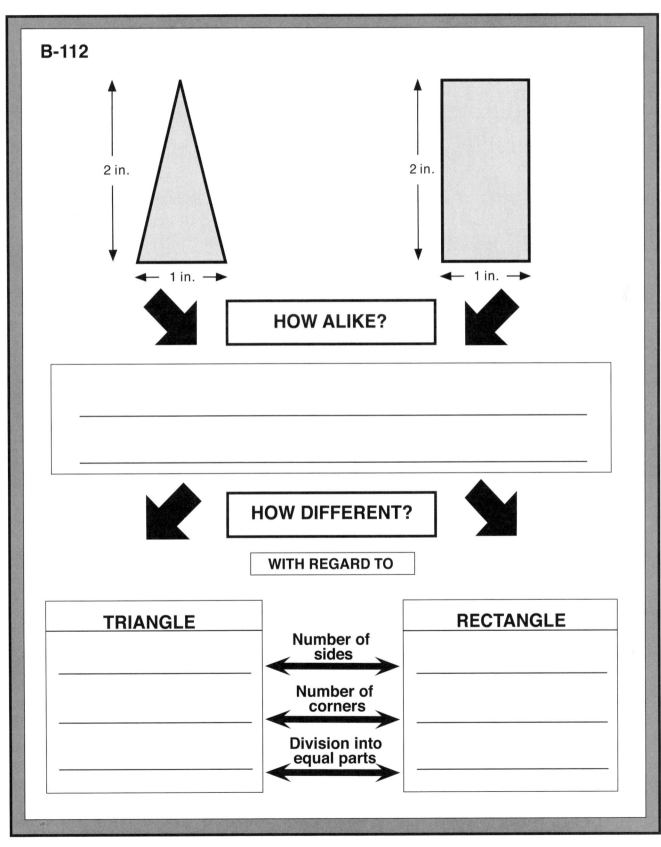

COMPARING SHAPES—EXPLAIN

DIRECTIONS: Use this diagram to organize your thinking about how the triangle and rectangle are alike and how they are different.

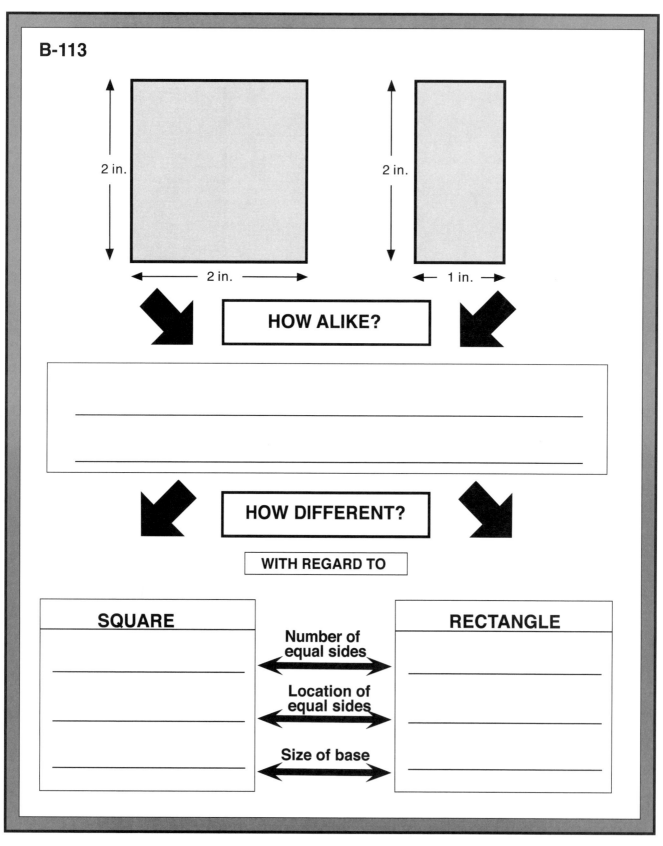

CHAPTER THREE

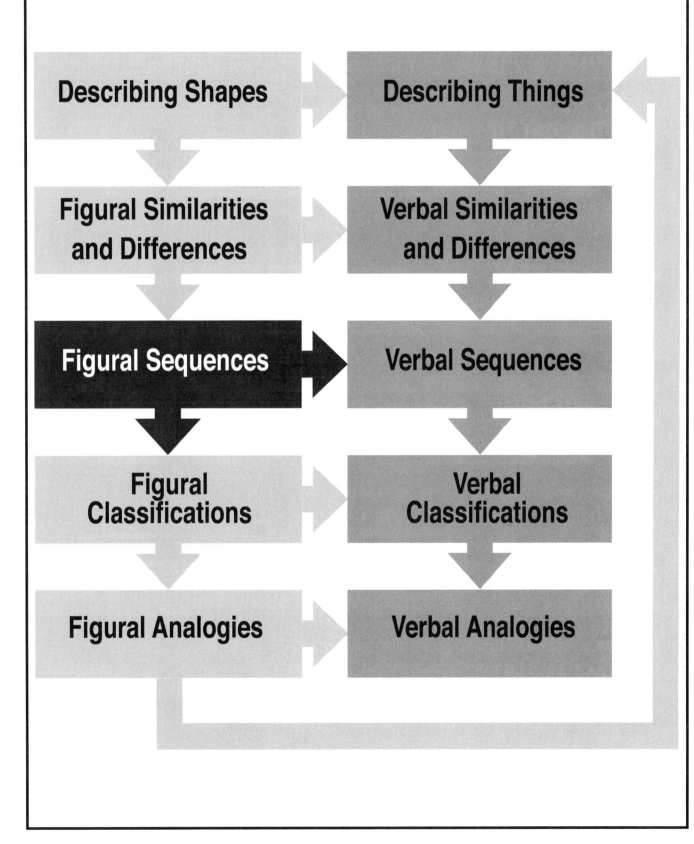

COPYING A PATTERN

DIRECTIONS: Use a pencil and the grid to copy each figure.

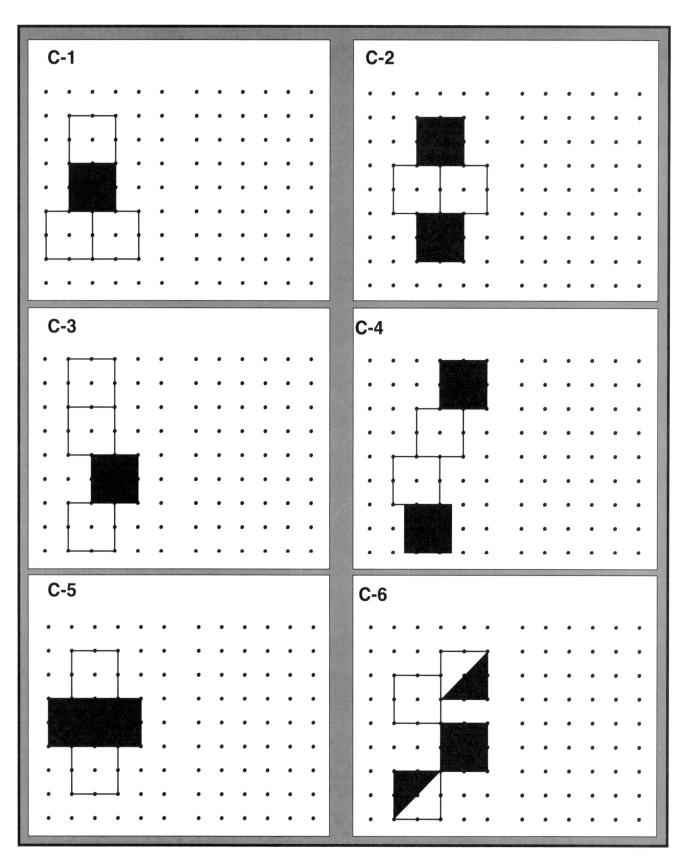

COPYING A PATTERN

DIRECTIONS: Copy each figure pattern.

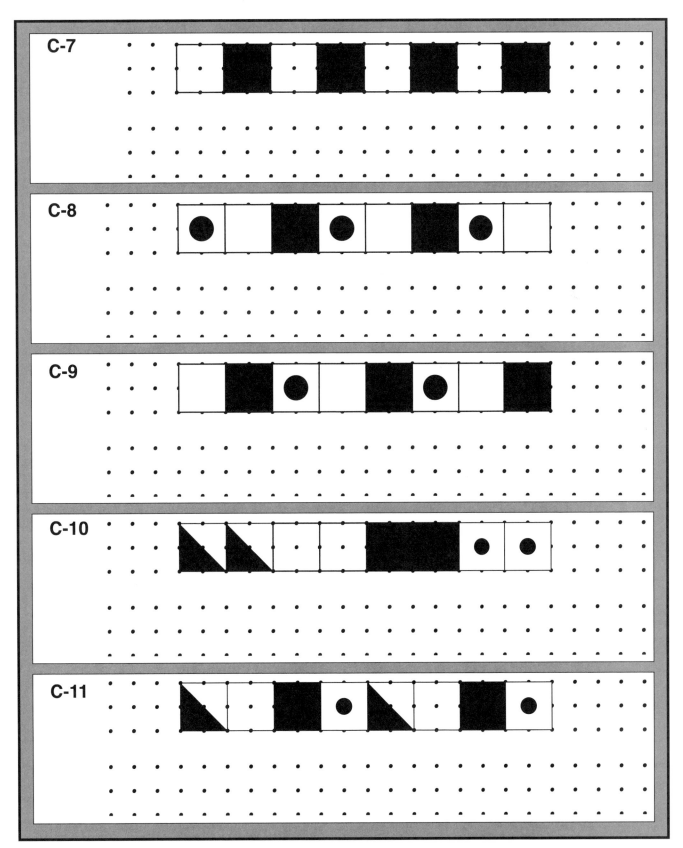

WHICH CUBE COMES NEXT?—SELECT

DIRECTIONS: Circle the cube that comes next.

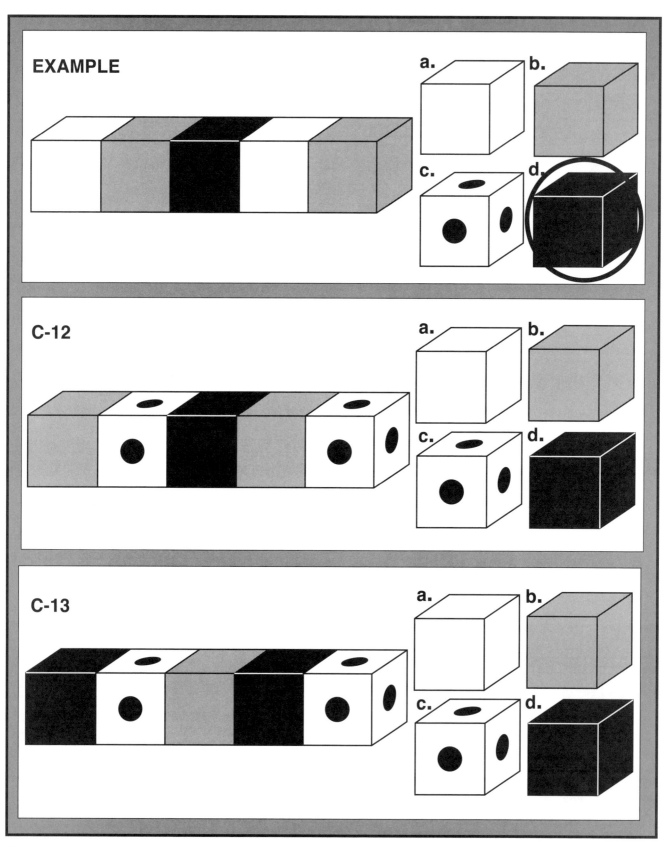

WHICH CUBE COMES NEXT?—SELECT

DIRECTIONS: Circle the cube that comes next.

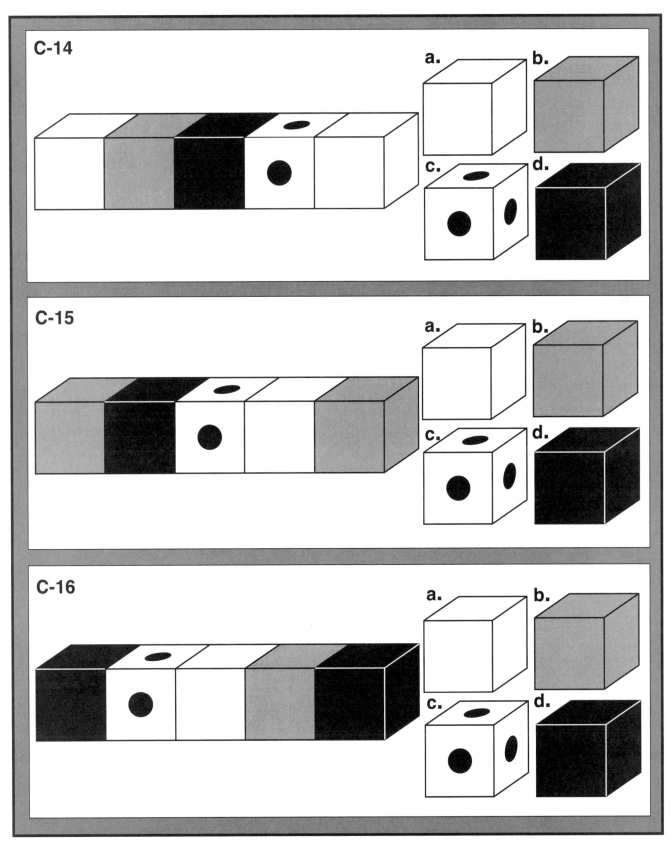

WHICH COLOR COMES NEXT?—SELECT

DIRECTIONS: Color the last cube in each row to continue the pattern.

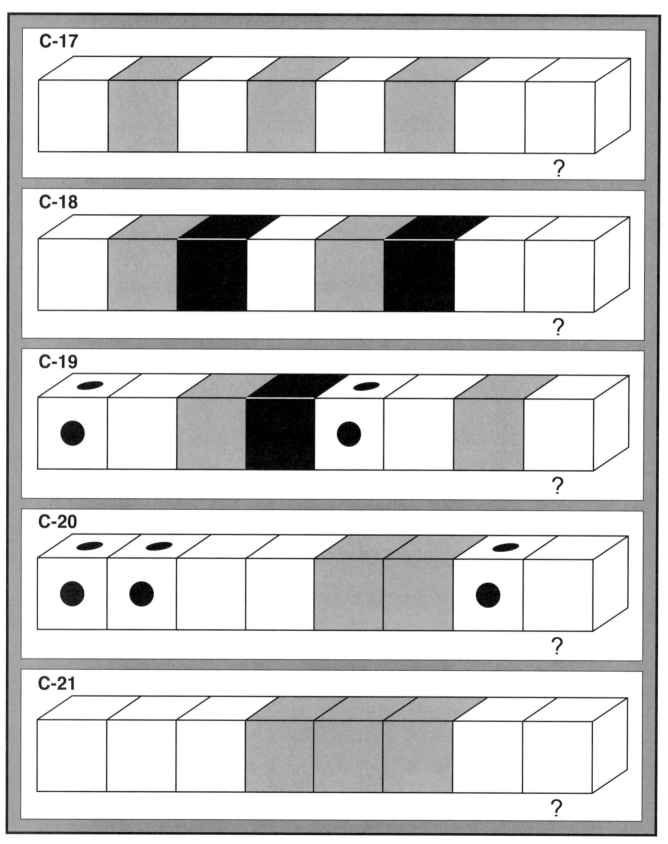

WHICH COLORS COME NEXT?—SELECT

DIRECTIONS: Use a pencil to draw the two squares that continue the pattern.

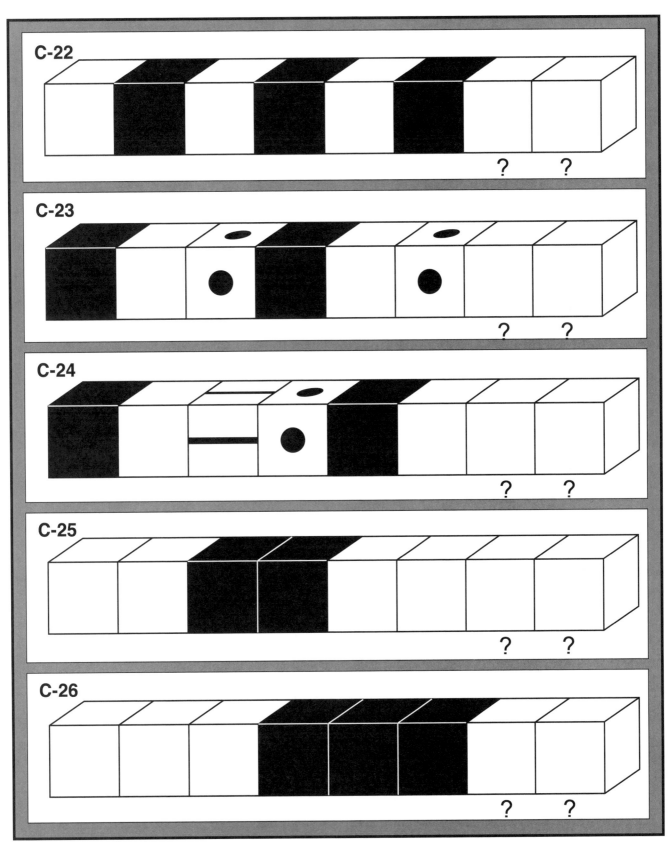

WHICH SHAPE COMES NEXT?—SELECT

DIRECTIONS: Circle the shape that comes next.

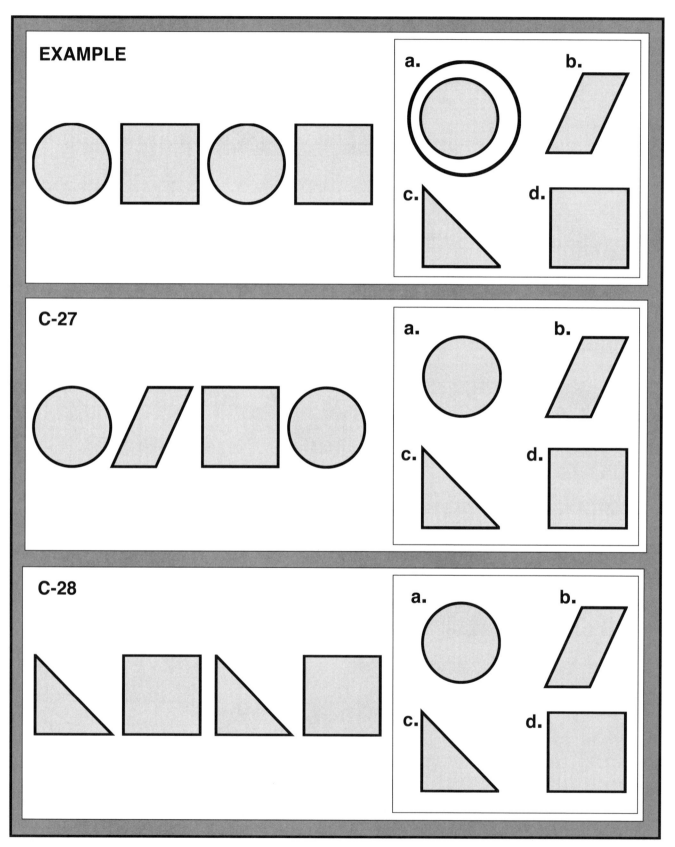

WHICH SHAPE COMES NEXT?—SELECT

DIRECTIONS: Circle the shape that comes next.

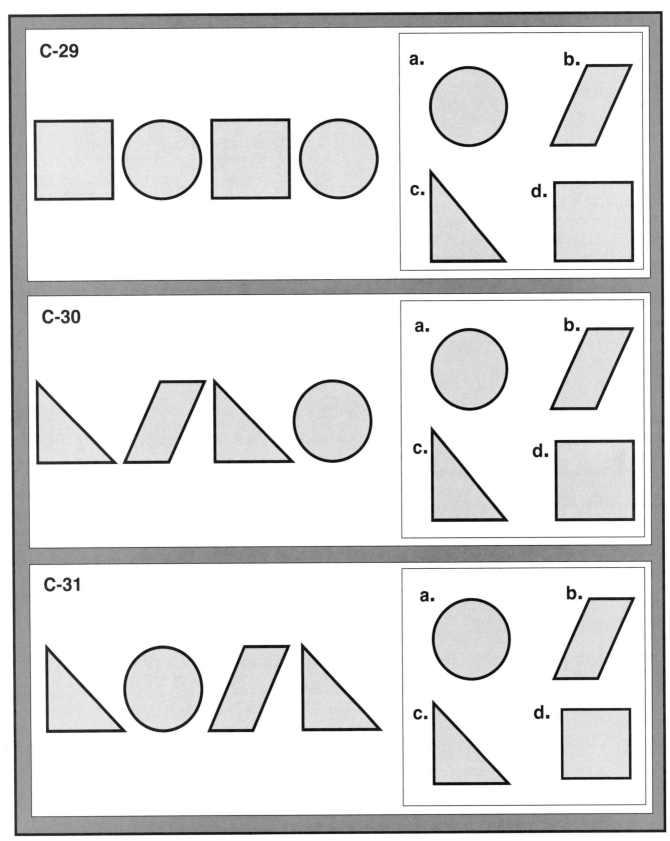

WHICH SHAPE COMES NEXT?—SELECT

DIRECTIONS: Each line contains a pattern of shapes. In the choice box, find the shape that continues the pattern. In the box at the right, write the letter that belongs to the correct shape.

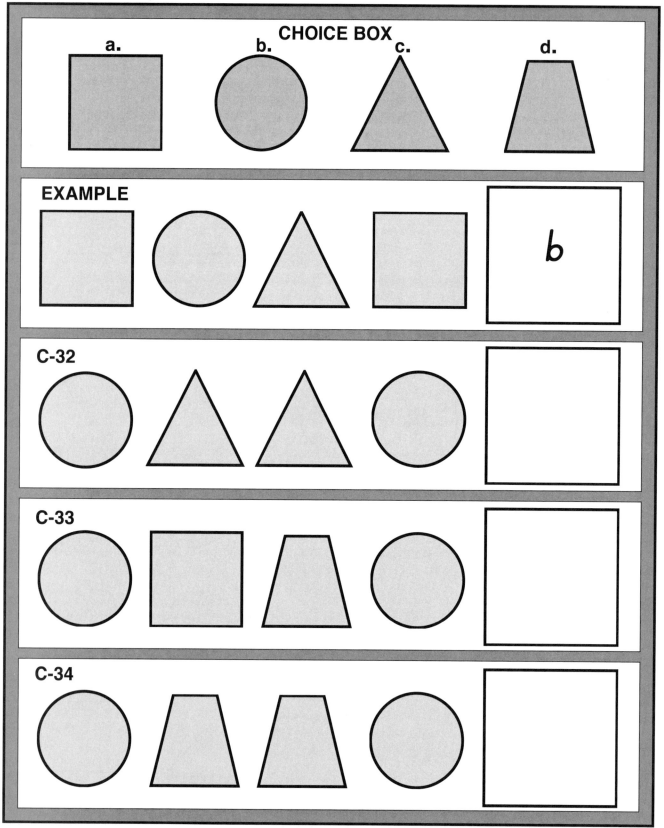

WHICH SHAPE COMES NEXT?—SELECT

DIRECTIONS: Each line contains a pattern of shapes. In the choice box, find the shape that continues the pattern. In the box at the right, write the letter that belongs to the correct shape.

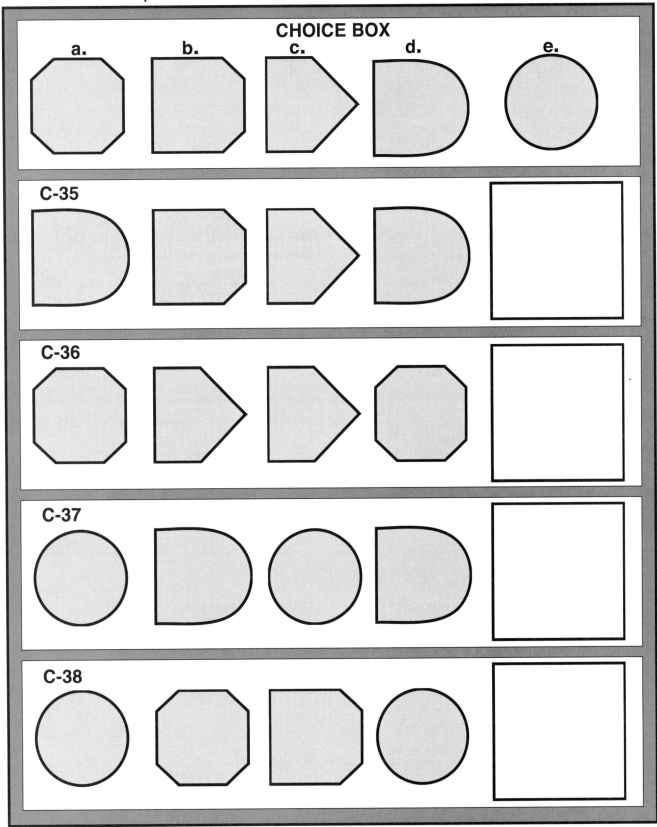

TUMBLING—COLORING

DIRECTIONS: As a figure tumbles along, the side that is on the ground changes. Tumble the blocks as shown. Color the following figures to show how they look as they tumble.

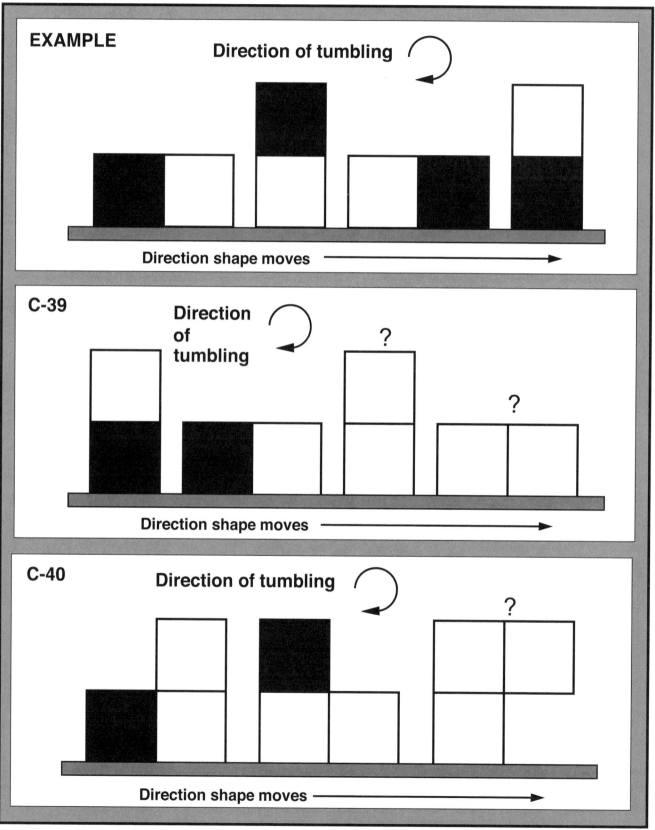

TUMBLING—SHADING

DIRECTIONS: As a shape tumbles along, the side that is on the ground changes. Darken the final two figures to show how they look as they tumble across the page.

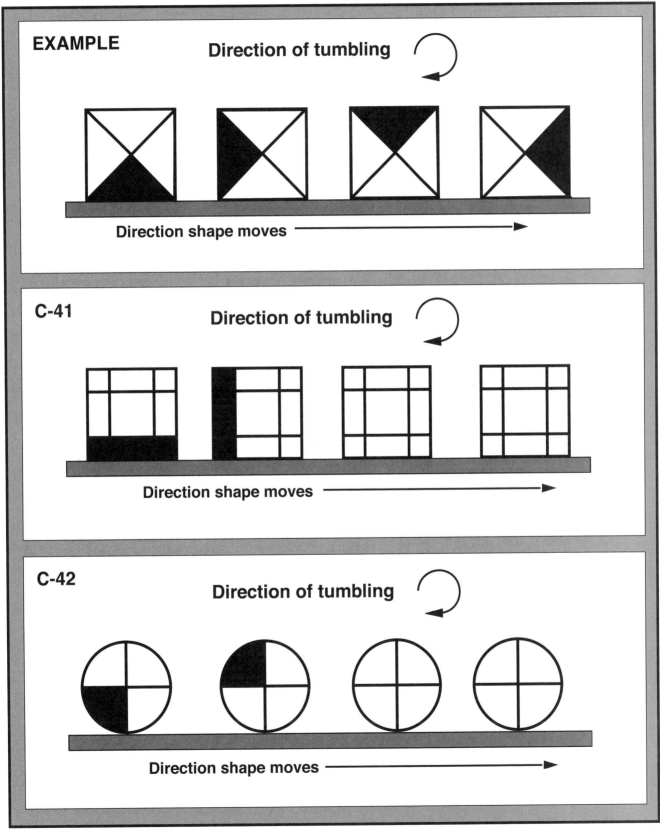

TUMBLING—SHADING

DIRECTIONS: As a shape tumbles along, the side that is on the ground changes. Darken the final two figures to show how they look as they tumble across the page.

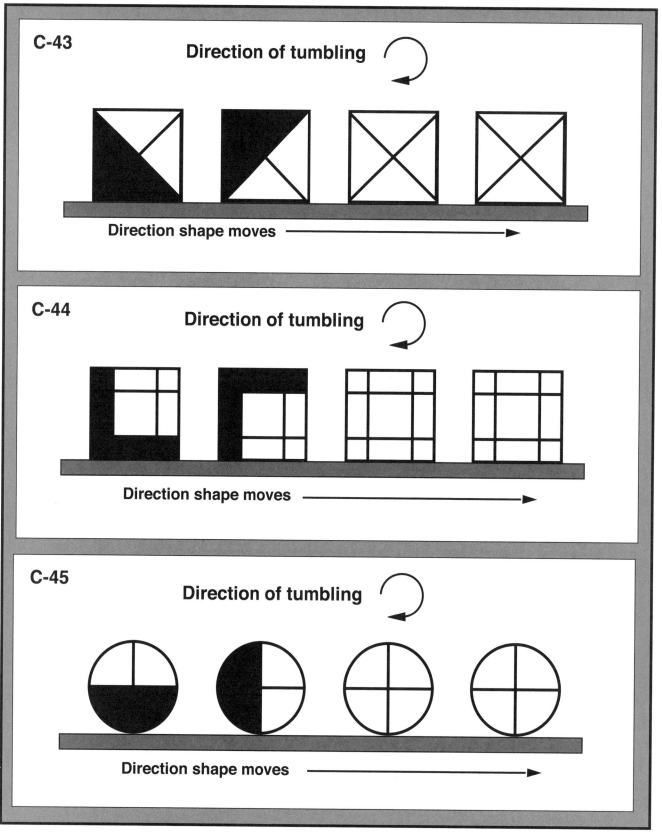

TUMBLING—DRAWING

DIRECTIONS: Color the figure to show what it will look like when it tumbles.

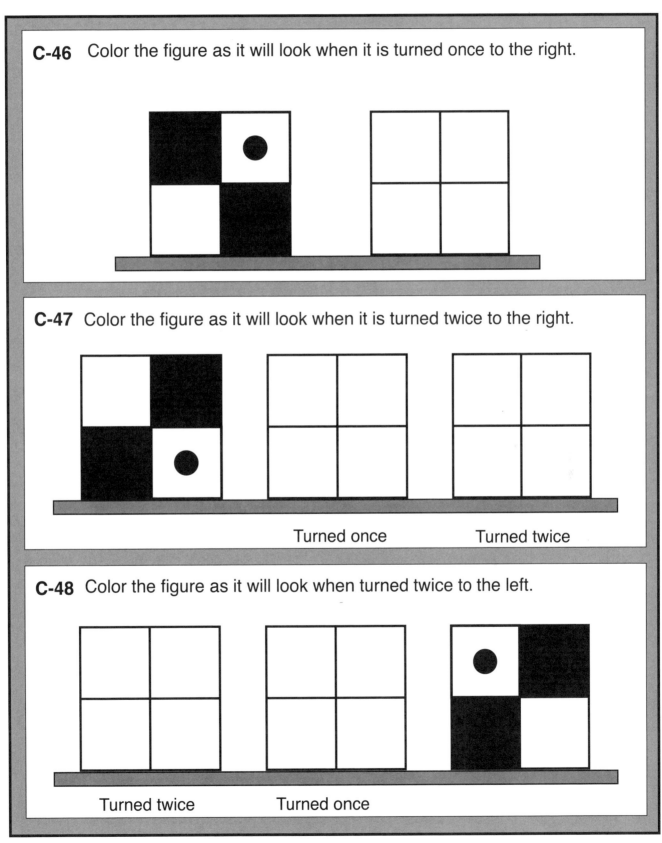

C-46 Color the figure as it will look when it is turned once to the right.

C-47 Color the figure as it will look when it is turned twice to the right.

Turned once   Turned twice

C-48 Color the figure as it will look when turned twice to the left.

Turned twice   Turned once

TUMBLING—DRAWING

DIRECTIONS: Draw and color the figure to show how it will look after it is tumbled.

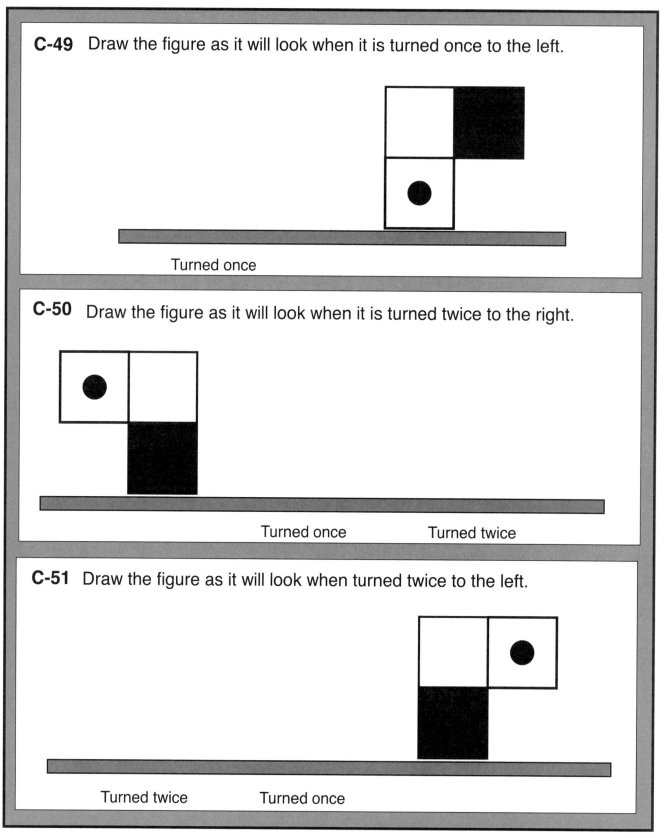

C-49 Draw the figure as it will look when it is turned once to the left.

Turned once

C-50 Draw the figure as it will look when it is turned twice to the right.

Turned once   Turned twice

C-51 Draw the figure as it will look when turned twice to the left.

Turned twice   Turned once

WHICH FIGURE COMES NEXT?—SELECT

DIRECTIONS: Circle the figure that comes next.

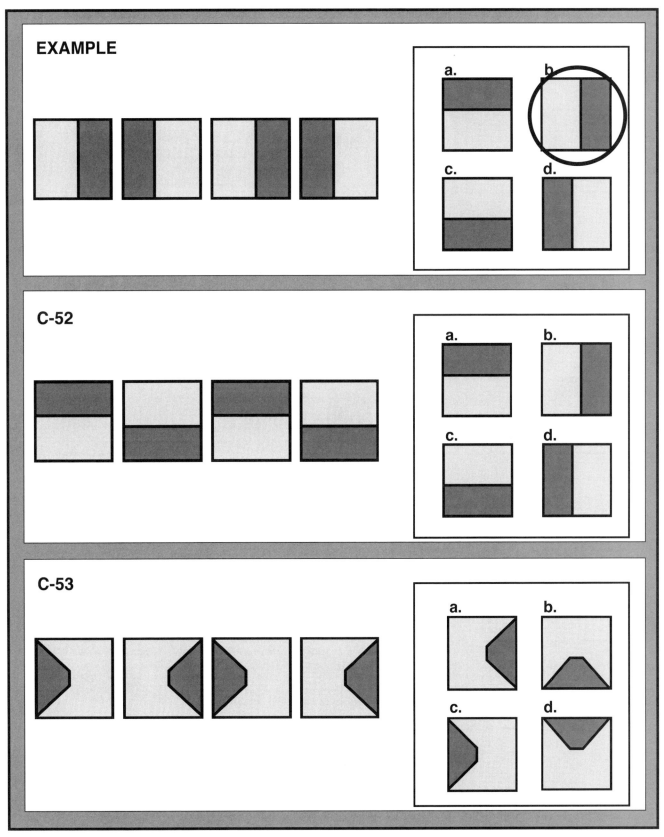

WHICH FIGURE COMES NEXT?—SELECT

DIRECTIONS: Circle the figure that comes next.

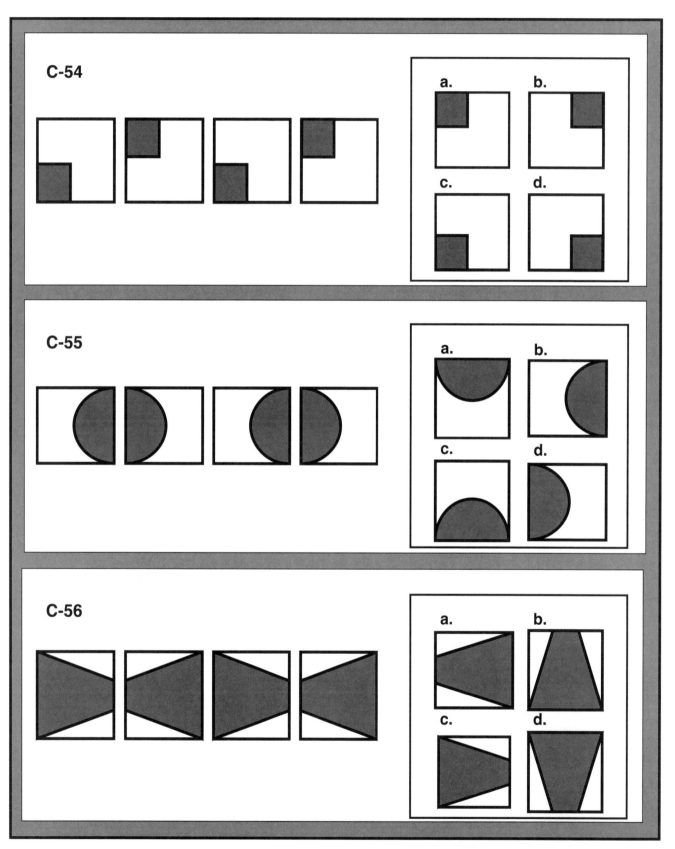

© 2006 The Critical Thinking Co.™ • www.CriticalThinking.com • 800-458-4849

WHICH FIGURE COMES NEXT?—SELECT

DIRECTIONS: Circle the figure that comes next.

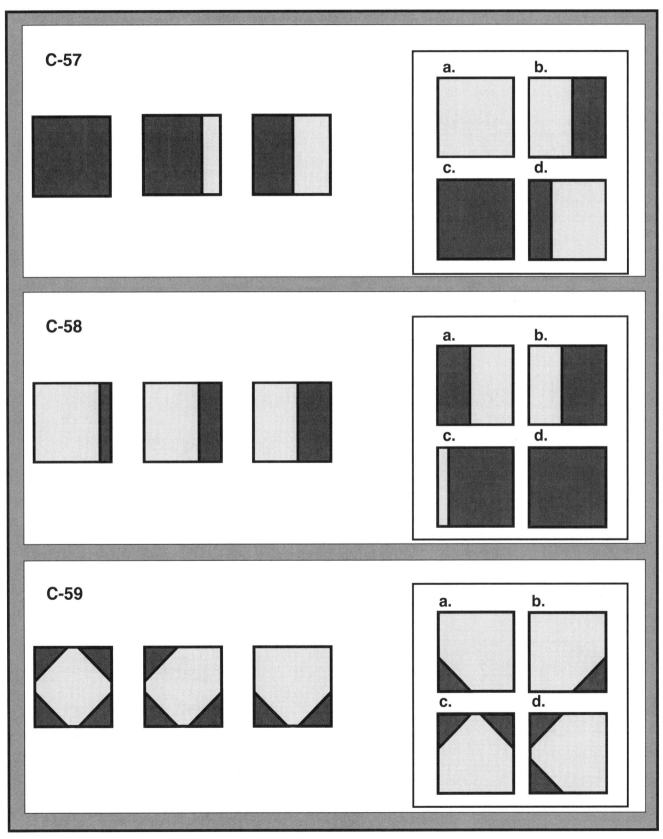

WHICH FIGURE COMES NEXT?—SELECT

DIRECTIONS: Circle the figure that comes next.

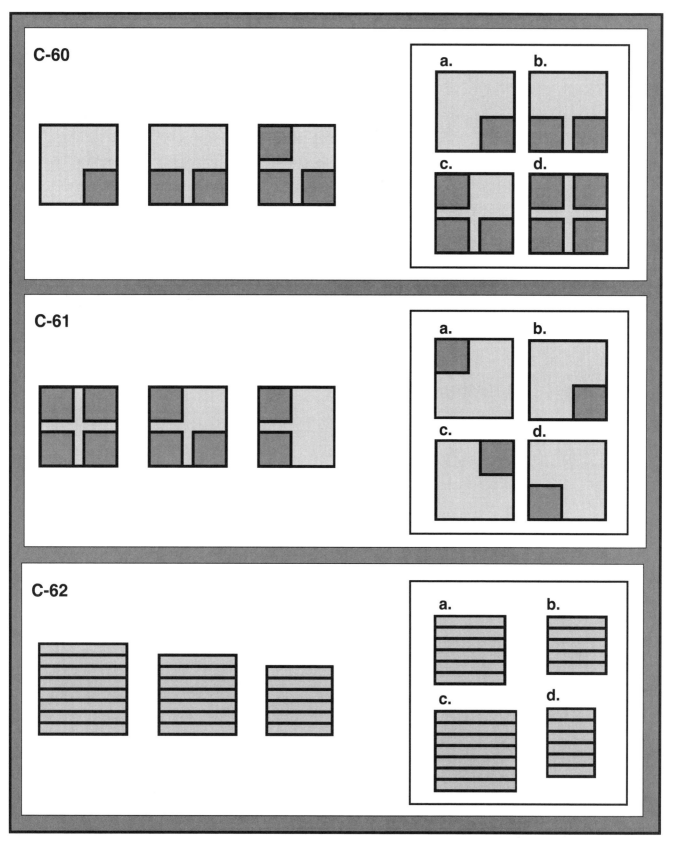

WHICH FIGURE COMES NEXT?—DRAW IT!

DIRECTIONS: Complete the sequence. Finish drawing the figure that comes next.

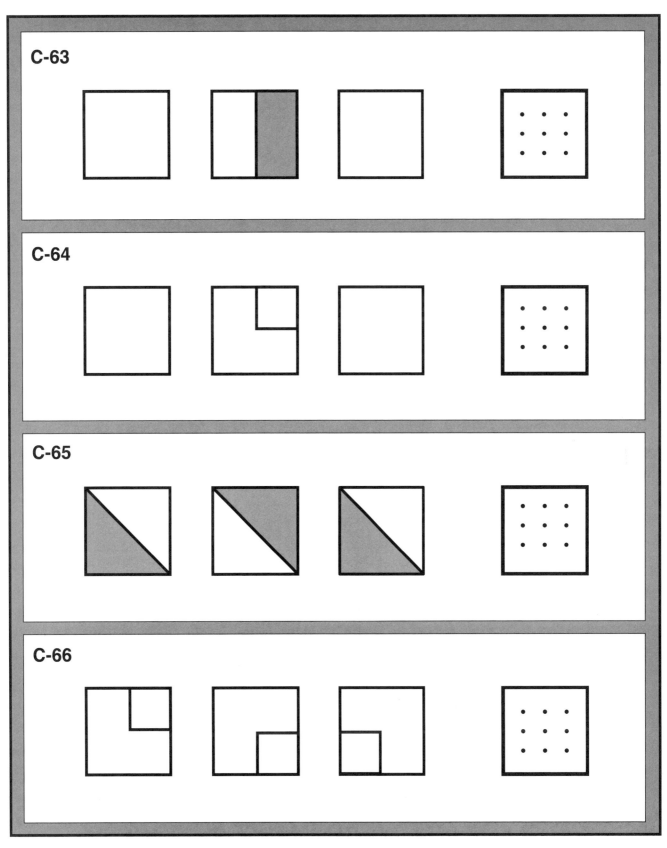

WHICH FIGURE COMES NEXT?—DRAW IT!

DIRECTIONS: Complete the sequence. Finish drawing the figure that comes next.

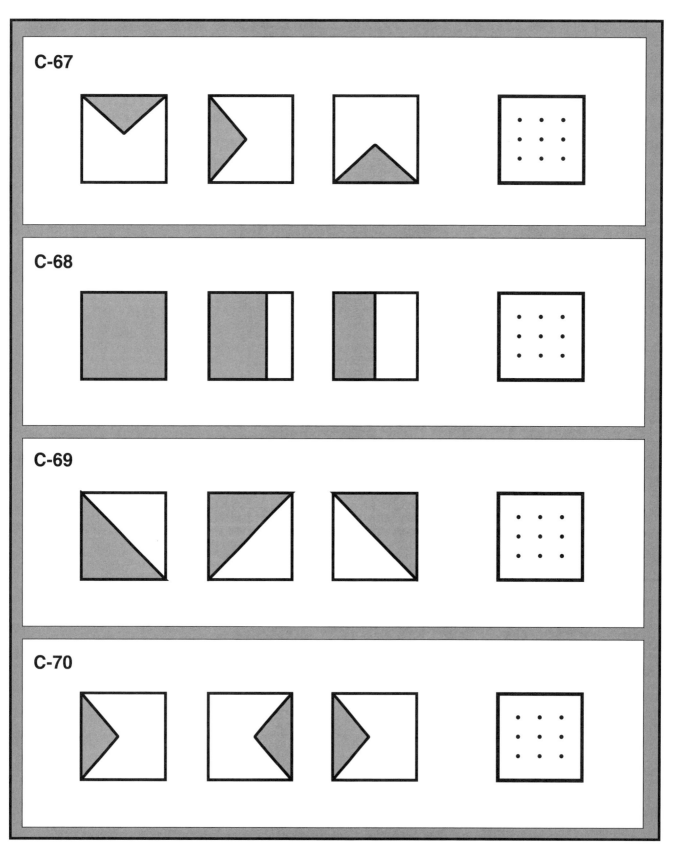

WHICH FIGURE COMES NEXT?—DRAW IT!

DIRECTIONS: Complete the sequence. Finish drawing the figure that comes next.

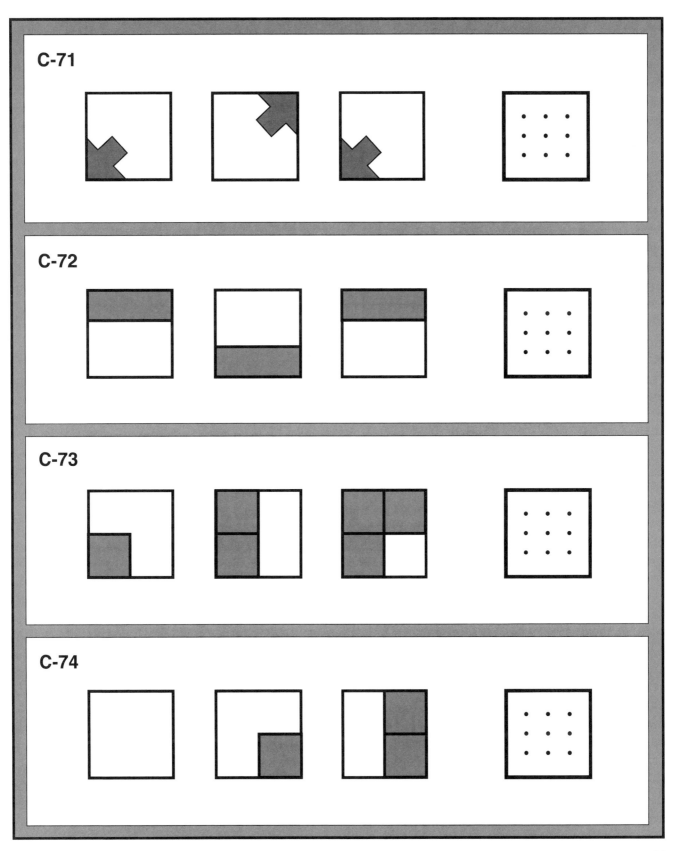

DESCRIBE A SEQUENCE

DIRECTIONS: Look at each sequence. Decide how the figures are changing. Write a description of the sequence on the lines below. Use complete sentences in your descriptions.

EXAMPLE

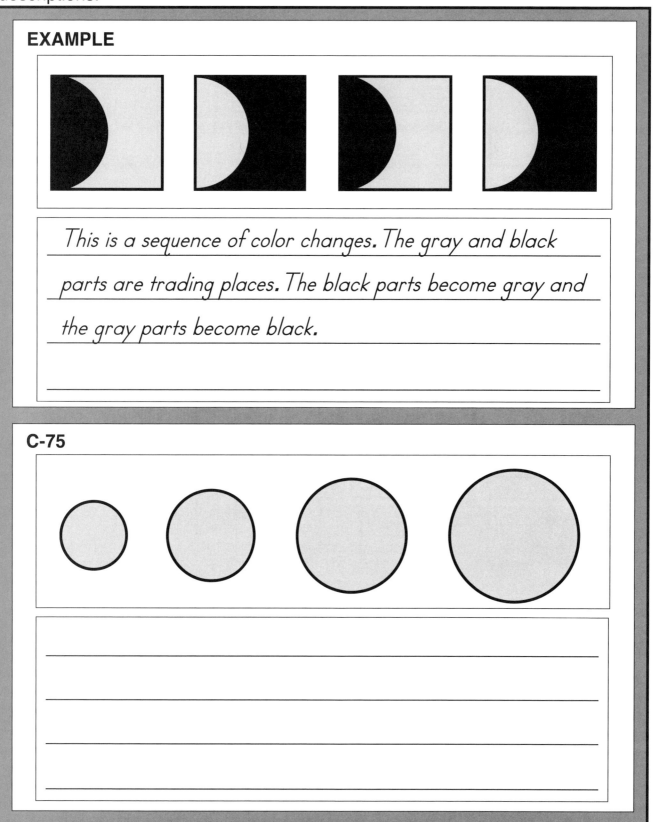

This is a sequence of color changes. The gray and black parts are trading places. The black parts become gray and the gray parts become black.

C-75

DESCRIBE A SEQUENCE

DIRECTIONS: Look at each sequence. Decide how the figures are changing. Write a description of the sequence on the lines below. Use complete sentences in your descriptions.

C-76

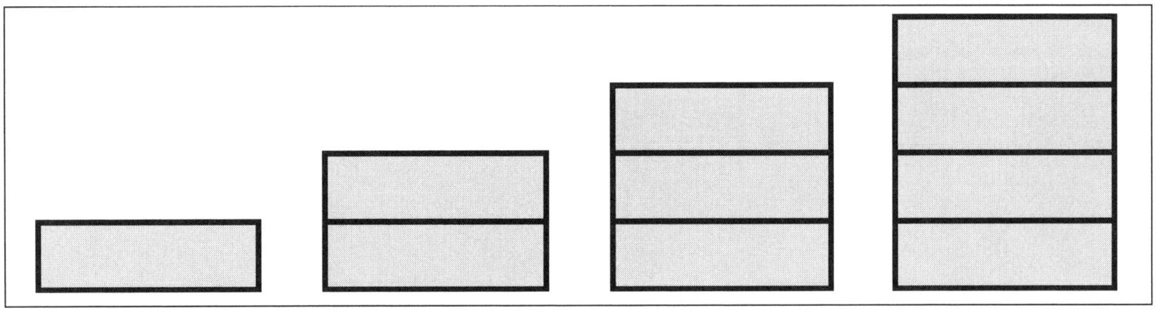

C-77

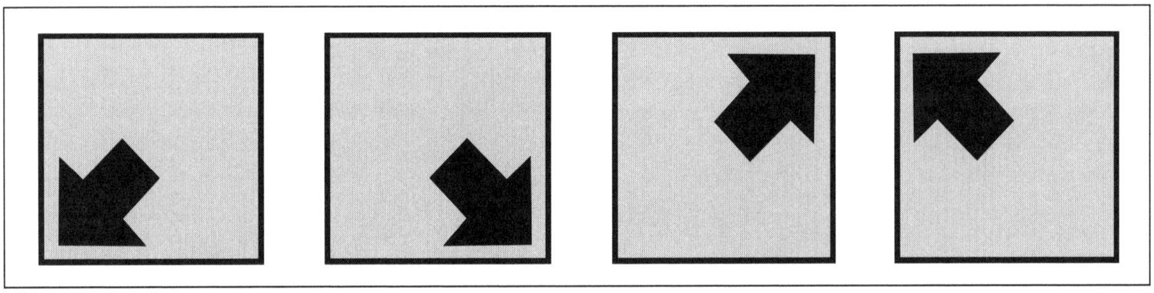

DESCRIBE A SEQUENCE

DIRECTIONS: Look at each sequence. Decide how the figures are changing. Write a description of the sequence on the lines below. Use complete sentences in your descriptions.

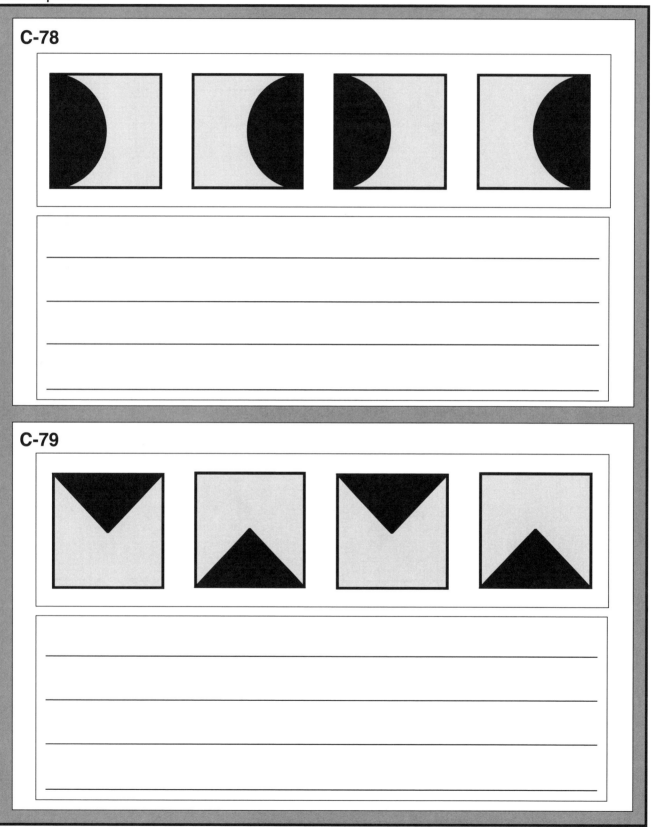

C-78

C-79

DESCRIBE A SEQUENCE

DIRECTIONS: Look at each sequence. Decide how the figures are changing. Write a description of the sequence on the lines below. Use complete sentences in your descriptions.

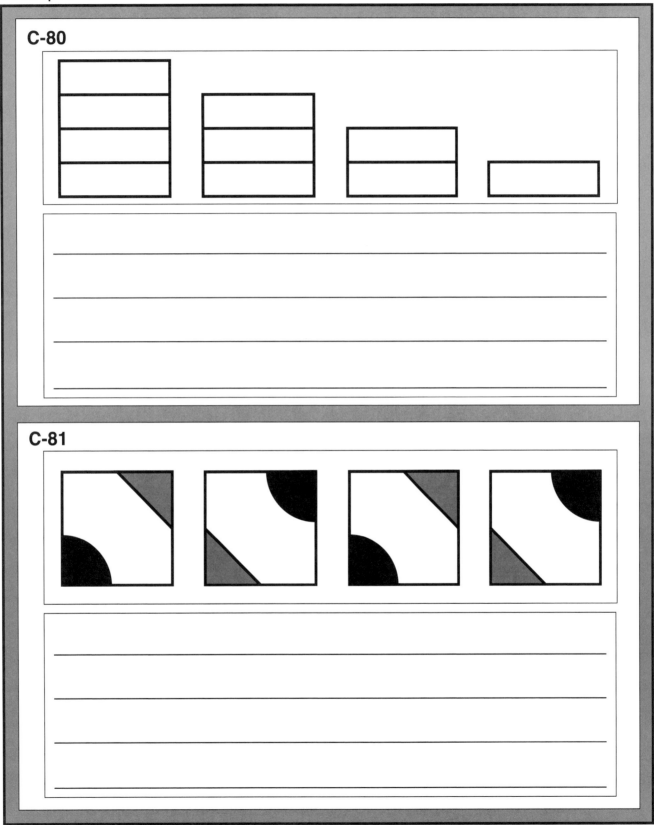

C-80

C-81

A SEQUENCE OF POLYGONS

DIRECTIONS: Look at the three polygons in the box. Cut the shapes apart. Arrange or draw them on the diagram.

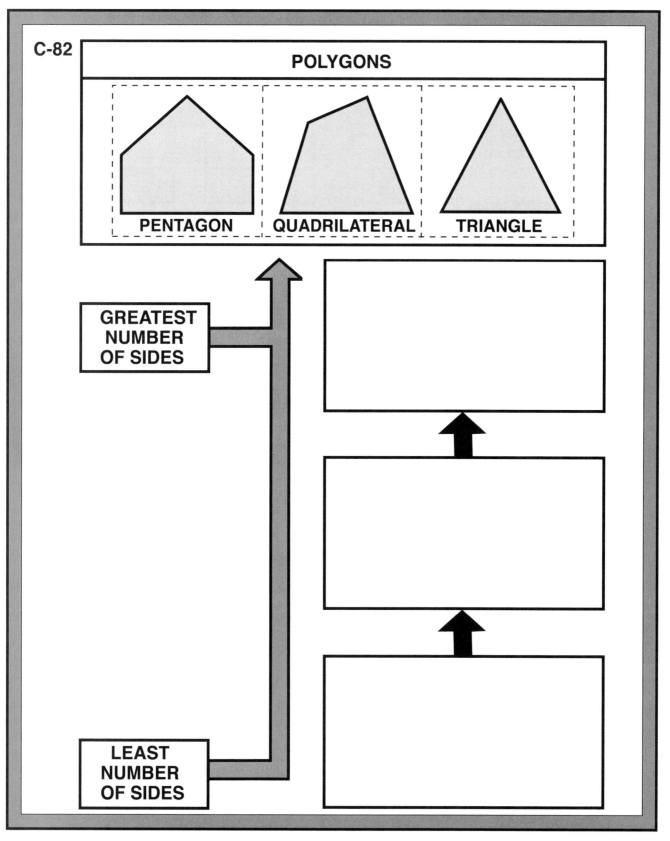

A SEQUENCE OF ANGLES

DIRECTIONS: Look at the three kinds of angles in the box. An angle is the shape made when two straight lines meet. On the diagram below, draw and label the angles from smallest to largest.

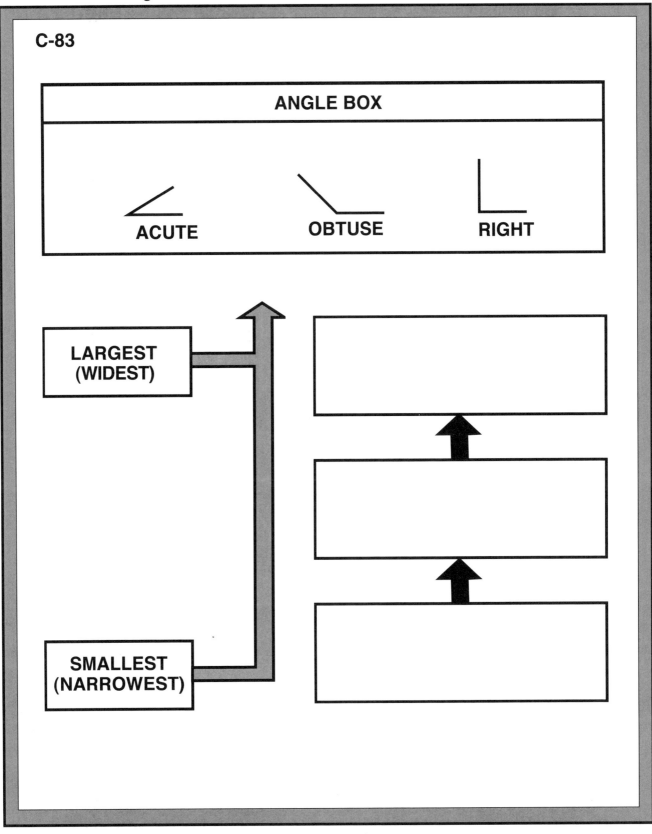

PAPER FOLDING-SELECT

DIRECTIONS: The figure on the left represents a sheet of paper with holes punched in it. How will the sheet look when folded along the dotted line? Circle the correct answer in the choice box.

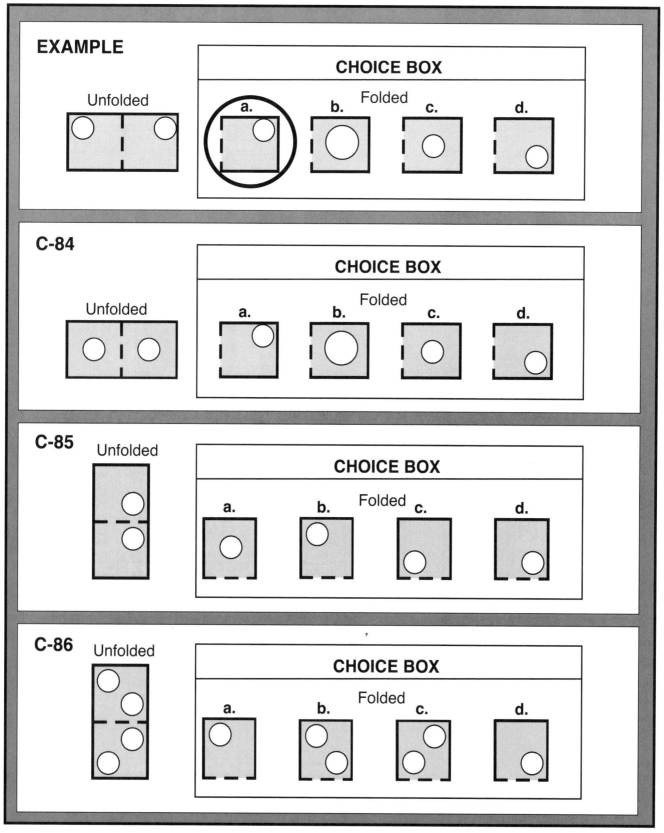

PAPER FOLDING-SELECT

DIRECTIONS: The figure on the left represents a sheet of paper with holes punched in it that has been folded along the dotted line. How will the sheet look when it is unfolded? Circle the correct answer in the choice box.

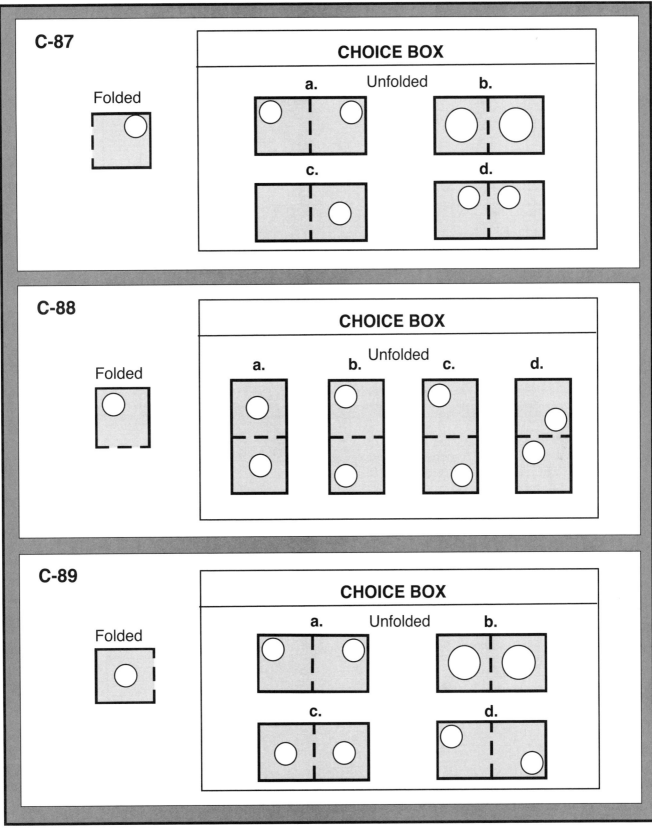

PAPER FOLDING—DRAW

DIRECTIONS: The figures on the left represent sheets of paper with holes punched in them. They are to be folded along the dotted line. Draw each sheet the way it will look after being folded.

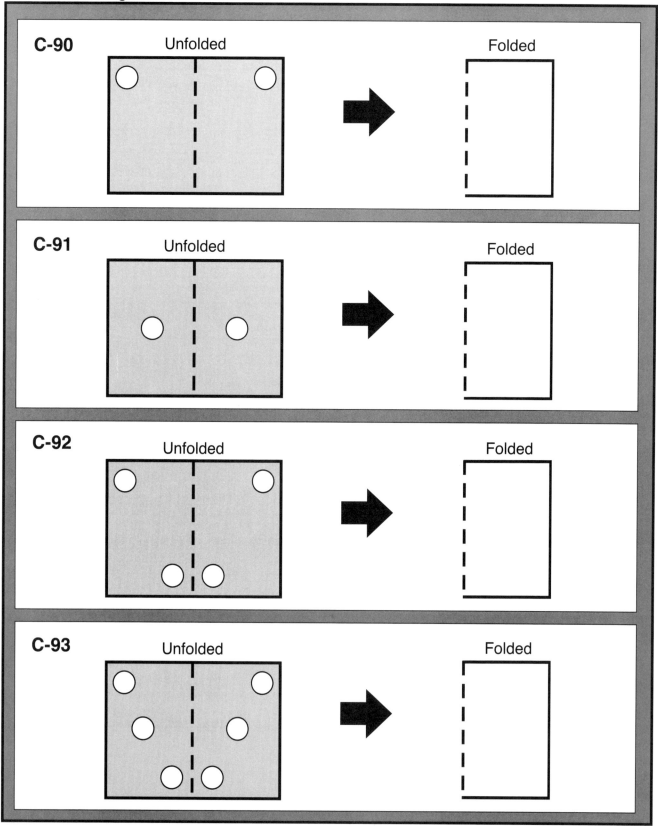

© 2006 The Critical Thinking Co.™ • www.CriticalThinking.com • 800-458-4849

PAPER FOLDING—DRAW

DIRECTIONS: The figures on the left represent sheets of paper with holes punched in them. They are folded along the dotted line. Draw each sheet as it will look when it is unfolded.

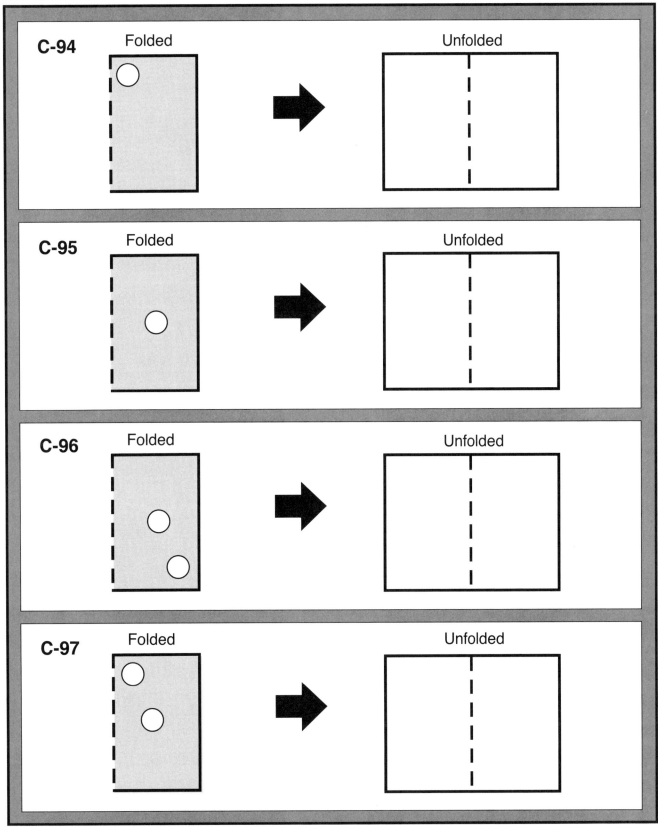

CHAPTER FOUR

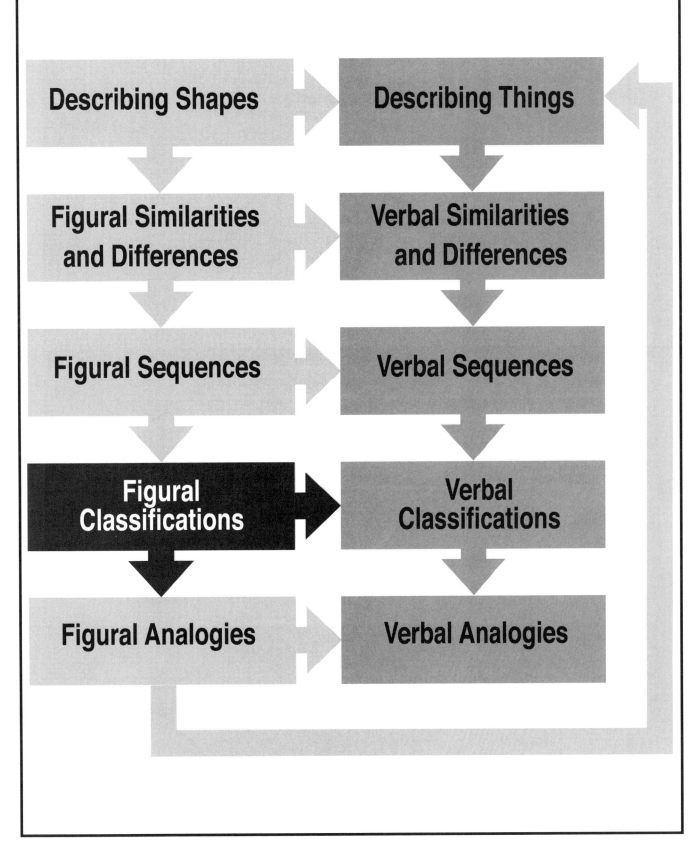

Describing Shapes

Describing Things

Figural Similarities and Differences

Verbal Similarities and Differences

Figural Sequences

Verbal Sequences

Figural Classifications

Verbal Classifications

Figural Analogies

Verbal Analogies

MATCH A SHAPE TO A GROUP

DIRECTIONS: Draw a line from each shape at the left to the group on the right in which it belongs.

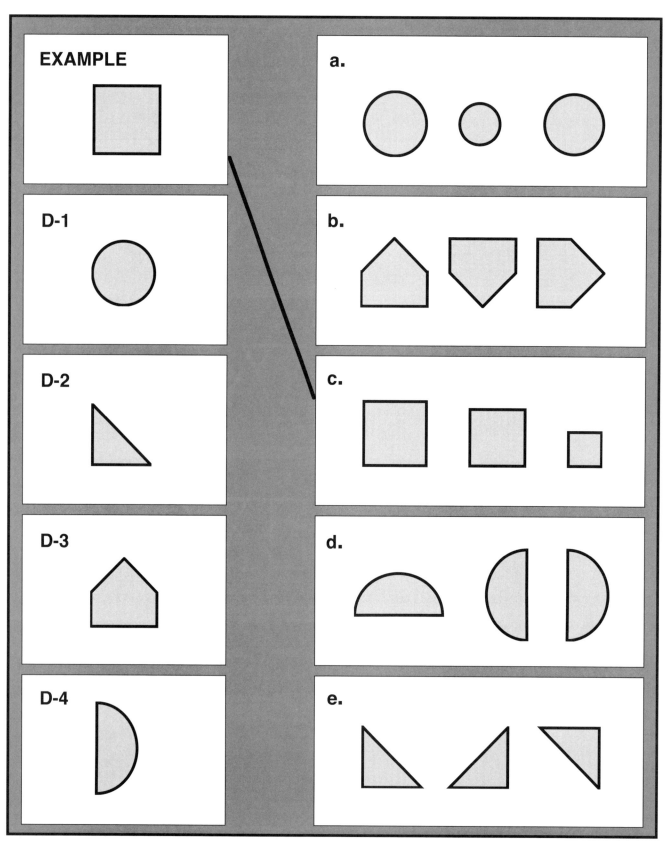

EXAMPLE

D-1

D-2

D-3

D-4

a.

b.

c.

d.

e.

MATCH A SHAPE TO A GROUP

DIRECTIONS: Draw a line from each shape on the left to the group on the right in which it belongs.

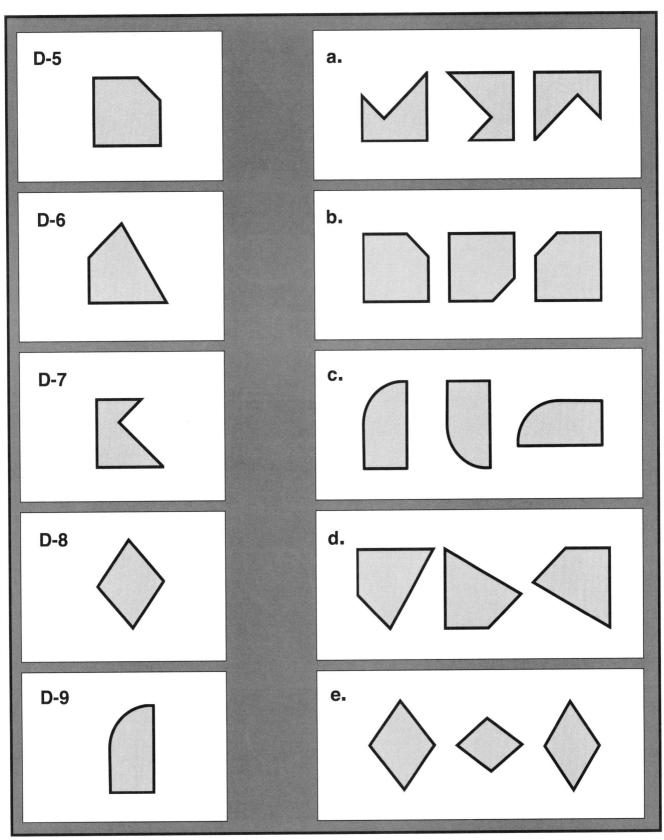

MATCH A PATTERN TO A GROUP

DIRECTIONS: Sometimes figures are grouped by patterns. Match each shape on the left with the correct group on the right by drawing a line from the shape to the group (class) having the same pattern.

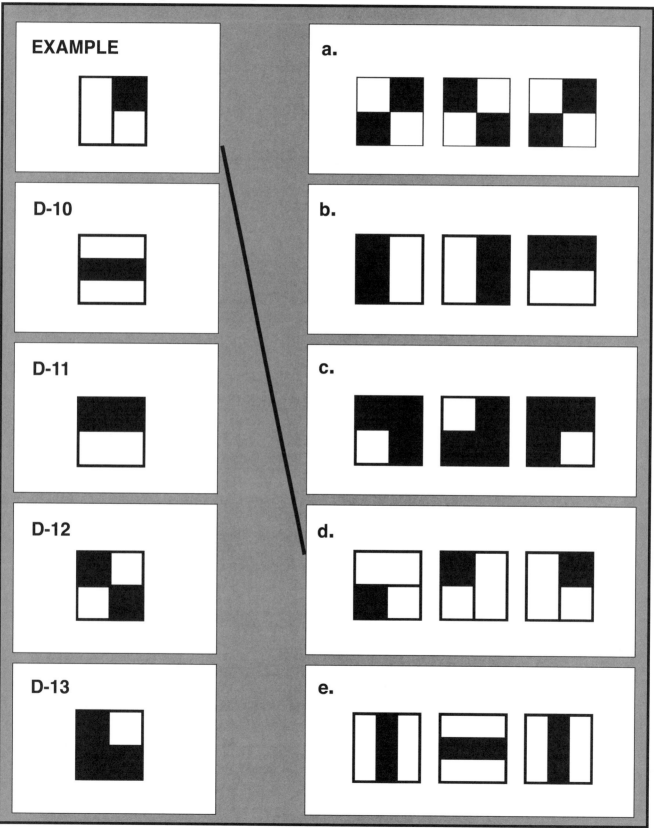

MATCH A PATTERN TO A GROUP

DIRECTIONS: Sometimes figures are grouped by patterns. Match each shape on the left with the correct group on the right by drawing a line from the shape to the group (class) having the same pattern.

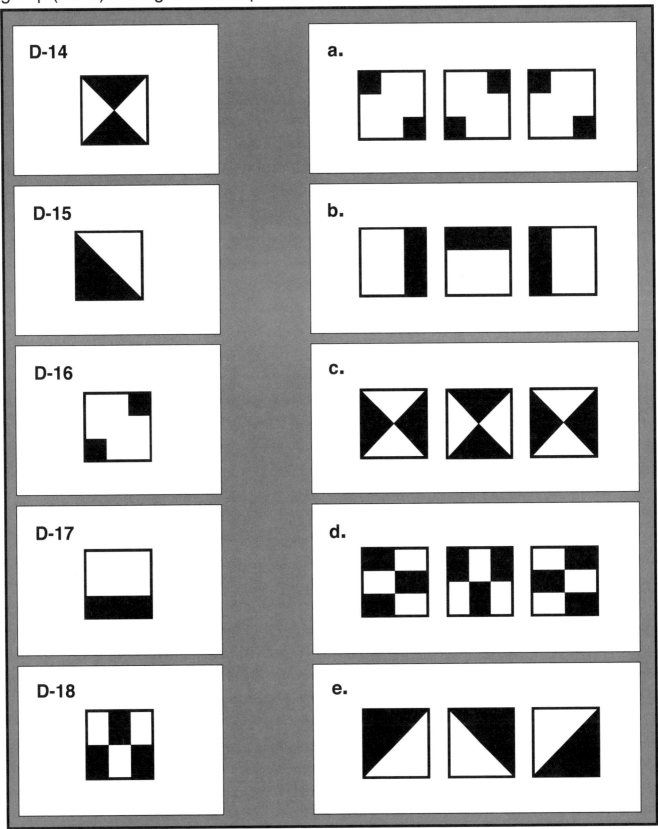

SELECT A SHAPE THAT BELONGS TO A GROUP

DIRECTIONS: The box on the left contains several figures of the same shape. The box on the right contains several lettered shapes. Check or circle the shape on the right that belongs to the group at the left.

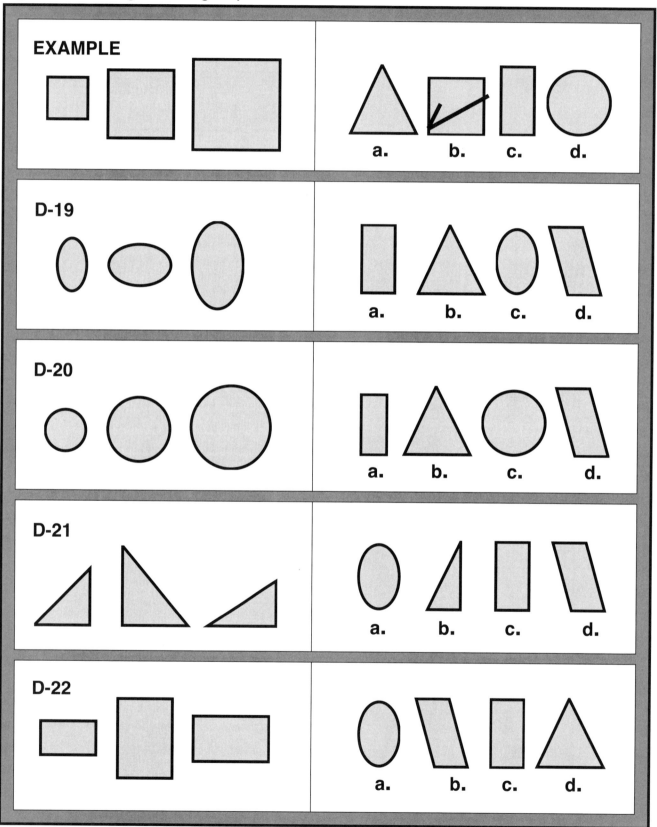

SELECT A SHAPE THAT BELONGS TO A GROUP

DIRECTIONS: The box on the left contains several figures of the same shape. The box on the right contains several lettered shapes. Check or circle the shape on the right that belongs to the group at the left.

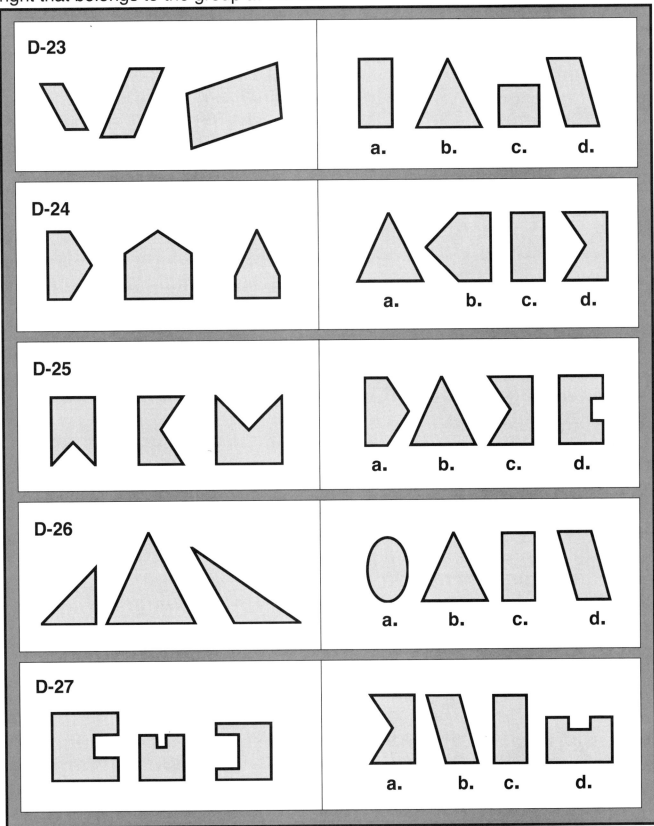

DESCRIBING CLASSES

DIRECTIONS: Circle the letter in front of each true statement.

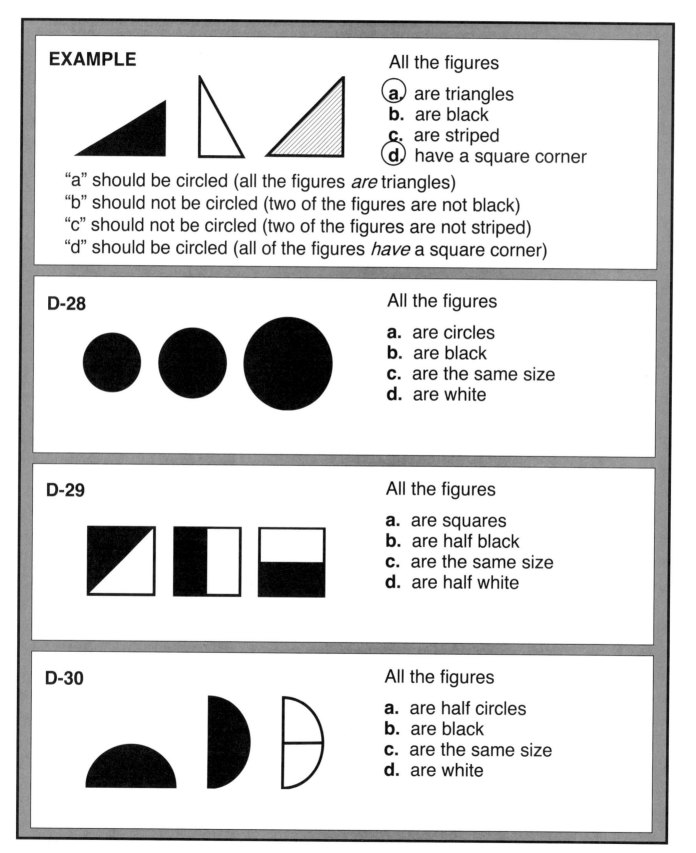

EXAMPLE

All the figures

a. are triangles
b. are black
c. are striped
d. have a square corner

"a" should be circled (all the figures *are* triangles)
"b" should not be circled (two of the figures are not black)
"c" should not be circled (two of the figures are not striped)
"d" should be circled (all of the figures *have* a square corner)

D-28

All the figures

a. are circles
b. are black
c. are the same size
d. are white

D-29

All the figures

a. are squares
b. are half black
c. are the same size
d. are half white

D-30

All the figures

a. are half circles
b. are black
c. are the same size
d. are white

DESCRIBING CLASSES

DIRECTIONS: Circle the letter in front of each true statement.

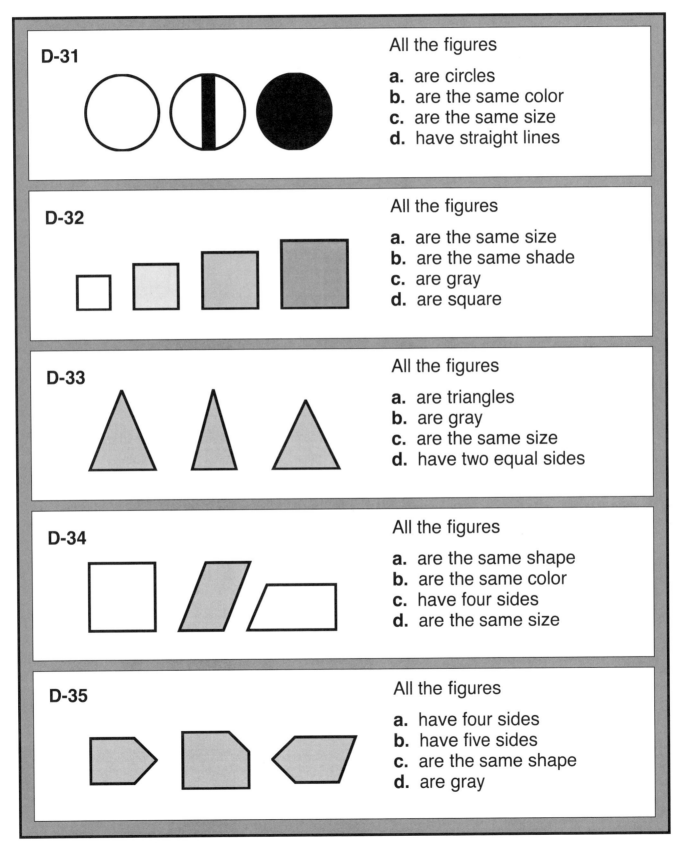

D-31

All the figures

a. are circles
b. are the same color
c. are the same size
d. have straight lines

D-32

All the figures

a. are the same size
b. are the same shade
c. are gray
d. are square

D-33

All the figures

a. are triangles
b. are gray
c. are the same size
d. have two equal sides

D-34

All the figures

a. are the same shape
b. are the same color
c. have four sides
d. are the same size

D-35

All the figures

a. have four sides
b. have five sides
c. are the same shape
d. are gray

MATCHING CLASSES BY SHAPE

DIRECTIONS: For every box on the left, there is a box on the right with the same shape. Draw lines between boxes that have shapes of the same class.

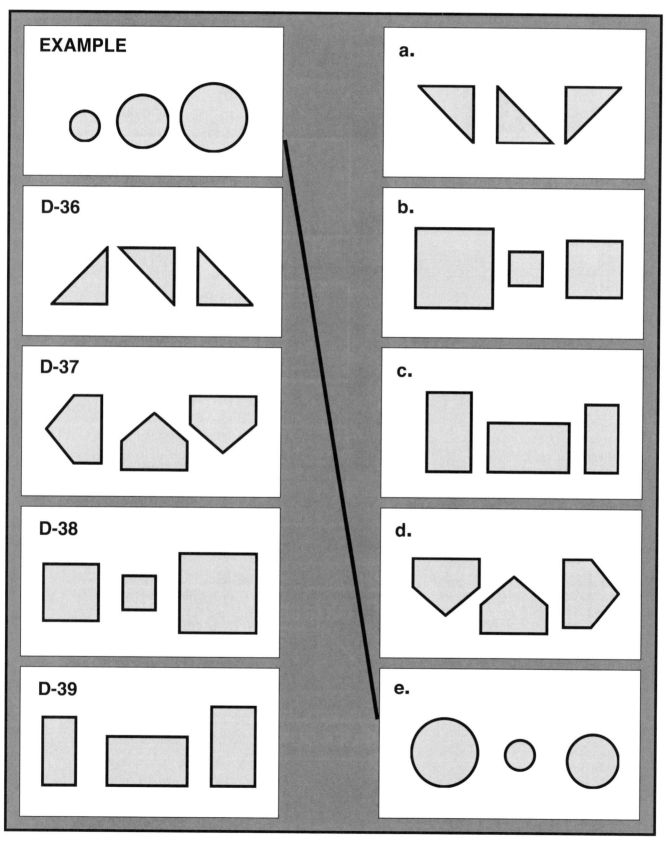

EXAMPLE

D-36

D-37

D-38

D-39

a.

b.

c.

d.

e.

MATCHING CLASSES BY SHAPE

DIRECTIONS: Draw lines between boxes that have shapes that belong to the same class.

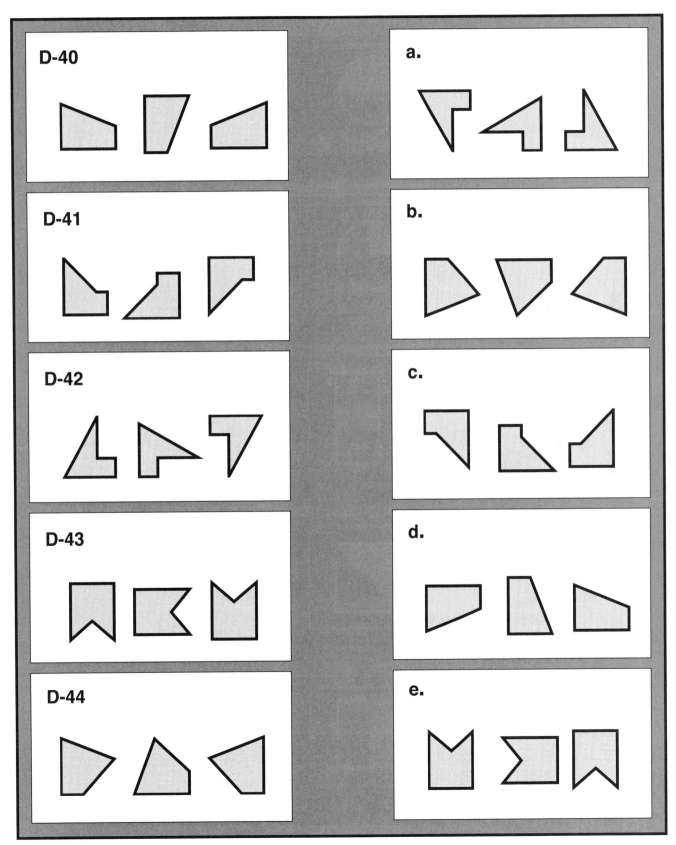

MATCHING CLASSES BY PATTERN

DIRECTIONS: Draw a line from each pattern on the left to a pattern on the right that belongs to the same class.

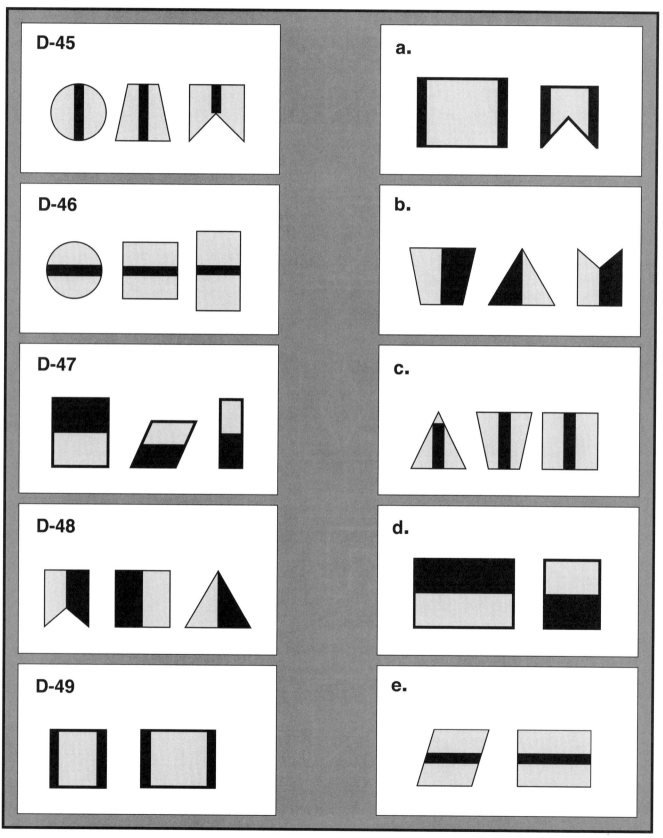

CLASSIFYING BY SHAPE—FIND THE EXCEPTION

DIRECTIONS: In each row, cross out the shape that does <u>not</u> belong to the class.

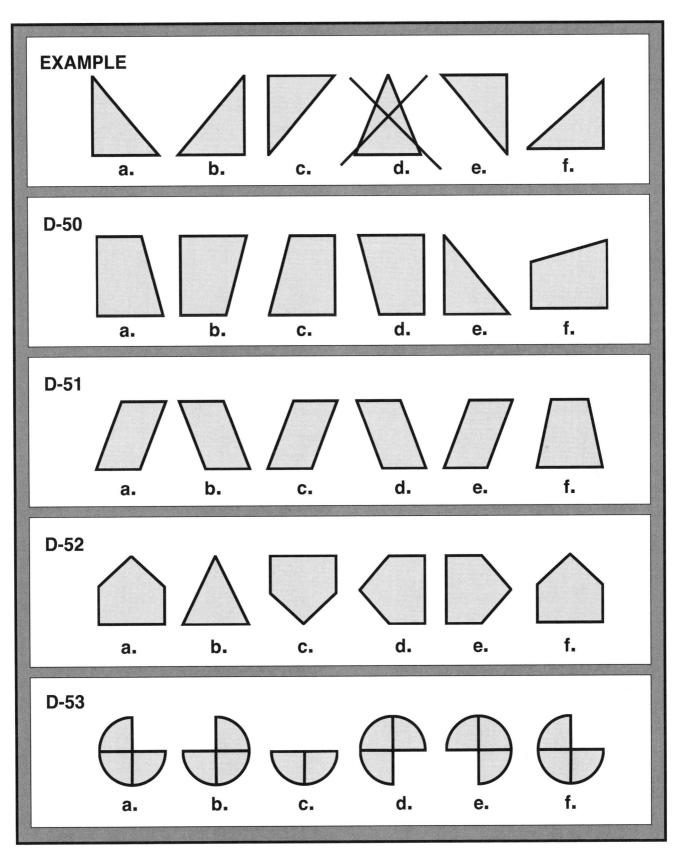

CLASSIFYING BY SHAPE—FIND THE EXCEPTION

DIRECTIONS: In each row, cross out the shape that does <u>not</u> belong to the class.

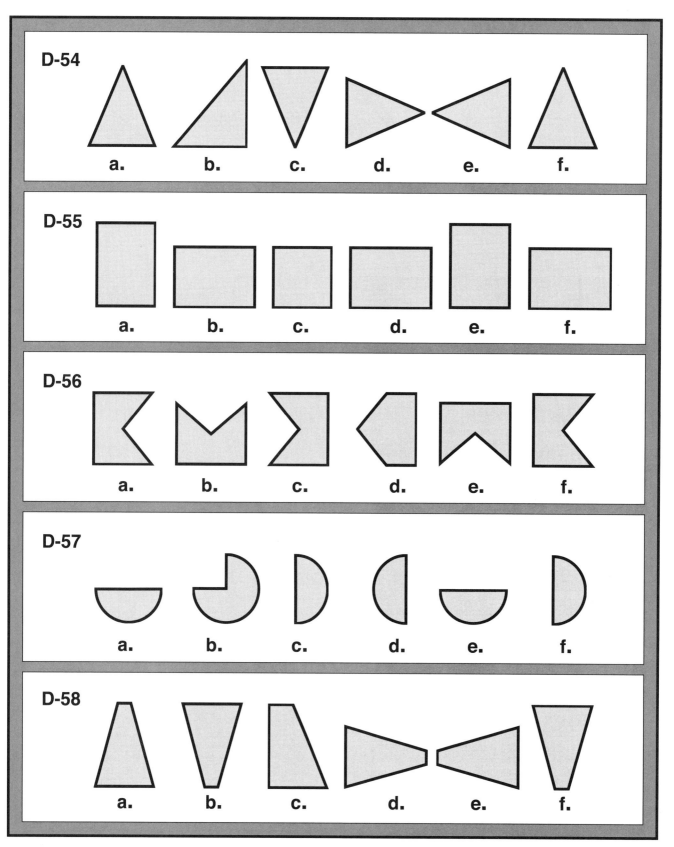

CLASSIFYING BY PATTERN—FIND THE EXCEPTION

DIRECTIONS: In each row, cross out the figure that does <u>not</u> belong to the class.

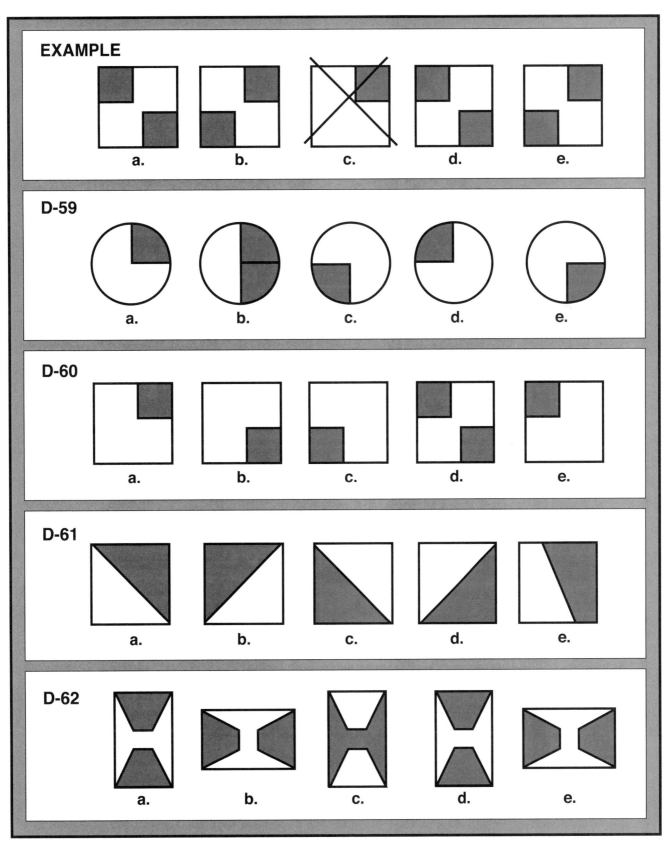

CLASSIFYING BY PATTERN—FIND THE EXCEPTION

DIRECTIONS: In each row, cross out the figure that does <u>not</u> belong to the class.

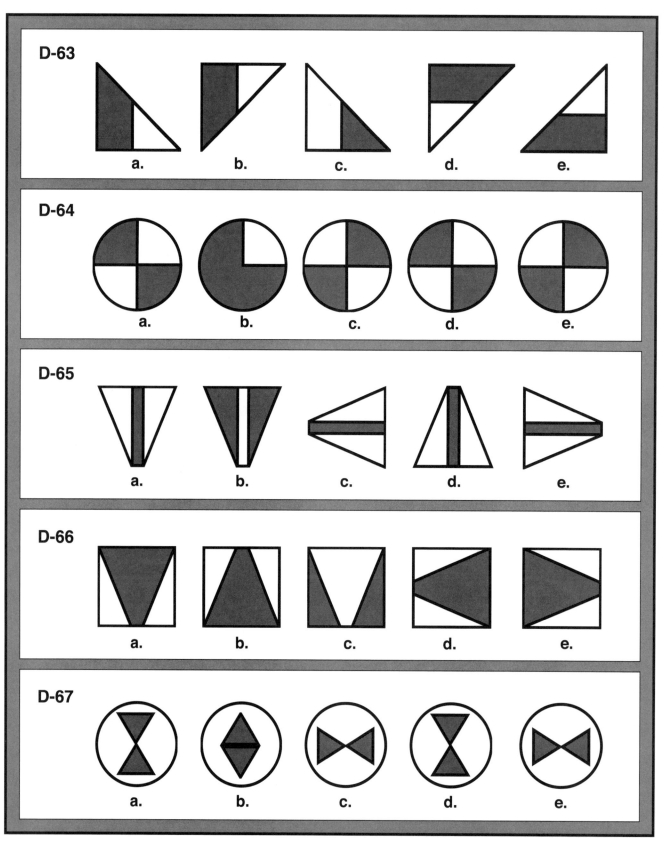

CLASSIFYING MORE THAN ONE WAY

DIRECTIONS: On the line beside each figure, write the letters of all classes to which the figure can belong. Classes are shown at the bottom of the page.

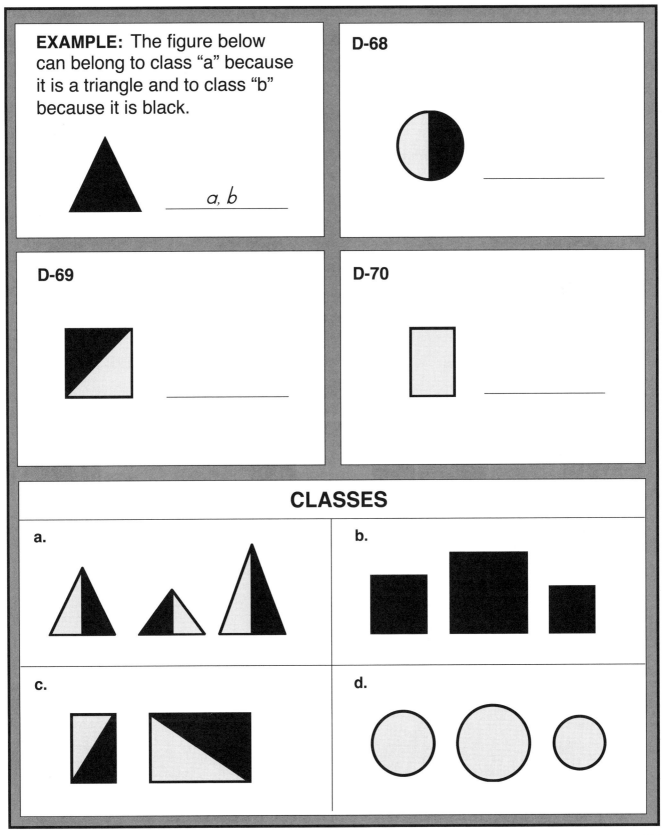

EXAMPLE: The figure below can belong to class "a" because it is a triangle and to class "b" because it is black.

_a, b_

D-68

D-69

D-70

CLASSES

a.

b.

c.

d.

CLASSIFYING MORE THAN ONE WAY

DIRECTIONS: On the line beside each figure, write the letters of all classes to which the figure can belong. Classes are shown at the bottom of the page.

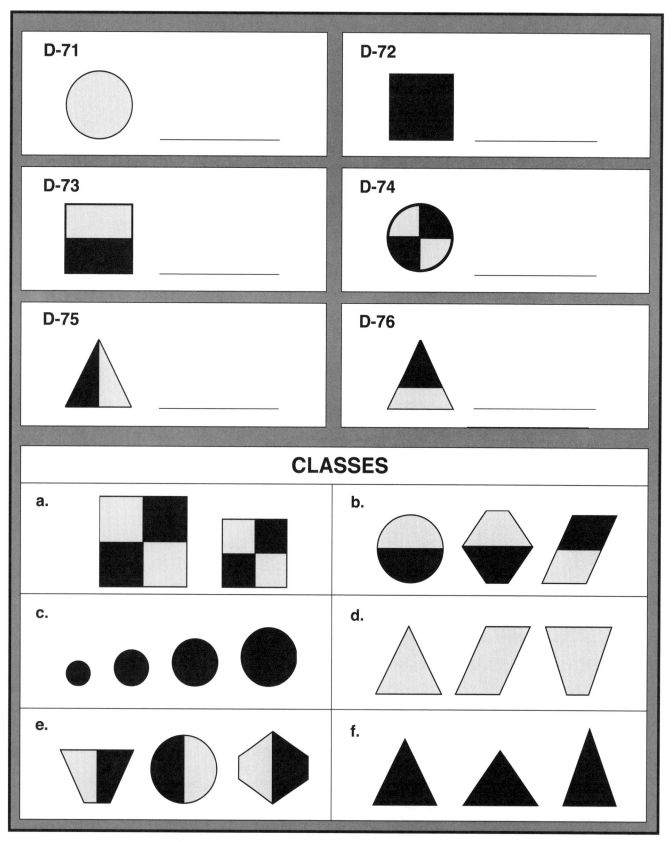

CLASSIFYING BY COLOR—SORTING

DIRECTIONS: Each shape below is made of several squares. In the boxes at the bottom, draw and color the shapes that belong in each class.

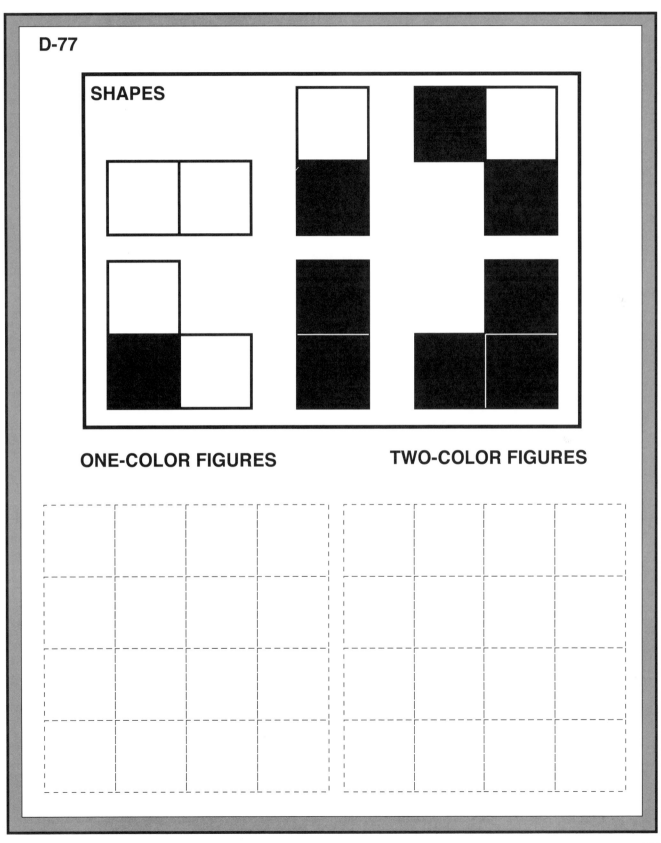

CLASSIFYING BY SHAPE—SORTING

DIRECTIONS: Each shape below is made of several squares. In the boxes at the bottom, draw and color the shapes that belong in each class.

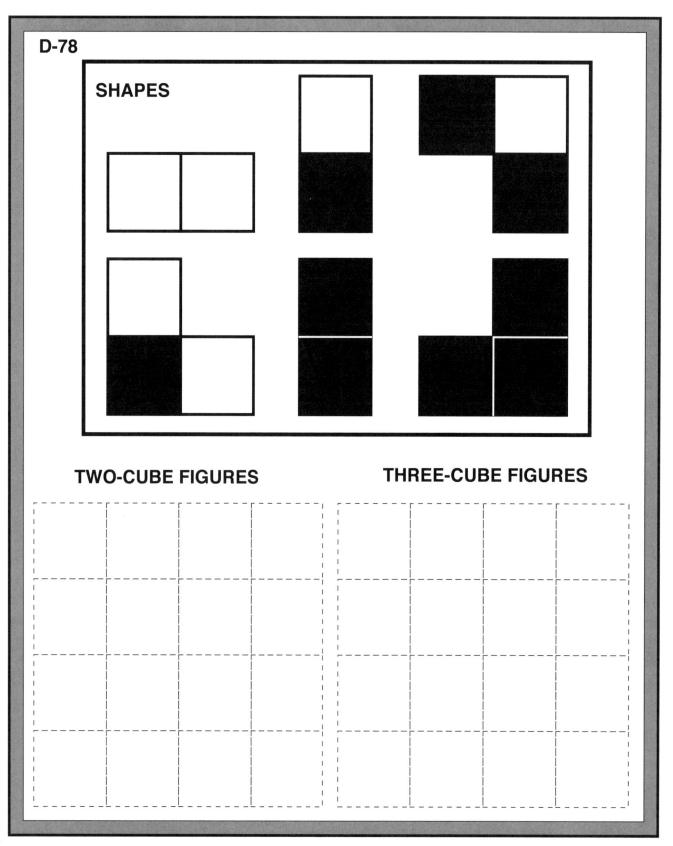

D-78

SHAPES

TWO-CUBE FIGURES   **THREE-CUBE FIGURES**

COMPLETE THE CLASS

DIRECTIONS: The shapes at the top of the page can be classified in many ways. At the bottom of the page, list the numbers of the shapes that complete each group.

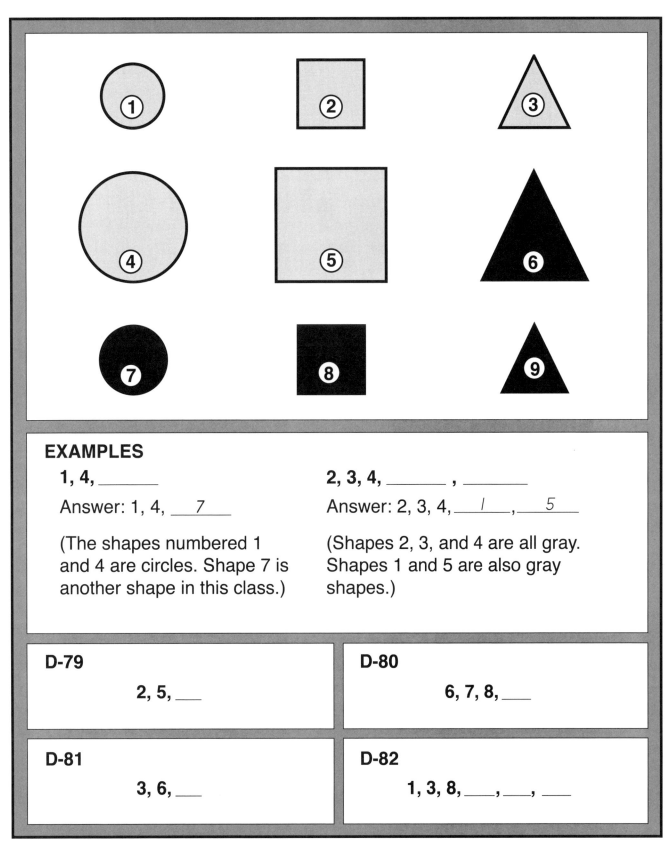

EXAMPLES

1, 4, _____

Answer: 1, 4, ___7___

(The shapes numbered 1 and 4 are circles. Shape 7 is another shape in this class.)

2, 3, 4, _____ , _____

Answer: 2, 3, 4, ___1___ , ___5___

(Shapes 2, 3, and 4 are all gray. Shapes 1 and 5 are also gray shapes.)

D-79

2, 5, ___

D-80

6, 7, 8, ___

D-81

3, 6, ___

D-82

1, 3, 8, ___ , ___ , ___

COMPLETE THE CLASS

DIRECTIONS: The figures at the left can be classified in many ways. Fill in each blank with the number of the figure that completes the given group.

FIGURES FOR D-83 to D-88

D-83	1, 6, _____
D-84	1, 3, _____
D-85	2, 4, _____
D-86	2, 5, _____
D-87	7, 8, _____
D-88	3, 4, _____

FIGURES FOR D-89 to D-94

D-89	1, 2, _____
D-90	3, 6, _____
D-91	7, 8, _____
D-92	1, 4, _____
D-93	2, 5, _____
D-94	4, 5, _____

FORM A CLASS

DIRECTIONS: The figures at the left can be classified in many ways. Fill in each blank with the numbers of the figures that belong to the group described.

FIGURES FOR D-95 to D-98

EXAMPLE	Squares
	1, 6, 8

D-95	Rectangles that are not squares
	_____

D-96	Gray shapes
	_____

D-97	Circles
	_____

D-98	Black shapes
	_____

FIGURES FOR D-99 to D-103

D-99	Circles
	_____

D-100	Squares
	_____

D-101	Black shapes
	_____

D-102	Triangles
	_____

D-103	Hexagons
	_____

DRAW ANOTHER

DIRECTIONS: In each grid on the right, draw a different figure that belongs to the group on the left.

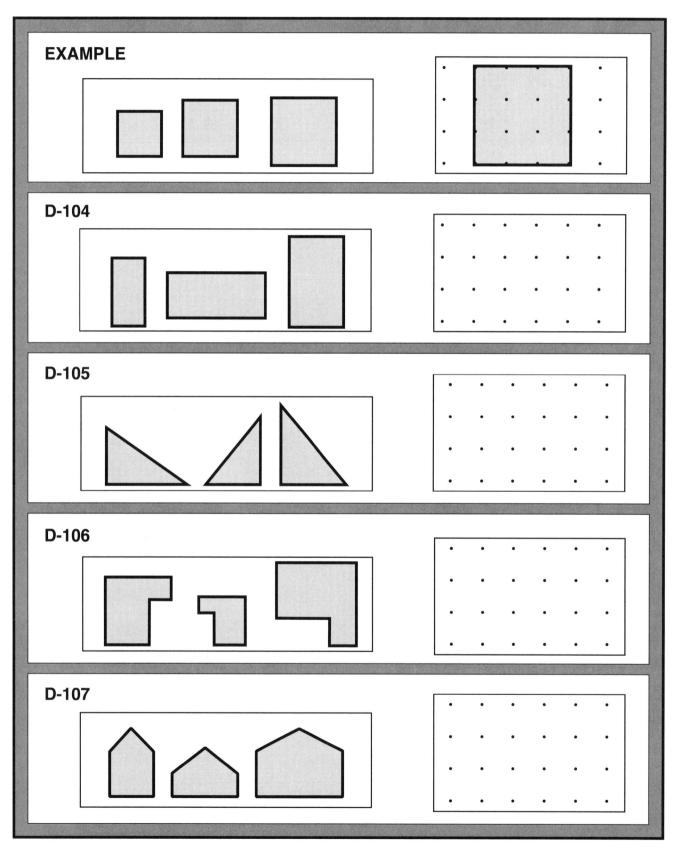

DRAW ANOTHER

DIRECTIONS: In each grid on the right, draw a different figure that belongs to the group on the left.

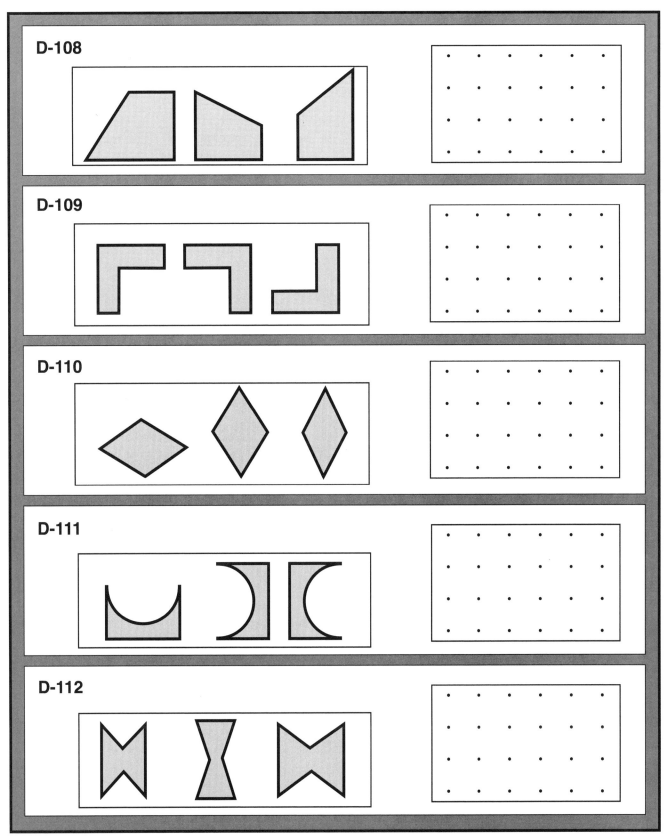

DRAW ANOTHER

DIRECTIONS: In each grid on the right, draw a different figure that belongs to the group on the left.

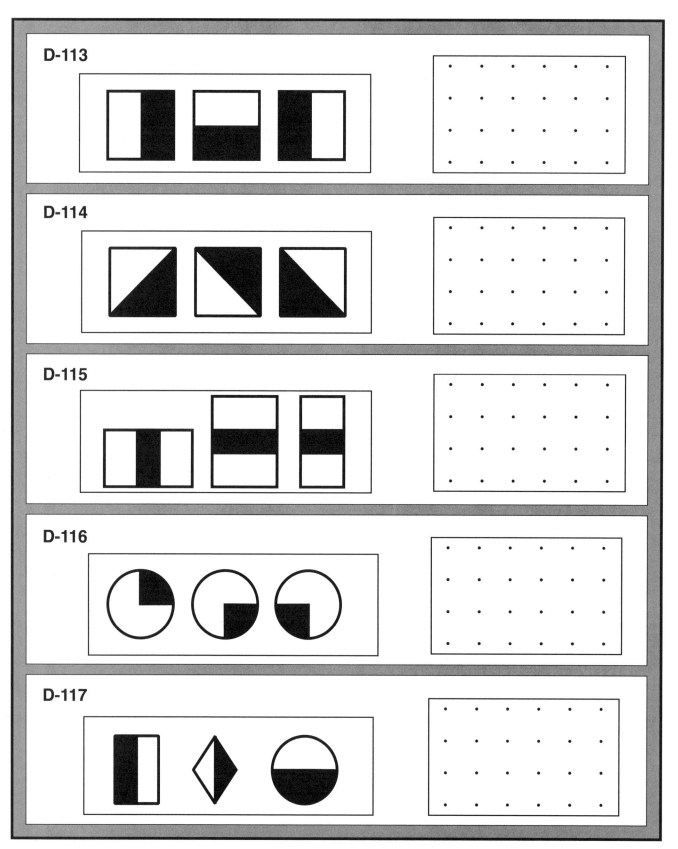

CLASSIFYING BY SHAPE—SORTING

DIRECTIONS: The figures at the top can be sorted into classes in more than one way. In the boxes at the bottom, draw and color the figures that belong in each class.

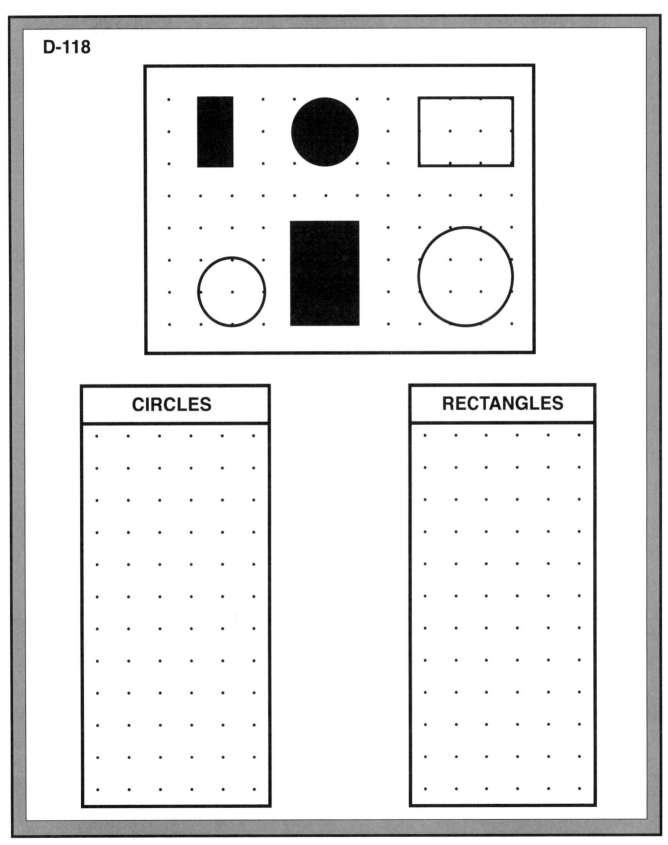

CLASSIFYING BY COLOR—SORTING

DIRECTIONS: The figures at the top can be sorted into classes in more than one way. In the boxes at the bottom, draw and color the figures that belong in each class.

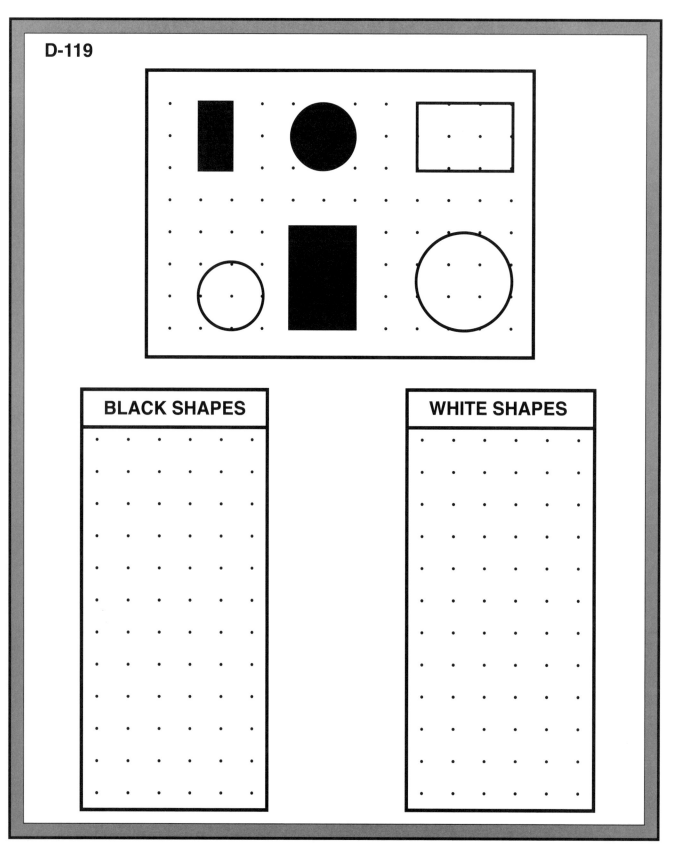

D-119

BLACK SHAPES

WHITE SHAPES

CLASSIFYING BY SIZE—SORTING

DIRECTIONS: The figures at the top can be sorted into classes in more than one way. In the boxes at the bottom, draw and color the figures that belong in each class.

D-120

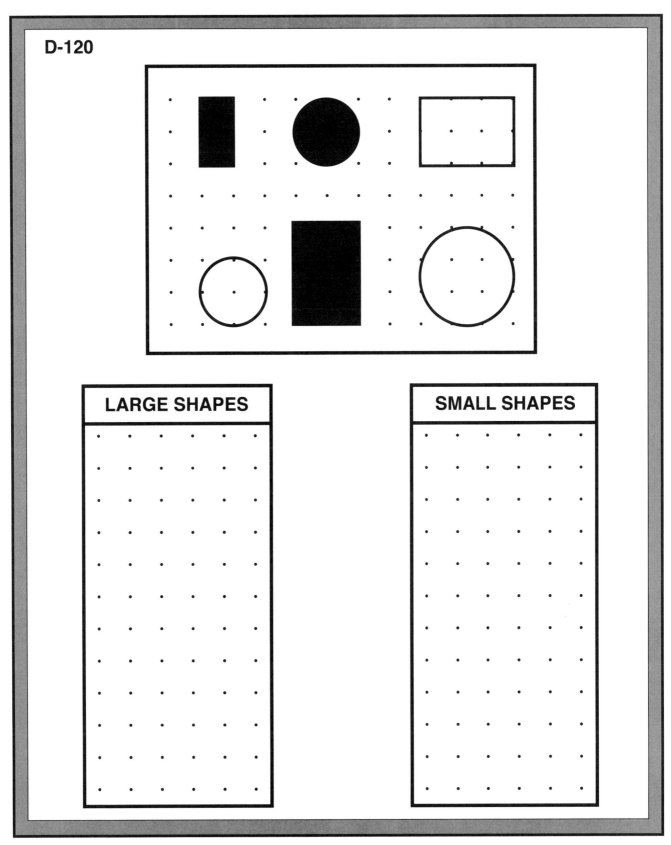

LARGE SHAPES	SMALL SHAPES

OVERLAPPING CLASSES—INTERSECTION

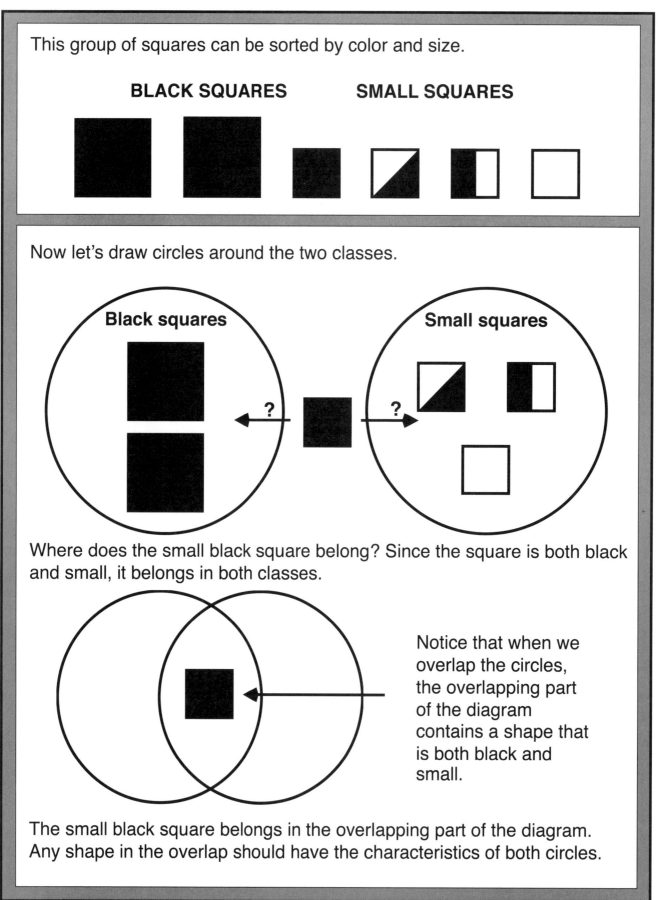

This group of squares can be sorted by color and size.

BLACK SQUARES   **SMALL SQUARES**

Now let's draw circles around the two classes.

Black squares   **Small squares**

Where does the small black square belong? Since the square is both black and small, it belongs in both classes.

Notice that when we overlap the circles, the overlapping part of the diagram contains a shape that is both black and small.

The small black square belongs in the overlapping part of the diagram. Any shape in the overlap should have the characteristics of both circles.

OVERLAPPING CLASSES—INTERSECTION

DIRECTIONS: Notice where the shapes are placed in the circles at the top. In the exercises below, use your pencil to darken the part of the circle's diagram to which the figure belongs (see example).

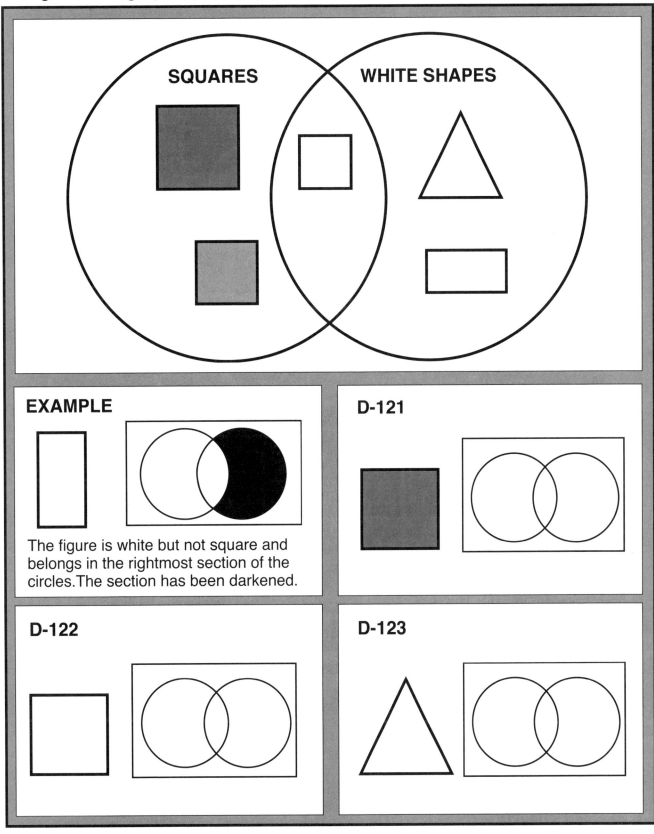

EXAMPLE

The figure is white but not square and belongs in the rightmost section of the circles. The section has been darkened.

D-121

D-122

D-123

OVERLAPPING CLASSES—INTERSECTION

DIRECTIONS: Notice where the shapes are placed in the circles at the top. In the exercises below, use your pencil to darken the part of the circle's diagram to which the figure belongs.

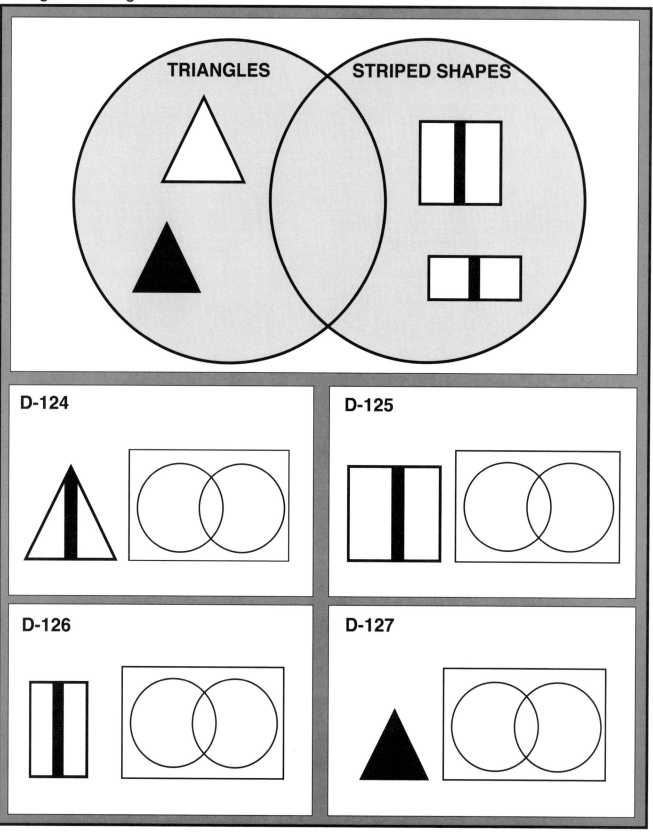

OVERLAPPING CLASSES—INTERSECTION

DIRECTIONS: Notice where the shapes are placed in the circles at the top. In the exercises below, use your pencil to darken the part of the circle's diagram to which the figure belongs.

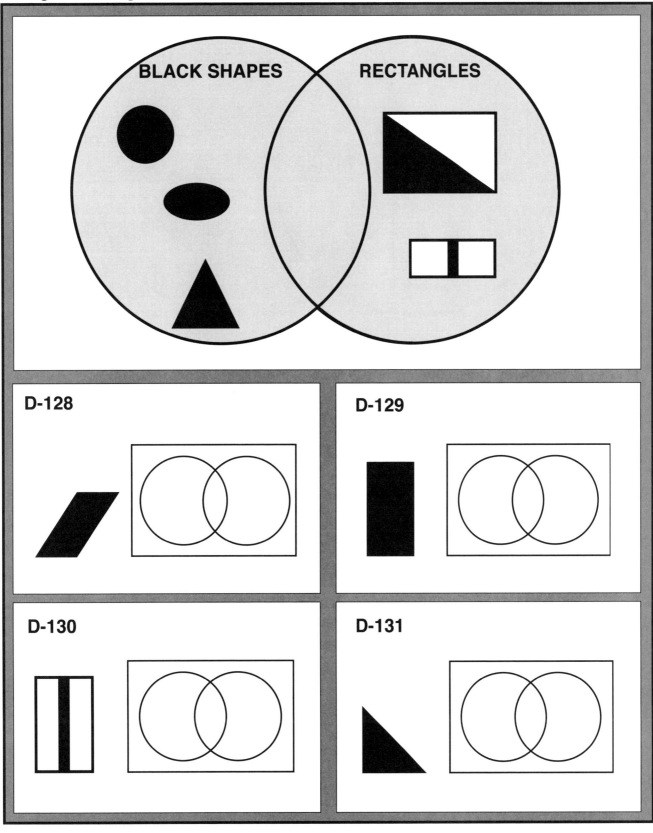

OVERLAPPING CLASSES—INTERSECTION

DIRECTIONS: Read the information about the circles and complete the exercises below. In each blank, write the characteristics for the group. In each small circle's diagram, darken the part where the given shape belongs.

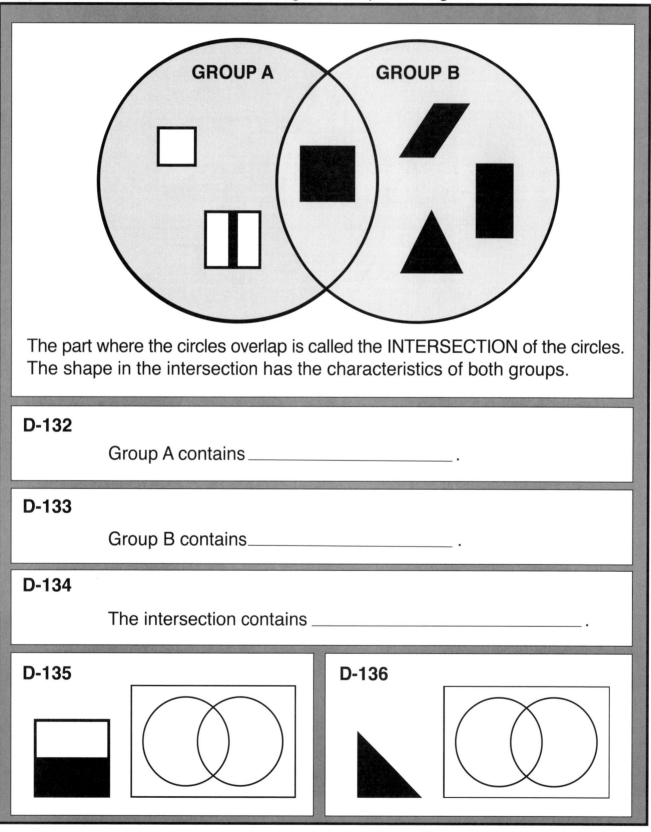

The part where the circles overlap is called the INTERSECTION of the circles. The shape in the intersection has the characteristics of both groups.

D-132

Group A contains _____ .

D-133

Group B contains_____ .

D-134

The intersection contains _____ .

D-135

D-136

OVERLAPPING CLASSES—MATRIX

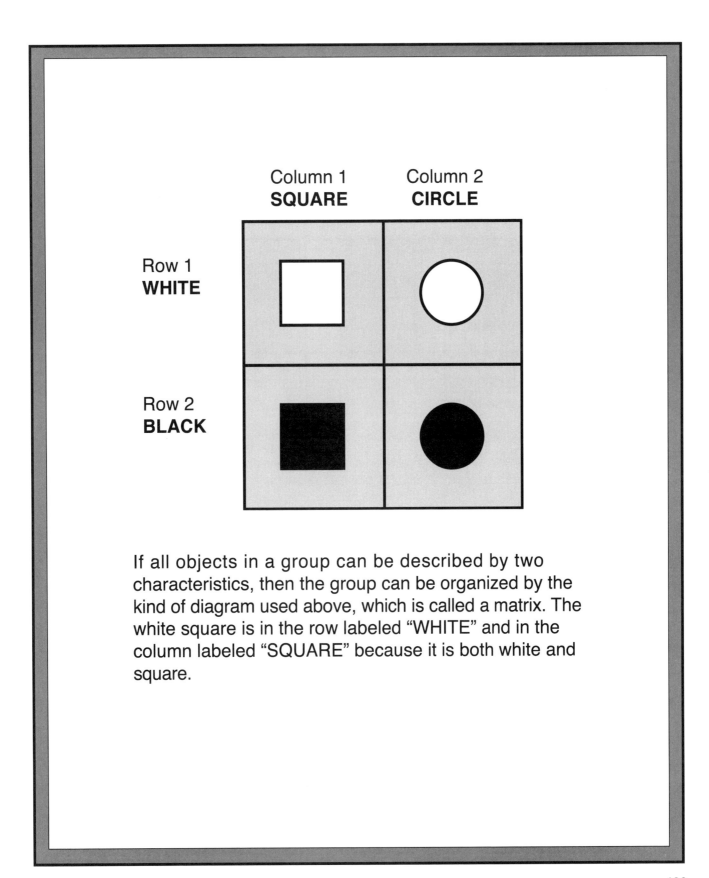

If all objects in a group can be described by two characteristics, then the group can be organized by the kind of diagram used above, which is called a matrix. The white square is in the row labeled "WHITE" and in the column labeled "SQUARE" because it is both white and square.

OVERLAPPING CLASSES—MATRIX

DIRECTIONS: Complete each matrix. The first matrix has been labeled for you.

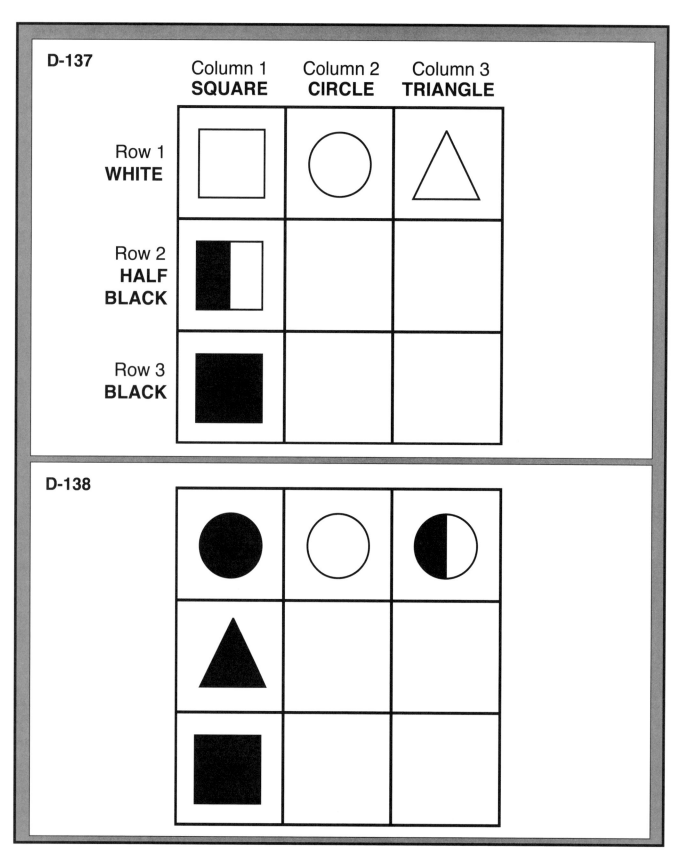

OVERLAPPING CLASSES—MATRIX

DIRECTIONS: Complete each matrix.

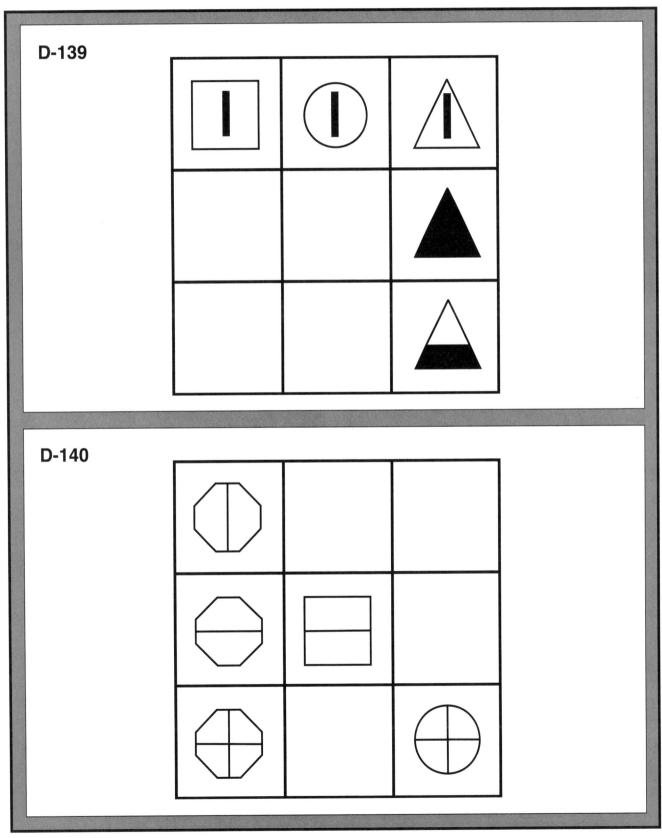

WRITING DESCRIPTIONS OF CLASSES

DIRECTIONS: Look at each group (class) of figures. Decide what characteristics all the figures have in common. Write a description of each class of figures in the description box. Use complete sentences in your description.

EXAMPLE

DESCRIPTION

This is a group of figures that are half black and half white.

D-141

DESCRIPTION

WRITING DESCRIPTIONS OF CLASSES

DIRECTIONS: Look at each group (class) of figures. Decide what characteristics all the figures have in common. Write a description of each class of figures in the description box. Use complete sentences in your description.

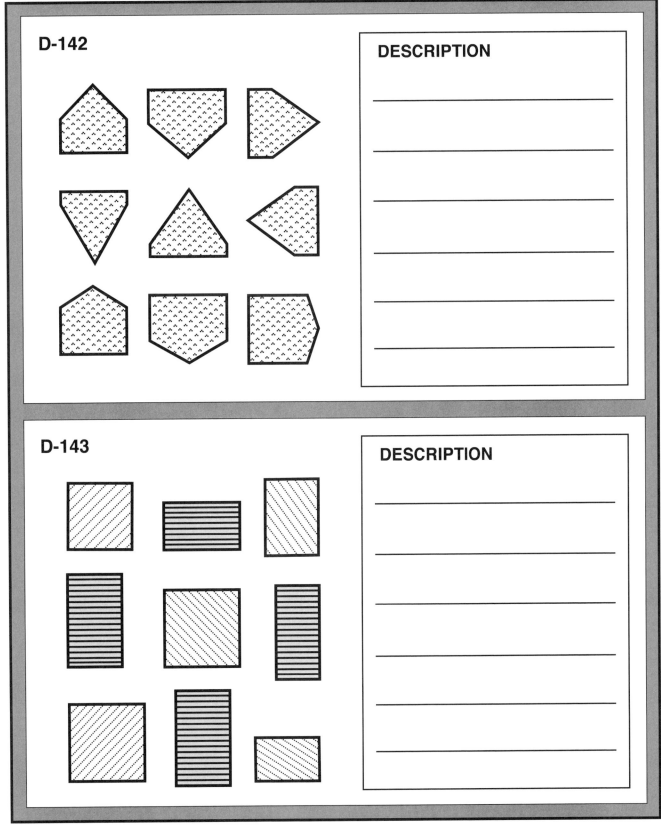

D-142

DESCRIPTION

D-143

DESCRIPTION

WRITING DESCRIPTIONS OF CLASSES

DIRECTIONS: Look at each group (class) of figures. Decide what characteristics all the figures have in common. Write a description of each class of figures in the description box. Use complete sentences in your description.

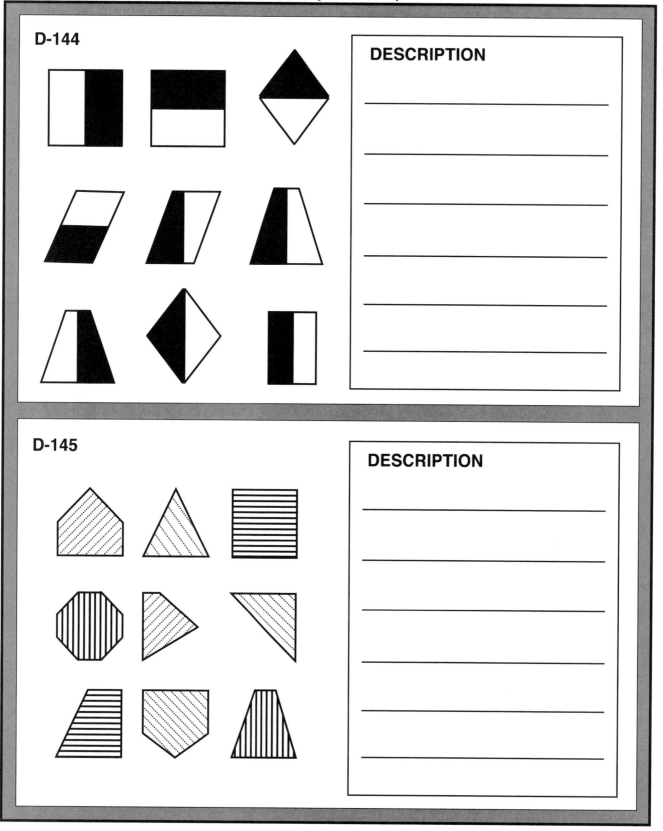

D-144

DESCRIPTION

_____

_____

_____

_____

_____

_____

D-145

DESCRIPTION

_____

_____

_____

_____

_____

_____

CHAPTER FIVE

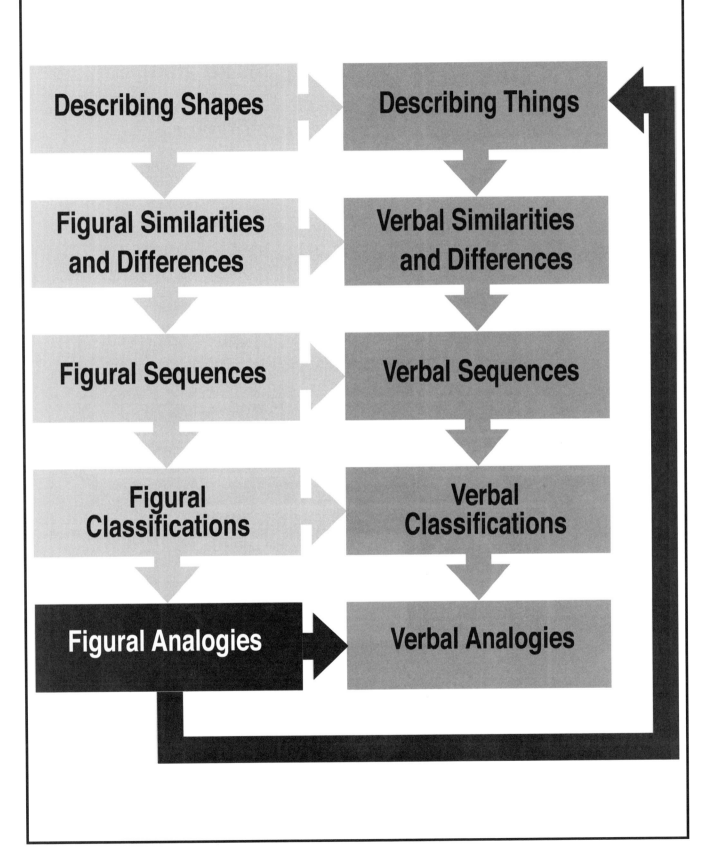

ANALOGIES WITH SHAPES

DIRECTIONS: Use the information in the diagrams below to fill in the blanks at the bottom of the page.

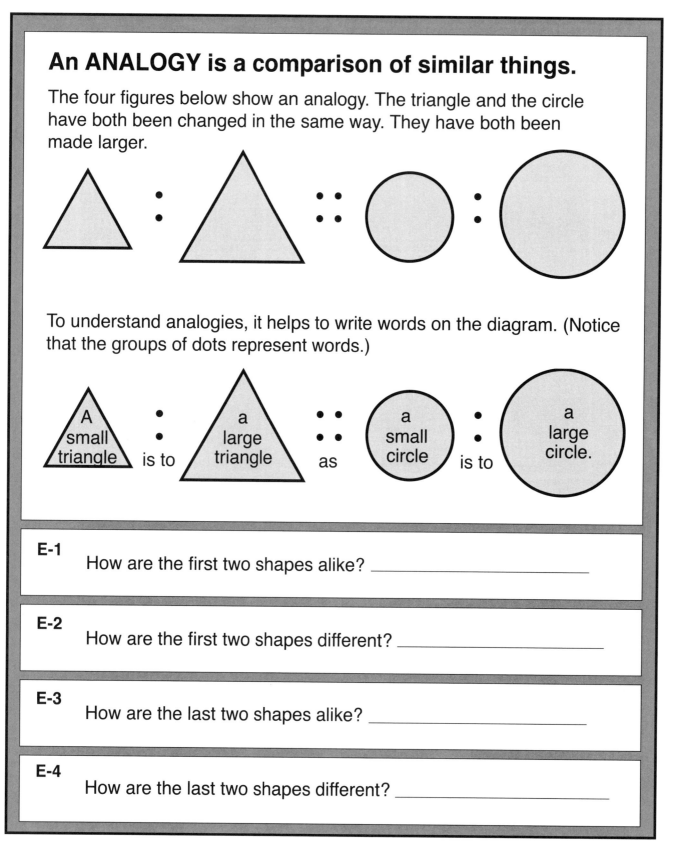

An ANALOGY is a comparison of similar things.

The four figures below show an analogy. The triangle and the circle have both been changed in the same way. They have both been made larger.

To understand analogies, it helps to write words on the diagram. (Notice that the groups of dots represent words.)

A small triangle   is to   a large triangle   as   a small circle   is to   a large circle.

E-1   How are the first two shapes alike? _____

E-2   How are the first two shapes different? _____

E-3   How are the last two shapes alike? _____

E-4   How are the last two shapes different? _____

BUILDING ANALOGIES WITH BLOCKS

DIRECTIONS: Fill in the blanks with "size," "shape," and "color."

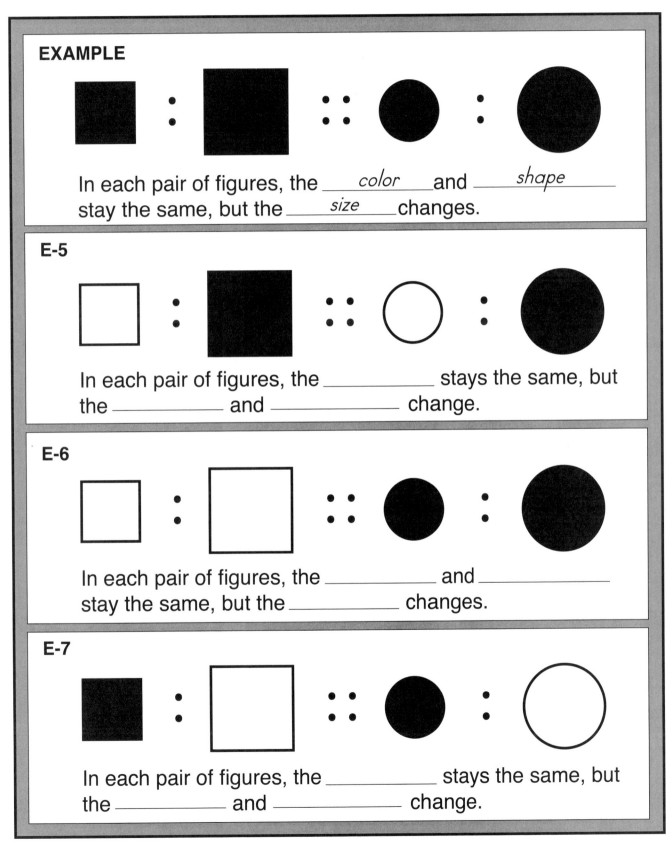

EXAMPLE

In each pair of figures, the ___*color*___ and ___*shape*___ stay the same, but the ___*size*___ changes.

E-5

In each pair of figures, the _____ stays the same, but the _____ and _____ change.

E-6

In each pair of figures, the _____ and _____ stay the same, but the _____ changes.

E-7

In each pair of figures, the _____ stays the same, but the _____ and _____ change.

ANALOGIES WITH SHAPES—SELECT

DIRECTIONS: Circle the figure that completes the analogy.

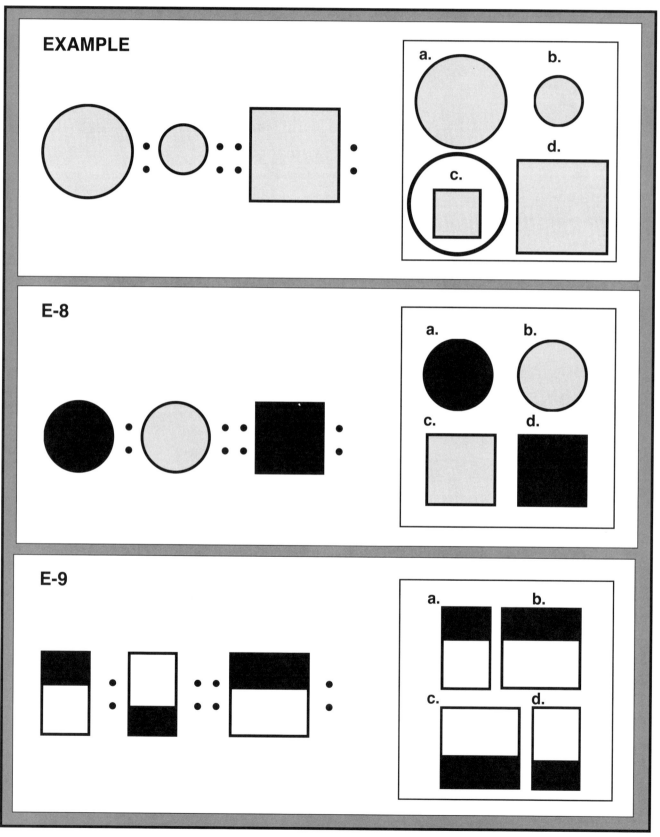

ANALOGIES WITH SHAPES—SELECT

DIRECTIONS: Circle the figure that completes the analogy.

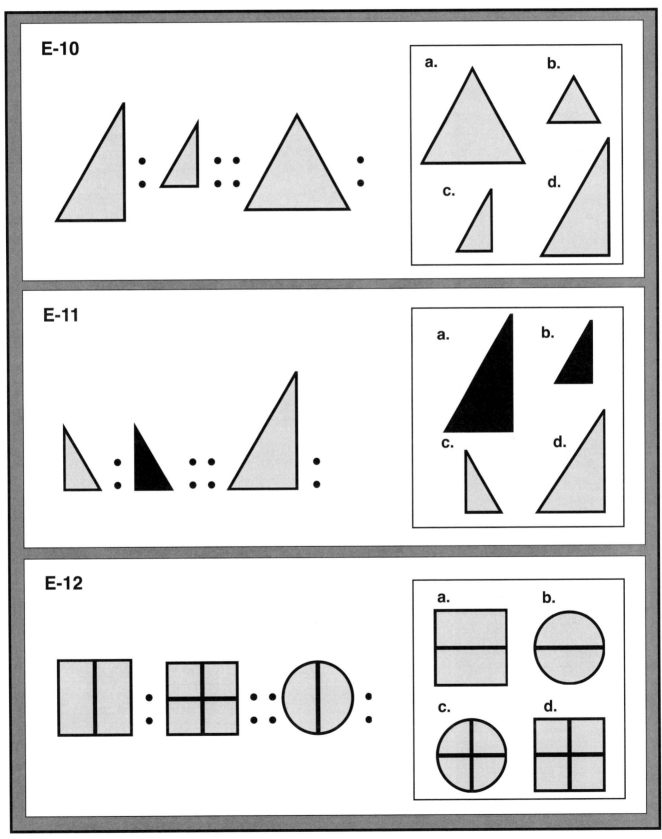

ANALOGIES WITH SHAPES—SELECT

DIRECTIONS: Circle the figure that completes the analogy.

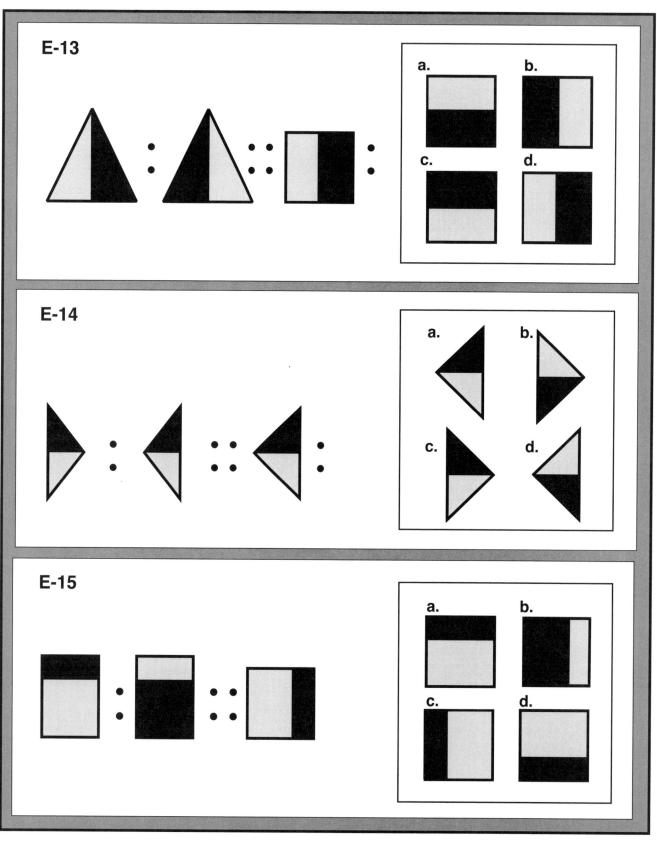

ANALOGIES WITH SHAPES—SELECT

DIRECTIONS: Circle the figure that completes the analogy.

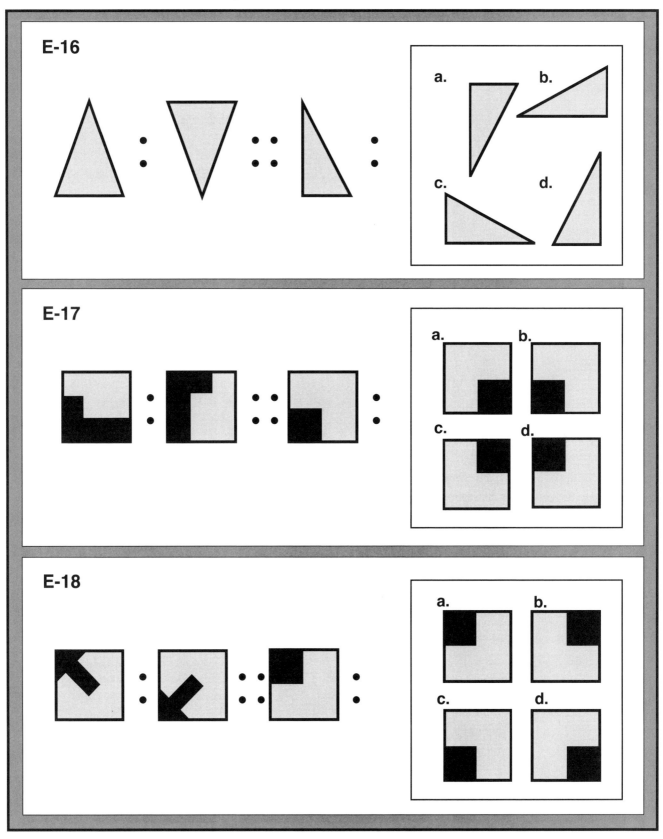

E-16

E-17

E-18

KINDS OF ANALOGIES

DIRECTIONS: Study the five types of analogies illustrated below.

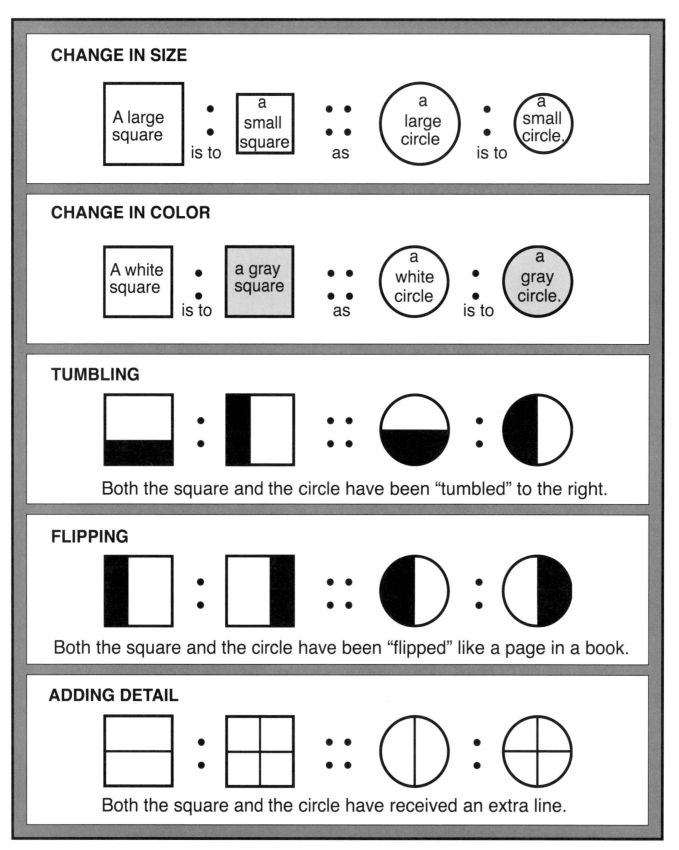

CHANGE IN SIZE

A large square **:** a small square **::** a large circle **:** a small circle.
is to   as   is to

CHANGE IN COLOR

A white square **:** a gray square **::** a white circle **:** a gray circle.
is to   as   is to

TUMBLING

Both the square and the circle have been "tumbled" to the right.

FLIPPING

Both the square and the circle have been "flipped" like a page in a book.

ADDING DETAIL

Both the square and the circle have received an extra line.

ANALOGIES WITH SHAPES—COMPLETE

DIRECTIONS: In the grid at the end of each row, draw the last figure to complete the analogy. As you draw the figure, think about what has changed.

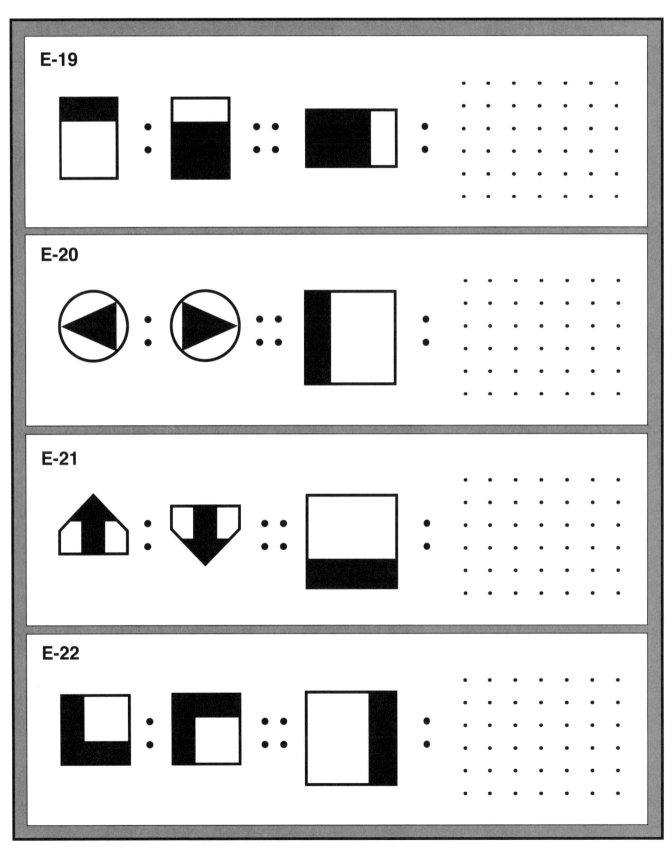

ANALOGIES WITH SHAPES—COMPLETE

DIRECTIONS: In the grid at the end of each row, draw the last figure to complete the analogy. As you draw the figure, think about what has changed.

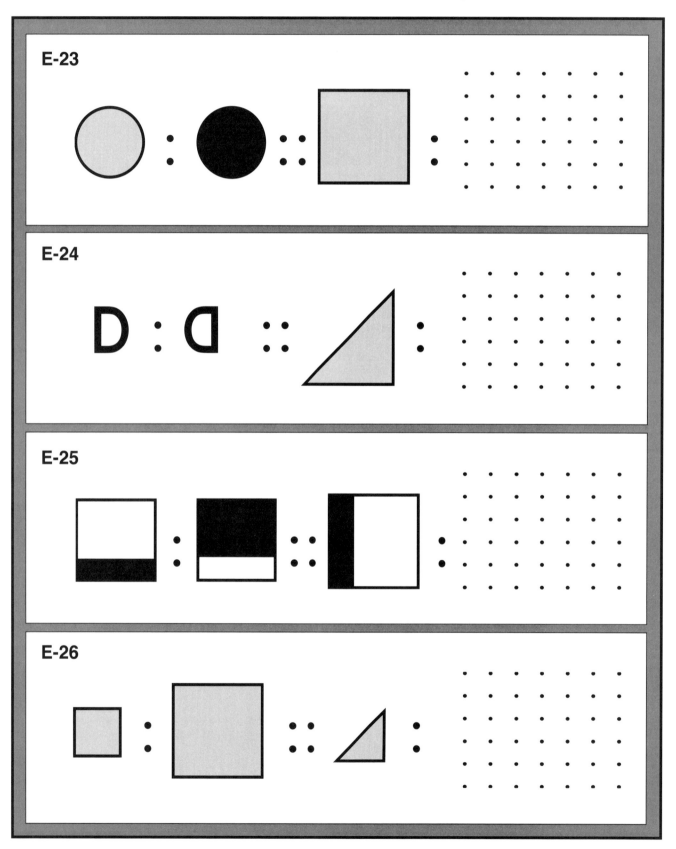

ANALOGIES WITH SHAPES—COMPLETE

DIRECTIONS: In the grid at the end of each row, draw the last figure to complete the analogy. As you draw the figure, think about what has changed.

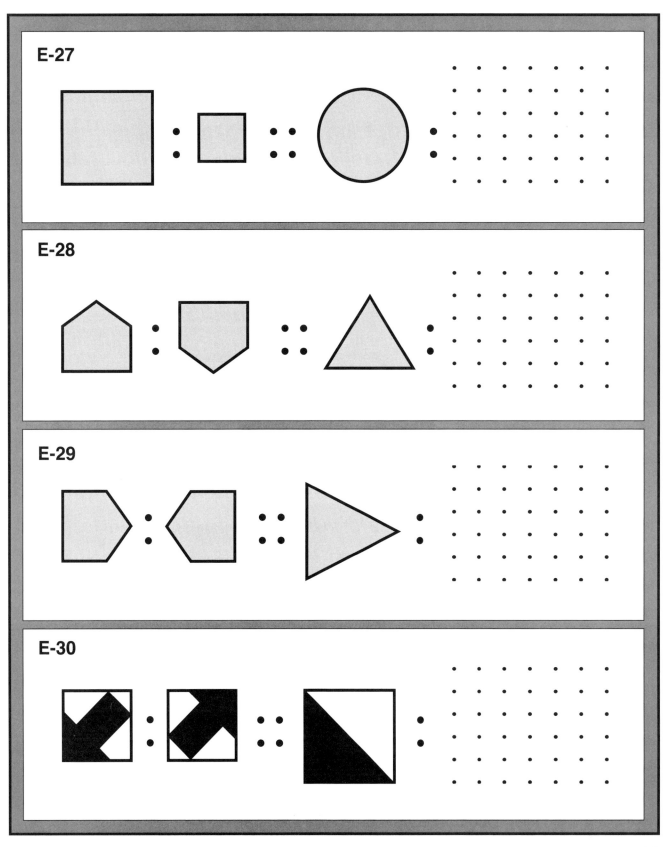

CHAPTER SIX

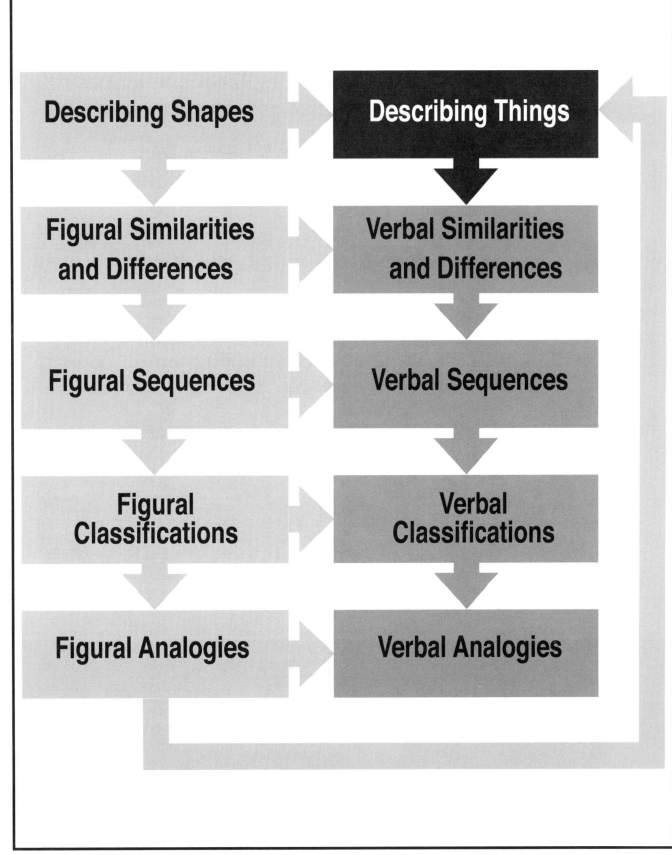

DESCRIBING FOODS—SELECT

DIRECTIONS: Look at the three pictures of foods. Read each description below the pictures and decide which of the pictures it describes. Write the letter of the correct picture on the line.

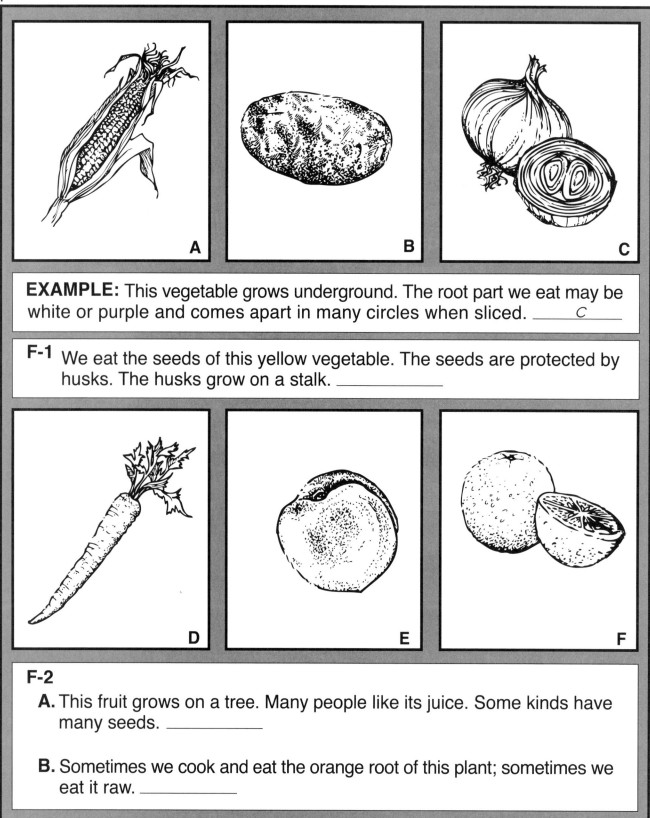

EXAMPLE: This vegetable grows underground. The root part we eat may be white or purple and comes apart in many circles when sliced. _____C_____

F-1 We eat the seeds of this yellow vegetable. The seeds are protected by husks. The husks grow on a stalk. _____

F-2

   A. This fruit grows on a tree. Many people like its juice. Some kinds have many seeds. _____

   B. Sometimes we cook and eat the orange root of this plant; sometimes we eat it raw. _____

DESCRIBING ANIMALS—SELECT

DIRECTIONS: Look at the three pictures of animals. Read each description below the pictures and decide which of the pictures it describes. Write the letter of the correct picture on the line.

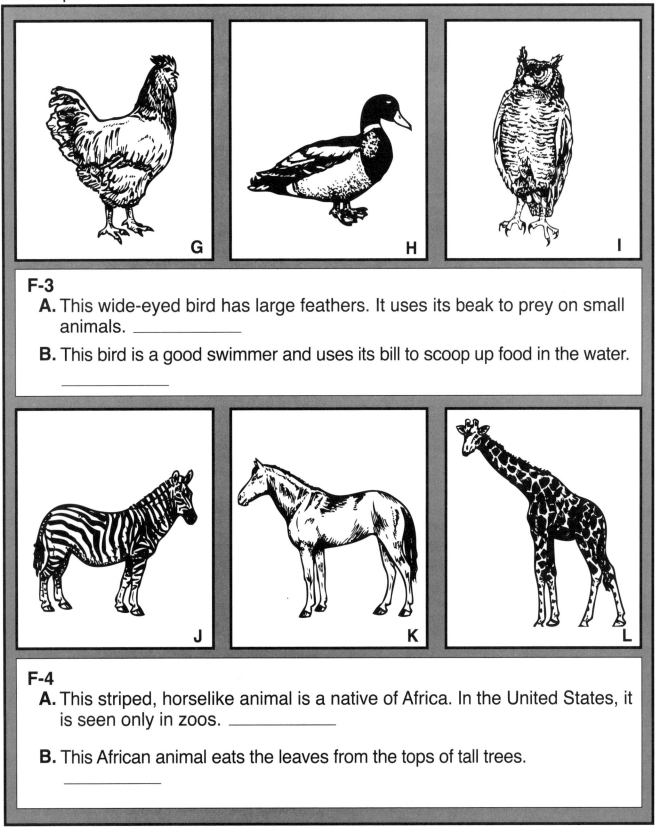

F-3

   A. This wide-eyed bird has large feathers. It uses its beak to prey on small animals. _____

   B. This bird is a good swimmer and uses its bill to scoop up food in the water.

_____

F-4

   A. This striped, horselike animal is a native of Africa. In the United States, it is seen only in zoos. _____

   B. This African animal eats the leaves from the tops of tall trees.

_____

DESCRIBING VEHICLES—SELECT

DIRECTIONS: Look at the three pictures of vehicles. Read each description below the pictures and decide which of the pictures it describes. Write the letter of the correct picture on the line.

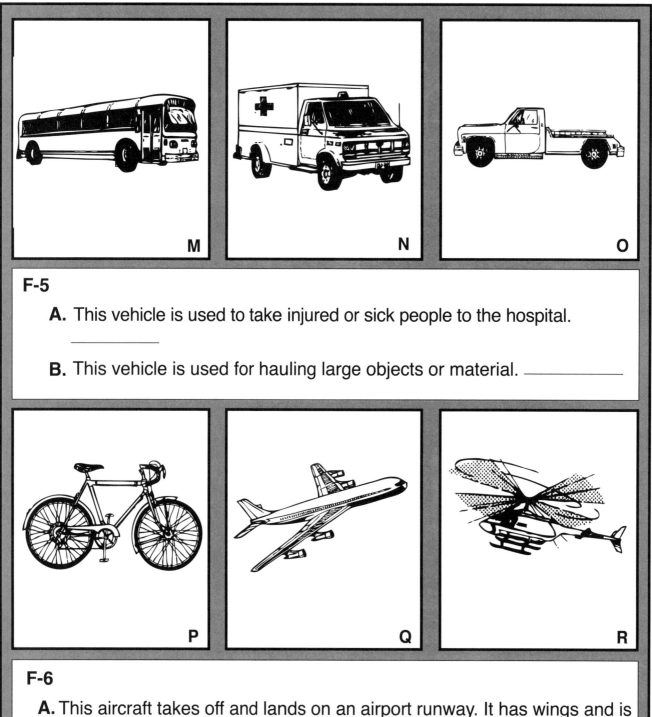

M

N

O

F-5

A. This vehicle is used to take injured or sick people to the hospital.

B. This vehicle is used for hauling large objects or material. _____

P

Q

R

F-6

A. This aircraft takes off and lands on an airport runway. It has wings and is moved by propellers or by jet engines. _____

B. This aircraft can take off straight up and land in very small areas. It is used for police patrol and sightseeing. _____

DESCRIBING PLACES—SELECT

DIRECTIONS: Look at the three pictures of places. Read each description and decide which of the pictures it describes. Write the letter of the correct picture on the line.

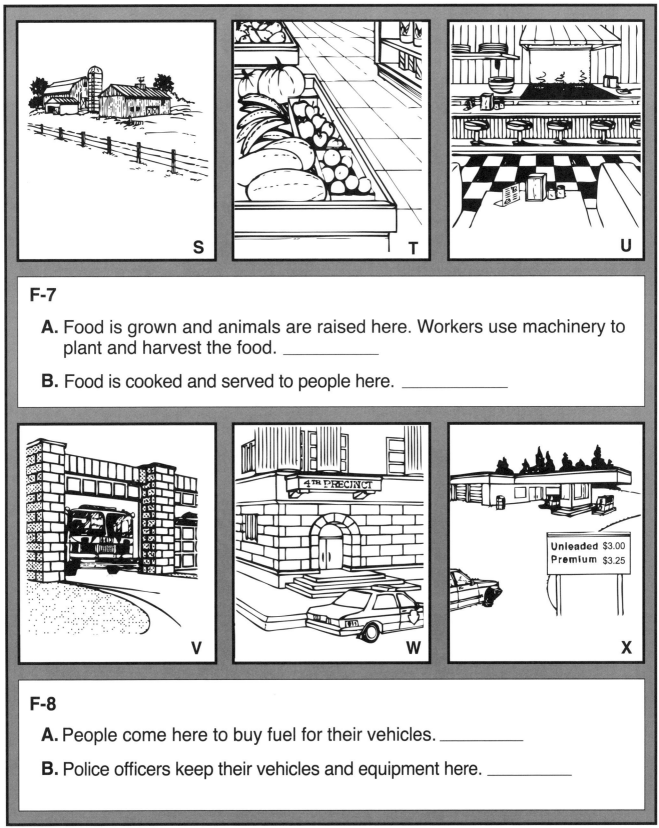

F-7

A. Food is grown and animals are raised here. Workers use machinery to plant and harvest the food. _____

B. Food is cooked and served to people here. _____

F-8

A. People come here to buy fuel for their vehicles. _____

B. Police officers keep their vehicles and equipment here. _____

DESCRIBING OCCUPATIONS—SELECT

DIRECTIONS: Look at the three pictures of people working. Read each description and decide which of the pictures it describes. Write the letter of the correct picture on the line.

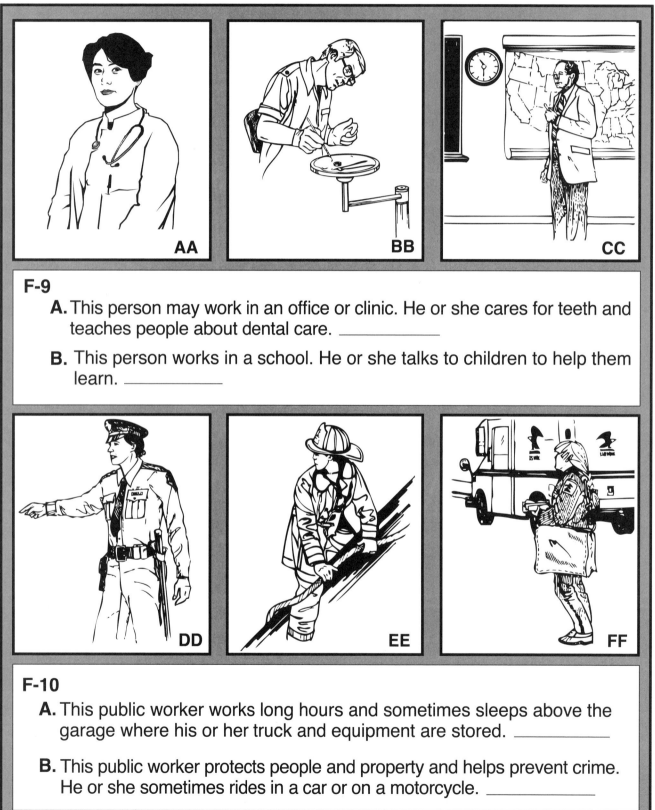

F-9

   A. This person may work in an office or clinic. He or she cares for teeth and teaches people about dental care. _____

   B. This person works in a school. He or she talks to children to help them learn. _____

F-10

   A. This public worker works long hours and sometimes sleeps above the garage where his or her truck and equipment are stored. _____

   B. This public worker protects people and property and helps prevent crime. He or she sometimes rides in a car or on a motorcycle. _____

DESCRIBING FOODS—EXPLAIN

DIRECTIONS: In each box, describe the food in the picture.

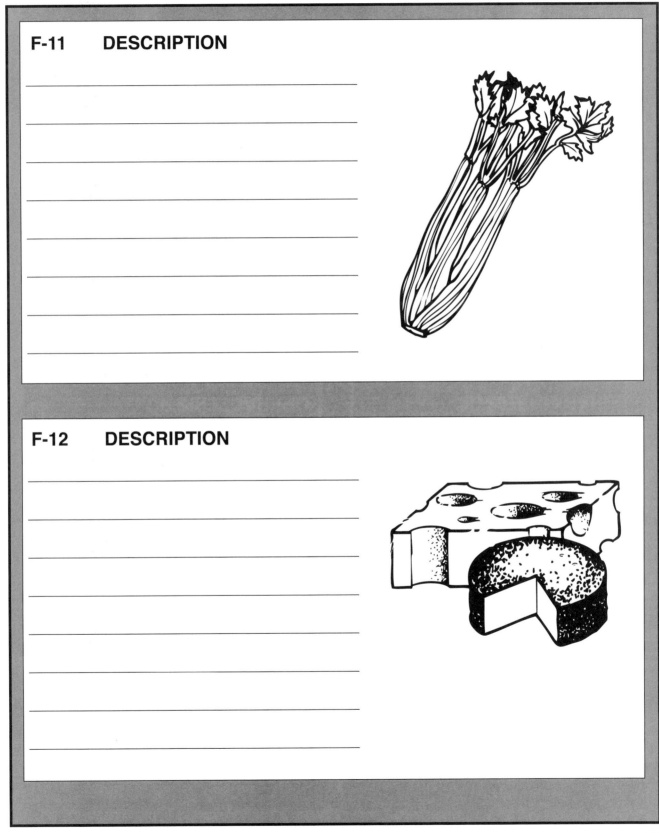

F-11   DESCRIPTION

_____

_____

_____

_____

_____

_____

_____

_____

F-12   DESCRIPTION

_____

_____

_____

_____

_____

_____

_____

DESCRIBING PLACES—EXPLAIN

DIRECTIONS: In each box, describe the building in the picture.

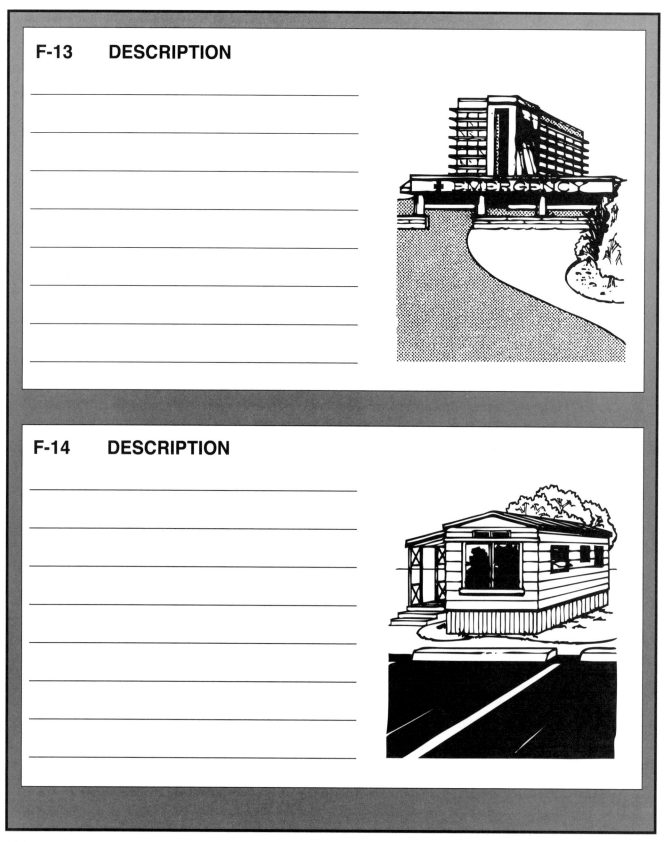

F-13   **DESCRIPTION**

_____
_____
_____
_____
_____
_____
_____

F-14   **DESCRIPTION**

_____
_____
_____
_____
_____
_____
_____

DESCRIBING PLACES ON EARTH—EXPLAIN

DIRECTIONS: In each box, describe the land form in the picture.

F-15   **DESCRIPTION**

_____
_____
_____
_____
_____
_____
_____
_____

F-16   **DESCRIPTION**

_____
_____
_____
_____
_____
_____
_____
_____

DESCRIBING ANIMALS—EXPLAIN

DIRECTIONS: In each box, describe the animal in the picture.

F-17   **DESCRIPTION**

_____

_____

_____

_____

_____

_____

_____

F-18   **DESCRIPTION**

_____

_____

_____

_____

_____

_____

_____

DESCRIBING OCCUPATIONS—EXPLAIN

DIRECTIONS: In each box, describe the job of the person in the picture.

F-19   **DESCRIPTION**

_____
_____
_____
_____
_____
_____
_____
_____
_____

F-20   **DESCRIPTION**

_____
_____
_____
_____
_____
_____
_____
_____
_____

DESCRIBING WORDS—SELECT

DIRECTIONS: Each exercise contains three words used in social studies followed by descriptions of two of the words. For each description, select the matching word and write it in the blank.

F-21

WORD CHOICES: country, map, photograph

Example: A drawing of all or part of the surface of the earth

_____*map*_____

A. A picture taken by a camera _____

F-22

WORD CHOICES: lake, river, ocean

A. A body of water completely surrounded by land

_____

B. The body of salt water that covers a large part of the surface of the earth _____

F-23

WORD CHOICES: continent, country, state

A. A nation made up of states _____

B. A land mass made up of countries _____

DESCRIBING WORDS—SELECT

DIRECTIONS: Each exercise contains three words used in social studies followed by descriptions of two of the words. For each description, select the matching word and write it in the blank.

F-24

WORD CHOICES: blade, leaf, needle

A. The long, thin, pointed leaf of a pine tree

_____

B. The broad leaf of a grass plant _____

F-25

WORD CHOICES: cloud, rainbow, star

A. A large, fluffy mass of water vapor in the sky _____

B. A half circle of colors that sometimes appears in the sky. It is formed by the light of the sun passing through rain droplets.

_____

F-26

WORD CHOICES: clock, thermometer, yardstick

A. A measuring device that is three feet long. It is divided into thirty-six parts. _____

B. A measuring device made of a glass tube containing a liquid. The liquid expands when heated and shows changes in temperature.

_____

NAME THE ANIMAL—SUPPLY

DIRECTIONS: Each exercise contains a description of an animal. Read each description, then decide what is being described. Write the answer in the blank.

F-27

This large bird is raised to be eaten. It is often purchased for holiday celebrations. Many meat products are made from this bird.

_____

F-28

This large cat is a good hunter. It is tan or light brown with a large mane on its head. _____

F-29

This large fish lives in the ocean. The meat from this fish is often canned and used to make salad-type sandwiches. _____

F-30

This beast of burden has two humps and can go days between drinks of water. _____

F-31

This insect builds hives and makes honey. _____

F-32

This reptile has two surfaces of hard shell. Its head and legs come out of the shell. _____

NAME THE PLANT—SUPPLY

DIRECTIONS: Each exercise contains a description of a plant. Read each description, then decide what is being described. Write the answer in the blank.

F-33

This dark-green leafy vegetable is eaten cooked or served as a salad.

_____

F-34

This long yellow fruit is peeled before being eaten. It grows in bunches in warm countries. _____

F-35

This grain is grown on huge farms in the center of the United States. It is made into bread, baking flour, and many breakfast cereals.

_____

F-36

This large tree has beautiful hard wood which is used to make furniture. Its seeds are called acorns. _____

F-37

This plant grows in the desert. It has many long, sharp points.

_____

F-38

This tree has soft wood which is used as lumber to build houses. Its seeds grow in a bunch called a "cone." Young trees of this kind are decorated at Christmas. _____

NAME THE VEHICLE/PLACE—SUPPLY

DIRECTIONS: Each exercise below contains a description of a vehicle or a place. Read each description, then decide what is being described. Write the answer in the blank.

F-39

This vehicle is used on farms to plow fields and tend the land.

_____

F-40

This vehicle is used to take injured or sick people to the hospital.

_____

F-41

This large vehicle flies through the air at 500 miles per hour by pushing hot gas out of a tube. It carries more than one hundred passengers.

_____

F-42

People come here to buy stamps and mail letters and packages.

_____

F-43

People come here to put money in their accounts. You can cash a check here. You can store valuable papers here. _____

F-44

This very large building contains a few large department stores and many small shops. _____

NAME THE OCCUPATION—SUPPLY

DIRECTIONS: Each exercise contains a description of a worker in a particular occupation. Read each description, then decide what worker is being described. Write the answer in the blank.

F-45

This public worker delivers letters and packages to homes.

_____

F-46

This person washes, cuts, and combs hair. _____

F-47

This person works in an office where he or she examines, cleans, fills, or removes teeth. _____

F-48

This person grows the food that we eat. _____

F-49

This person works in a store and sells food. _____

F-50

This person works in a restaurant and prepares the food that we eat at the restaurant. _____

F-51

This person works in a school and helps children learn.

_____

F-52

This person works in an office or hospital. He or she finds out why a person is sick and gives advice on what medicine the person should take. _____

IDENTIFYING CHARACTERISTICS

DIRECTIONS: Read the passage about frogs. Identify the characteristics of a frog and write them in the blanks.

F-53

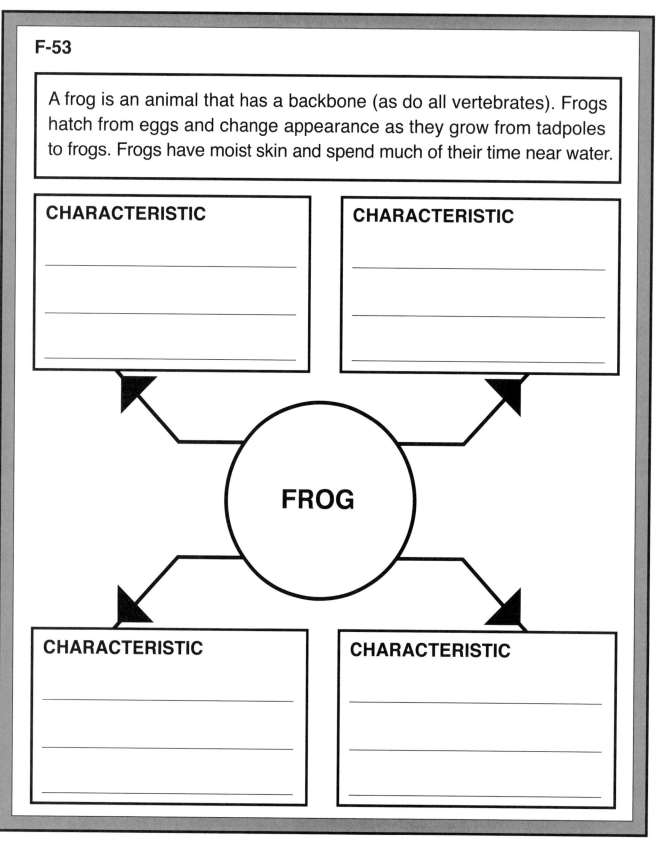

A frog is an animal that has a backbone (as do all vertebrates). Frogs hatch from eggs and change appearance as they grow from tadpoles to frogs. Frogs have moist skin and spend much of their time near water.

CHARACTERISTIC

CHARACTERISTIC

FROG

CHARACTERISTIC

CHARACTERISTIC

CHAPTER SEVEN

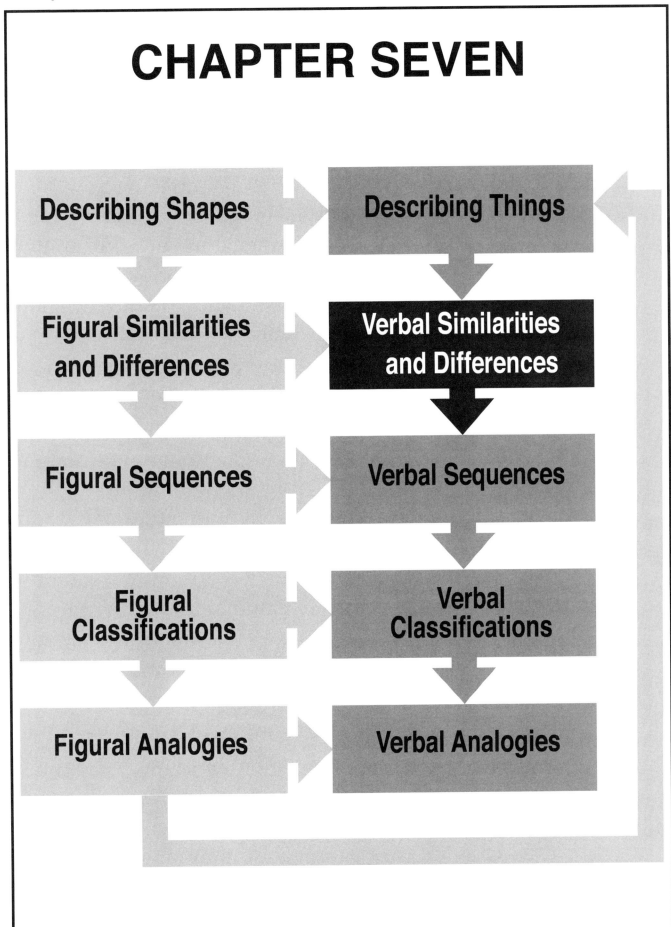

OPPOSITES—SELECT

DIRECTIONS: Each line contains four words describing directions or locations. Read the first word and think about what it means. Of the next three words, circle the opposite word or the word that is <u>most</u> <u>unlike</u> the first word.

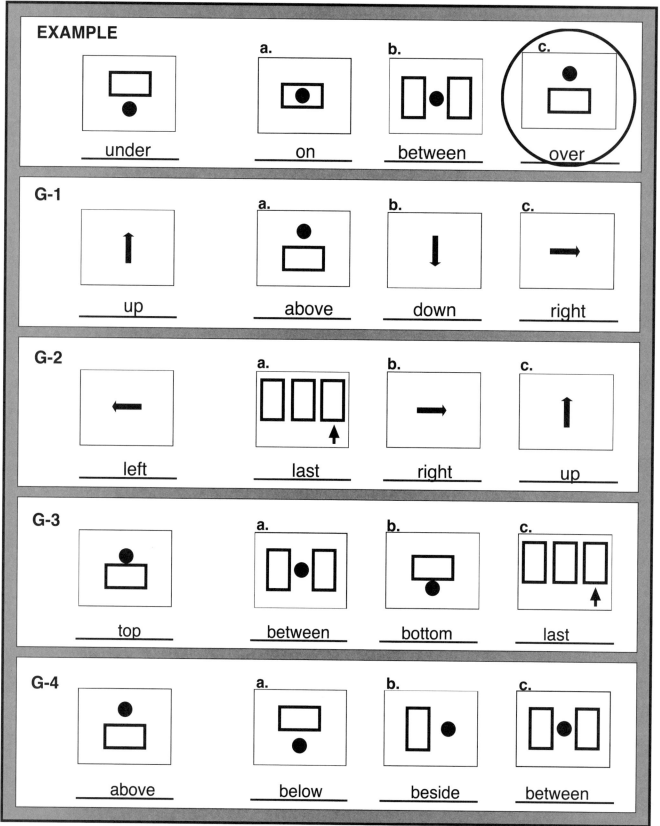

EXAMPLE

under   **a.** on   **b.** between   **c.** over

G-1 up   **a.** above   **b.** down   **c.** right

G-2 left   **a.** last   **b.** right   **c.** up

G-3 top   **a.** between   **b.** bottom   **c.** last

G-4 above   **a.** below   **b.** beside   **c.** between

OPPOSITES—SELECT

DIRECTIONS: Each line contains four words. Read the first word and think about what it means. One of the next three words will mean the <u>opposite</u> of the first word. Circle the word that is opposite or <u>most</u> <u>unlike</u> the first word.

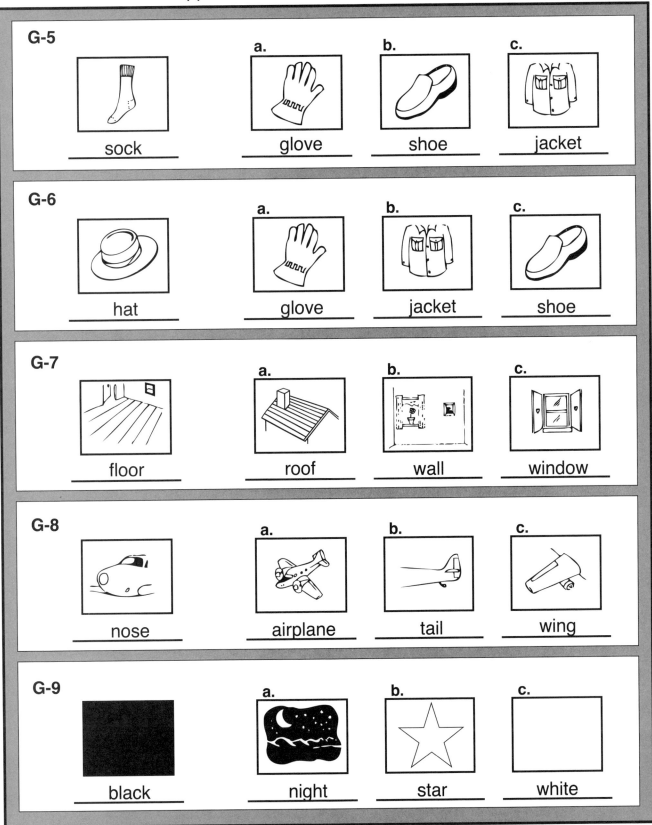

G-5

| | a. | b. | c. |
| sock | glove | shoe | jacket |

G-6

| | a. | b. | c. |
| hat | glove | jacket | shoe |

G-7

| | a. | b. | c. |
| floor | roof | wall | window |

G-8

| | a. | b. | c. |
| nose | airplane | tail | wing |

G-9

| | a. | b. | c. |
| black | night | star | white |

OPPOSITES—SELECT

DIRECTIONS: Each line contains four words. Read the first word and think about what it means. One of the next three words will mean the <u>opposite</u> of the first word. Circle the word that is opposite or <u>most</u> <u>unlike</u> the first word.

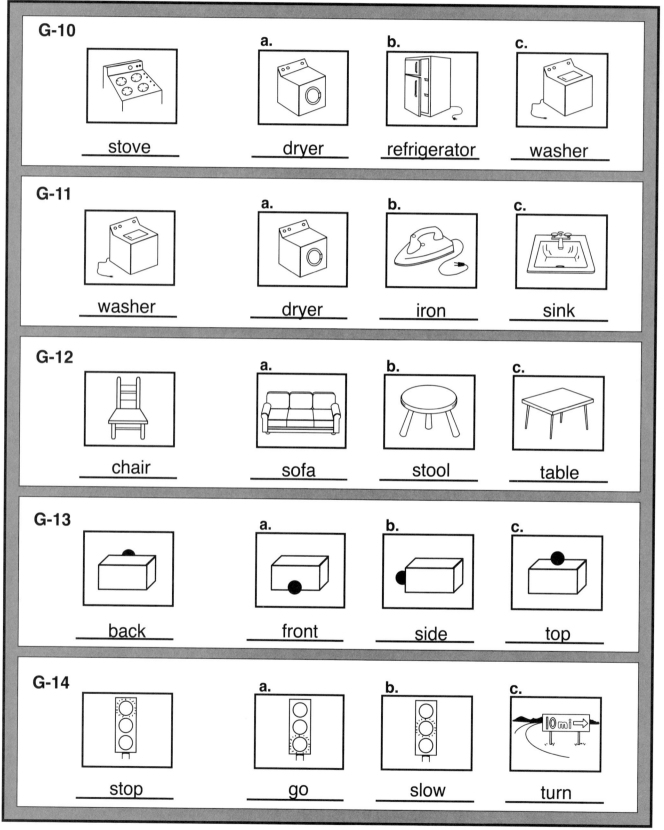

G-10

stove

a. dryer

b. refrigerator

c. washer

G-11

washer

a. dryer

b. iron

c. sink

G-12

chair

a. sofa

b. stool

c. table

G-13

back

a. front

b. side

c. top

G-14

stop

a. go

b. slow

c. turn

OPPOSITES—SELECT

DIRECTIONS: Each line contains four words we use in science. Read the first word and think about what it means. One of the next three words will mean the <u>opposite</u> of the first word. Circle the word that is opposite or <u>most</u> <u>unlike</u> the first word.

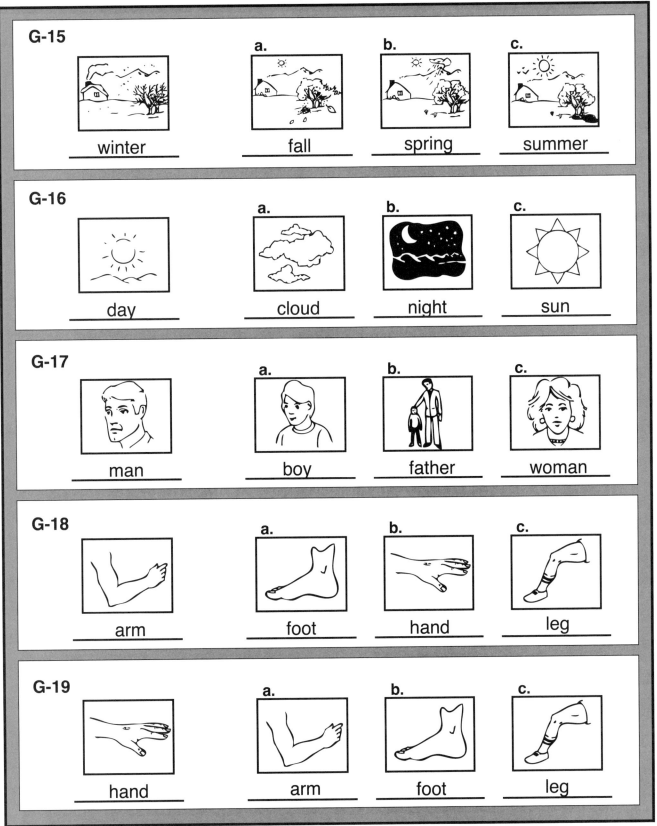

G-15

winter   **a.** fall   **b.** spring   **c.** summer

G-16

day   **a.** cloud   **b.** night   **c.** sun

G-17

man   **a.** boy   **b.** father   **c.** woman

G-18

arm   **a.** foot   **b.** hand   **c.** leg

G-19

hand   **a.** arm   **b.** foot   **c.** leg

OPPOSITES—SELECT

DIRECTIONS: Each line contains four words we use in science. Read the first word and think about what it means. One of the next three words will mean the opposite of the first word. Circle the word that is opposite or most unlike the first word.

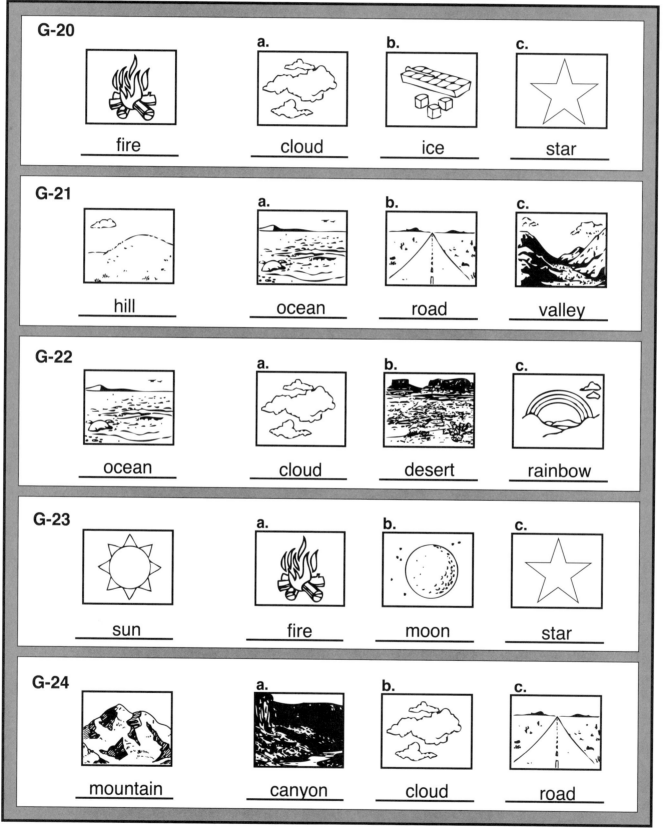

G-20
fire   a. cloud   b. ice   c. star

G-21
hill   a. ocean   b. road   c. valley

G-22
ocean   a. cloud   b. desert   c. rainbow

G-23
sun   a. fire   b. moon   c. star

G-24
mountain   a. canyon   b. cloud   c. road

OPPOSITES—SELECT

DIRECTIONS: Each line contains four words. Read the first word and think about what it means. One of the next three words will mean the <u>opposite</u> of the first word. Underline the word that is the opposite of the first word.

G-25

clean   **a.** dirty   **b.** new   **c.** old

G-26

lost   **a.** found   **b.** gone   **c.** look

G-27

catch   **a.** ball   **b.** play   **c.** throw

G-28

die   **a.** live   **b.** old   **c.** sick

G-29

enter   **a.** leave   **b.** open   **c.** stay

G-30

hard   **a.** difficult   **b.** easy   **c.** problem

G-31

dull   **a.** boring   **b.** exciting   **c.** long

G-32

hard   **a.** brittle   **b.** sharp   **c.** soft

G-33

dull   **a.** blunt   **b.** sharp   **c.** worn

OPPOSITES—SELECT

DIRECTIONS: Each line contains four "direction" words. Read the first word and think about what it means. One of the next three words will mean the <u>opposite</u> of the first word. Underline the word that is the opposite of the first word.

G-34

    back   **a.** bone   **b.** end   **c.** front

G-35

    upper   **a.** class   **b.** lower   **c.** story

G-36

    begin   **a.** end   **b.** go   **c.** start

G-37

    north   **a.** east   **b.** south   **c.** west

G-38

    give   **a.** present   **b.** receive   **c.** rent

G-39

    right   **a.** above   **b.** below   **c.** left

G-40

    head   **a.** first   **b.** foot   **c.** strong

G-41

    leave   **a.** arrive   **b.** exit   **c.** run

G-42

    go   **a.** come   **b.** exit   **c.** leave

OPPOSITES—SELECT

DIRECTIONS: Each line contains four science or weather words. Read the first word and think about what it means. One of the next three words will mean the <u>opposite</u> of the first word. Underline the word that is the opposite of the first word.

G-43

dry **a.** bright **b.** hot **c.** wet

G-44

clear **a.** bright **b.** cloudy **c.** sunny

G-45

hot **a.** cold **b.** heat **c.** warm

G-46

sunny **a.** bright **b.** cloudy **c.** hot

G-47

rainy **a.** cloudy **b.** cold **c.** sunny

G-48

big **a.** large **b.** little **c.** tall

G-49

warm **a.** bright **b.** clothes **c.** cool

G-50

boiling **a.** baking **b.** cooking **c.** freezing

G-51

heavy **a.** firm **b.** light **c.** weight

OPPOSITES—SELECT

DIRECTIONS: Each line contains four words about amount or time. Read the first word and think about what it means. One of the next three words will mean the opposite of the first word. Underline the word that is the opposite of the first word.

G-52			
often	**a.** again	**b.** repeat	**c.** seldom

G-53			
always	**a.** never	**b.** often	**c.** some

G-54			
tight	**a.** loose	**b.** close	**c.** sharp

G-55			
none	**a.** empty	**b.** nothing	**c.** some

G-56			
all	**a.** every	**b.** none	**c.** some

G-57			
now	**a.** here	**b.** often	**c.** then

G-58			
many	**a.** all	**b.** few	**c.** none

G-59			
past	**a.** before	**b.** future	**c.** then

G-60			
everything	**a.** all	**b.** nothing	**c.** something

OPPOSITES—SELECT

DIRECTIONS: Each line contains four words used in art lessons. Read the first word and think about what it means. One of the next three words will mean the <u>opposite</u> of the first word. Underline the word that is the opposite of the first.

G-61

    dark   **a.** dim   **b.** heavy   **c.** light

G-62

    small   **a.** heavy   **b.** large   **c.** little

G-63

    dull   **a.** bright   **b.** dim   **c.** light

G-64

    smooth   **a.** glass   **b.** rough   **c.** slick

G-65

    tall   **a.** high   **b.** short   **c.** round

G-66

    easy   **a.** soft   **b.** simple   **c.** hard

G-67

    fine   **a.** coarse   **b.** dim   **c.** soft

G-68

    thick   **a.** fat   **b.** thin   **c.** wide

G-69

    zigzag   **a.** bumpy   **b.** straight   **c.** up and down

OPPOSITES—SUPPLY

DIRECTIONS: Each line contains a word. Read the given word and think about what it means. Think of a word that means the <u>opposite</u>. Write the word that you think of. (If you can think of other opposites, write them all down.)

G-70

fast _____

G-71

love _____

G-72

leader _____

G-73

clean _____

G-74

happy _____

G-75

whisper _____

G-76

lost _____

G-77

work _____

G-78

asleep _____

OPPOSITES—SUPPLY

DIRECTIONS: Each line contains a "direction" word. Read the given word and think about what it means. Think of a word that means the <u>opposite</u>. Write the word that you think of. (If you can think of other opposites, write them all down.)

G-79

close _____

G-80

start _____

G-81

true _____

G-82

ahead _____

G-83

front _____

G-84

top _____

G-85

later _____

G-86

remember _____

G-87

receive _____

OPPOSITES—SUPPLY

DIRECTIONS: Each line contains a word about action, amount, or order. Read the given word and think about what it means. Think of a word that means the <u>opposite</u> and write it. (If you can think of other opposites, write them all down.)

G-88

dark _____

G-89

go _____

G-90

run _____

G-91

many _____

G-92

none _____

G-93

more _____

G-94

after _____

G-95

last _____

G-96

never _____

SIMILARITIES—SELECT

DIRECTIONS: Each line contains four words. Read the first word and think about what it means. One of the next three words will mean almost the same thing. Circle the word that is <u>most</u> <u>like</u> the first word.

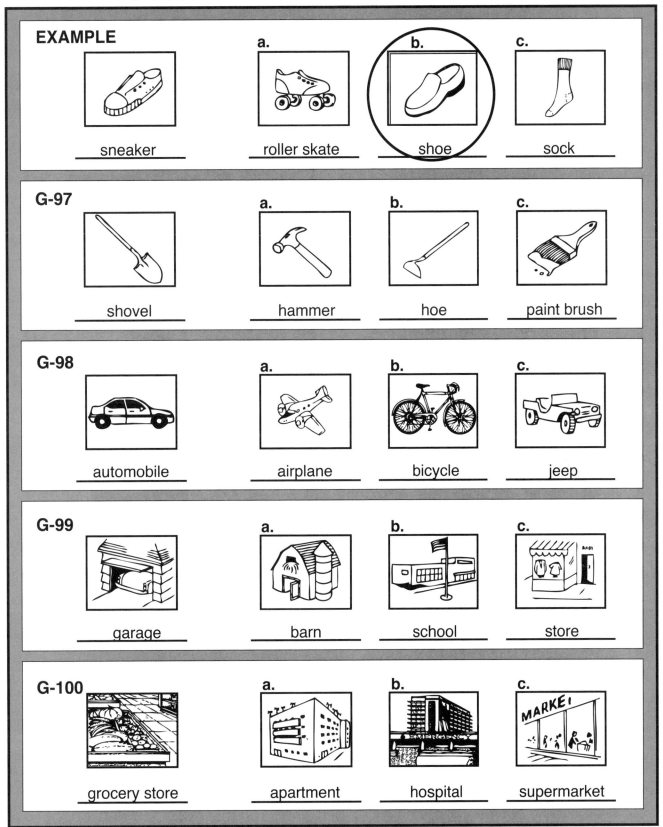

EXAMPLE

sneaker

a. roller skate

b. shoe

c. sock

G-97

shovel

a. hammer

b. hoe

c. paint brush

G-98

automobile

a. airplane

b. bicycle

c. jeep

G-99

garage

a. barn

b. school

c. store

G-100

grocery store

a. apartment

b. hospital

c. supermarket

189

SIMILARITIES—SELECT

DIRECTIONS: Each line contains four science or health words. Read the first word and think about what it means. One of the next three words will mean almost the same thing. Circle the word that is <u>most</u> <u>like</u> the first word.

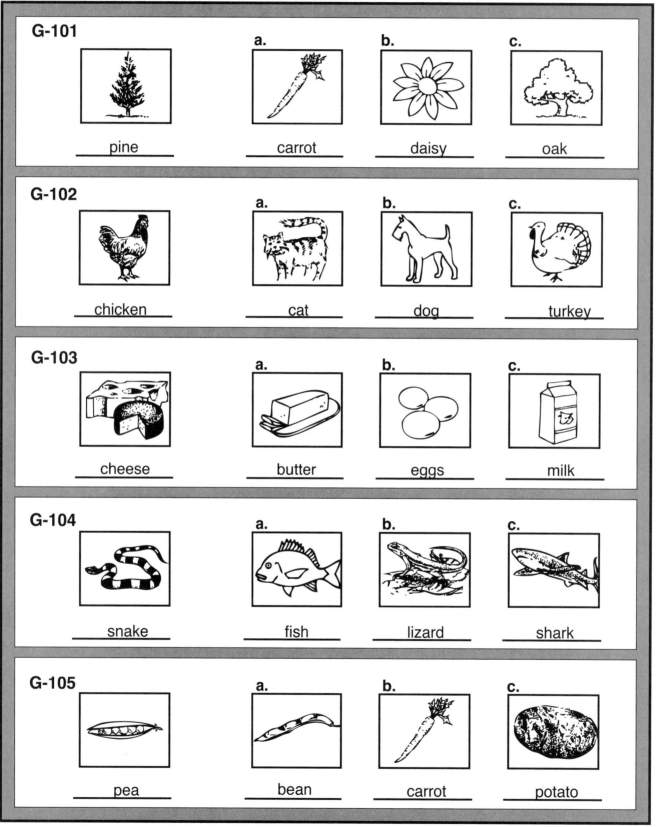

G-101

pine   **a.** carrot   **b.** daisy   **c.** oak

G-102

chicken   **a.** cat   **b.** dog   **c.** turkey

G-103

cheese   **a.** butter   **b.** eggs   **c.** milk

G-104

snake   **a.** fish   **b.** lizard   **c.** shark

G-105

pea   **a.** bean   **b.** carrot   **c.** potato

SIMILARITIES—SELECT

DIRECTIONS: Each line contains four words that tell what you do at school. Read the first word and think about what it means. One of the next three words will mean almost the same thing. Underline the word that is <u>most</u> <u>like</u> the first word.

G-106

listen | **a.** hear | **b.** speak | **c.** talk

G-107

talk | **a.** read | **b.** say | **c.** sing

G-108

draw | **a.** around | **b.** color | **c.** work

G-109

study | **a.** learn | **b.** lesson | **c.** talk

G-110

act | **a.** do | **b.** relax | **c.** rest

G-111

learn | **a.** discover | **b.** reply | **c.** show

G-112

ask | **a.** about | **b.** receive | **c.** question

G-113

answer | **a.** hear | **b.** reply | **c.** question

G-114

solve | **a.** ask | **b.** figure out | **c.** problem

SIMILARITIES—SELECT

DIRECTIONS: Each line contains four household words. Read the first word and think about what it means. One of the next three words will mean almost the same thing. Underline the word that is <u>most</u> <u>like</u> the first word.

G-115

newspaper   **a.** book   **b.** dictionary   **c.** magazine

G-116

cook   **a.** bake   **b.** dinner   **c.** soup

G-117

fix   **a.** build   **b.** repair   **c.** wreck

G-118

door   **a.** gate   **b.** roof   **c.** window

G-119

rug   **a.** carpet   **b.** floor   **c.** sweeper

G-120

curtains   **a.** drapes   **b.** door   **c.** window

G-121

clean   **a.** clothes   **b.** house   **c.** wash

G-122

meal   **a.** cook   **b.** dinner   **c.** vegetable

G-123

broom   **a.** sponge   **b.** handle   **c.** sweeper

SIMILARITIES—SELECT

DIRECTIONS: Each line contains four action words. Read the first word and think about what it means. One of the next three words will mean almost the same thing. Underline the word that is <u>most</u> <u>like</u> the first word.

G-124

pay   **a.** owe   **b.** spend   **c.** take

G-125

run   **a.** jog   **b.** sit   **c.** walk

G-126

look   **a.** hear   **b.** talk   **c.** watch

G-127

stay   **a.** go   **b.** leave   **c.** remain

G-128

call   **a.** say   **b.** shout   **c.** tell

G-129

take   **a.** carry   **b.** give   **c.** keep

G-130

throw   **a.** toss   **b.** catch   **c.** hit

G-131

build   **a.** fix   **b.** make   **c.** repair

G-132

hide   **a.** cover   **b.** seek   **c.** show

SIMILARITIES—SELECT

DIRECTIONS: Each line contains four words from science. Read the first word and think about what it means. One of the next three words will mean almost the same thing. Underline the word that is <u>most</u> <u>like</u> the first word.

G-133			
sound	**a.** noise	**b.** quiet	**c.** silence

G-134			
heat	**a.** light	**b.** stove	**c.** warmth

G-135			
sun	**a.** beam	**b.** shine	**c.** star

G-136			
rock	**a.** mountain	**b.** ocean	**c.** stone

G-137			
fog	**a.** cloud	**b.** ice	**c.** snow

G-138			
beak	**a.** bill	**b.** claw	**c.** wing

G-139			
baby	**a.** brother	**b.** child	**c.** sister

G-140			
earth	**a.** continent	**b.** country	**c.** world

G-141			
map	**a.** country	**b.** drawing	**c.** photograph

SIMILARITIES—SUPPLY

DIRECTIONS: Each line contains a word used to describe something. Read the word and think about what it means. Think of a word or phrase that means <u>almost</u> the same and write it down. Write as many similar words as you can think of.

G-142

short _____

G-143

big _____

G-144

friendly _____

G-145

heavy _____

G-146

happy _____

G-147

good _____

G-148

sweet _____

G-149

beautiful _____

G-150

safe _____

SIMILARITIES—SUPPLY

DIRECTIONS: Each line contains an action word. Read the word and think about what it means. Think of a word or phrase that means <u>almost</u> the same and write it down. Write as many similar words as you can think of.

G-151

touch _____

G-152

see _____

G-153

hear _____

G-154

speak _____

G-155

work _____

G-156

study _____

G-157

build _____

G-158

fix _____

G-159

destroy _____

SIMILARITIES—SUPPLY

DIRECTIONS: Each line contains a word used in instructions. Read the word and think about what it means. Think of a word or phrase that means <u>almost</u> the same and write it down. Write as many similar words as you can think of.

G-160

leave _____

G-161

above _____

G-162

enter _____

G-163

below _____

G-164

continue _____

G-165

stop _____

G-166

choose _____

G-167

listen _____

G-168

fasten _____

HOW ALIKE?—SELECT

DIRECTIONS: Each activity contains two pictures. Think about the ways these two things are alike. Circle the letters of the sentences that are true of both items.

EXAMPLE

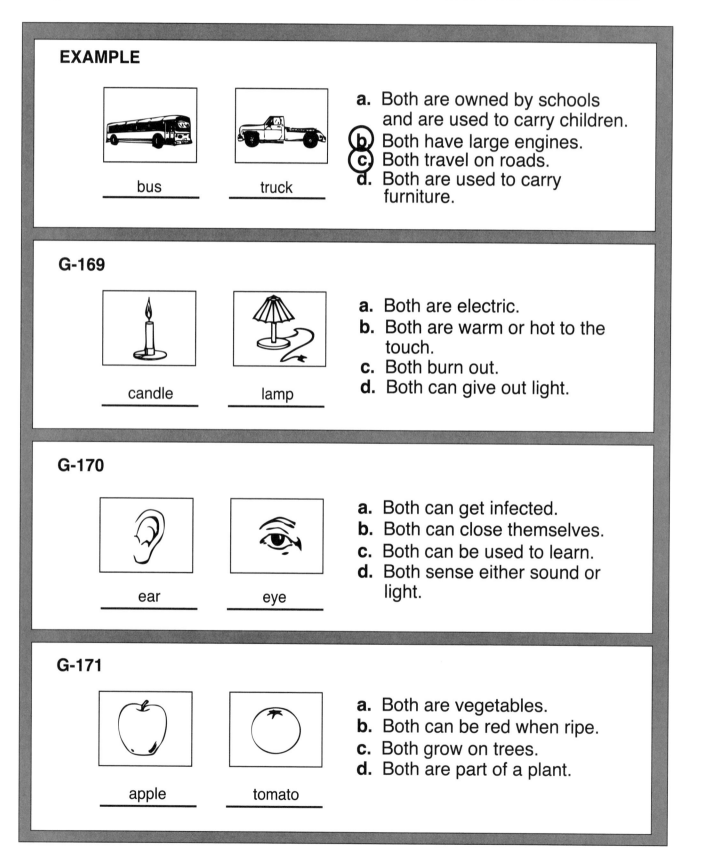

bus   truck

a. Both are owned by schools and are used to carry children.
b. Both have large engines.
c. Both travel on roads.
d. Both are used to carry furniture.

G-169

candle   lamp

a. Both are electric.
b. Both are warm or hot to the touch.
c. Both burn out.
d. Both can give out light.

G-170

ear   eye

a. Both can get infected.
b. Both can close themselves.
c. Both can be used to learn.
d. Both sense either sound or light.

G-171

apple   tomato

a. Both are vegetables.
b. Both can be red when ripe.
c. Both grow on trees.
d. Both are part of a plant.

HOW ALIKE?—SELECT

DIRECTIONS: Each activity contains two pictures. Think about the ways these two things are alike. Circle the letters of the sentences that are true of both items.

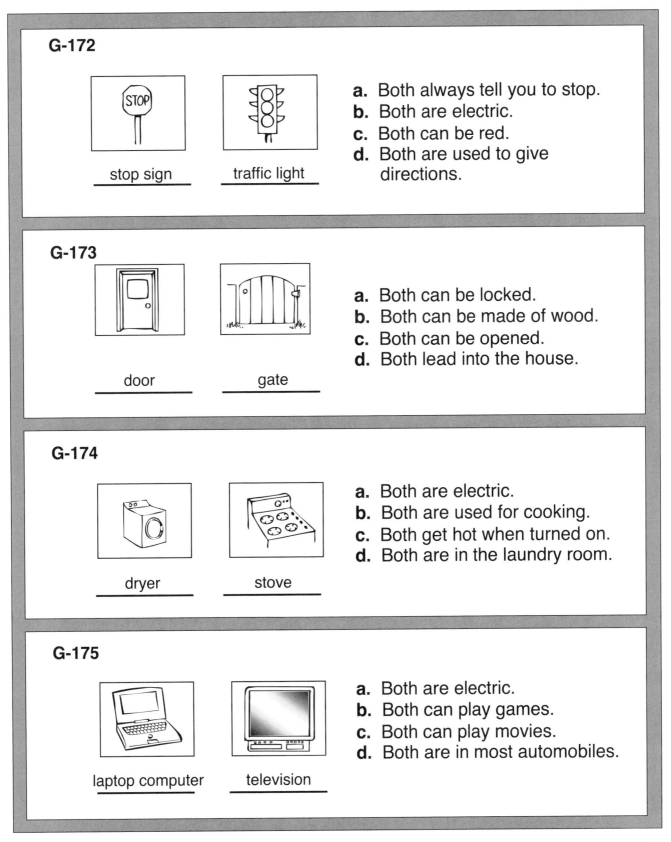

G-172

stop sign   traffic light

a. Both always tell you to stop.
b. Both are electric.
c. Both can be red.
d. Both are used to give directions.

G-173

door   gate

a. Both can be locked.
b. Both can be made of wood.
c. Both can be opened.
d. Both lead into the house.

G-174

dryer   stove

a. Both are electric.
b. Both are used for cooking.
c. Both get hot when turned on.
d. Both are in the laundry room.

G-175

laptop computer   television

a. Both are electric.
b. Both can play games.
c. Both can play movies.
d. Both are in most automobiles.

HOW ALIKE AND HOW DIFFERENT?

DIRECTIONS: Each activity contains two pictures. Think about the ways these two things are alike and different. Tell how they are alike and how they are different, and give your reasons why.

G-176

bicycle   car

How alike?

_____

_____

_____

How different?

_____

_____

_____

G-177

boat   ship

How alike?

_____

_____

_____

How different?

_____

_____

_____

G-178

fire truck   police car

How alike?

_____

_____

_____

How different?

_____

_____

_____

HOW ALIKE AND HOW DIFFERENT?

DIRECTIONS: Each activity contains two pictures. Think about the ways these two things are alike and different. Tell how they are alike and how they are different, and give your reasons why.

G-179

book   television

How alike?

_____

_____

_____

How different?

_____

_____

_____

G-180

baseball   football

How alike?

_____

_____

_____

How different?

_____

_____

_____

G-181

mother   teacher

How alike?

_____

_____

_____

How different?

_____

_____

_____

HOW ALIKE AND HOW DIFFERENT?

DIRECTIONS: Each activity contains two pictures. Think about the ways these two things are alike and different. Tell how they are alike and how they are different, and give your reasons why.

G-182

arm   branch

How alike?

_____
_____
_____

How different?

_____
_____
_____

G-183

can   can

How alike?

_____
_____
_____

How different?

_____
_____
_____

G-184

legs   legs

How alike?

_____
_____
_____

How different?

_____
_____
_____

HOW ALIKE AND HOW DIFFERENT?

DIRECTIONS: Each activity contains two pictures. Think about the ways these two things are alike and different. Tell how they are alike and how they are different, and give your reasons why.

G-185

snake   lizard

How alike?

_____

_____

_____

How different?

_____

_____

_____

G-186

deer   horse

How alike?

_____

_____

_____

How different?

_____

_____

_____

G-187

shark   whale

How alike?

_____

_____

_____

How different?

_____

_____

_____

COMPARE AND CONTRAST—GRAPHIC ORGANIZER

DIRECTIONS: Read the passage carefully to decide how nouns and verbs are alike and different. Record the information on the diagram.

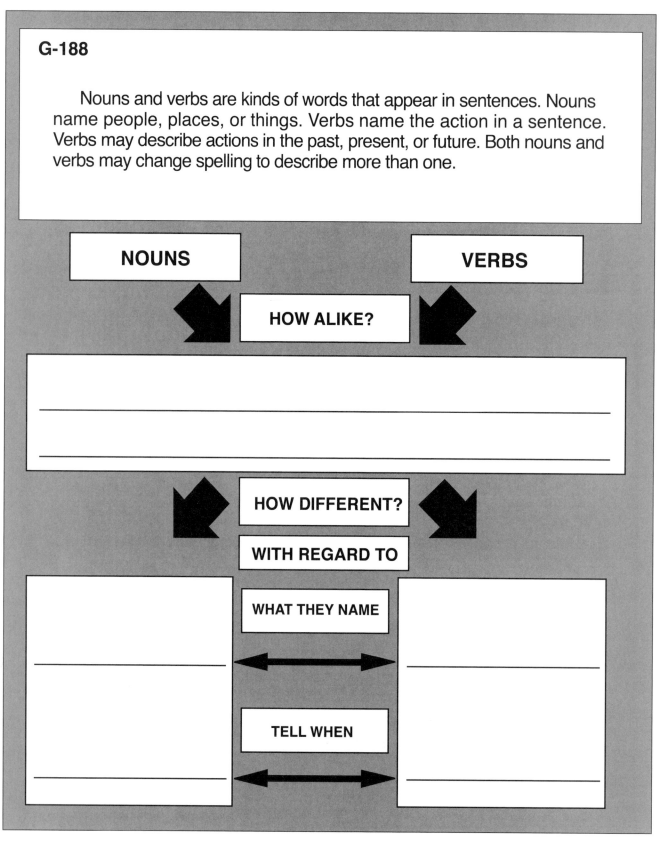

G-188

Nouns and verbs are kinds of words that appear in sentences. Nouns name people, places, or things. Verbs name the action in a sentence. Verbs may describe actions in the past, present, or future. Both nouns and verbs may change spelling to describe more than one.

NOUNS

VERBS

HOW ALIKE?

HOW DIFFERENT?

WITH REGARD TO

WHAT THEY NAME

TELL WHEN

COMPARE AND CONTRAST—GRAPHIC ORGANIZER

DIRECTIONS: Use the diagram to show how statements and questions are alike and how they are different.

G-189

Statements and questions are kinds of sentences and tell whole thoughts. Both contain a subject and a verb and end with a punctuation mark. Both are used to give or get information. Paragraphs can have both statements and questions.

Statements give information about people, places, things, or ideas. They usually end with a period. The whole verb usually follows the subject; for example, "The motor is running."

Questions ask for information about people, places, things, or ideas. They always end with a question mark. The subject usually comes between parts of the verb; for example, "Is the motor running?"

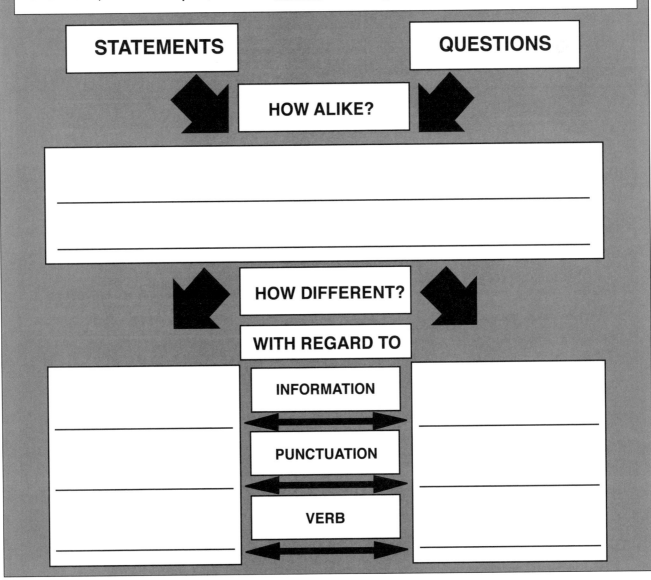

COMPARE AND CONTRAST—GRAPHIC ORGANIZER

DIRECTIONS: Locate your state on a map of the United States of America. Read the passage carefully to see how the United States of America and your state are alike and how they are different. Record the information on the diagram.

G-190

The United States government and your state government each have a chief official, meet in a particular city, and have a special building. The governor is the chief official of a state. The governor sees that the laws made by the state legislature are carried out. The state government is located in the state capital. The state legislature meets in the state capitol building.

The chief official of the national government is the president of the United States, who carries out laws passed by the Congress. Congress meets in the Capitol in Washington, D.C.

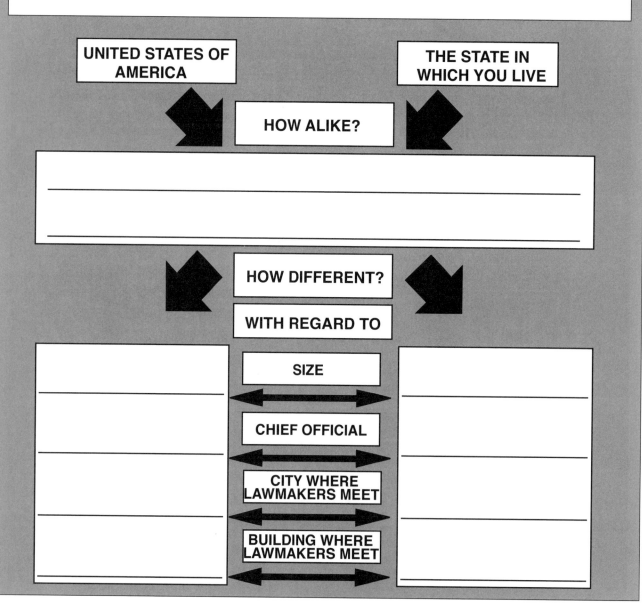

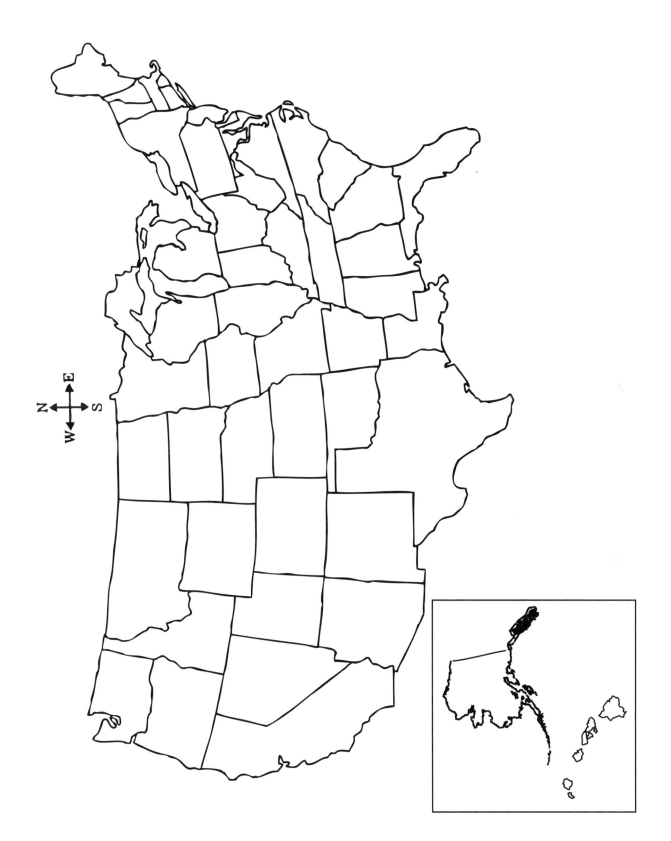

COMPARING LIVING AND NONLIVING THINGS

DIRECTIONS: Read the passage carefully, then use the diagram below to record how living and nonliving things are alike and how they are different.

G-191

All things have weight and take up space. Both living and nonliving things come in many sizes and shapes. There are tiny plants, tiny animals, and tiny grains of sand as well as large plants, large animals, and large mountains.

Most animals can move themselves around. Plants must be moved by wind or animals. No nonliving thing can move by itself.

All living things breathe, but plants breathe differently from animals. Nonliving things do not breathe. Breathing is called respiration.

Nonliving things do not eat and do not give birth. Giving birth is known as reproduction. All plants and animals reproduce themselves. Plants and animals need nourishment but get their food in different ways.

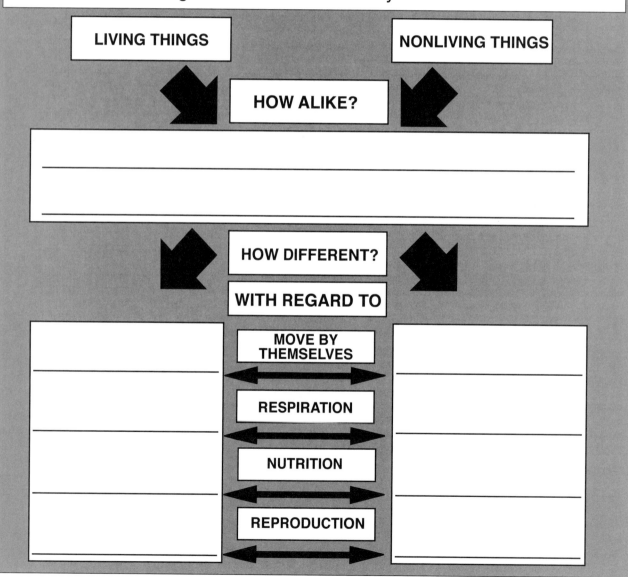

CHAPTER EIGHT

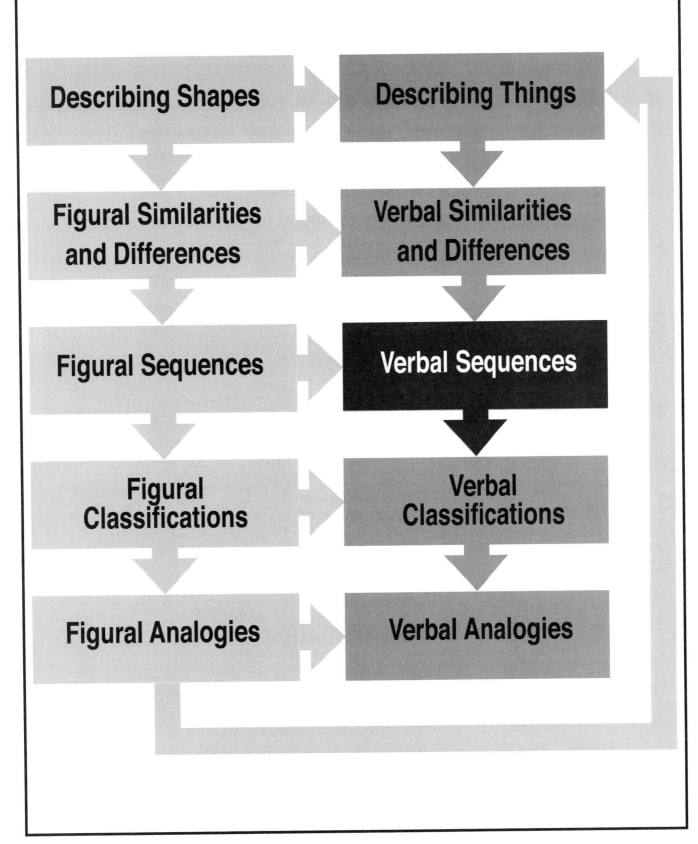

FOLLOWING YES-NO RULES—A

DIRECTIONS: You will be following rules about circles. **YES** is used to show that the two circles are the same size, and **NO** is used to show that the circles are not the same size. Draw circles of the right size to follow the yes-or-no rule.

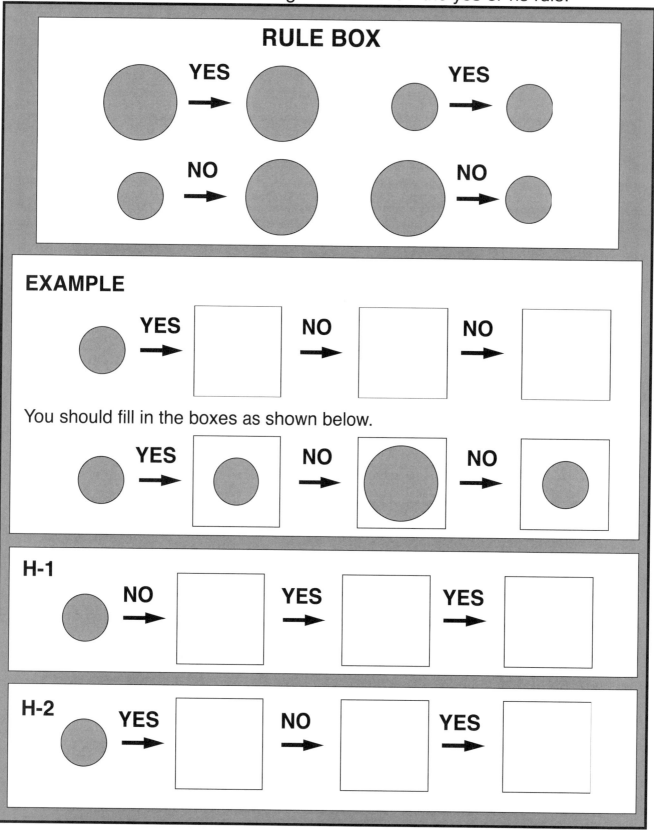

You should fill in the boxes as shown below.

FOLLOWING YES-NO RULES—A

DIRECTIONS: In the blank boxes, draw dark or white circles to correctly illustrate the yes-or-no rules.

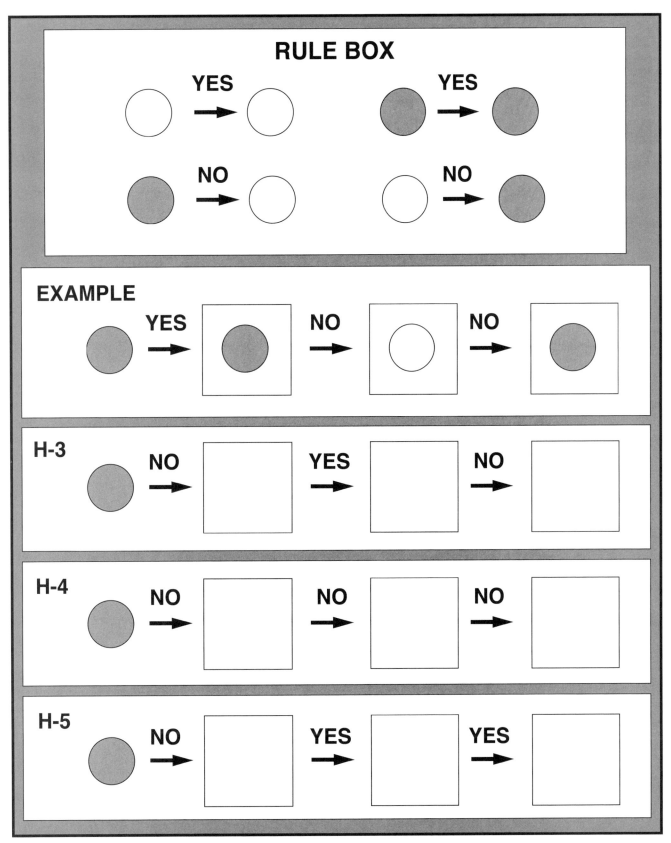

WRITING YES-NO RULES

DIRECTIONS: In the boxes above the arrows, write yes or no to correctly label the illustrated rules.

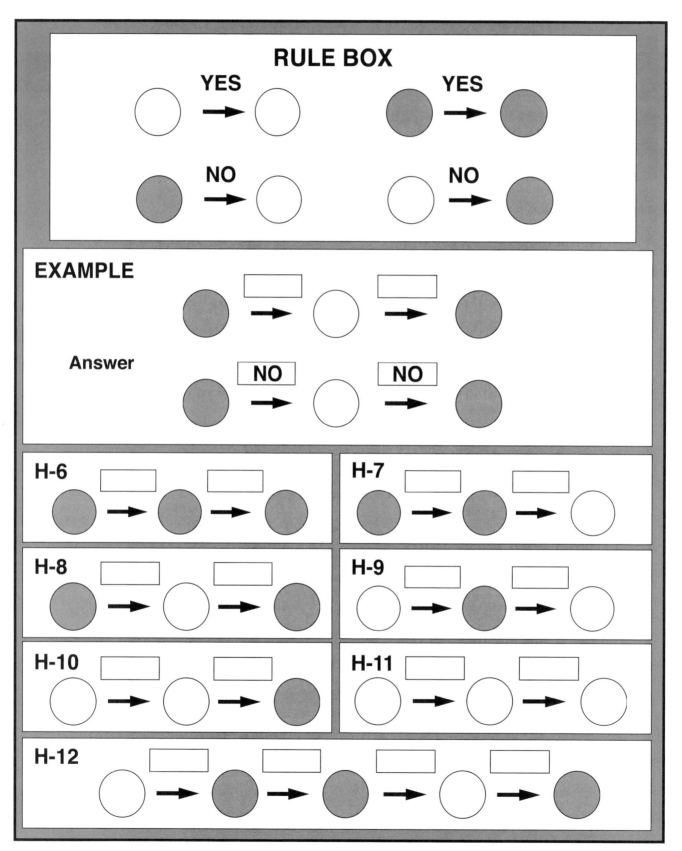

WRITING YES-NO RULES

DIRECTIONS: In the blank boxes, write yes or no to correctly label the yes-or-no rules.

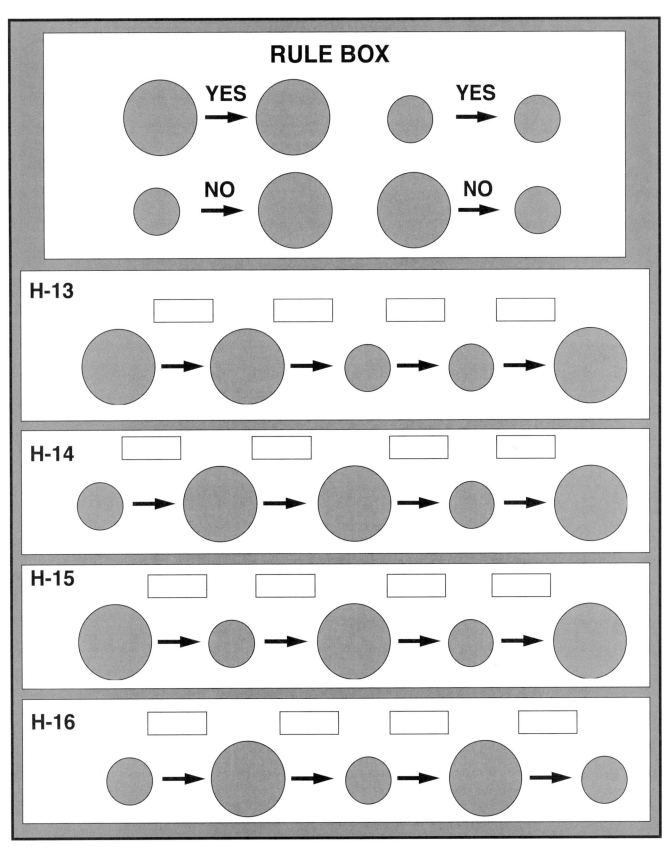

FOLLOWING YES-NO RULES—B

DIRECTIONS: Following the yes-or-no rule, darken the correct circles along the path from start to finish.

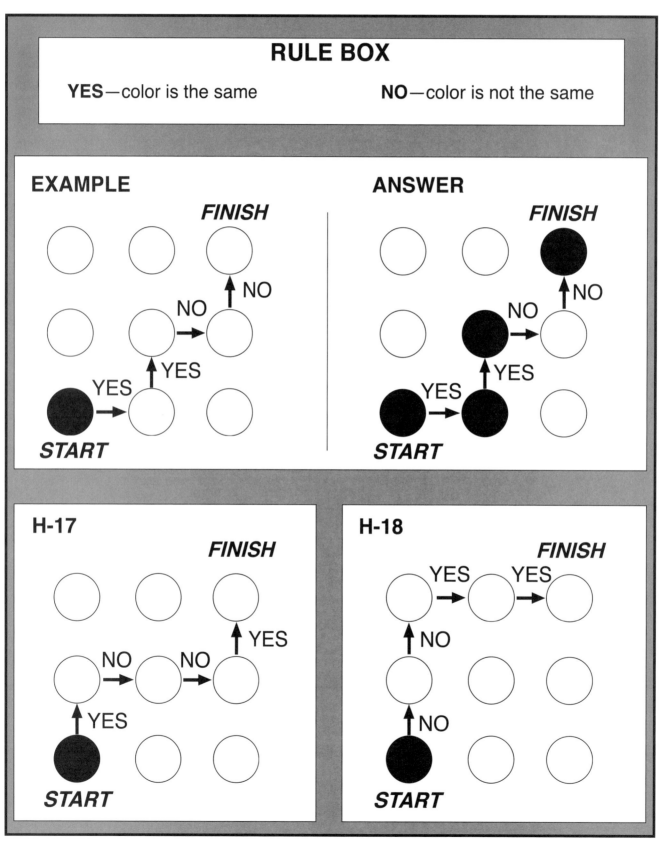

FOLLOWING YES-NO RULES—B

DIRECTIONS: Following the yes-or-no rule, darken the correct circles along the path from start to finish.

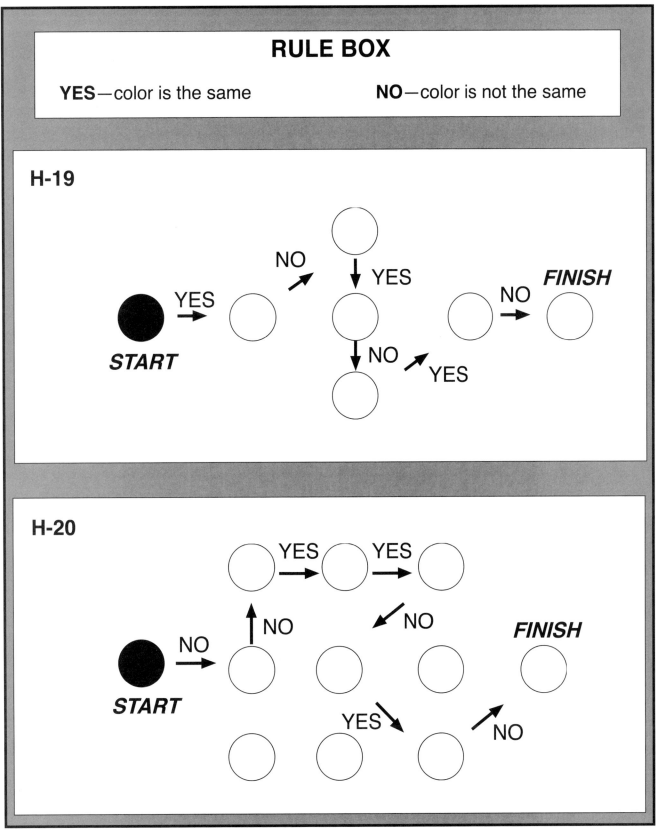

RULE BOX

YES—color is the same   **NO**—color is not the same

H-19

H-20

COMPLETING TRUE-FALSE TABLES

DIRECTIONS: Study the given true-false table and then complete the blank table.

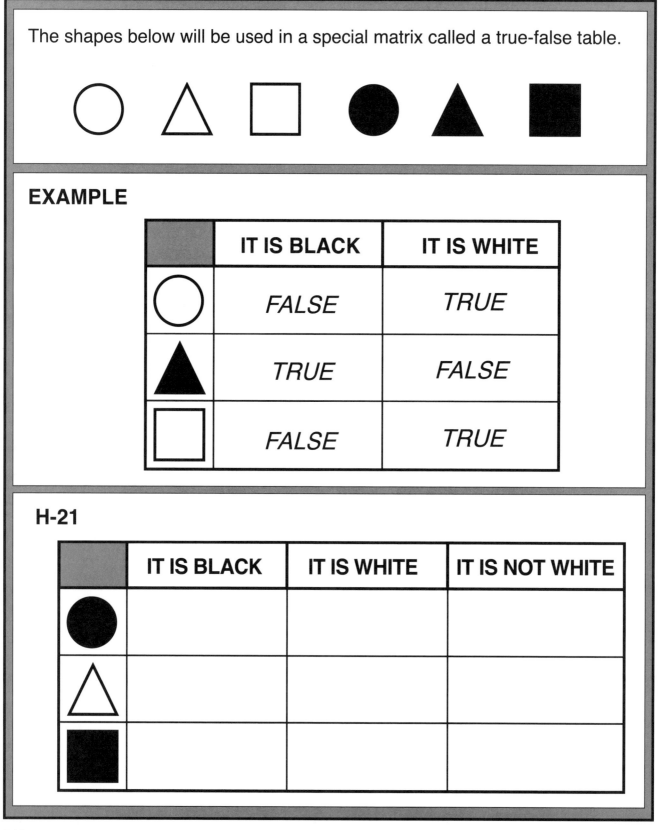

The shapes below will be used in a special matrix called a true-false table.

EXAMPLE

	IT IS BLACK	IT IS WHITE
◯	*FALSE*	*TRUE*
▲	*TRUE*	*FALSE*
▢	*FALSE*	*TRUE*

H-21

	IT IS BLACK	IT IS WHITE	IT IS NOT WHITE
●			
△			
■			

COMPLETING TRUE-FALSE TABLES

DIRECTIONS: Complete the blank true-false tables.

H-22

	IT IS WHITE	IT IS BLACK	IT IS NOT BLACK
▲			
◯			
☐			

H-23

	IT IS A SQUARE	IT IS A CIRCLE	IT IS NOT A CIRCLE
■			
◯			
●			

COMPLETING TRUE-FALSE TABLES

DIRECTIONS: Complete the blank true-false tables.

H-24

	IT IS ALL BLACK	IT IS ALL WHITE	IT IS NOT ALL WHITE
■			
○			
◐			

H-25

	IT IS HALF BLACK	IT IS HALF WHITE	IT IS NOT A CIRCLE
●			
▮			
◖			

FINDING LOCATIONS ON MAPS

DIRECTIONS: Using the map, follow the directions or answer the question in each exercise.

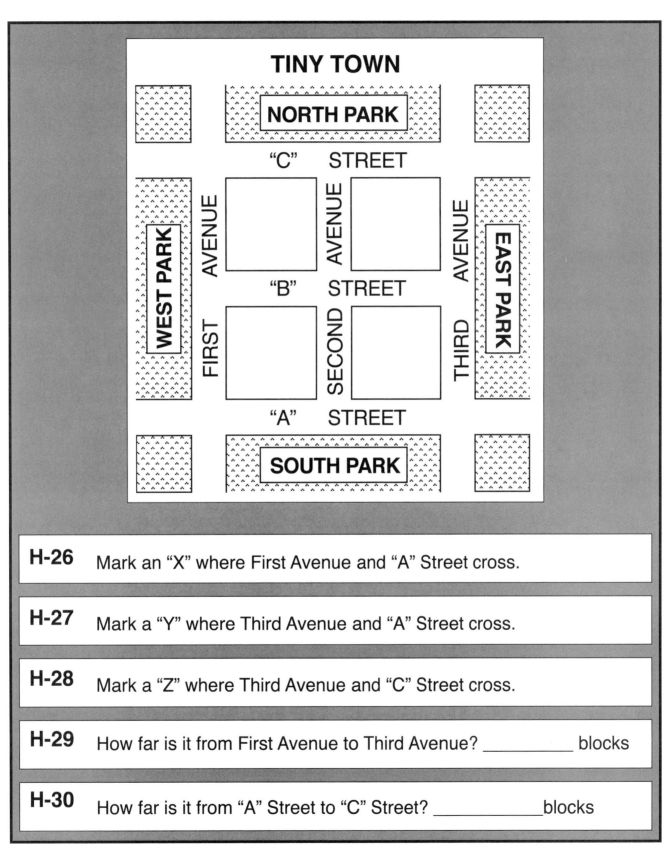

H-26   Mark an "X" where First Avenue and "A" Street cross.

H-27   Mark a "Y" where Third Avenue and "A" Street cross.

H-28   Mark a "Z" where Third Avenue and "C" Street cross.

H-29   How far is it from First Avenue to Third Avenue? _____ blocks

H-30   How far is it from "A" Street to "C" Street? _____ blocks

FINDING LOCATIONS ON MAPS

DIRECTIONS: Using the map, follow the directions or answer the question in each exercise.

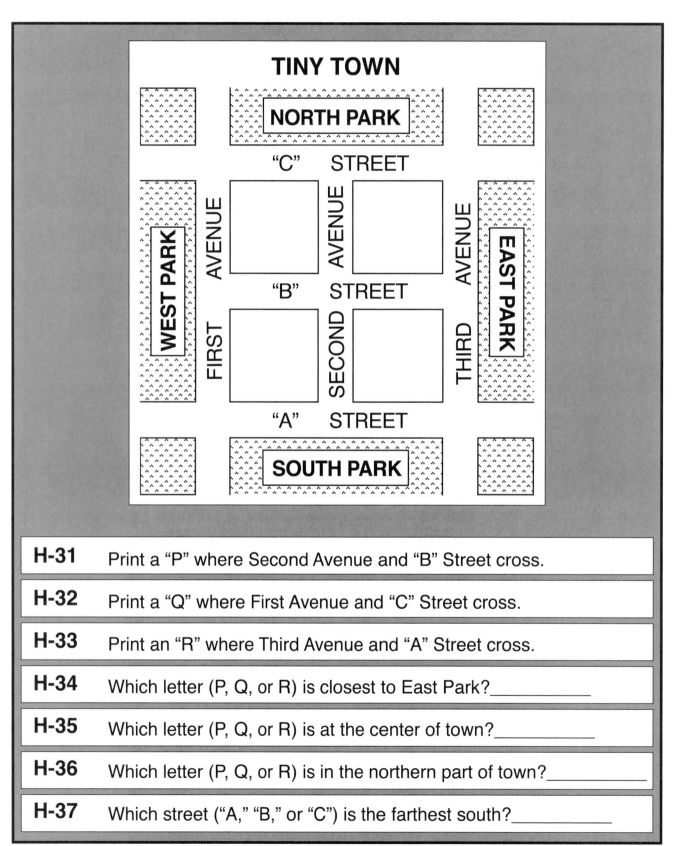

H-31	Print a "P" where Second Avenue and "B" Street cross.
H-32	Print a "Q" where First Avenue and "C" Street cross.
H-33	Print an "R" where Third Avenue and "A" Street cross.
H-34	Which letter (P, Q, or R) is closest to East Park?_____
H-35	Which letter (P, Q, or R) is at the center of town?_____
H-36	Which letter (P, Q, or R) is in the northern part of town?_____
H-37	Which street ("A," "B," or "C") is the farthest south?_____

DESCRIBING LOCATIONS—A

DIRECTIONS: Look at the map and pretend you are standing at Second Avenue and "C" Street facing North Park. Based on that information, answer the questions below.

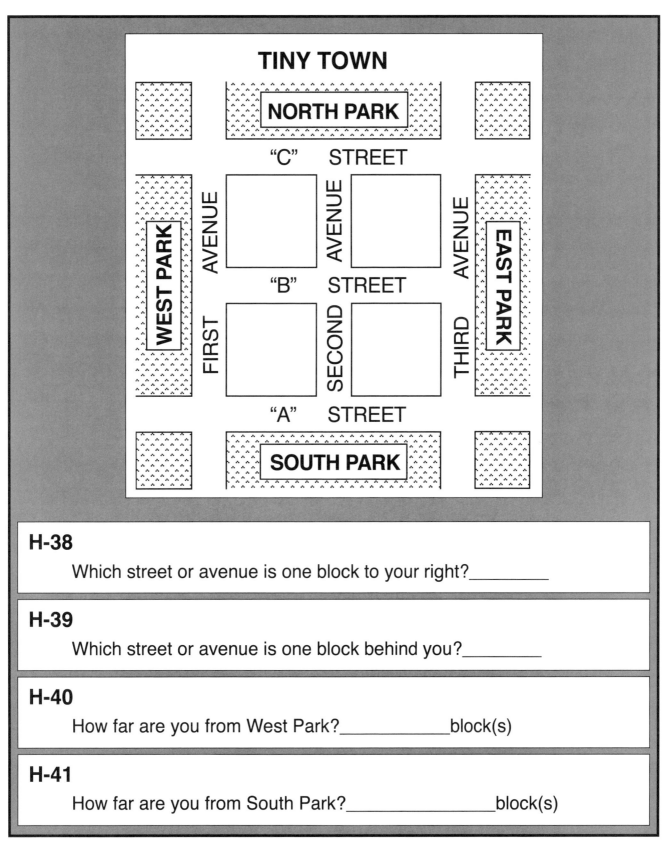

H-38

    Which street or avenue is one block to your right?_____

H-39

    Which street or avenue is one block behind you?_____

H-40

    How far are you from West Park?_____block(s)

H-41

    How far are you from South Park?_____block(s)

DESCRIBING LOCATIONS—A

DIRECTIONS: Look at the map and pretend you are standing at Third Avenue and "B" Street facing East Park. Based on that information, answer the questions below.

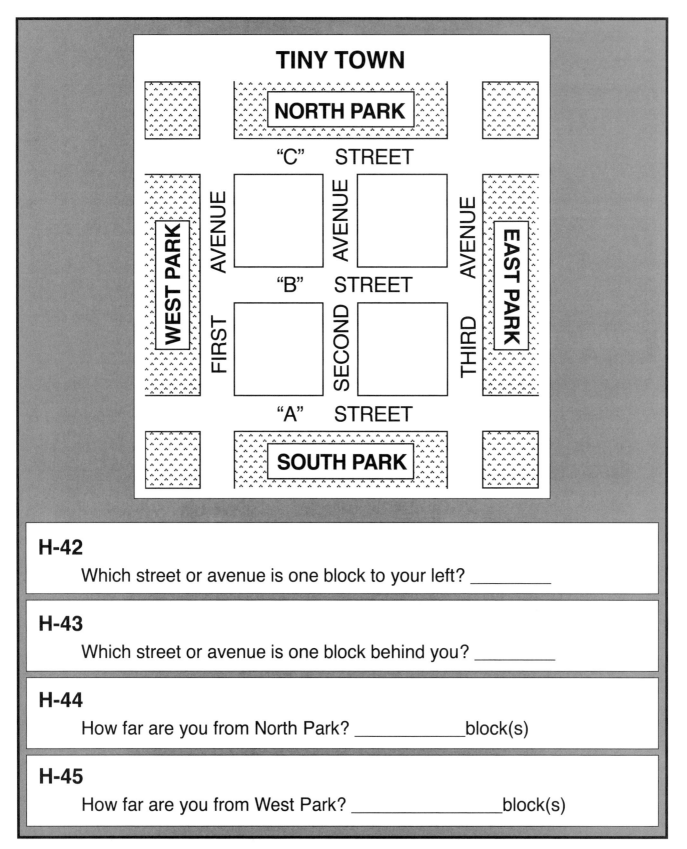

H-42

Which street or avenue is one block to your left? _____

H-43

Which street or avenue is one block behind you? _____

H-44

How far are you from North Park? _____ block(s)

H-45

How far are you from West Park? _____ block(s)

DESCRIBING DIRECTIONS—A

DIRECTIONS: Look at the path along the arrows from "P" to "Q" to "R." Answer the following questions about parts of the path.

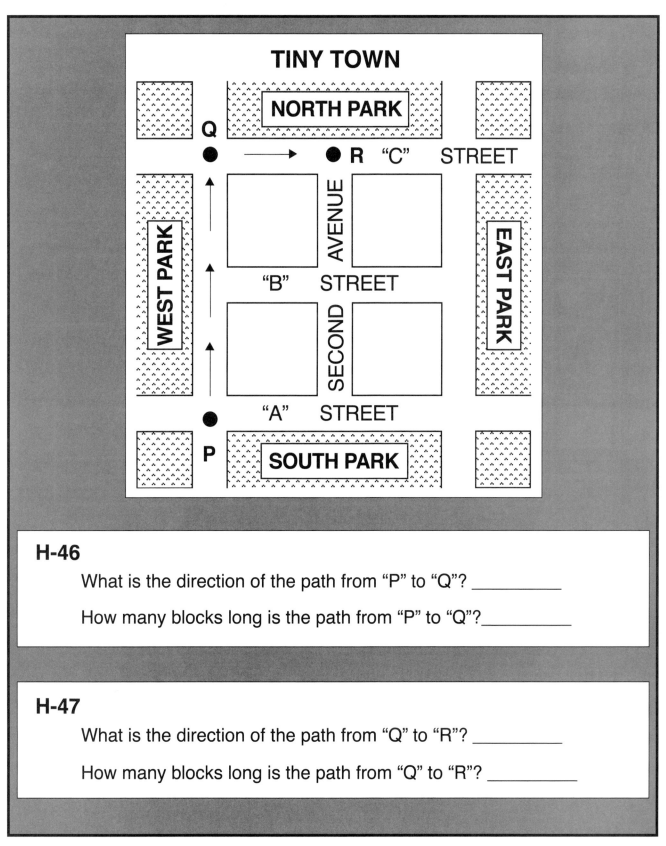

H-46

What is the direction of the path from "P" to "Q"? _____

How many blocks long is the path from "P" to "Q"? _____

H-47

What is the direction of the path from "Q" to "R"? _____

How many blocks long is the path from "Q" to "R"? _____

DESCRIBING DIRECTIONS—A

DIRECTIONS: Look at the path along the arrows from "L" to "M" to "O." Answer the following questions about parts of the path.

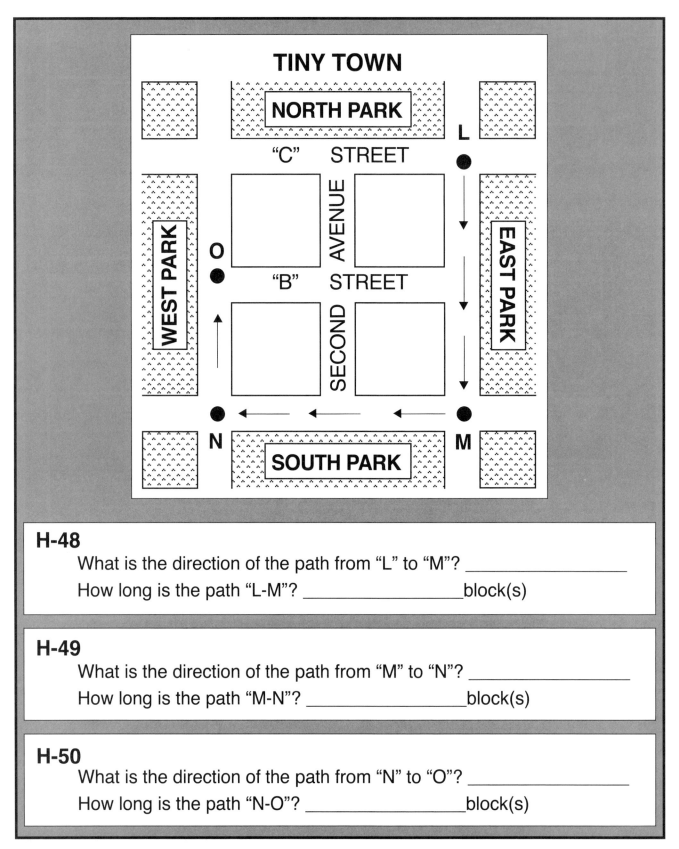

H-48

What is the direction of the path from "L" to "M"? _____

How long is the path "L-M"? _____block(s)

H-49

What is the direction of the path from "M" to "N"? _____

How long is the path "M-N"? _____block(s)

H-50

What is the direction of the path from "N" to "O"? _____

How long is the path "N-O"? _____block(s)

DESCRIBING LOCATIONS—B

DIRECTIONS: Use the map to answer the questions below.

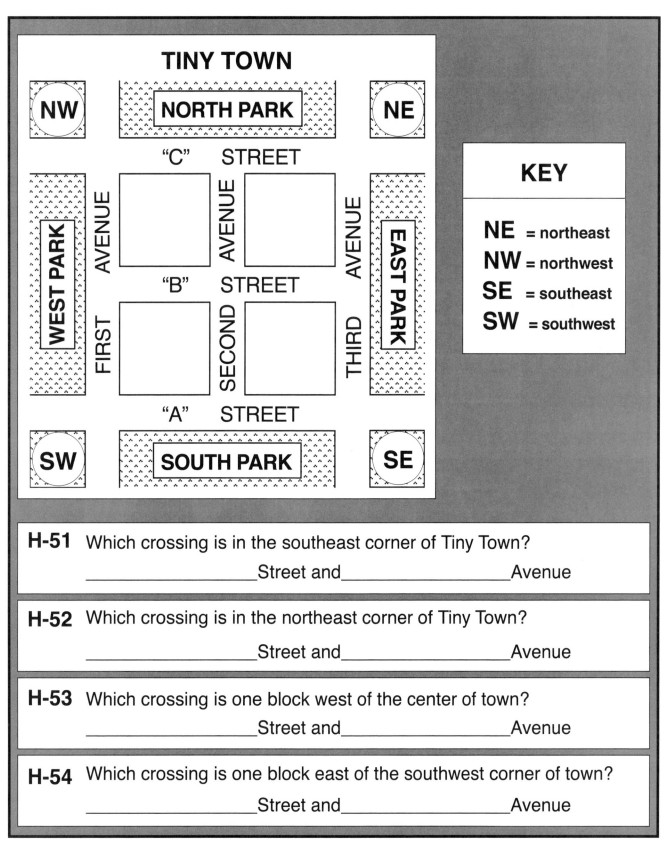

TINY TOWN

NW   NORTH PARK   NE

"C"   STREET

KEY

NE = northeast
NW = northwest
SE = southeast
SW = southwest

WEST PARK   "B"   STREET   EAST PARK

"A"   STREET

SW   SOUTH PARK   SE

H-51 Which crossing is in the southeast corner of Tiny Town?

_____Street and_____Avenue

H-52 Which crossing is in the northeast corner of Tiny Town?

_____Street and_____Avenue

H-53 Which crossing is one block west of the center of town?

_____Street and_____Avenue

H-54 Which crossing is one block east of the southwest corner of town?

_____Street and_____Avenue

DESCRIBING DIRECTIONS—B

DIRECTIONS: If you start at Second Avenue and "C" Street and travel two blocks south, you will be on the corner of Second Avenue and "A" Street (follow the arrow from *START to FINISH*.) Answer the questions below.

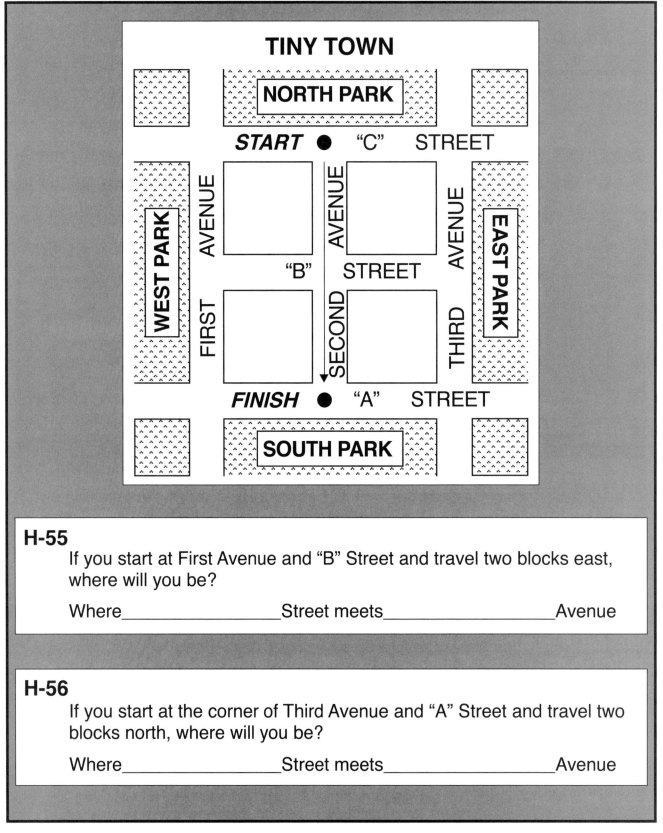

H-55

If you start at First Avenue and "B" Street and travel two blocks east, where will you be?

Where_____Street meets_____Avenue

H-56

If you start at the corner of Third Avenue and "A" Street and travel two blocks north, where will you be?

Where_____Street meets_____Avenue

DESCRIBING DIRECTIONS—B

DIRECTIONS: Use the map to answer the questions below.

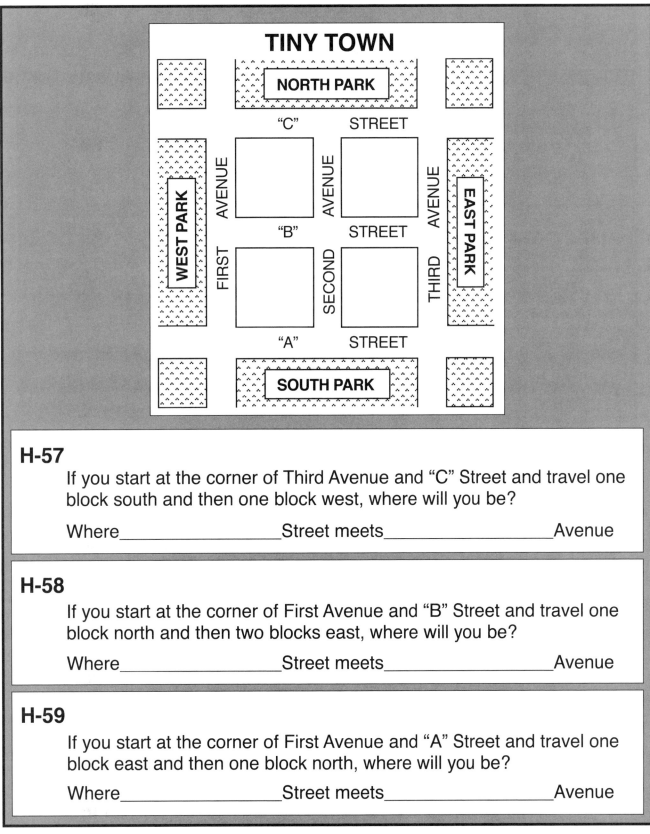

H-57

If you start at the corner of Third Avenue and "C" Street and travel one block south and then one block west, where will you be?

Where_____Street meets_____Avenue

H-58

If you start at the corner of First Avenue and "B" Street and travel one block north and then two blocks east, where will you be?

Where_____Street meets_____Avenue

H-59

If you start at the corner of First Avenue and "A" Street and travel one block east and then one block north, where will you be?

Where_____Street meets_____Avenue

DESCRIBING DIRECTIONS—B

DIRECTIONS: Use the map to answer the questions below.

TINY TOWN

NORTH PARK

"C"   STREET

WEST PARK   FIRST AVENUE   "B"   AVENUE   STREET   SECOND AVENUE   THIRD AVENUE   EAST PARK

"A"   STREET

SOUTH PARK

H-60

If you start at the corner of First Avenue and "C" Street and travel one block east and then two blocks south, where will you be?

Where_____Street meets_____Avenue

H-61

If you start at the corner of Second Avenue and "B" Street and travel one block south and then one block west, where will you be?

Where_____Street meets_____Avenue

H-62

If you start at the corner of First Avenue and "A" Street and travel two blocks north and then one block east, where will you be?

Where_____Street meets_____Avenue

SELECT THE WORD THAT CONTINUES THE SEQUENCE

DIRECTIONS: The first two words in each group suggest a time sequence. From the box, choose the word that should come next in the sequence. Write the word in the blank.

H-63

before, during, _____

> after
> beside
> whole

H-64

Monday, Tuesday, _____

> Saturday
> Sunday
> Wednesday

H-65

day, month, _____

> hour
> week
> year

H-66

first, second, _____

> beginning
> last
> third

H-67

Halloween, Thanksgiving, _____

> April Fool's Day
> Christmas
> Labor Day

SELECT THE WORD THAT CONTINUES THE SEQUENCE

DIRECTIONS: The first two words in each group suggest a sequence of amount. From the box, choose the word that should come next in the sequence. Write the word in the blank.

H-68

pint, quart, _____

| cup |
| gallon |
| teaspoon |

H-69

more, same, _____

| equal |
| less |
| most |

H-70

small, medium, _____

| large |
| regular |
| tiny |

H-71

some, more, _____

| few |
| many |
| most |

H-72

inch, foot, _____

| minute |
| pound |
| yard |

SELECT THE WORD THAT CONTINUES THE SEQUENCE

DIRECTIONS: The first two words in each group suggest a sequence of rank, degree, size, or order. From the box, choose the word that should come next in the sequence. Write the word in the blank.

H-73

above, beside, _____

> below
> between
> over

H-74

bad, worse, _____

> better
> less
> worst

H-75

boy, teen, _____

> baby
> child
> man

H-76

enter, stay, _____

> arrive
> leave
> remain

H-77

good, better, _____

> best
> well
> worst

RANKING

DIRECTIONS: On the line under each group of words, rewrite the group in order from lowest or smallest to highest or largest in size, degree, rank, or order.

EXAMPLE

all, none, some

none, some, all
_____

H-78

afternoon, morning, night

_____

H-79

always, never, sometimes

_____

H-80

giant, large, regular

_____

H-81

many, more, most

_____

H-82

first, last, middle

_____

RANKING

DIRECTIONS: On the line under each group of words, rewrite the group in order from lowest or smallest to highest or largest in size, degree, rank, or order.

H-83

dime, dollar, quarter

_____

H-84

highway, sidewalk, street

_____

H-85

lake, ocean, pond

_____

H-86

city, nation, state

_____

H-87

century, month, year

_____

H-88

dime, nickel, penny

_____

RANKING

DIRECTIONS: On the line under each group of words, rewrite the group in order from lowest or smallest to highest or largest in size, degree, rank, or order.

H-89

body, head, tail

_____

H-90

rope, string, thread

_____

H-91

game, inning, out

_____

H-92

continue, finish, start

_____

H-93

book, page, word

_____

H-94

baseball, basketball, Ping-Pong ball

_____

SUPPLY A WORD THAT CONTINUES A SEQUENCE

DIRECTIONS: The first two words in each sequence suggest a degree, rank, size, or order. Think of a word that will continue the sequence and write it on the line. You may use a dictionary to get help.

H-95

second, minute, _____

H-96

ready, set, _____

H-97

March, April, _____

H-98

breakfast, lunch, _____

H-99

inch, foot, _____

H-100

small, medium, _____

H-101

beginning, middle, _____

H-102

spring, summer, _____

H-103

penny, nickel, _____

SUPPLY A WORD THAT CONTINUES A SEQUENCE

DIRECTIONS: The first two words in each sequence suggest a degree, rank, size, or order. Think of a word that will continue the sequence and write it on the line. You may use a dictionary to get help.

H-104

ten, twenty, _____

H-105

yesterday, today, _____

H-106

second, third, _____

H-107

baby, girl, _____

H-108

ounce, pound, _____

H-109

go, going, _____

H-110

white, gray, _____

H-111

cook, serve, _____

H-112

one, three, _____

WARM-UP DEDUCTIVE REASONING

DIRECTIONS: The example below shows how to complete the exercises on the following pages, in which people are being compared. Given the clues in the sentences, you can determine who is the fastest swimmer (see the directions below).

EXAMPLE

Maria swims faster than Fred. Kim swims faster than Maria.

Who swims the fastest? _____

HOW TO FIGURE IT OUT

STEP 1: Read the first clue and write the names, with the faster swimmer on top, in the space below.

Maria swims faster than Fred. Kim swims faster than Maria.

Maria
Fred

STEP 2: Read the second clue and decide how Kim compares to the other two. Since Kim is faster than Maria, her name should be on top.

Maria swims faster than Fred. **Kim swims faster than Maria.**

Kim
Maria
Fred

Now you can answer that Kim swims the fastest (see below).

EXAMPLE

Maria swims faster than Fred. Kim swims faster than Maria.

Who swims the fastest? _____ Kim _____

Kim
Maria
Fred

WARM-UP DEDUCTIVE REASONING

DIRECTIONS: In the sentences below, people are being compared according to some characteristic (weight, age, height, score, etc.). Read the sentences; in the space below the sentences, write the names in order, then answer the question.

H-113

Charlie is heavier than Bill. Bill is heavier than Albert.

Who is the heaviest? _____

H-114

James is younger than Alice. Betty is younger than James.

Who is the youngest? _____

H-115

Sally has more cats than Clare. Irene has more cats than Sally.

Who has the most cats? _____

WARM-UP DEDUCTIVE REASONING

DIRECTIONS: In the sentences below, people are being compared according to some characteristic (weight, age, height, score, etc.). Read the sentences and fill in the blanks.

H-116

Doug runs faster than Ivan. Ivan runs faster than Lee.

List the runners in order from fastest to slowest.

_____ _____ _____

List the runners in order from slowest to fastest.

_____ _____ _____

H-117

John is older than Sam but younger than Lois.

List the people in order from oldest to youngest.

_____ _____ _____

List the people in order from youngest to oldest.

_____ _____ _____

H-118

David is taller than Fred. Fred is taller than George. George is

taller than Harold.

Who is the tallest? _____

WARM-UP DEDUCTIVE REASONING

DIRECTIONS: In the sentences below, people are being compared according to some characteristic (weight, age, height, score, etc.). Read the sentences and fill in the blanks.

H-119

Delores is shorter than Mary. June is shorter than Delores. Mary is shorter than Nancy.

Who is the shortest? _____

Who is the tallest? _____

H-120

Gina caught fewer fish than Spiro. Nick caught fewer fish than Gina.

List the people in order from the one who caught the most fish to the one who caught the fewest fish.

_____ _____ _____

List the people in order from the one who caught the fewest fish to the one who caught the most fish.

_____ _____ _____

H-121

Pedro is older than Jose but younger than Manuel.

List the people in order from youngest to oldest.

_____ _____ _____

WARM-UP DEDUCTIVE REASONING

DIRECTIONS: In the sentences below, people are being compared according to some characteristic (weight, age, height, score, etc.). Read the sentences and fill in the blanks.

H-122

Emil made more points in a basketball game than Carlos. Emil did not make as many points as Larry.

List the boys in order from high scorer to low scorer.

_____   _____   _____

List the boys in order from low scorer to high scorer.

_____   _____   _____

H-123

Pedro got more hits than Sol but fewer than Nina.

List the players in order from the one who made the most hits to the one who made the fewest hits.

_____   _____   _____

List the players in order from the one who made the fewest hits to the one who made the most hits.

_____   _____   _____

H-124

John is taller than Marna but shorter than Larry.

List the people in order from tallest to shortest.

_____   _____   _____

List the people in order from shortest to tallest.

_____   _____   _____

DEDUCTIVE REASONING

DIRECTIONS: The example below shows how to solve a Mind Benders® problem. Study it before going on to the next pages.

A Mind Benders® problem asks you to match items with their characteristics. Making a matrix helps you work the problem. The easiest Mind Bender® is one involving two things.

Here is an example.

Spot and Prince are two pets. One pet is a dog and the other a horse. Spot is not the dog. Find the names of the pets.

Step 1 From the clue "Spot is not the dog," we can put NO in the dog column in the Spot row on the chart.

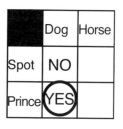

Step 2 Look down the dog column on the chart. There is only one blank place. Remember the clue, "One pet is a dog and the other a horse"? Since Spot is not the dog, Prince must be the dog. Put YES in the blank.

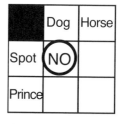

Step 3 Look across the row having a YES. YES is in the Prince row. Since Prince is a dog, you can write NO in the horse column.

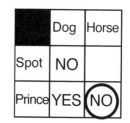

Step 4 The only choice left is to put YES in the last open space.

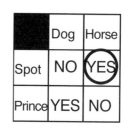

Now the Mind Bender® is complete. Spot is the horse, and Prince is the dog.

DEDUCTIVE REASONING

DIRECTIONS: Using the method given in the previous example, complete each of the following Mind Benders® problems.

H-125

Hernando, Isaac, and Juanita are in a spelling contest.

Who was first, second, and third in each contest?

1. Isaac spells three words correctly.

2. Juanita spells correctly one more word than Isaac.

3. The winner spells five words correctly.

	1st	2nd	3rd
Hernando			
Isaac			
Juanita	N	Y	N

Hernando was _____.

Isaac was _____.

Juanita was _____.

H-126

Donna, Ernie, and Frank run a race. Who was first, second, and third in each contest?

1. Ernie drops out on the first lap.

2. Frank finishes behind Donna.

	1st	2nd	3rd
Donna			
Ernie			
Frank			

Donna was _____.

Ernie was _____.

Frank was _____.

DEDUCTIVE REASONING

DIRECTIONS: Complete each of the following Mind Benders® problems.

H-127

Juan, Kyle, and Lori own bikes. The bikes are a one-speed, a three-speed, and a ten-speed.

Find out the owners of the three kinds of bikes.

1. Juan and Lori have bikes with more than one gear speed.

2. Lori's bike has the most gear speeds.

	1	3	10
Juan			
Kyle			
Lori			

The one-speed is owned by _____.

The three-speed is owned by _____.

The ten-speed is owned by _____.

H-128

Three students—Green, Jones, and Perez—ride to school together. The students are in the second, third, and fourth grades.

Find out which student is in each grade.

1. Jones is in an odd-numbered grade.

2. Green is in a higher grade than Jones.

	Green	Jones	Perez
2			
3			
4			

Green is in the_____grade.

Jones is in the_____grade.

Perez is in the_____grade.

DEDUCTIVE REASONING

DIRECTIONS: Complete each of the following Mind Benders® problems.

H-129

Mrs. Grant is giving her grandchildren presents from her bicycle store. Her grandchildren are 3, 6, and 12 years old.
Find out which of the children are boys and which are girls.

1. Mrs. Grant gave her grandson a tricycle.

2. The oldest received a 10-speed bicycle, but her sister was unhappy because she got a bicycle with training wheels.

	Boy	Girl
3		
6		
12		

The 3-year-old is a _____.

The 6-year-old is a _____.

The 12-year-old is a _____.

H-130

Amanda, Desiree, and Jose listed their favorite foots. One liked beef burgers, one liked chicken, and one liked salads.

Find out the favorite food of each person.

Amanda does not eat meat, and Jose does not eat beef.

	Beef Burgers	Chicken	Salads
A			
D			
J			

Amanda likes_____.

Desiree likes _____.

Jose likes_____.

DEDUCTIVE REASONING

DIRECTIONS: Complete each of the following Mind Benders® problems.

H-131

Three boys named Nick, Pablo, and Tim own athletic shoes. One boy has basketball shoes, another has running shoes, and another has sneakers.

Find out the owners of each shoe size and style.

1. The basketball shoes are the largest.

2. Tim has the smallest feet.

3. Nick wears a larger shoe than Pablo, who owns the sneakers.

Shoe size	Shoe style
	Basketball
	Running
	Sneakers

	Basketball	Running	Sneakers
Nick			
Pablo			
Tim			

The basketball shoes are owned by_____.

The running shoes are owned by_____.

The sneakers are owned by _____.

RANKING TIME MEASURES

DIRECTIONS: Use the chart below to list time measures in order from shortest to longest. Remember that 1 day equals 24 hours, 1 month equals 28-31 days, and 1 year equals 12 months or 365 days.

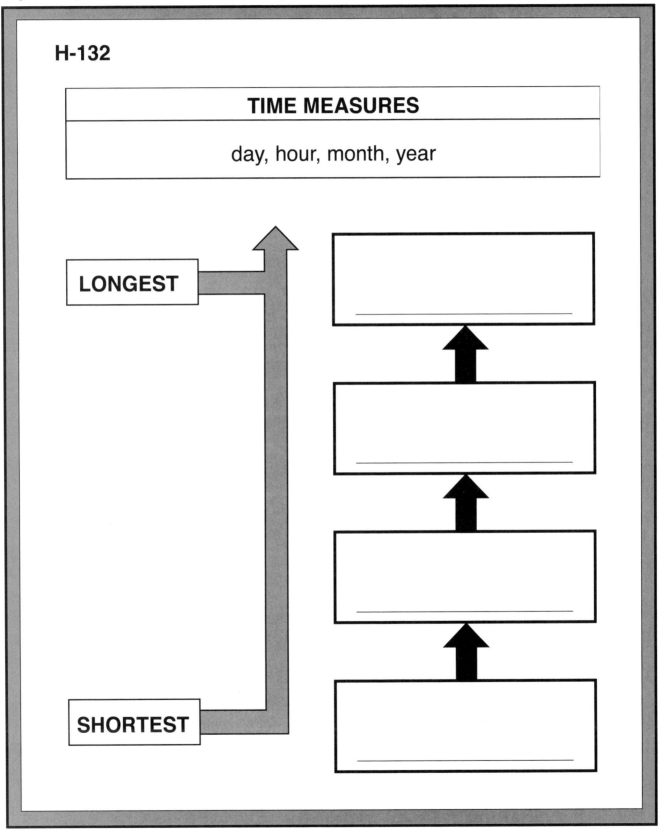

H-132

TIME MEASURES
day, hour, month, year

LONGEST

SHORTEST

RANKING LENGTH MEASURES

DIRECTIONS: Use the chart below to list length measures in order from smallest to largest. Remember that 1 foot equals 12 inches, 1 yard equals 3 feet, 3 feet equals 36 inches, and 1 mile equals 5,280 feet.

H-133

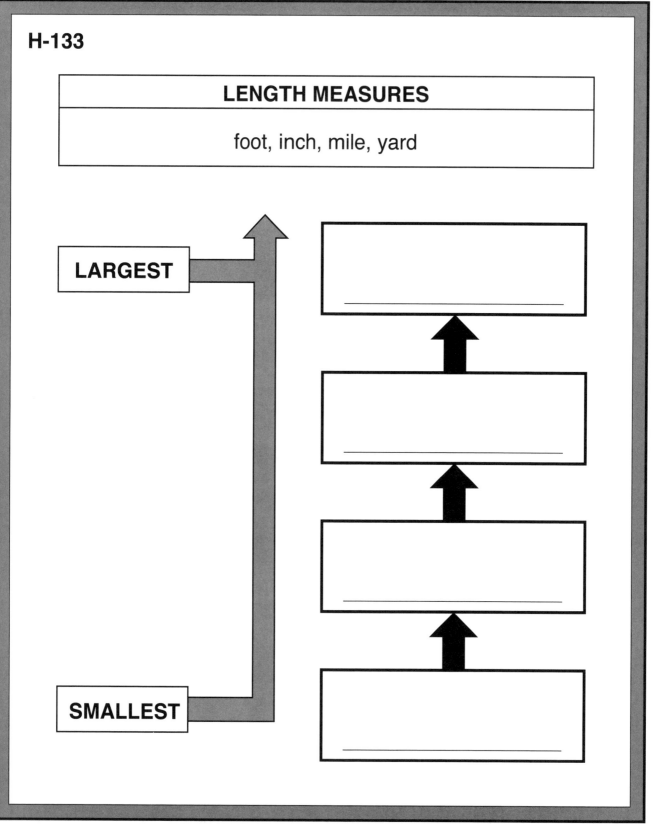

LENGTH MEASURES
foot, inch, mile, yard

LARGEST

SMALLEST

RANKING IN GEOGRAPHY

DIRECTIONS: Use the chart below to list the geographic regions in order from smallest to largest.

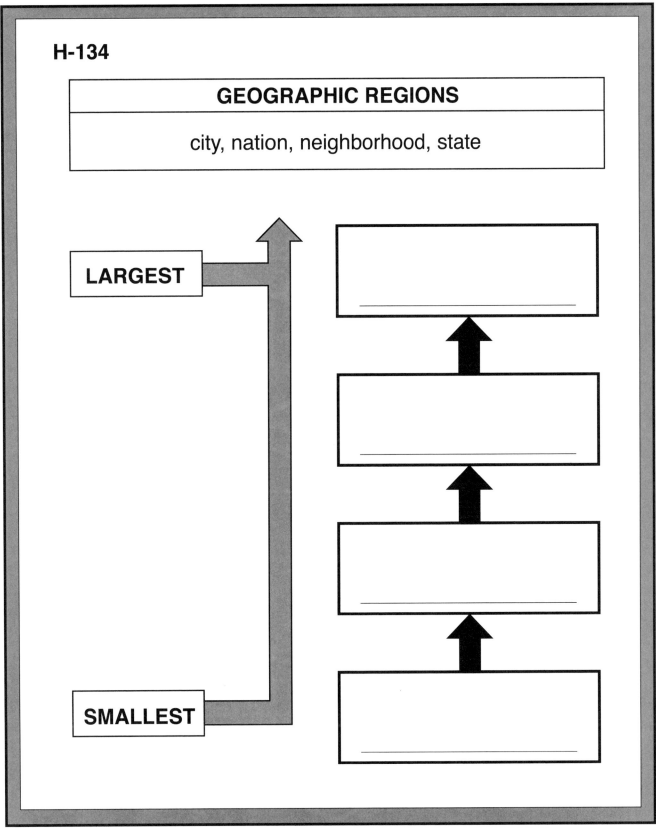

H-134

GEOGRAPHIC REGIONS

city, nation, neighborhood, state

LARGEST

SMALLEST

FLOWCHART—EXAMPLE

DIRECTIONS: Look at the "flowchart symbols." Next, read the example question and follow the flowchart to see how the problem is solved. Since the answer to the question "Are all times in days?" is "No," you need to read the left "loop" first.

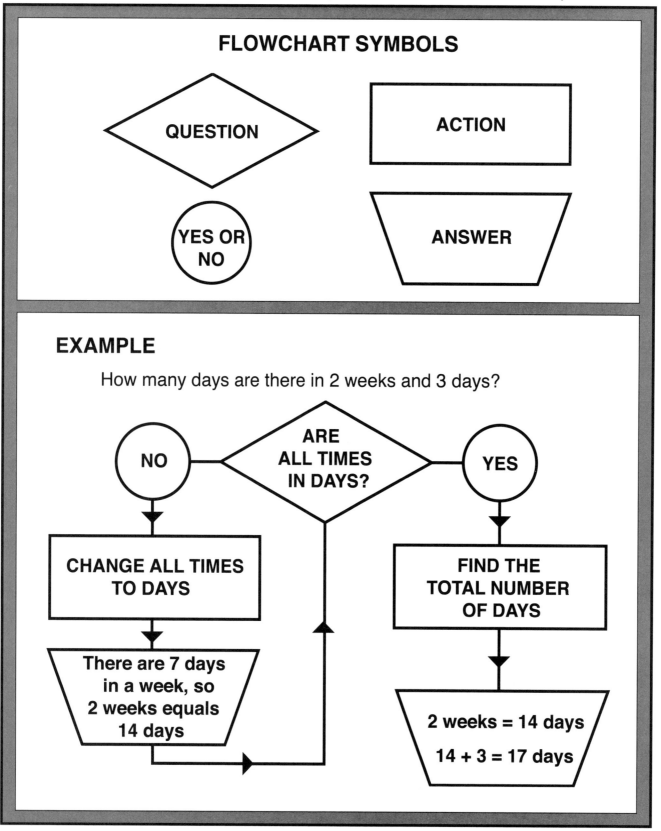

FLOWCHART SYMBOLS

QUESTION

ACTION

YES OR NO

ANSWER

EXAMPLE

How many days are there in 2 weeks and 3 days?

NO

ARE ALL TIMES IN DAYS?

YES

CHANGE ALL TIMES TO DAYS

FIND THE TOTAL NUMBER OF DAYS

There are 7 days in a week, so 2 weeks equals 14 days

2 weeks = 14 days

14 + 3 = 17 days

FLOWCHART—ARITHMETIC

DIRECTIONS: A flowchart can show a sequence of steps to be followed. Use the flowchart below to help you solve arithmetic problems.

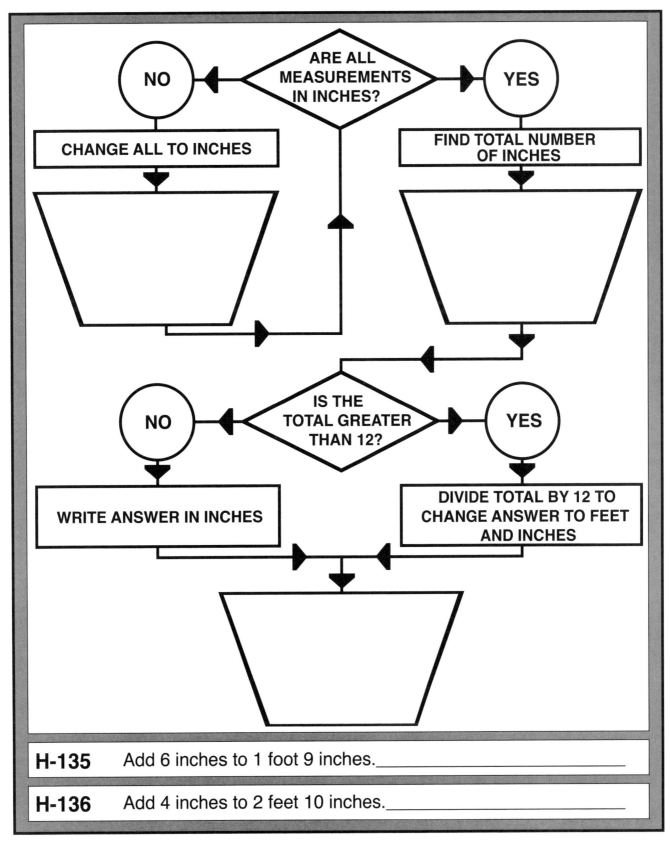

| **H-135** | Add 6 inches to 1 foot 9 inches._____ |
| **H-136** | Add 4 inches to 2 feet 10 inches._____ |

FLOWCHART—ARITHMETIC

DIRECTIONS: A flowchart can show a sequence of steps to be followed. Think about how to add hours and minutes. Fill in the blanks on the decision diamond and the action rectangles, and complete the flowchart to solve the problem below.

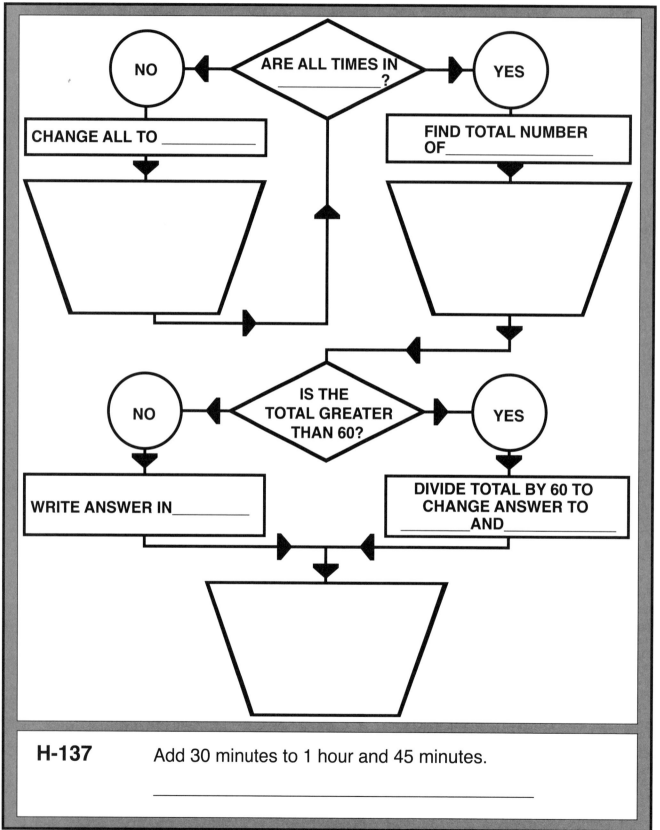

ARE ALL TIMES IN _____?

NO

YES

CHANGE ALL TO _____

FIND TOTAL NUMBER OF_____

IS THE TOTAL GREATER THAN 60?

NO

YES

WRITE ANSWER IN_____

DIVIDE TOTAL BY 60 TO CHANGE ANSWER TO _____ AND_____

H-137   Add 30 minutes to 1 hour and 45 minutes.

_____

CHAPTER NINE

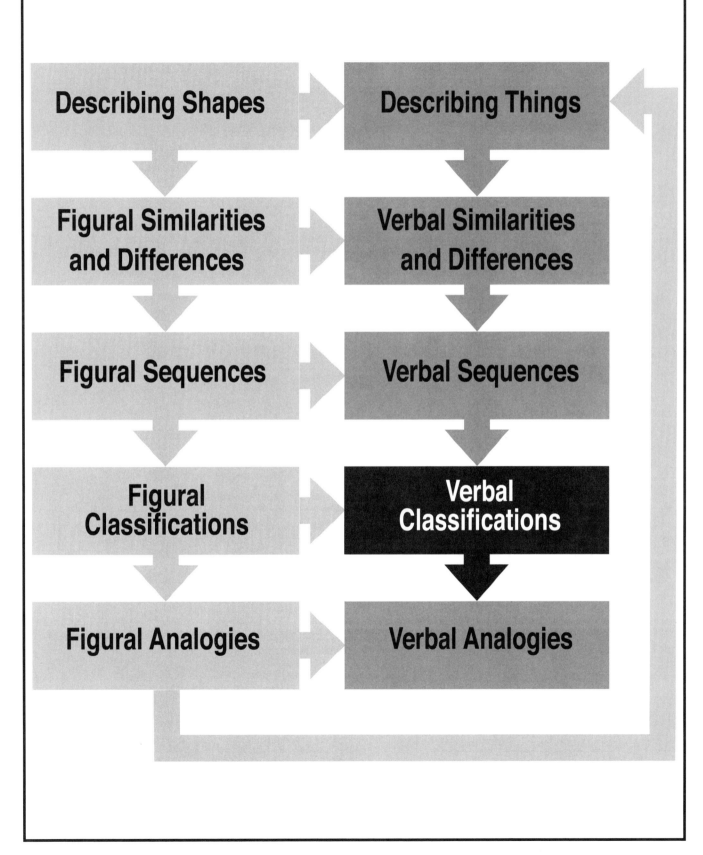

PARTS OF A WHOLE—SELECT

DIRECTIONS: Each exercise has four words. Read the words and decide which represents a whole thing and which are parts of the whole. In the blanks below each group, write the word that is the whole thing and then the words that are the parts.

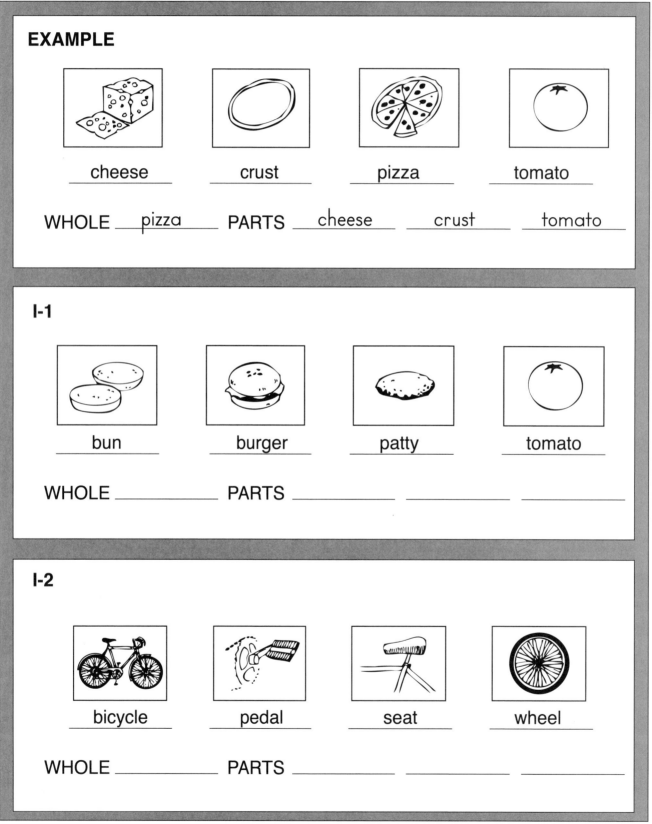

EXAMPLE

cheese   crust   pizza   tomato

WHOLE _pizza_   PARTS _cheese_   _crust_   _tomato_

I-1

bun   burger   patty   tomato

WHOLE _____   PARTS _____   _____   _____

I-2

bicycle   pedal   seat   wheel

WHOLE _____   PARTS _____   _____   _____

PARTS OF A WHOLE—SELECT

DIRECTIONS: Each exercise has four words. Read the words and decide which represents a whole thing and which are parts of the whole. In the blanks below each group, write the word that is the whole thing and then the words that are the parts.

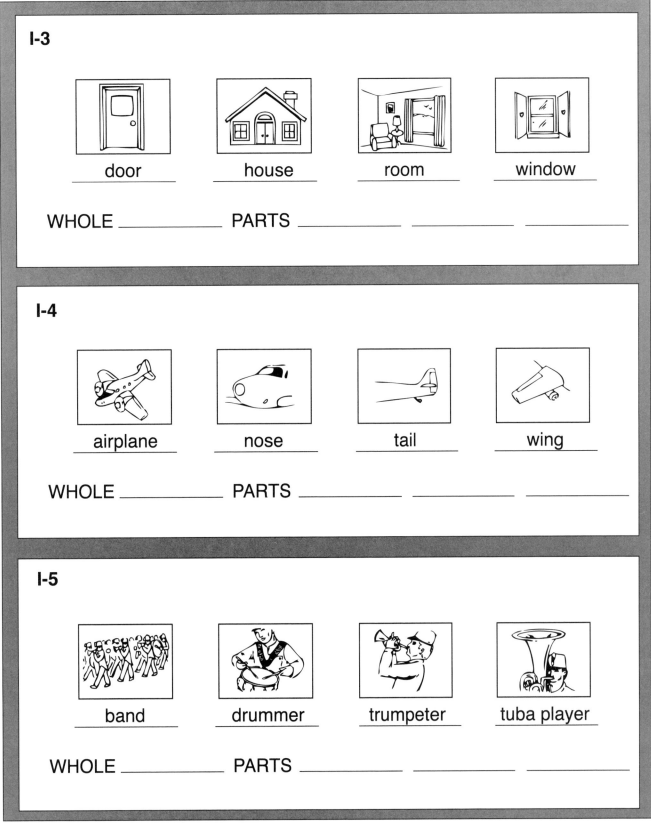

I-3

door   house   room   window

WHOLE _____ PARTS _____ _____ _____

I-4

airplane   nose   tail   wing

WHOLE _____ PARTS _____ _____ _____

I-5

band   drummer   trumpeter   tuba player

WHOLE _____ PARTS _____ _____ _____

PARTS OF A WHOLE—SELECT

DIRECTIONS: Each exercise has four words. Read the words and decide which represents a whole thing and which are parts of the whole. In the blanks below each group, write the word that is the whole thing and then the words that are the parts.

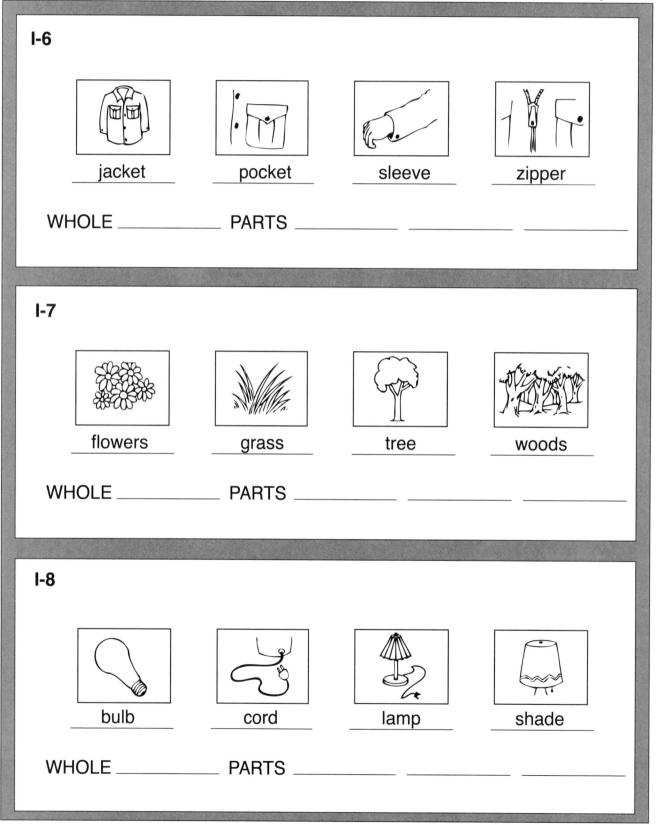

I-6

jacket

pocket

sleeve

zipper

WHOLE _____ PARTS _____ _____ _____

I-7

flowers

grass

tree

woods

WHOLE _____ PARTS _____ _____ _____

I-8

bulb

cord

lamp

shade

WHOLE _____ PARTS _____ _____ _____

PARTS OF A WHOLE—SELECT

DIRECTIONS: Each exercise has four words. Read the words and decide which represents a whole thing and which are parts of the whole. In the blanks below each group, write the word that is the whole thing and then the words that are the parts.

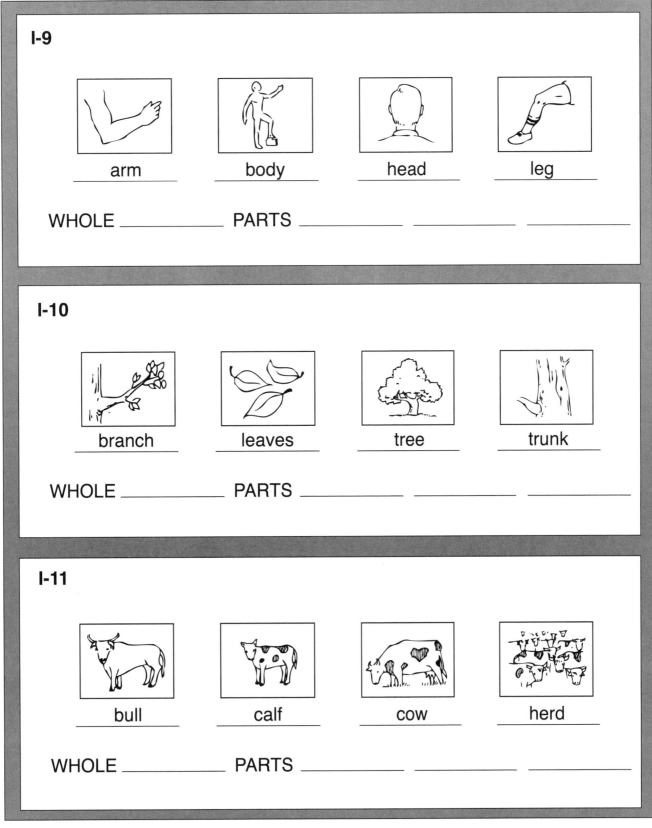

I-9

arm   body   head   leg

WHOLE _____ PARTS _____ _____ _____

I-10

branch   leaves   tree   trunk

WHOLE _____ PARTS _____ _____ _____

I-11

bull   calf   cow   herd

WHOLE _____ PARTS _____ _____ _____

PARTS OF A WHOLE—SELECT

DIRECTIONS: Each exercise has four words. Read the words and decide which represents a whole thing and which are parts of the whole. In the blanks below each group, write the word that is the whole thing and then the words that are the parts.

EXAMPLE

drink	meal	meat	salad

WHOLE ___meal___   PARTS ___drink___   ___meat___   ___salad___

I-12

body	car	engine	wheel

WHOLE _____   PARTS _____   _____   _____

I-13

army	trucks	soldiers	tanks

WHOLE _____   PARTS _____   _____   _____

I-14

cashier	market	meat	vegetables

WHOLE _____   PARTS _____   _____   _____

I-15

beans	chili	onions	tomatoes

WHOLE _____   PARTS _____   _____   _____

I-16

dial	radio	switch	volume control

WHOLE _____   PARTS _____   _____   _____

PARTS OF A WHOLE—SELECT

DIRECTIONS: Each exercise has four words. Read the words and decide which represents a whole thing and which are parts of the whole. In the blanks below each group, write the word that is the whole thing and then the words that are the parts.

I-17

cord   power button   screen   television

WHOLE _____ PARTS _____ _____ _____

I-18

dressing   lettuce   salad   tomato

WHOLE _____ PARTS _____ _____ _____

I-19

blade   engine   handle   lawnmower

WHOLE _____ PARTS _____ _____ _____

I-20

cap   ink   pen   point

WHOLE _____ PARTS _____ _____ _____

I-21

acrobats   animals   clowns   circus

WHOLE _____ PARTS _____ _____ _____

I-22

principal   school   students   teachers

WHOLE _____ PARTS _____ _____ _____

PARTS OF A WHOLE—SELECT

DIRECTIONS: Each exercise has four words. Read the words and decide which represents a whole thing and which are parts of the whole. In the blanks below each group, write the word that is the whole thing and then the words that are the parts.

I-23

addition   arithmetic   numbers   subtraction

WHOLE _____   PARTS _____   _____   _____

I-24

adjectives   language   nouns   verbs

WHOLE _____   PARTS _____   _____   _____

I-25

government   judge   president   senator

WHOLE _____   PARTS _____   _____   _____

I-26

cover   book   pages   words

WHOLE _____   PARTS _____   _____   _____

I-27

schools   houses   stores   city

WHOLE _____   PARTS _____   _____   _____

I-28

key   map   mountains   rivers

WHOLE _____   PARTS _____   _____   _____

PARTS OF A WHOLE—GRAPHIC ORGANIZER

DIRECTIONS: The words in the choice box represent the parts of a nation. Fill in the blank boxes of the diagram to show how these parts are related. Write a statement about their relationships, starting with the smallest part of the whole.

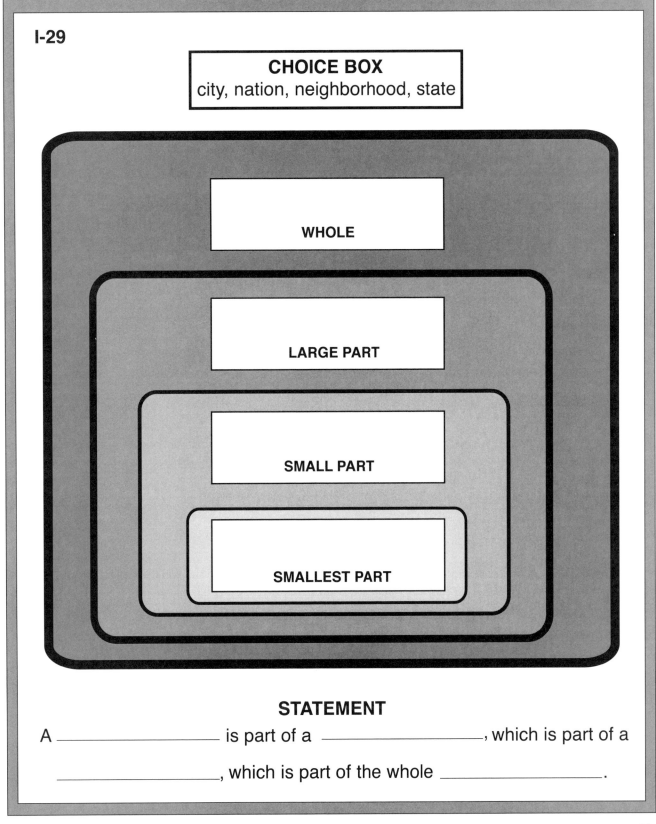

I-29

CHOICE BOX
city, nation, neighborhood, state

WHOLE

LARGE PART

SMALL PART

SMALLEST PART

STATEMENT

A _____ is part of a _____, which is part of a

_____, which is part of the whole _____.

PARTS OF A WHOLE—GRAPHIC ORGANIZER

DIRECTIONS: Decide how the words in the choice box are related, and fill in the blank boxes of the diagram. Write a statement about their relationships, starting with the smallest part of the whole.

I-30

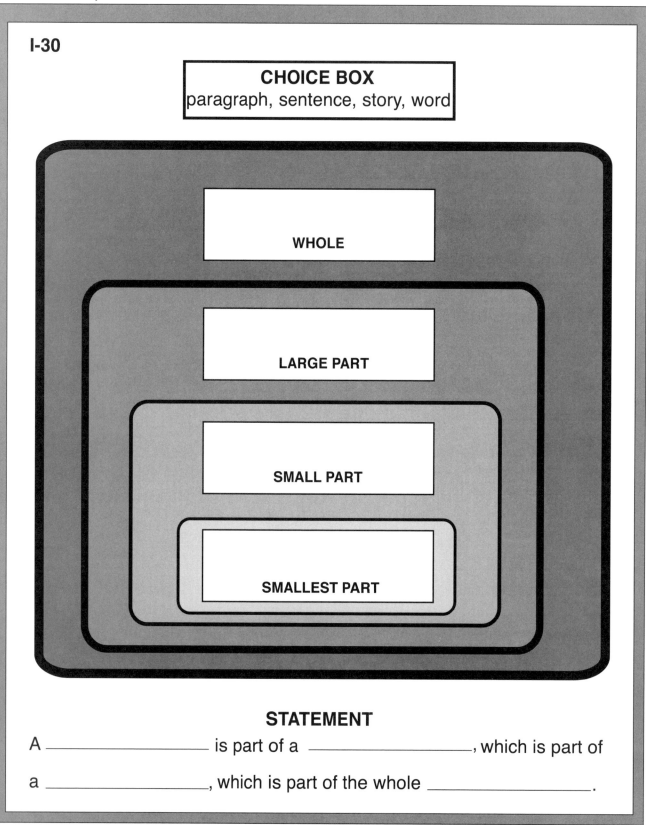

CHOICE BOX
paragraph, sentence, story, word

WHOLE

LARGE PART

SMALL PART

SMALLEST PART

STATEMENT

A _____ is part of a _____, which is part of

a _____, which is part of the whole _____.

CLASS AND MEMBERS—SELECT

DIRECTIONS: In each exercise are four words. Read the words and decide which represents a class to which the others belong. In the blanks below each group, write the word that represents the class and then the words that are its members.

EXAMPLE

_____coin_____   _____dime_____   _____nickel_____   _____penny_____

CLASS _____coin_____   MEMBERS _____dime_____   _____nickel_____   _____penny_____

I-31

_____clothing_____   _____coat_____   _____hat_____   _____pants_____

CLASS _____   MEMBERS _____   _____   _____

I-32

_____baseball_____   _____basketball_____   _____football_____   _____sport_____

CLASS _____   MEMBERS _____   _____   _____

I-33

_____blue_____   _____color_____   _____green_____   _____red_____

CLASS _____   MEMBERS _____   _____   _____

I-34

_____hammer_____   _____saw_____   _____screwdriver_____   _____tool_____

CLASS _____   MEMBERS _____   _____   _____

I-35

_____arithmetic_____   _____reading_____   _____school subject_____   _____writing_____

CLASS _____   MEMBERS _____   _____   _____

CLASS AND MEMBERS—SELECT

DIRECTIONS: Each exercise has four words. Read the words and decide which represents a class to which the others belong. In the blanks below each group, write the word that represents the class and then the words that are its members.

I-36

English   French   language   Spanish

CLASS _____   MEMBERS _____ _____ _____

I-37

corn   grain   oats   wheat

CLASS _____   MEMBERS _____ _____ _____

I-38

bass   fish   salmon   tuna

CLASS _____   MEMBERS _____ _____ _____

I-39

fruit   grain   plant   vegetable

CLASS _____   MEMBERS _____ _____ _____

I-40

animal   bird   fish   reptile

CLASS _____   MEMBERS _____ _____ _____

I-41

oak   palm   pine   tree

CLASS _____   MEMBERS _____ _____ _____

WHAT IS TRUE OF BOTH WORDS?—SELECT

DIRECTIONS: Decide what the following pairs of words have in common. Circle the letters of the characteristics that are true of both items.

EXAMPLE

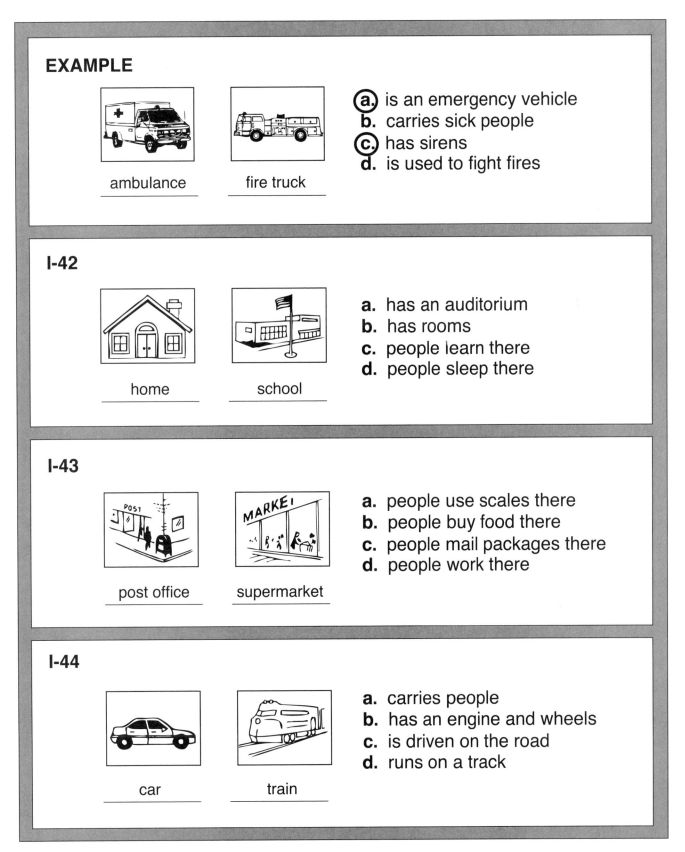

ambulance   fire truck

(a.) is an emergency vehicle
 b. carries sick people
(c.) has sirens
 d. is used to fight fires

I-42

home   school

a. has an auditorium
b. has rooms
c. people learn there
d. people sleep there

I-43

post office   supermarket

a. people use scales there
b. people buy food there
c. people mail packages there
d. people work there

I-44

car   train

a. carries people
b. has an engine and wheels
c. is driven on the road
d. runs on a track

WHAT IS TRUE OF BOTH WORDS?—SELECT

DIRECTIONS: Decide what the following pairs of words have in common. Circle the letters of the characteristics that are true of both items.

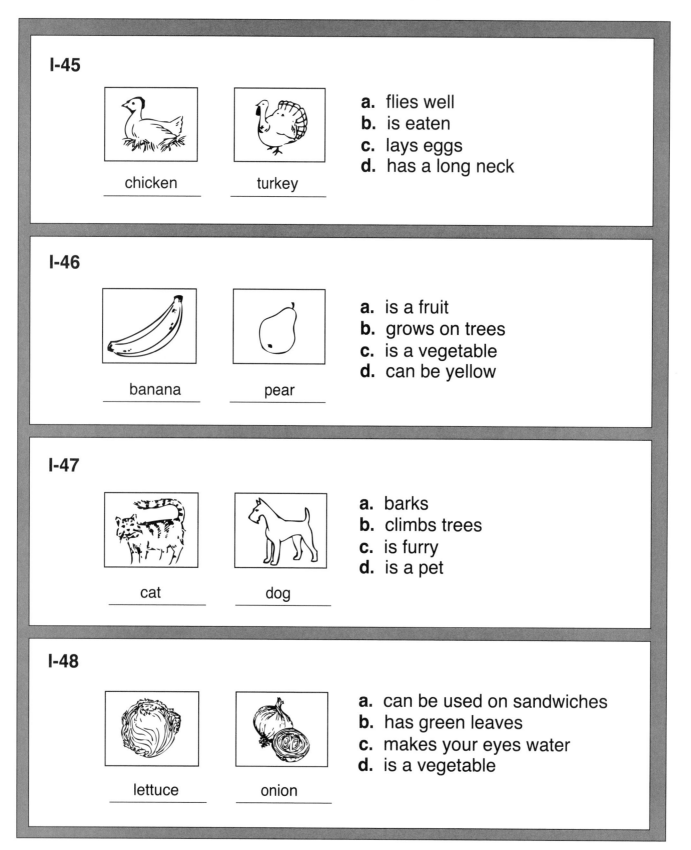

I-45

chicken   turkey

a. flies well
b. is eaten
c. lays eggs
d. has a long neck

I-46

banana   pear

a. is a fruit
b. grows on trees
c. is a vegetable
d. can be yellow

I-47

cat   dog

a. barks
b. climbs trees
c. is furry
d. is a pet

I-48

lettuce   onion

a. can be used on sandwiches
b. has green leaves
c. makes your eyes water
d. is a vegetable

WHAT IS TRUE OF BOTH WORDS?—SELECT

DIRECTIONS: Decide what the following pairs of words have in common. Circle the letters of the characteristics that are true of both items.

I-49

clock   watch

a. fits on the wrist
b. is often round in shape
c. plugs into an electric socket
d. tells time

I-50

boat   duck

a. is an animal
b. grows on trees
c. can float
d. is a vehicle

I-51

moon   sun

a. always looks round
b. is in the sky
c. is round
d. shines only during the day

I-52

horse   motorcycle

a. is an animal
b. can carry one or two people
c. can move
d. is a vehicle

HOW ARE THESE WORDS ALIKE?—SELECT

DIRECTIONS: Decide what the words in each group have in common. Circle the letter of the one answer that best describes the class of the words.

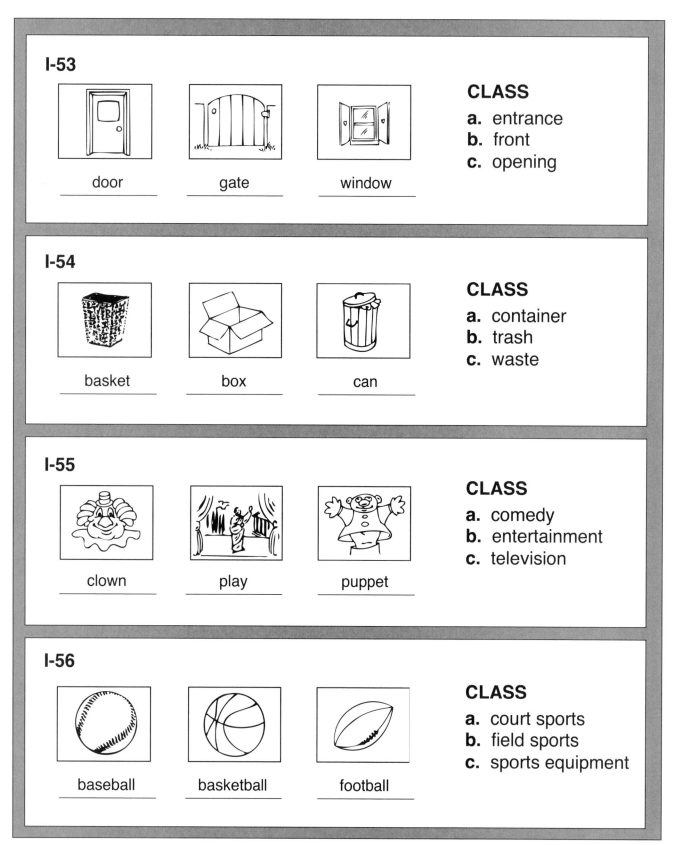

I-53

door   gate   window

CLASS
a. entrance
b. front
c. opening

I-54

basket   box   can

CLASS
a. container
b. trash
c. waste

I-55

clown   play   puppet

CLASS
a. comedy
b. entertainment
c. television

I-56

baseball   basketball   football

CLASS
a. court sports
b. field sports
c. sports equipment

HOW ARE THESE WORDS ALIKE?—SELECT

DIRECTIONS: Decide what the words in each group have in common. Circle the letter of the one answer that best describes the class of the words.

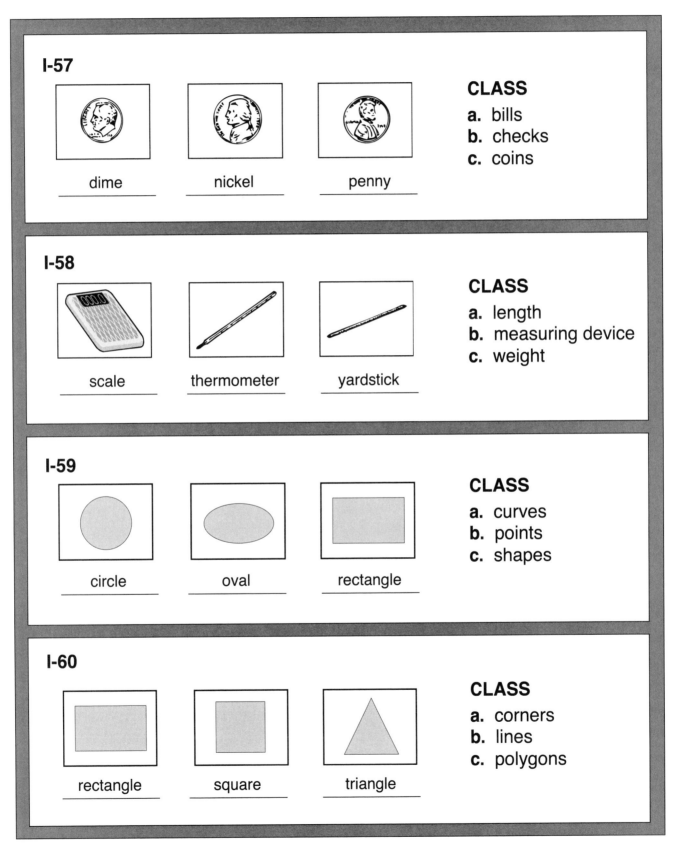

I-57

dime   nickel   penny

CLASS
a. bills
b. checks
c. coins

I-58

scale   thermometer   yardstick

CLASS
a. length
b. measuring device
c. weight

I-59

circle   oval   rectangle

CLASS
a. curves
b. points
c. shapes

I-60

rectangle   square   triangle

CLASS
a. corners
b. lines
c. polygons

HOW ARE THESE WORDS ALIKE?—SELECT

DIRECTIONS: Decide what the words in each group have in common. Circle the letter of the one answer that best describes the class of the words.

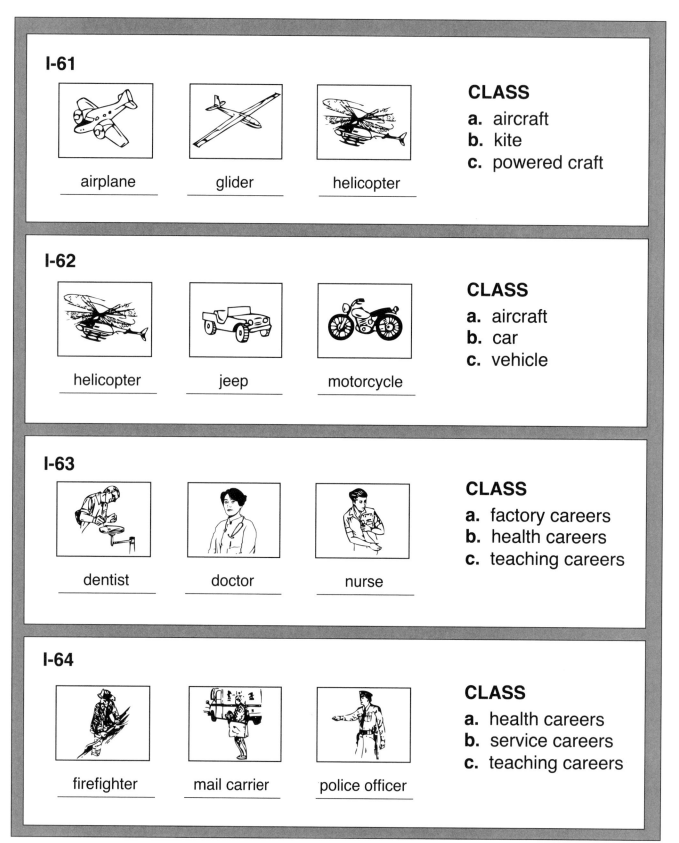

I-61

airplane

glider

helicopter

CLASS

a. aircraft
b. kite
c. powered craft

I-62

helicopter

jeep

motorcycle

CLASS

a. aircraft
b. car
c. vehicle

I-63

dentist

doctor

nurse

CLASS

a. factory careers
b. health careers
c. teaching careers

I-64

firefighter

mail carrier

police officer

CLASS

a. health careers
b. service careers
c. teaching careers

HOW ARE THESE WORDS ALIKE?—SELECT

DIRECTIONS: Decide what the words in each group have in common. Circle the letter of the one answer that best describes the class of the words.

EXAMPLE

cake	cookie	pie

CLASS
- **a.** dessert *(circled)*
- **b.** dinner
- **c.** fruit

Dinner is not the best answer; these foods are usually eaten after dinner. Fruit is not the answer, even though these foods can be made of fruit. Dessert is the best answer because it is a term which describes all three foods.

I-65

boxer	poodle	shepherd

CLASS
- **a.** clothing
- **b.** dog
- **c.** job

I-66

button	snap	zipper

CLASS
- **a.** fastener
- **b.** hardware
- **c.** tool

I-67

bed	desk	table

CLASS
- **a.** chair
- **b.** furniture
- **c.** kitchen

I-68

curtains	drapes	shades

CLASS
- **a.** floor covering
- **b.** furniture covering
- **c.** window covering

HOW ARE THESE WORDS ALIKE?—SELECT

DIRECTIONS: Decide what the words in each group have in common. Circle the letter of the one answer that best describes the class of the words.

I-69

letter   poem   song

CLASS

a. things people sing
b. things people speak
c. things people write

I-70

grow   increase   swell

CLASS

a. become higher
b. become larger
c. become lighter

I-71

baby   boy   girl

CLASS

a. children
b. mother
c. student

I-72

bush   flower   tree

CLASS

a. blossom
b. plant
c. wood

I-73

blue   rose   violet

CLASS

a. bird
b. color
c. flower

I-74

decrease   reduce   shrink

CLASS

a. become colder
b. become larger
c. become smaller

HOW ARE THESE WORDS ALIKE?—EXPLAIN

DIRECTIONS: Decide what the words in each group have in common. On the line below the group, explain how the words in the class are alike.

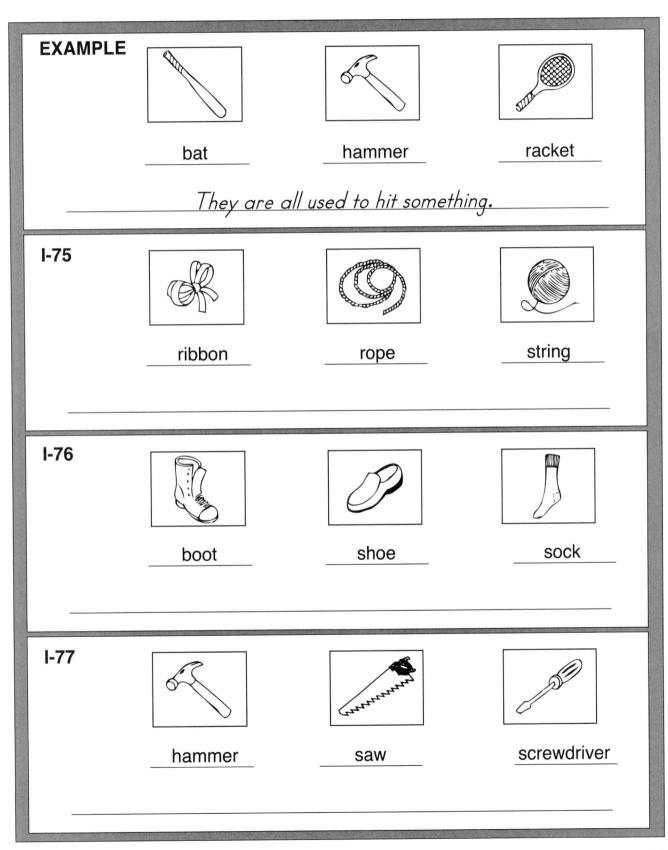

EXAMPLE

bat   hammer   racket

They are all used to hit something.

I-75

ribbon   rope   string

_____

I-76

boot   shoe   sock

_____

I-77

hammer   saw   screwdriver

_____

HOW ARE THESE WORDS ALIKE?—EXPLAIN

DIRECTIONS: Decide what the words in each group have in common. On the line below the group, explain how the words in the class are alike.

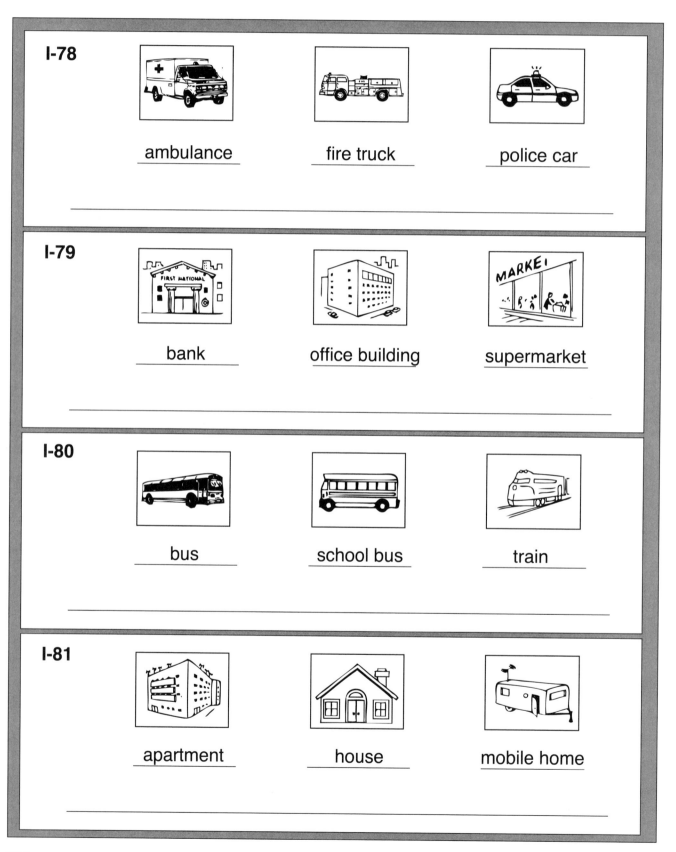

I-78

ambulance

fire truck

police car

_____

I-79

bank

office building

supermarket

_____

I-80

bus

school bus

train

_____

I-81

apartment

house

mobile home

_____

HOW ARE THESE WORDS ALIKE?—EXPLAIN

DIRECTIONS: Decide what the words in each group have in common. On the line below the group, explain how the words in the class are alike.

I-82

dryer

heater

stove

_____

I-83

foot

hoof

paw

_____

I-84

leaves

root

stem

_____

I-85

desert

island

mountain

_____

HOW ARE THESE WORDS ALIKE?—EXPLAIN

DIRECTIONS: Decide what the words in each group have in common. On the line below the group, explain how the words in the class are alike.

EXAMPLE

___diamond___   ___square___   ___triangle___

_____These words name different shapes._____

I-86

___cap___   ___cork___   ___lid___

_____

I-87

___drip___   ___leak___   ___spill___

_____

I-88

___glue___   ___paste___   ___tape___

_____

I-89

___float___   ___sail___   ___swim___

_____

I-90

___bang___   ___boom___   ___pop___

_____

HOW ARE THESE WORDS ALIKE?—EXPLAIN

DIRECTIONS: Decide what the words in each group have in common. On the line below the group, explain how the words in the class are alike.

I-91

iron   stove   toaster

_____

I-92

grapefruit   lemon   orange

_____

I-93

eye   ear   nose

_____

I-94

blade   leaf   needle

_____

I-95

clouds   ice   rain

_____

I-96

leopard   lion   tiger

_____

EXPLAIN THE EXCEPTION

DIRECTIONS: Each group of words contains one member that is an exception to the class. On the lines under the group, explain how the similar words are alike and how the exception is different.

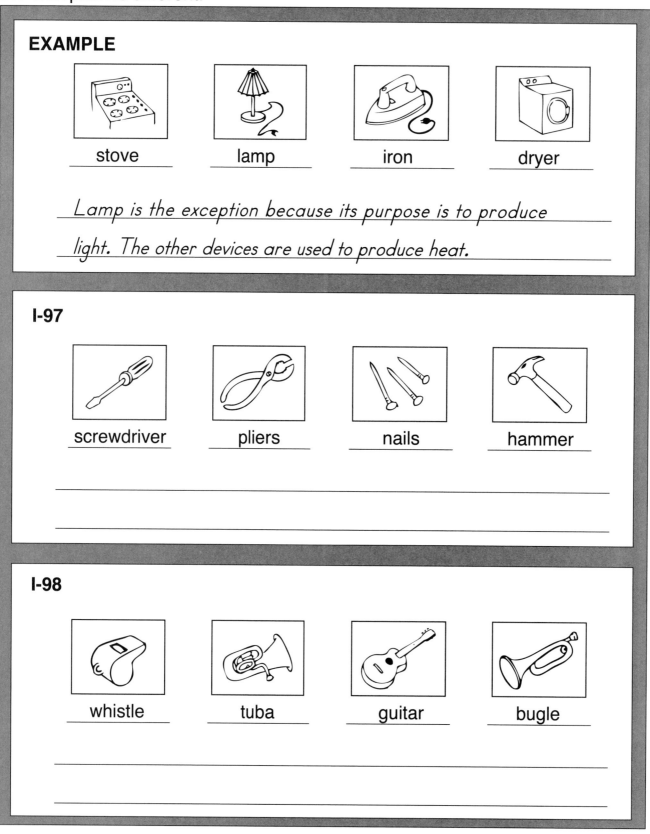

EXAMPLE

stove   lamp   iron   dryer

Lamp is the exception because its purpose is to produce
light. The other devices are used to produce heat.

I-97

screwdriver   pliers   nails   hammer

I-98

whistle   tuba   guitar   bugle

EXPLAIN THE EXCEPTION

DIRECTIONS: Each group of words contains one member that is an exception to the class. On the lines under the group, explain how the similar words are alike and how the exception is different.

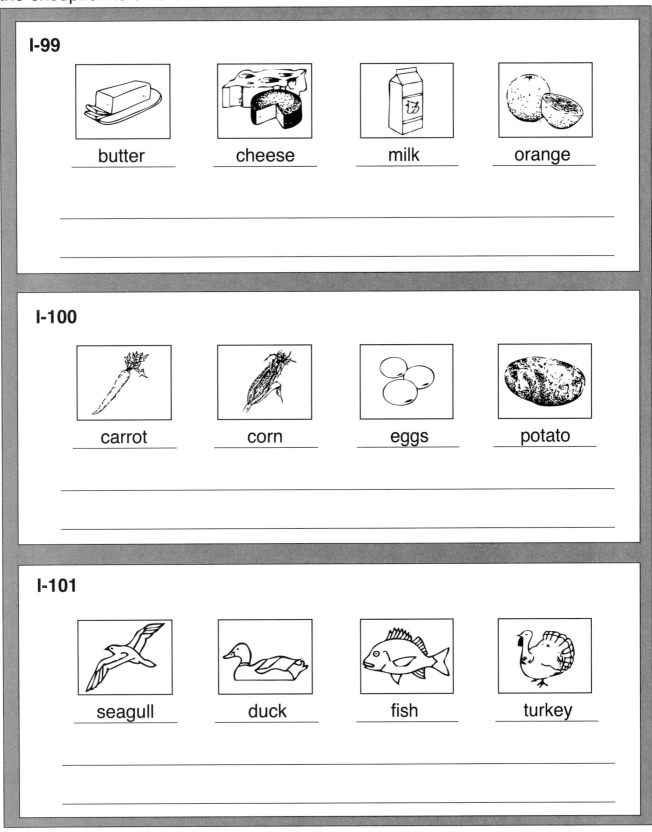

I-99

butter   cheese   milk   orange

_____

_____

I-100

carrot   corn   eggs   potato

_____

_____

I-101

seagull   duck   fish   turkey

_____

_____

EXPLAIN THE EXCEPTION

DIRECTIONS: Each group of words contains one member that is an exception to the class. On the lines under the group, explain how the similar words are alike and how the exception is different.

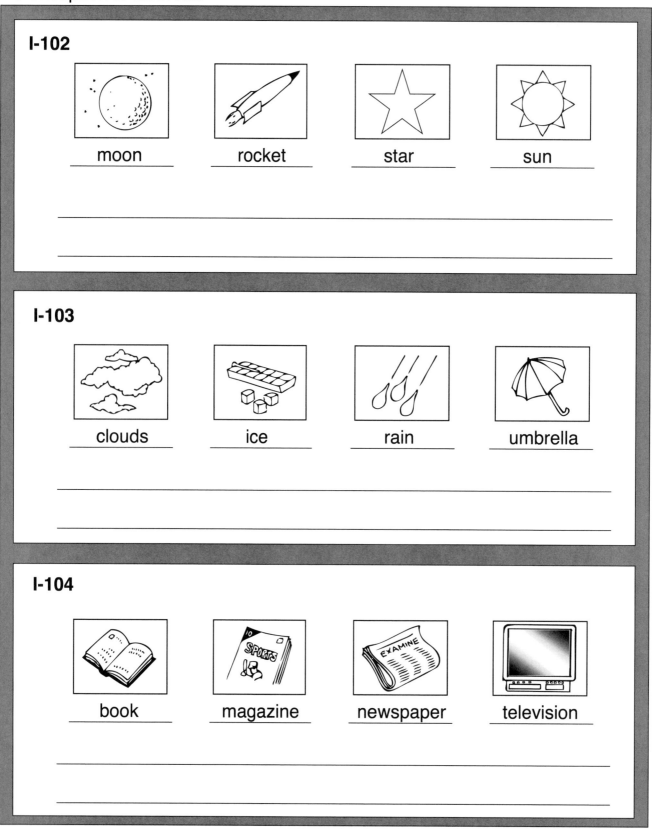

I-102

moon   rocket   star   sun

_____

_____

I-103

clouds   ice   rain   umbrella

_____

_____

I-104

book   magazine   newspaper   television

_____

EXPLAIN THE EXCEPTION

DIRECTIONS: Each group of words contains one member that is an exception to the class. On the lines under the group, explain how the similar words are alike and how the exception is different.

EXAMPLE

explain	listen	talk	tell

Listen is the exception because listening involves hearing. The other words represent forms of speaking.

I-105

jog	run	sleep	walk

I-106

chalk	crayons	pencil	ruler

I-107

fork	knife	scissors	spoon

I-108

reading	recess	spelling	writing

EXPLAIN THE EXCEPTION

DIRECTIONS: Each group of words contains one member that is an exception to the class. On the lines under the group, explain how the similar words are alike and how the exception is different.

I-109

color   draw   paint   write

_____

_____

I-110

few   many   none   some

_____

_____

I-111

banana   grapefruit   lemon   orange

_____

_____

I-112

bicycle   helicopter   jeep   motorcycle

_____

_____

I-113

chew   cook   drink   eat

_____

_____

PICTURE DICTIONARY—SORTING INTO CLASSES

DIRECTIONS: Each picture is labeled with a place name. Sort the names into three groups by writing each place name in the appropriate column on the chart.

I-114

apartment	barber shop	farm	fire station
gas station	hospital	house	mobile home
police station	post office	restaurant	supermarket

PLACES WHERE PEOPLE		
BUY THINGS	**LIVE**	**GET SERVICES**

PICTURE DICTIONARY—SORTING INTO CLASSES

DIRECTIONS: Using the picture dictionary on the next two pages, sort the animals on each chart below.

I-115

ANIMALS THAT

FLOAT/SWIM IN WATER

ANIMALS THAT

MOVE ON LAND

PICTURE DICTIONARY—SORTING INTO CLASSES

DIRECTIONS: Use the words from the picture dictionary to fill in the charts on page 284.

PICTURE DICTIONARY—SORTING INTO CLASSES

DIRECTIONS: Use the words from the picture dictionary to fill in the charts on page 284.

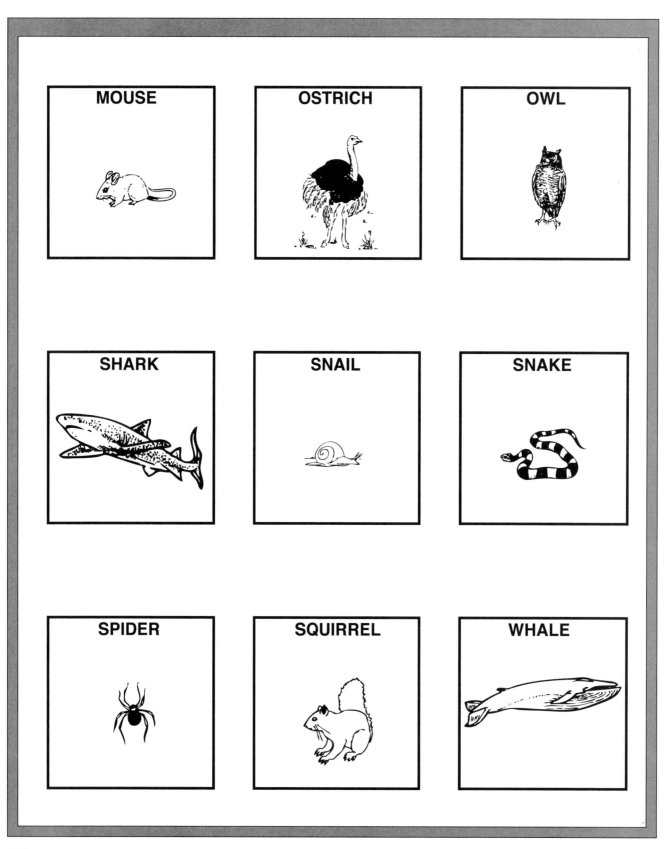

SORTING INTO CLASSES

DIRECTIONS: Sort the words in the choice box into "happy" words and "sad" words.

I-116

CHOICE BOX
bright, cheerful, crying, glad, gloomy, grumpy, jolly, joyous, merry, upset

HAPPY WORDS	SAD WORDS

SORTING INTO CLASSES

DIRECTIONS: Sort the words in the choice box into "when" words and "where" words.

I-117

CHOICE BOX	
above, across, already, always, behind, below, between, never, often, seldom	
WHEN	**WHERE**

PICTURE DICTIONARY—SORTING INTO CLASSES

DIRECTIONS: Use the words in the picture dictionary on page 290. Some words may be used more than once. Sort the words into the following four classes or groups.

I-118

THINGS THAT			
MAKE MUSIC	**ARE USED FOR INFORMATION**	**ARE USED FOR ENTERTAINMENT**	**WE RIDE ON**

PICTURE DICTIONARY—SORTING INTO CLASSES

DIRECTIONS: Use the words from the picture dictionary to fill in the chart on page 289.

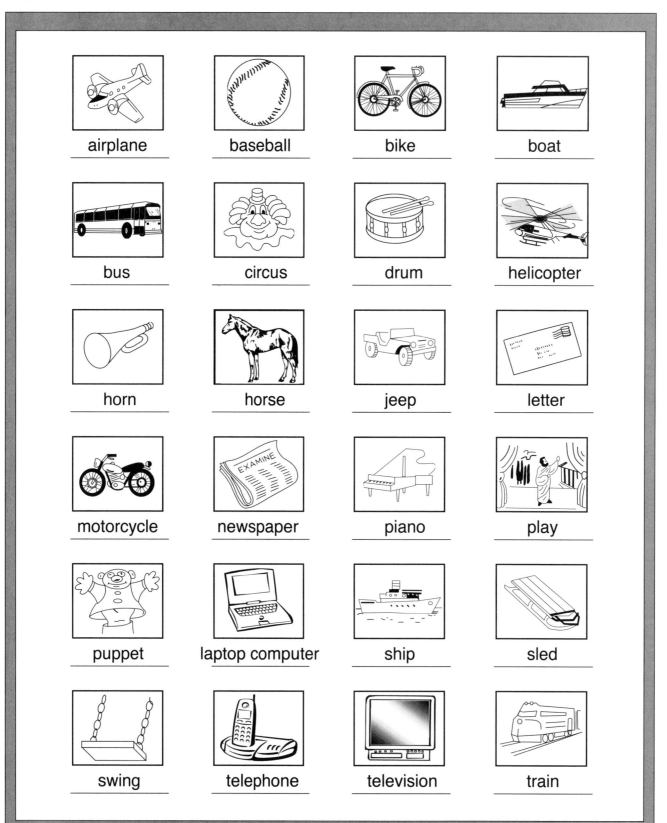

airplane	baseball	bike	boat
bus	circus	drum	helicopter
horn	horse	jeep	letter
motorcycle	newspaper	piano	play
puppet	laptop computer	ship	sled
swing	telephone	television	train

SORTING INTO CLASSES

DIRECTIONS: Sort the words in the choice box according to how they are used with the concepts of "open" and "closed."

I-119

CHOICE BOX	
clear, end, entrance, fence, finish, free, indoors, locked, lower, off, on, outdoors, raise, shut, start, stop, wall, wide	
OPEN	**CLOSED**

WORD CLASSES—SELECT

DIRECTIONS: Select a word from the choice box and write it on the line below the picture to which the word belongs. You may need to use some of the words more than once in order to fill in all the blanks.

I-120

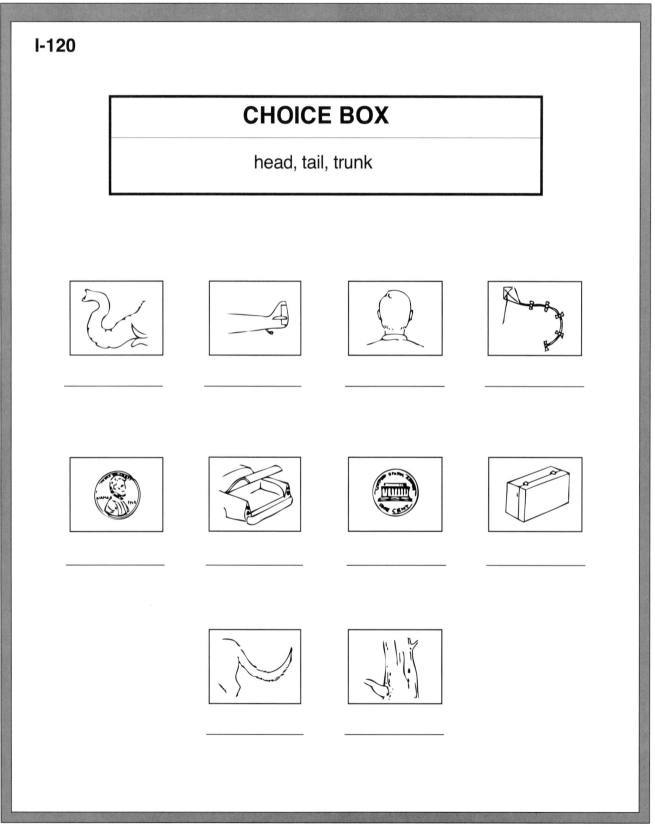

WORD CLASSES—SELECT

DIRECTIONS: Select a word from the choice box and write it on the line below the picture to which the word belongs. You may need to use some of the words more than once in order to fill in all the blanks.

I-121

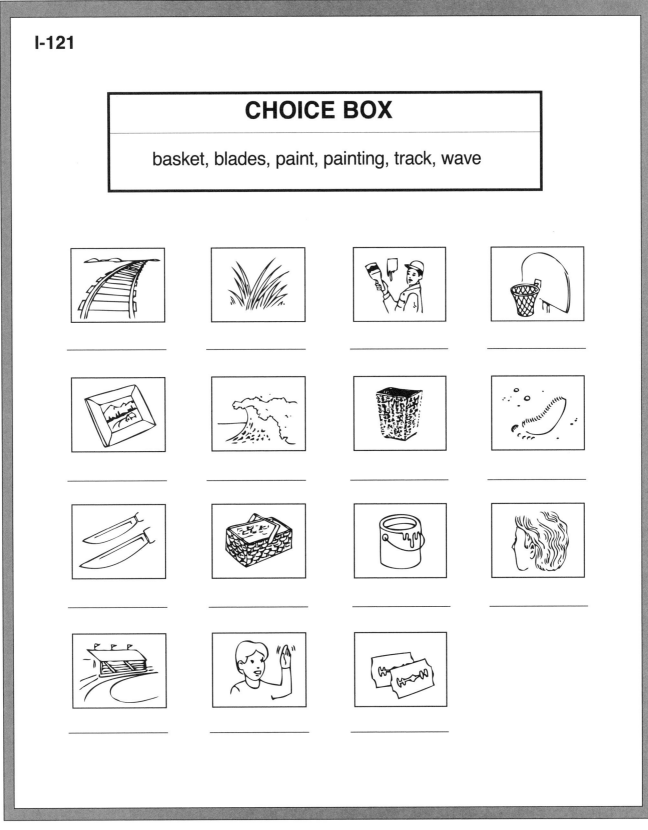

CHOICE BOX

basket, blades, paint, painting, track, wave

SORTING BY CLASS AND SIZE

DIRECTIONS: The words in the box are taken from the picture dictionary on the next two pages. In the chart below, write each word in the box that best describes it.

I-122

apartment building, barrel, cabin, cup, fast food restaurant, gallon, glass, guppy, house, hut, laundromat, minnow, perch, pint, quart, school, shark, shed, shopping center, supermarket, trout, tuna

	building	**container**	**fish**
small			
medium			
large			

PICTURE DICTIONARY

DIRECTIONS: Use the words from the picture dictionary to fill in the chart on page 294.

PICTURE DICTIONARY

DIRECTIONS: Use the words from the picture dictionary to fill in the chart on page 294.

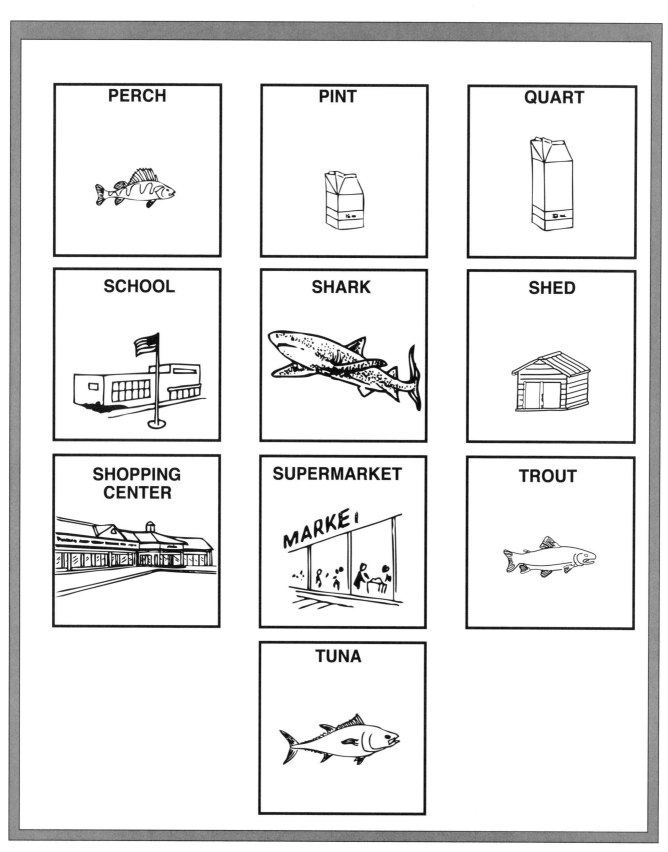

PERCH

PINT

QUART

SCHOOL

SHARK

SHED

SHOPPING CENTER

SUPERMARKET

MARKET

TROUT

TUNA

RECOGNIZING CLASSES—GRAPHIC ORGANIZER

DIRECTIONS: Fill in the diagram to show how the words in the choice box are related. The most general class belongs in the large rounded box. The most specialized class belongs in the small rounded box.

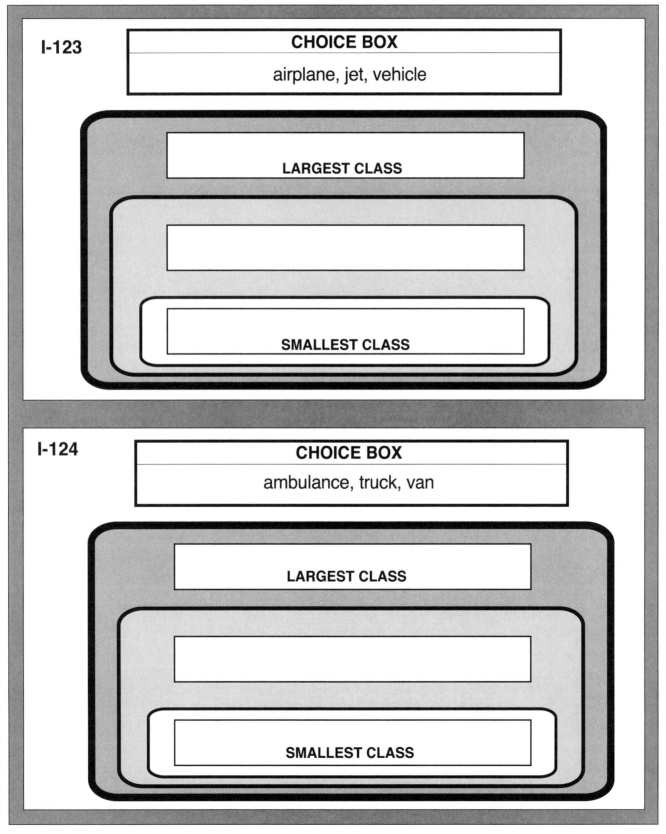

I-123

CHOICE BOX

airplane, jet, vehicle

LARGEST CLASS

SMALLEST CLASS

I-124

CHOICE BOX

ambulance, truck, van

LARGEST CLASS

SMALLEST CLASS

RECOGNIZING CLASSES—GRAPHIC ORGANIZER

DIRECTIONS: Fill in the diagram to show how the words in the choice box are related. The most general class belongs in the large rounded box. The most specialized class belongs in the small rounded box.

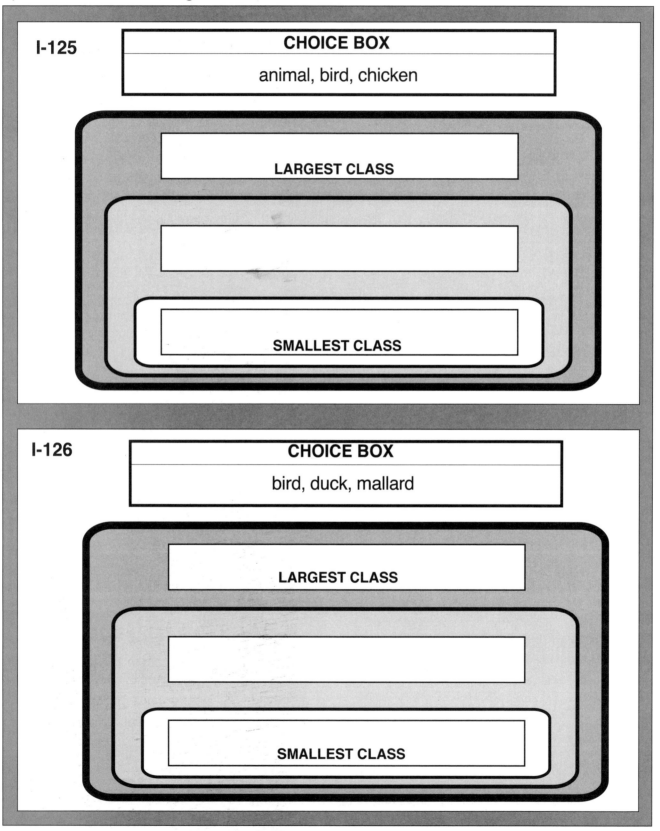

I-125

CHOICE BOX

animal, bird, chicken

LARGEST CLASS

SMALLEST CLASS

I-126

CHOICE BOX

bird, duck, mallard

LARGEST CLASS

SMALLEST CLASS

RECOGNIZING CLASSES—GRAPHIC ORGANIZER

DIRECTIONS: Read the passage carefully to decide how special four-sided closed figures are related. Record the information on the diagram. In each box, draw an example of the shape.

I-127

If the opposite sides of a four-sided figure are parallel, the figure is a parallelogram. A rectangle is a special parallelogram that has four right angles (square corners). A square is a special rectangle that has four equal sides.

MOST GENERAL CLASS

MOST SPECIALIZED CLASS

CHAPTER TEN

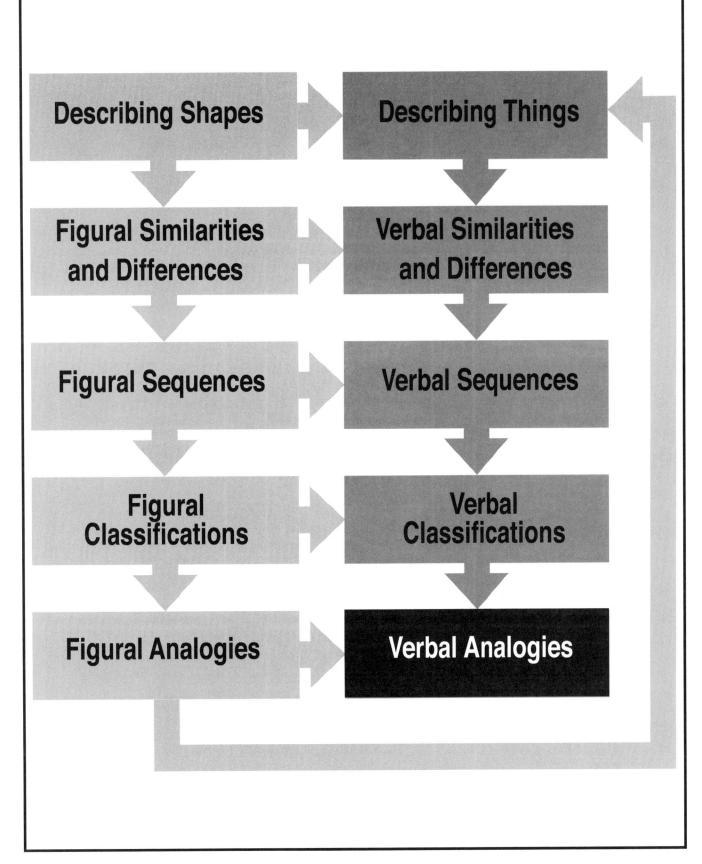

ANALOGIES

DIRECTIONS: Read the explanation of analogies below before going on to the next page.

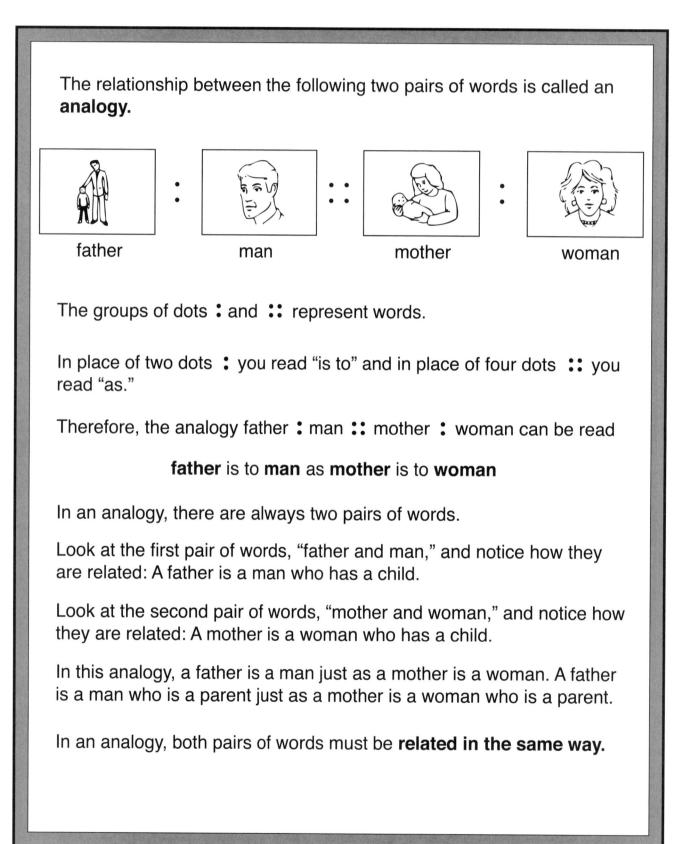

The relationship between the following two pairs of words is called an **analogy.**

father   man   mother   woman

The groups of dots **:** and **::** represent words.

In place of two dots **:** you read "is to" and in place of four dots **::** you read "as."

Therefore, the analogy father **:** man **::** mother **:** woman can be read

father is to **man** as **mother** is to **woman**

In an analogy, there are always two pairs of words.

Look at the first pair of words, "father and man," and notice how they are related: A father is a man who has a child.

Look at the second pair of words, "mother and woman," and notice how they are related: A mother is a woman who has a child.

In this analogy, a father is a man just as a mother is a woman. A father is a man who is a parent just as a mother is a woman who is a parent.

In an analogy, both pairs of words must be **related in the same way.**

PICTURE ANALOGIES—SELECT

DIRECTIONS: Look at the first two words and think about how they are related. Next, look at the third word and decide which word in the choice box is related to the third word in the same way the first two words are related. Write it in the blank.

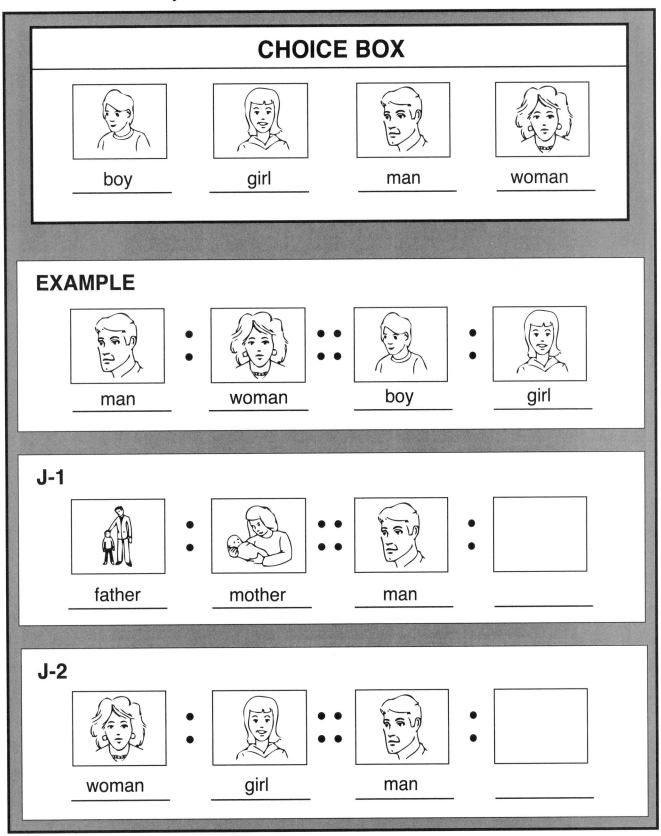

PICTURE ANALOGIES—SELECT

DIRECTIONS: Look at the first two words and think about how they are related. Next, look at the third word and decide which word in the choice box is related to the third word in the same way the first two words are related. Write it in the blank.

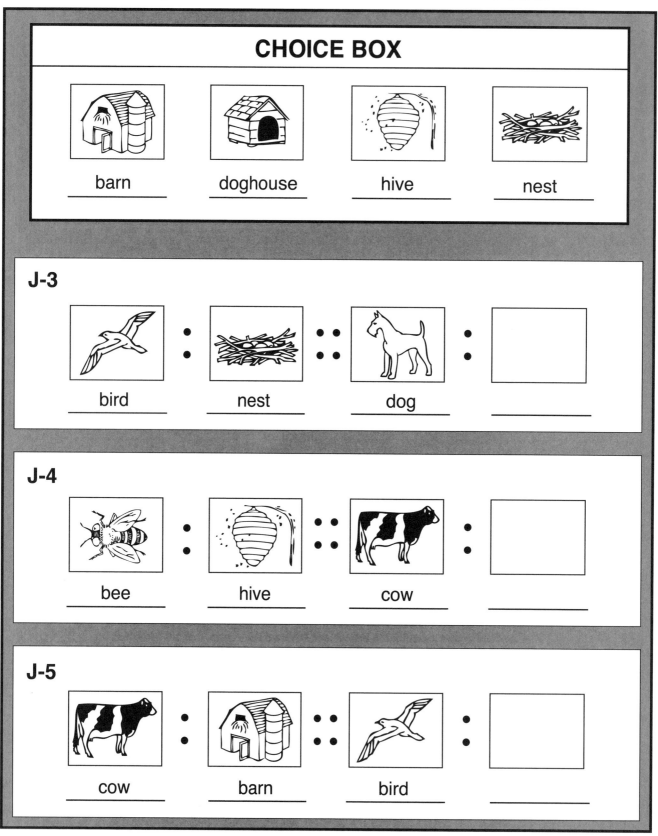

CHOICE BOX

barn   doghouse   hive   nest

J-3

bird   :   nest   ::   dog   :   _____

J-4

bee   :   hive   ::   cow   :   _____

J-5

cow   :   barn   ::   bird   :   _____

PICTURE ANALOGIES—SELECT

DIRECTIONS: Look at the first two words and think about how they are related. Next, look at the third word and decide which word in the choice box is related to the third word in the same way the first two words are related. Write it in the blank.

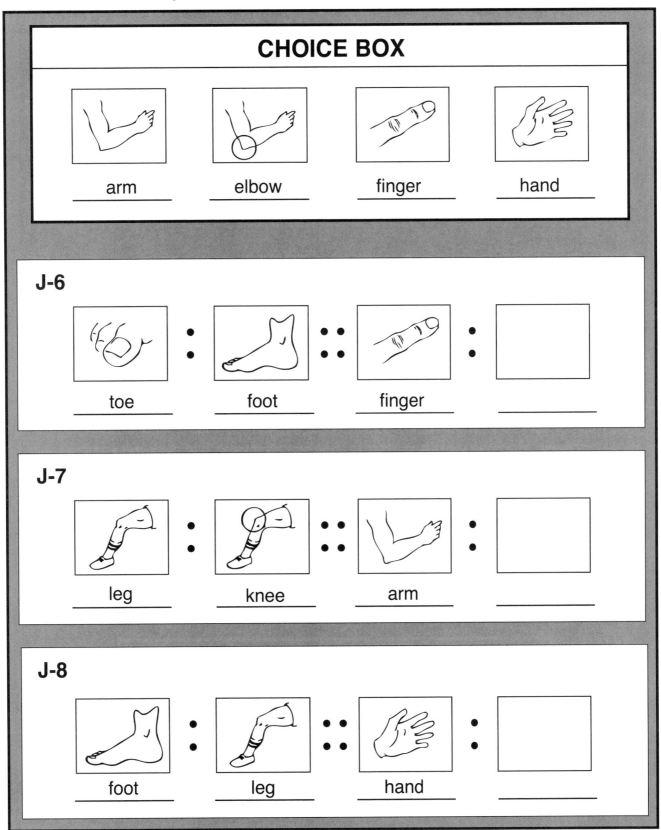

CHOICE BOX

arm   elbow   finger   hand

J-6

toe   :   foot   ::   finger   :

J-7

leg   :   knee   ::   arm   :

J-8

foot   :   leg   ::   hand   :

PICTURE ANALOGIES—NAME THE RELATIONSHIP

DIRECTIONS: Read the analogies and decide how the words in each pair are related. On the lines below each analogy, explain how the words are related.

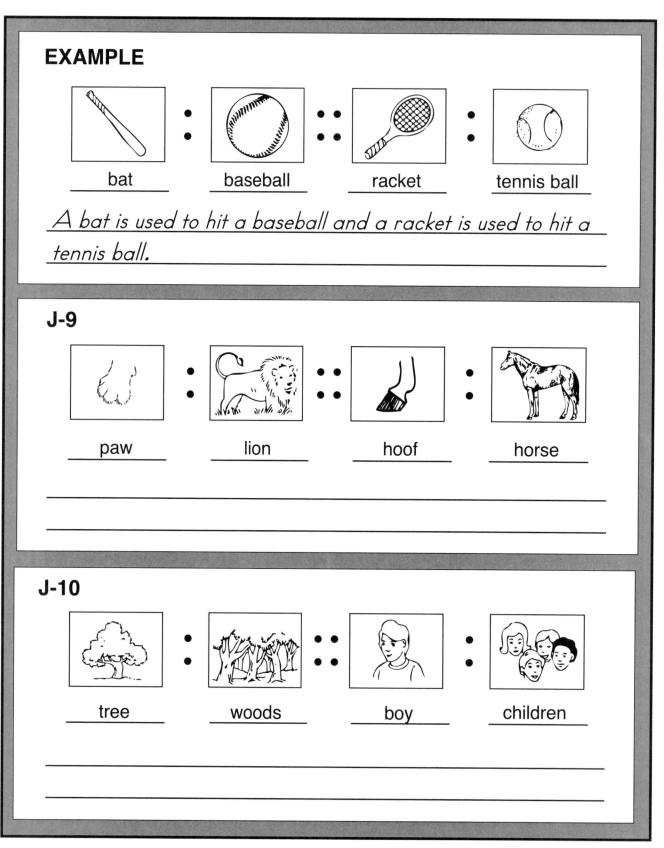

EXAMPLE

bat : baseball :: racket : tennis ball

A bat is used to hit a baseball and a racket is used to hit a tennis ball.

J-9

paw : lion :: hoof : horse

J-10

tree : woods :: boy : children

PICTURE ANALOGIES—NAME THE RELATIONSHIP

DIRECTIONS: Read the analogies and decide how the words in each pair are related. On the lines below each analogy, explain how the words are related.

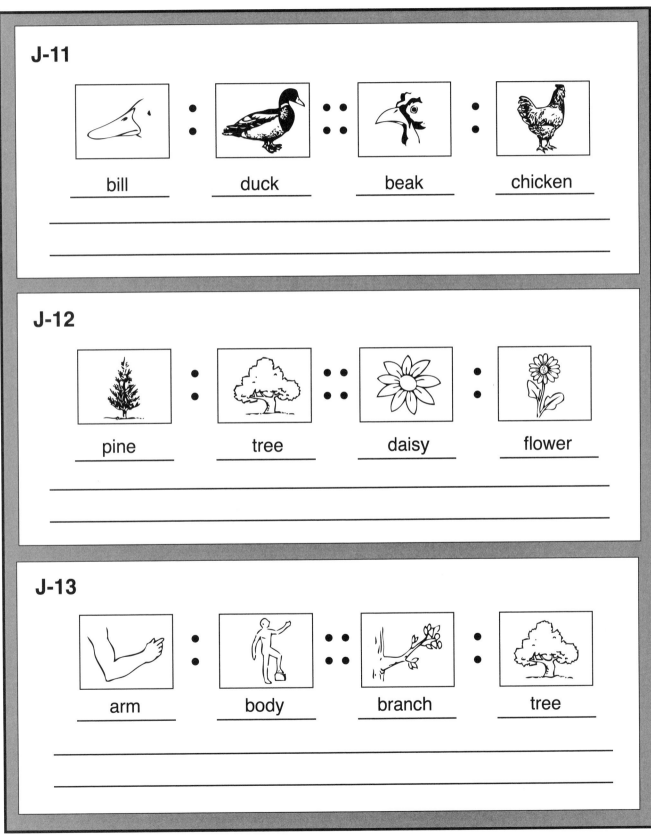

J-11

bill : duck :: beak : chicken

_____

J-12

pine : tree :: daisy : flower

_____

J-13

arm : body :: branch : tree

_____

PICTURE ANALOGIES—NAME THE RELATIONSHIP

DIRECTIONS: Read the analogies and decide how the words in each pair are related. On the lines below each analogy, explain how the words are related.

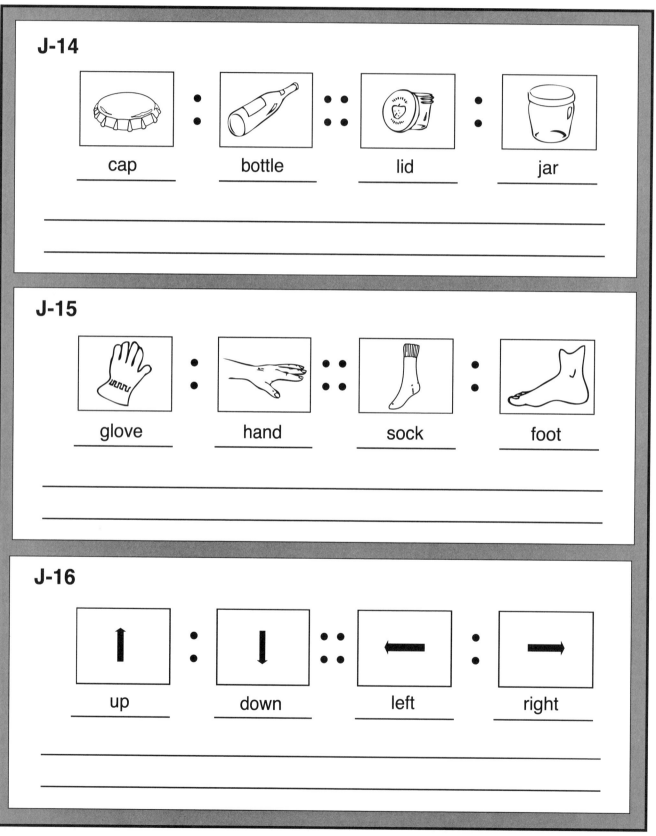

J-14

cap : bottle :: lid : jar

_____

_____

J-15

glove : hand :: sock : foot

_____

_____

J-16

up : down :: left : right

_____

_____

ANALOGIES—SELECT

DIRECTIONS: In each exercise, decide how the first two words are related. Next, look at the third word and find a word in the choice box that will complete a similar relationship. Some words may be used more than once; not all words must be used.

CHOICE BOX

between, bottom, far, follow, rear, side, under, upon

J-17

above **:** below **::** over **:** _____

J-18

first **:** front **::** last **:** _____

J-19

over **:** below **::** above **:** _____

J-20

here **:** there **::** near **:** _____

J-21

roof **:** top **::** base **:** _____

J-22

front **:** lead **::** rear **:** _____

ANALOGIES—SELECT

DIRECTIONS: In each exercise, decide how the first two words are related. Next, look at the third word and find a word in the choice box that will complete a similar relationship. Some words may be used more than once; not all words must be used.

CHOICE BOX

empty, full, half, low, quarter, small, tall, whole

J-23

more : less :: full : _____

J-24

pint : quart :: half : _____

J-25

nothing : everything :: empty : _____

J-26

tall : large :: short : _____

J-27

low : high :: short : _____

J-28

tall : short :: high : _____

ANALOGIES—SELECT

DIRECTIONS: In each exercise, decide how the first two words are related. Next, look at the third word and find a word in the choice box that will complete a similar relationship. Some words may be used more than once; not all words must be used.

CHOICE BOX

after, now, often, past, present, today, tomorrow, yesterday

J-29

today   :   present   ::   yesterday   :   _____

J-30

then   :   now   ::   past   :   _____

J-31

before   :   now   ::   yesterday   :   _____

J-32

today   :   yesterday   ::   present   :   _____

J-33

rarely   :   frequently   ::   seldom   :   _____

J-34

yesterday   :   before   ::   tomorrow   :   _____

ANALOGIES—SELECT

DIRECTIONS: In each exercise, decide how the first two words are related. Next, look at the third word and find a word in the choice box that will complete a similar relationship. Some words may be used more than once; not all words must be used.

CHOICE BOX

bird, cat, cow, deer, fish, horse, lion

J-35

puppy : dog :: colt : _____

J-36

antlers : deer :: mane : _____

J-37

meow : cat :: roar : _____

J-38

swim : fish :: fly : _____

J-39

fur : cat :: scales : _____

J-40

mare : horse :: doe : _____

ANALOGIES—SELECT

DIRECTIONS: In each exercise, decide how the first two words are related. Next, look at the third word and find a word in the choice box that will complete a similar relationship. Some words may be used more than once; not all words must be used.

CHOICE BOX

day, minute, month, week, year

J-41

minute **:** second **::** hour **:** _____

J-42

day **:** week **::** week **:** _____

J-43

hour **:** day **::** month **:** _____

J-44

week **:** day **::** month **:** _____

J-45

century **:** year **::** month **:** _____

J-46

minute **:** hour **::** second **:** _____

ANALOGIES—SELECT

DIRECTIONS: In each exercise, decide how the first two words are related. Next, look at the third word and find a word in the choice box that will complete a similar relationship. Some words may be used more than once; not all words must be used.

CHOICE BOX

heat, light, odor, sound

J-47

eye　**:**　light　**::**　ear　**:**　_____

J-48

hear　**:**　sound　**::**　feel　**:**　_____

J-49

fire　**:**　heat　**::**　speaker　**:**　_____

J-50

lamp　**:**　light　**::**　furnace　**:**　_____

J-51

eye　**:**　light　**::**　nose　**:**　_____

J-52

hear　**:**　sound　**::**　see　**:**　_____

ANALOGIES—SELECT

DIRECTIONS: In each exercise, decide how the first two words are related. Next, look at the third word and find a word in the choice box that will complete a similar relationship. Some words may be used more than once; not all words must be used.

CHOICE BOX
cup, gallon, pint, quart (Note: 2 cups = 1 pint; 2 pints = 1 quart; 4 quarts = 1 gallon)

J-53

two pints **:** quart **::** four quarts **:** _____

J-54

two quarts **:** gallon **::** pint **:** _____

J-55

gallon **:** quart **::** half-gallon **:** _____

J-56

pint **:** cup **::** quart **:** _____

J-57

gallon **:** quart **::** quart **:** _____

J-58

half-pint **:** cup **::** two pints **:** _____

ANALOGIES—SELECT

DIRECTIONS: In each exercise, decide how the first two words are related. Next, look at the third word and find a word in the list at right that will complete a similar relationship.

EXAMPLE

in　：　out　：：　down　：　___*up*___

outside
over
under
up

J-59

read　：　book　：：　listen　：　_____

magazine
newspaper
radio
picture

J-60

knife　：　cut　：：　hammer　：　_____

handle
picture
pound
slice

J-61

silo　：　grain　：：　tank　：　_____

brick
metal
water
wood

ANALOGIES—SELECT

DIRECTIONS: In each exercise, decide how the first two words are related. Next, look at the third word and find a word in the list at right that will complete a similar relationship.

J-62

this **:** that **::** these **:** _____

here
them
those
there

J-63

hot dog **:** sausage **::** orange **:** _____

blossom
cherry
fruit
sandwich

J-64

read **:** poem **::** sing **:** _____

song
talk
whisper
word

J-65

swim **:** water **::** fly **:** _____

air
land
ocean
sea

ANALOGIES—SELECT

DIRECTIONS: In each exercise, decide how the first two words are related. Next, look at the third word and find a word in the list at right that will complete a similar relationship.

J-66

buy : sell :: take : _____

bought
give
have
save

J-67

here : there :: this : _____

that
them
these
those

J-68

come : go :: enter : _____

bring
give
have
leave

J-69

car : garage :: tractor : _____

barn
cow
field
plow

ANALOGIES—SELECT

DIRECTIONS: In each exercise, decide how the first two words are related. Next, look at the third word and find a word in the list at right that will complete a similar relationship.

J-70

nose : smell :: tongue : _____

feel
see
taste
touch

J-71

mower : lawn :: saw : _____

blade
handle
nail
wood

J-72

overpass : highway :: bridge : _____

cards
rail
river
train

J-73

breakfast : lunch :: lunch : _____

eating
food
supper
vegetables

ANALOGIES—SUPPLY

DIRECTIONS: In each exercise, decide how the first two words are related. Next, look at the third word and pick a word from your memory that belongs in the blank. In this exercise, all the words have to do with things you wear.

J-74

　　shoe　:　sock　::　jacket　:　_____

J-75

　　button　:　shirt　::　lace or string　:　_____

J-76

　　bracelet　:　arm　::　ring　:　_____

J-77

　　shoe　:　foot　::　glove　:　_____

J-78

　　scarf　:　neck　::　hat　:　_____

J-79

　　pants　:　legs　::　sweater　:　_____

ANALOGIES—SUPPLY

DIRECTIONS: In each exercise, decide how the first two words are related. Next, look at the third word and pick a word from your memory that belongs in the blank.

J-80

above : below :: ceiling : _____

J-81

outside : inside :: porch : _____

J-82

door : wood :: window : _____

J-83

above : ceiling :: side : _____

J-84

shingles : roof :: rug : _____

J-85

chimney : roof :: window : _____

ANALOGIES—SUPPLY

DIRECTIONS: In each exercise, decide how the first two words are related. Next, look at the third word and pick a word from your memory that belongs in the blank.

J-86

cool : cold :: warm : _____

J-87

iron : heavy :: feathers : _____

J-88

penny : coin :: dollar : _____

J-89

rabbit : fast :: turtle : _____

J-90

lid : eye :: shade : _____

J-91

soldier : army :: sailor : _____

ANALOGIES—SUPPLY

DIRECTIONS: In each exercise, decide how the first two words are related. Next, look at the third word and pick a word from your memory that belongs in the blank.

J-92

tan : brown :: pink : _____

J-93

handlebar : bicycle :: steering wheel : _____

J-94

over : above :: under : _____

J-95

front : first :: rear : _____

J-96

sky : air :: lake : _____

J-97

knife : slice :: scissors : _____

ANALOGIES—SUPPLY

DIRECTIONS: In each exercise, decide how the first two words are related. Next, look at the third word and pick a word from your memory that belongs in the blank.

J-98

red **:** stop **::** green **:** _____

J-99

fast **:** slow **::** run **:** _____

J-100

side **:** wall **::** bottom **:** _____

J-101

enter **:** come **::** leave **:** _____

J-102

cotton **:** soft **::** steel **:** _____

J-103

bottle **:** cap **::** pan **:** _____

ANALOGIES—SUPPLY

DIRECTIONS: In each exercise, decide how the first two words are related. Next, look at the third word and pick a word from your memory that belongs in the blank.

J-104

late : last :: early : _____

J-105

last : first :: least : _____

J-106

rain : spring :: snow : _____

J-107

book : read :: pencil : _____

J-108

freeze : refrigerator :: boil : _____

J-109

boil : pot :: fry : _____

ANALOGIES—SELECT THE RIGHT PAIR

DIRECTIONS: In each exercise, decide how the first two words are related. Next, look at the pairs of words in the list at right; find the pair with a similar relationship. Fill in the blanks to complete the analogy.

J-110

below : under ::

_____ : _____

above : behind

above : over

between : over

beneath : over

J-111

dog : puppy ::

_____ : _____

calf : cow

cat : kitten

child : adult

colt : horse

J-112

now : then ::

_____ : _____

give : take

here : there

present : past

this : that

J-113

true : false ::

_____ : _____

lie : wrong

love : promise

right : answer

right : wrong

ANALOGIES—SELECT THE RIGHT PAIR

DIRECTIONS: In each exercise, decide how the first two words are related. Next, look at the pairs of words in the list at right; find the pair with a similar relationship. Fill in the blanks to complete the analogy.

J-114

up : down ::

_____ : _____

below : under

beneath : under

over : under

over : upper

J-115

more : less ::

_____ : _____

always : often

much : more

now : then

plus : minus

J-116

mother : child ::

_____ : _____

brother : sister

girl : boy

parent : baby

son : mother

J-117

slow : fast ::

_____ : _____

always : often

minus : less

much : more

seldom : often

ANSWER GUIDE

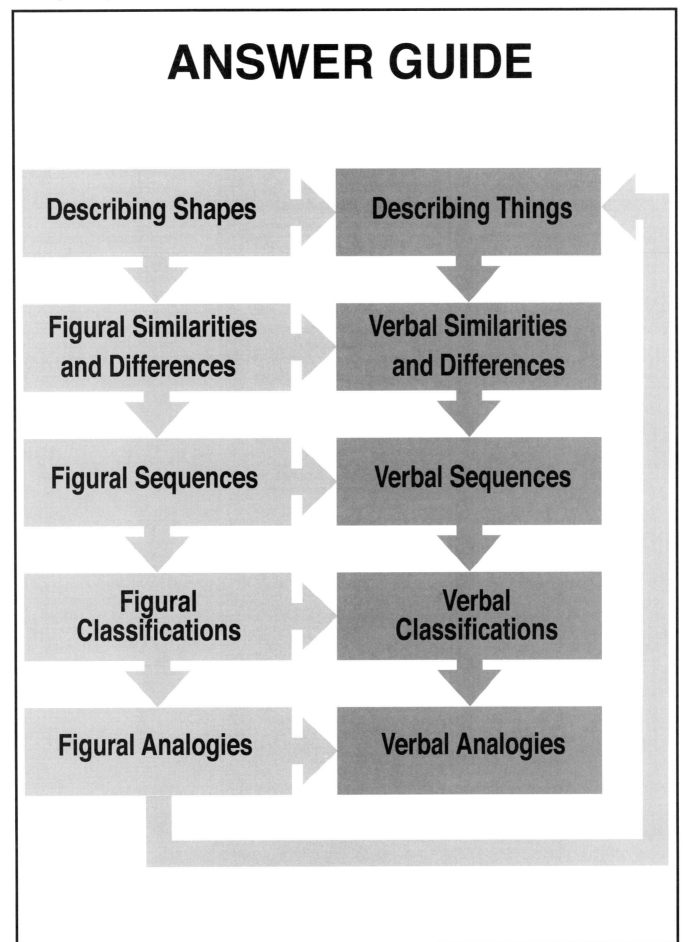

Describing Shapes → Describing Things

Figural Similarities and Differences → Verbal Similarities and Differences

Figural Sequences → Verbal Sequences

Figural Classifications → Verbal Classifications

Figural Analogies → Verbal Analogies

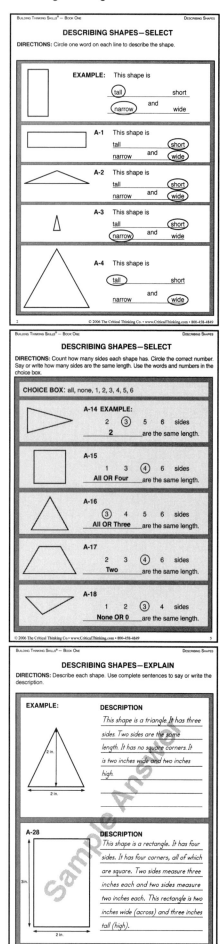

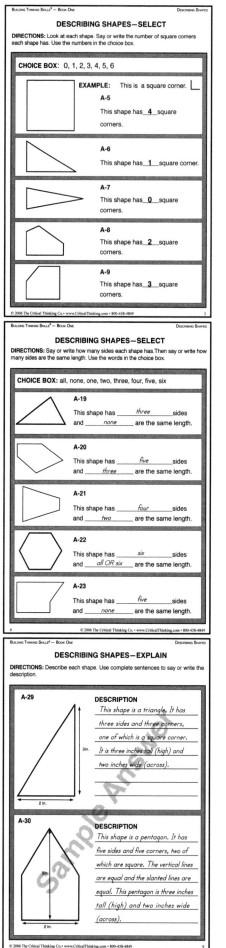

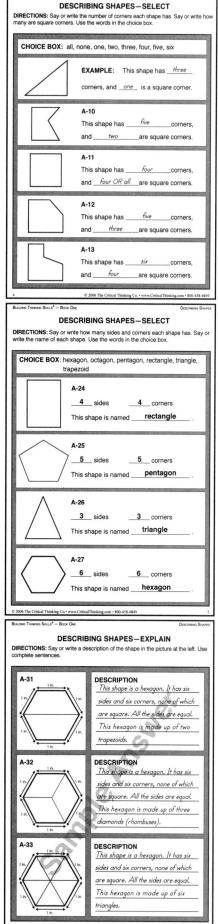

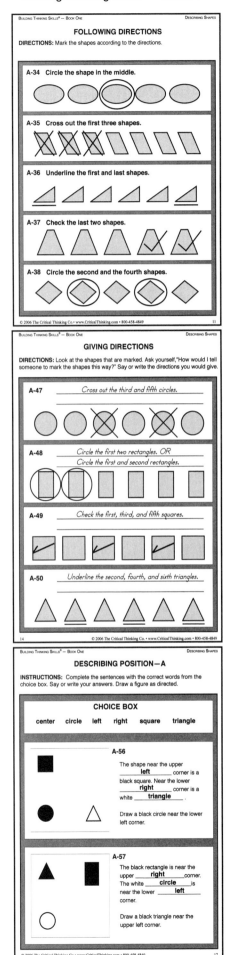

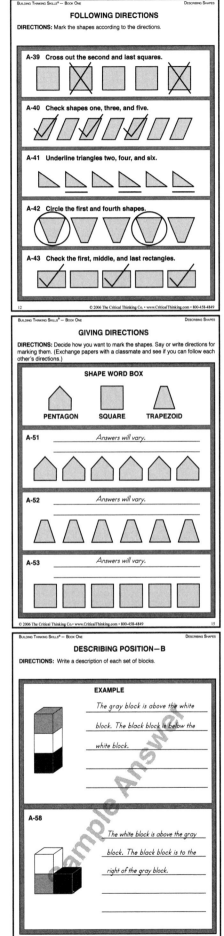

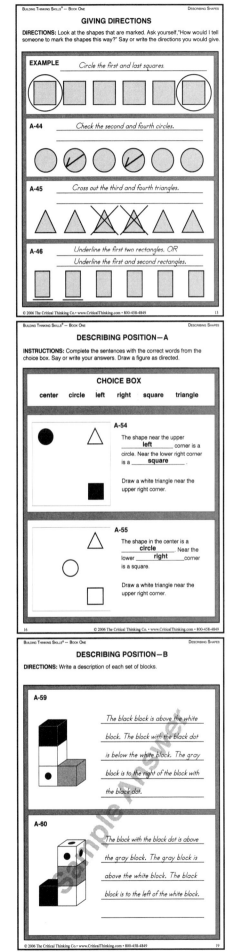

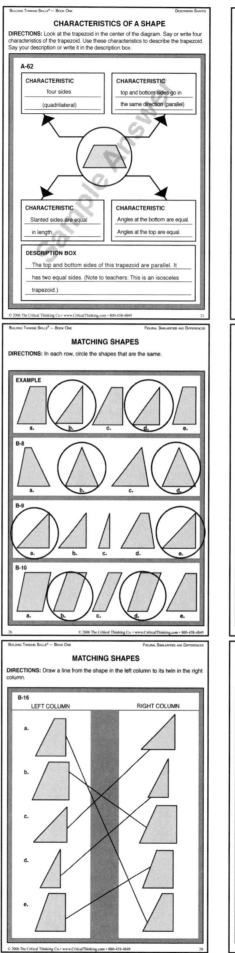
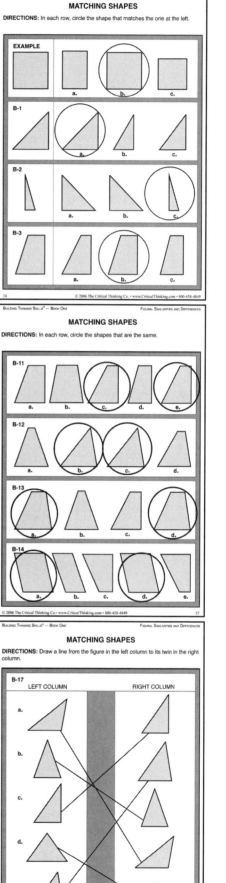

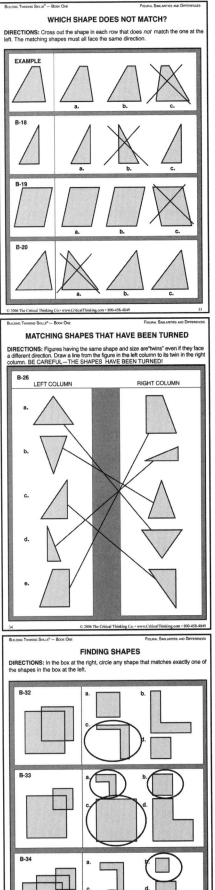

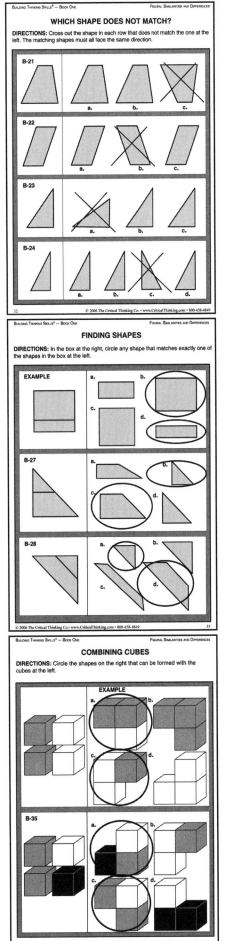

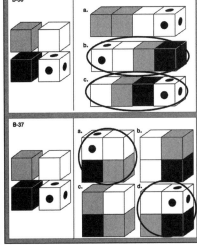

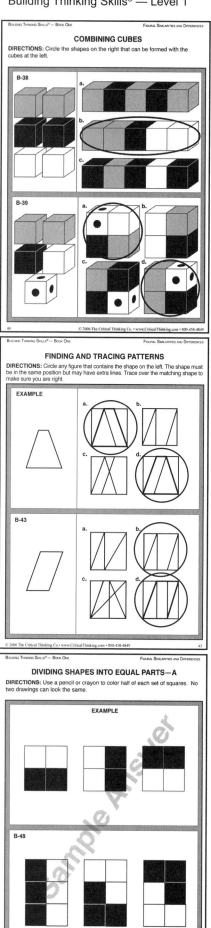

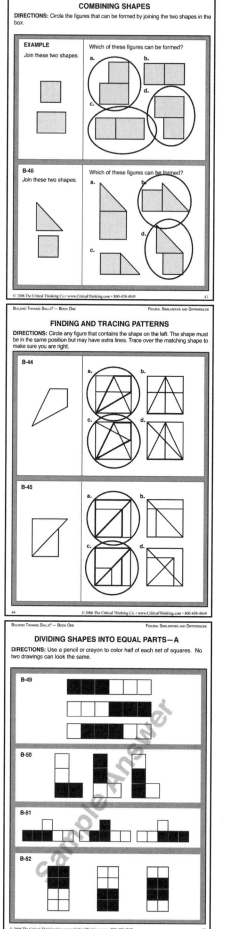

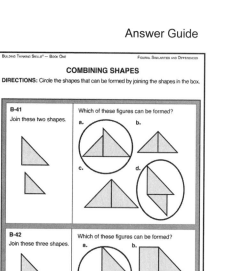

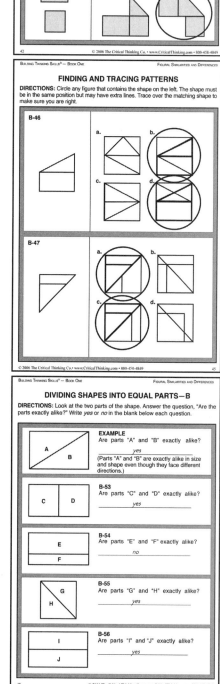

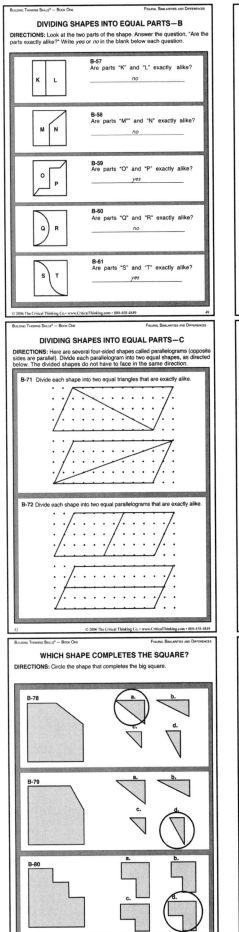

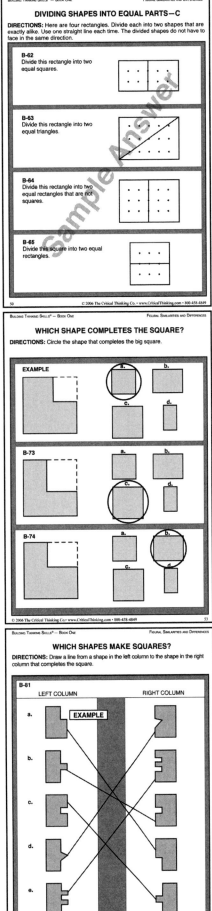

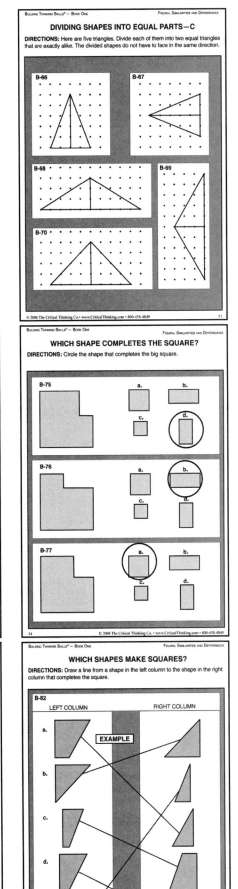

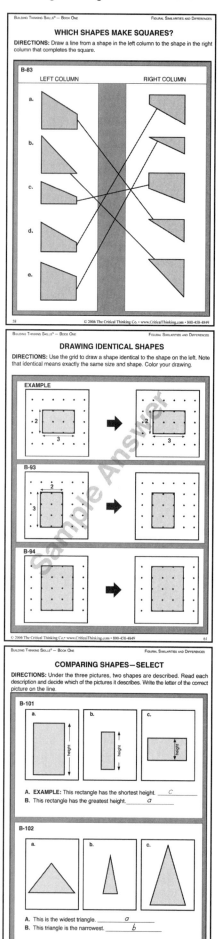

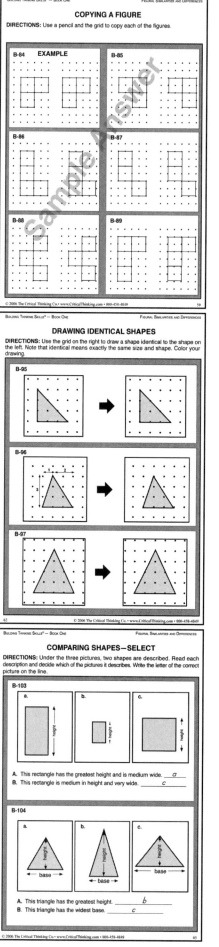

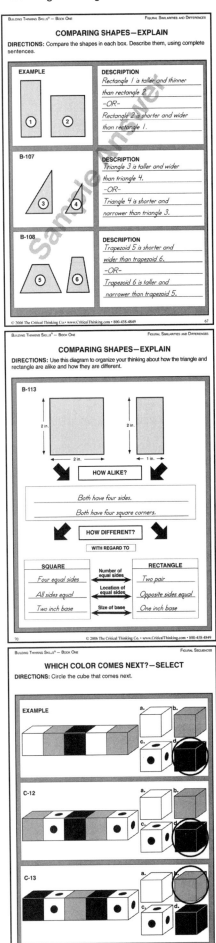

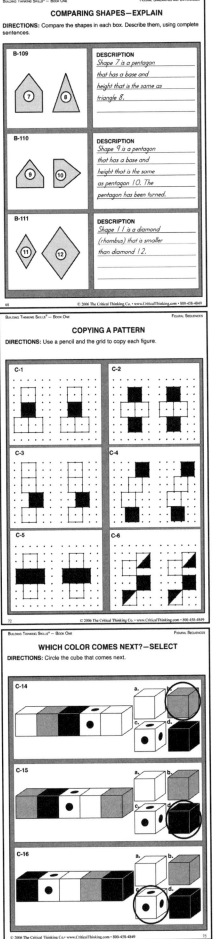

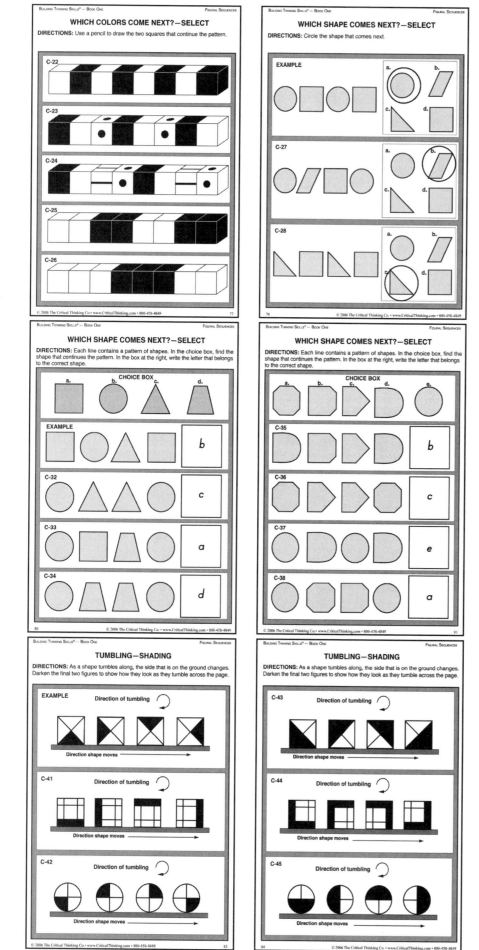

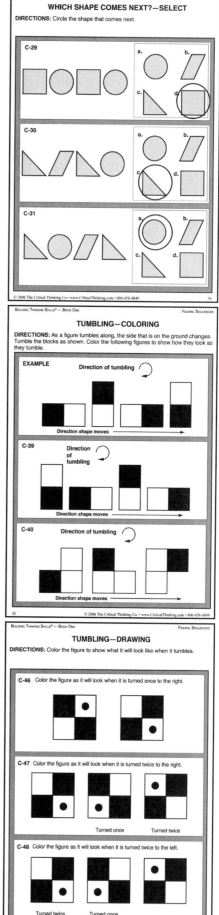

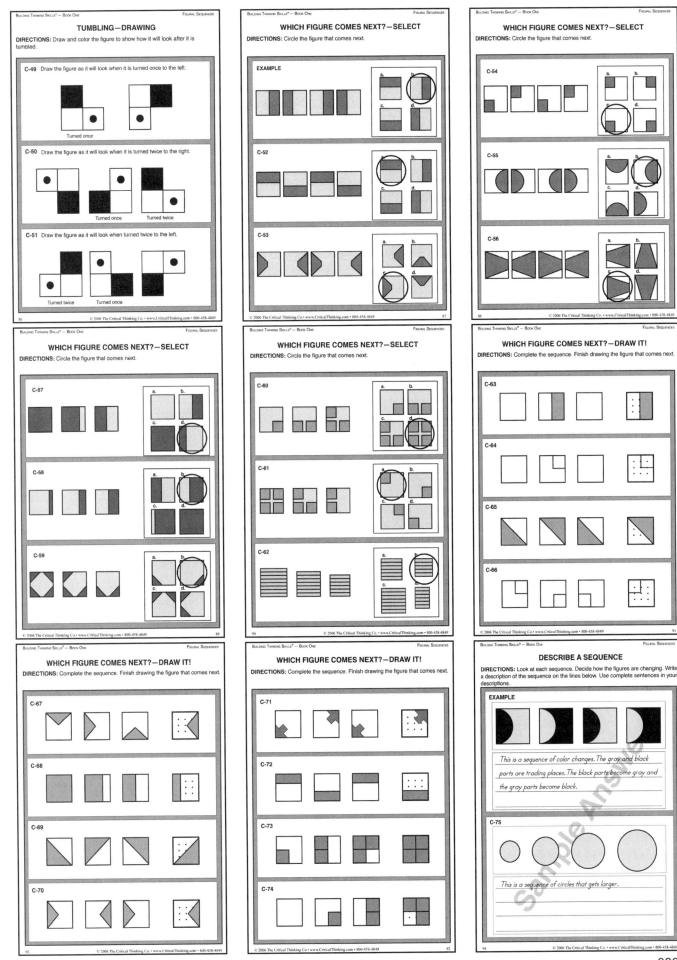

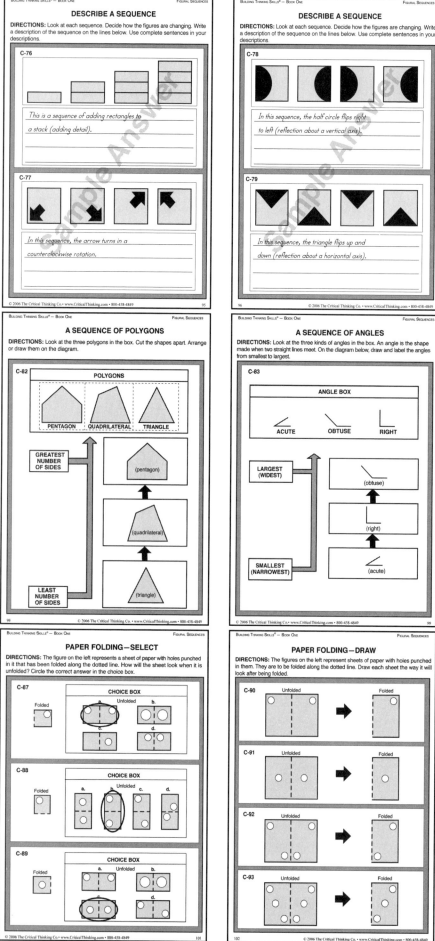

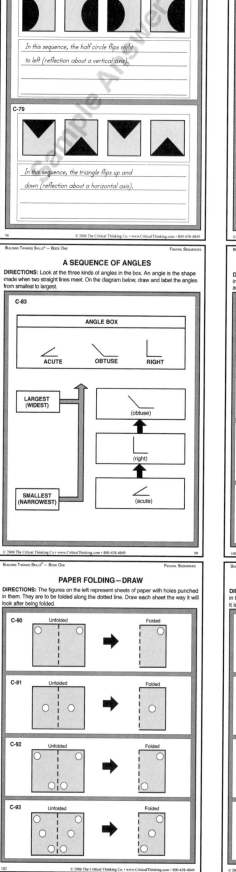

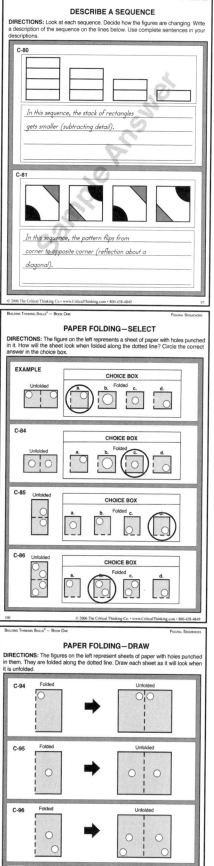

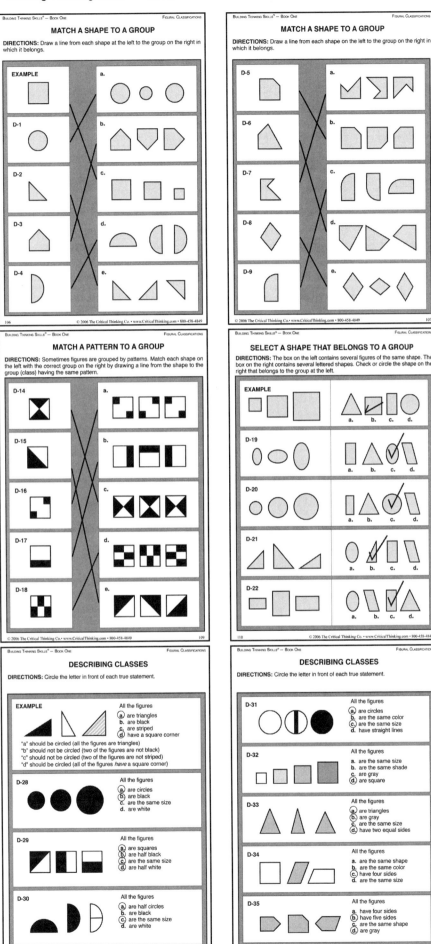

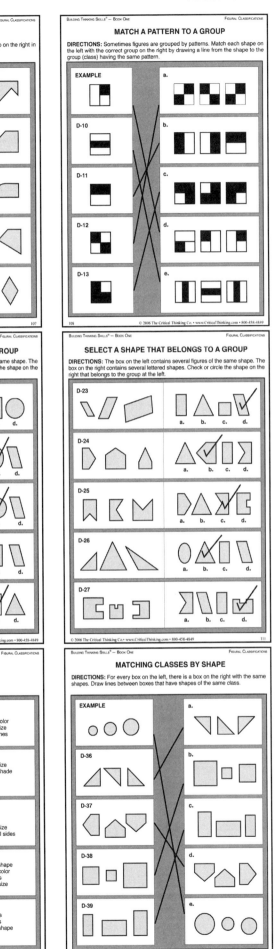

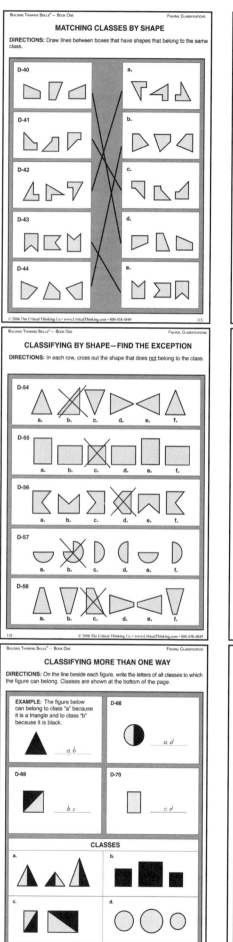

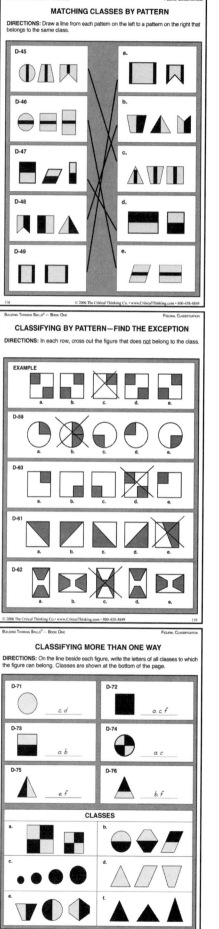

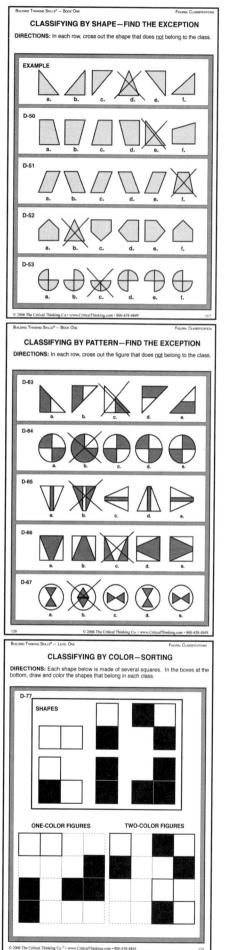

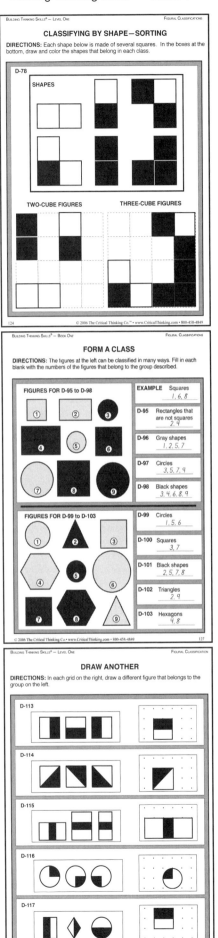

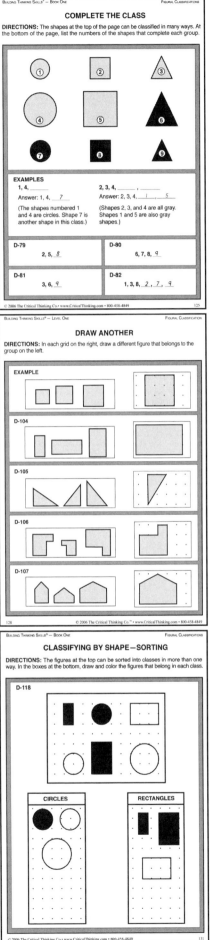

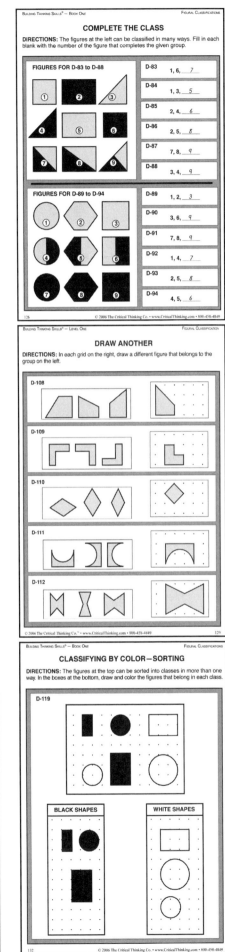

CLASSIFYING BY SIZE—SORTING

DIRECTIONS: The figures at the top can be sorted into classes in more than one way. In the boxes at the bottom, draw and color the figures that belong in each class.

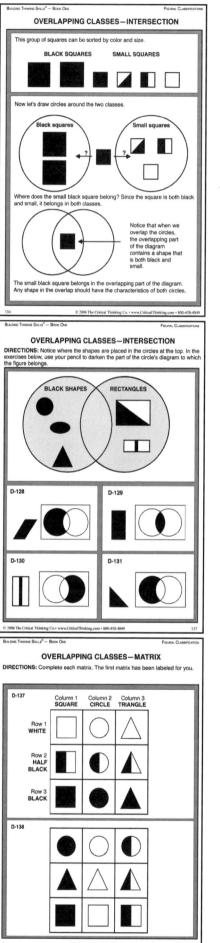

OVERLAPPING CLASSES—INTERSECTION

This group of squares can be sorted by color and size.

BLACK SQUARES   SMALL SQUARES

Now let's draw circles around the two classes.

Where does the small black square belong? Since the square is both black and small, it belongs in both classes.

Notice that when we overlap the circles, the overlapping part of the diagram contains a shape that is both black and small.

The small black square belongs in the overlapping part of the diagram. Any shape in the overlap should have the characteristics of both circles.

OVERLAPPING CLASSES—INTERSECTION

DIRECTIONS: Notice where the shapes are placed in the circles at the top. In the exercises below, use your pencil to darken the part of the circle's diagram to which the figure belongs (see example).

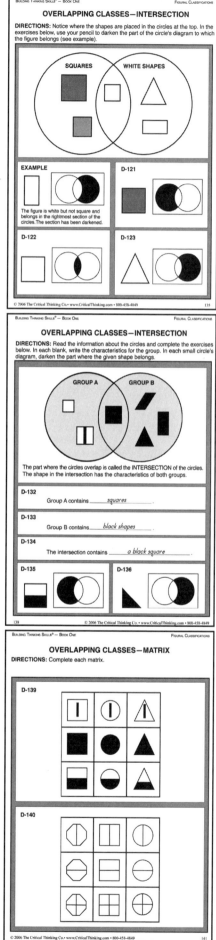

EXAMPLE

The figure is white but not square and belongs in the rightmost section of the circles. The section has been darkened.

D-121

D-122

D-123

OVERLAPPING CLASSES—INTERSECTION

DIRECTIONS: Notice where the shapes are placed in the circles at the top. In the exercises below, use your pencil to darken the part of the circle's diagram to which the figure belongs.

TRIANGLES   STRIPED SHAPES

D-124

D-125

D-126

D-127

OVERLAPPING CLASSES—INTERSECTION

DIRECTIONS: Notice where the shapes are placed in the circles at the top. In the exercises below, use your pencil to darken the part of the circle's diagram to which the figure belongs.

BLACK SHAPES   RECTANGLES

D-128

D-129

D-130

D-131

OVERLAPPING CLASSES—INTERSECTION

DIRECTIONS: Read the information about the circles and complete the exercises below. In each blank, write the characteristics for the group. In each small circle's diagram, darken the part where the given shape belongs.

GROUP A   GROUP B

The part where the circles overlap is called the INTERSECTION of the circles. The shape in the intersection has the characteristics of both groups.

D-132
Group A contains _____squares_____.

D-133
Group B contains _____black shapes_____.

D-134
The intersection contains _____a black square_____.

D-135

D-136

OVERLAPPING CLASSES—MATRIX

	Column 1 SQUARE	Column 2 CIRCLE
Row 1 WHITE		
Row 2 BLACK		

If all objects in a group can be described by two characteristics, then the group can be organized by the kind of diagram used above, which is called a matrix. The white square is in the row labeled "WHITE" and in the column labeled "SQUARE" because it is both white and square.

OVERLAPPING CLASSES—MATRIX

DIRECTIONS: Complete each matrix. The first matrix has been labeled for you.

D-137

	Column 1 SQUARE	Column 2 CIRCLE	Column 3 TRIANGLE
Row 1 WHITE			
Row 2 HALF BLACK			
Row 3 BLACK			

D-138

OVERLAPPING CLASSES—MATRIX

DIRECTIONS: Complete each matrix.

D-139

D-140

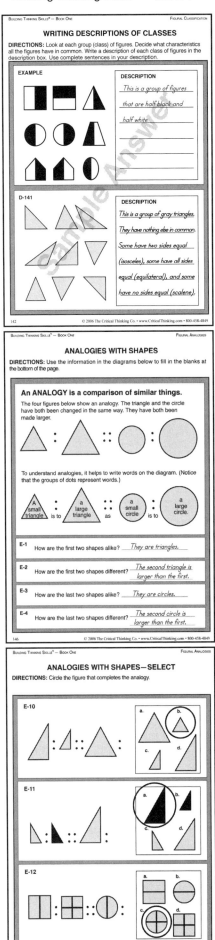

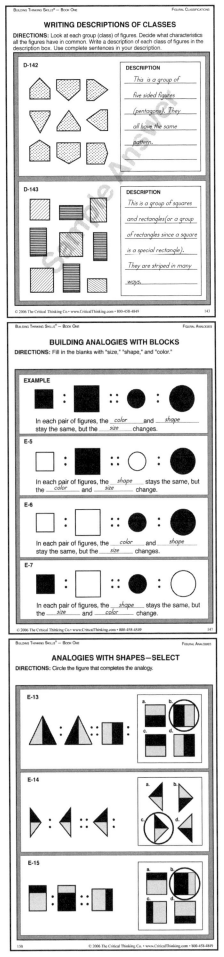

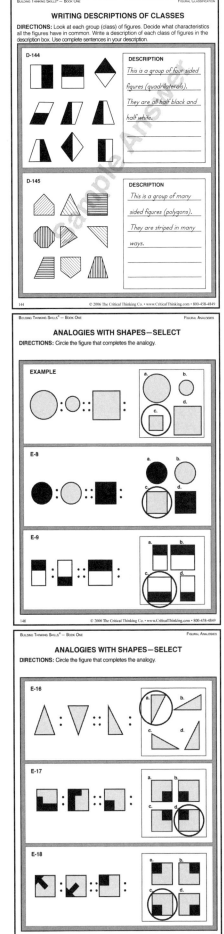

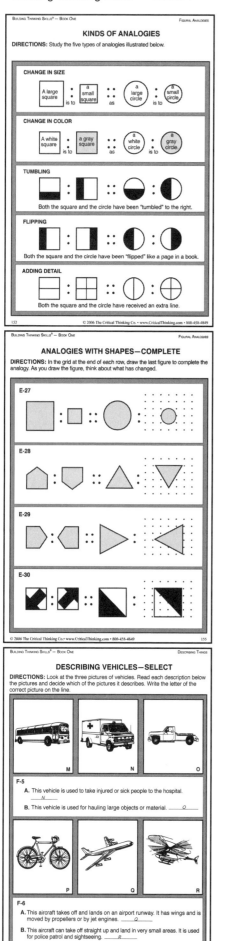

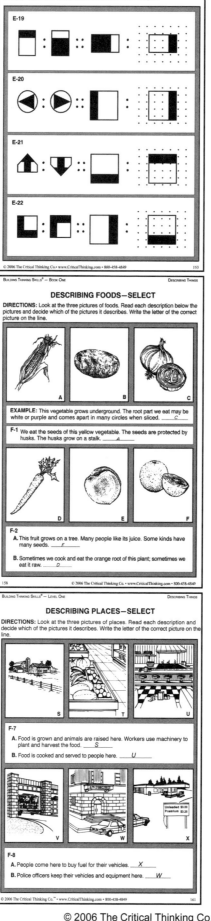

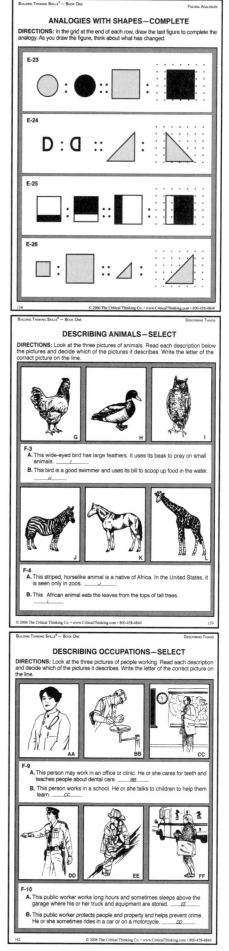

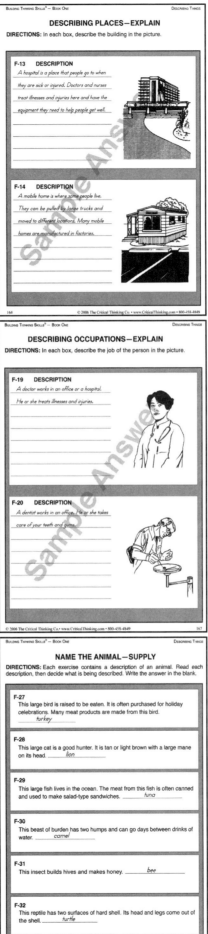

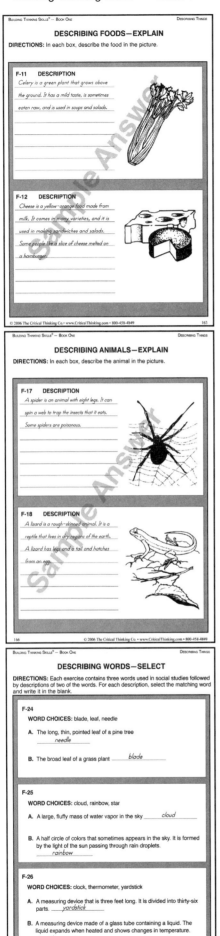

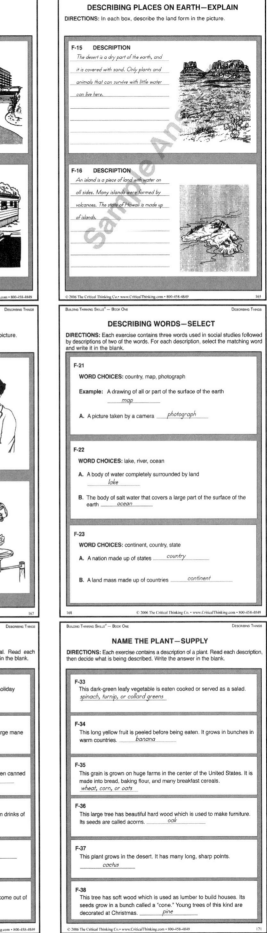

DESCRIBING FOODS—EXPLAIN
DIRECTIONS: In each box, describe the food in the picture.

F-11   DESCRIPTION
Celery is a green plant that grows above the ground. It has a mild taste, is sometimes eaten raw, and is used in soups and salads.

F-12   DESCRIPTION
Cheese is a yellow-orange food made from milk. It comes in many varieties, and it is used in making sandwiches and salads. Some people like a slice of cheese melted on a hamburger.

DESCRIBING PLACES—EXPLAIN
DIRECTIONS: In each box, describe the building in the picture.

F-13   DESCRIPTION
A hospital is a place that people go to when they are sick or injured. Doctors and nurses treat illnesses and injuries here and have the equipment they need to help people get well.

F-14   DESCRIPTION
A mobile home is where some people live. They can be pulled by large trucks and moved to different locations. Many mobile homes are manufactured in factories.

DESCRIBING PLACES ON EARTH—EXPLAIN
DIRECTIONS: In each box, describe the land form in the picture.

F-15   DESCRIPTION
The desert is a dry part of the earth, and it is covered with sand. Only plants and animals that can survive with little water can live here.

F-16   DESCRIPTION
An island is a piece of land with water on all sides. Many islands were formed by volcanoes. The state of Hawaii is made up of islands.

DESCRIBING ANIMALS—EXPLAIN
DIRECTIONS: In each box, describe the animal in the picture.

F-17   DESCRIPTION
A spider is an animal with eight legs. It can spin a web to trap the insects that it eats. Some spiders are poisonous.

F-18   DESCRIPTION
A lizard is a rough-skinned animal. It is a reptile that lives in dry regions of the earth. A lizard has legs and a tail and hatches from an egg.

DESCRIBING OCCUPATIONS—EXPLAIN
DIRECTIONS: In each box, describe the job of the person in the picture.

F-19   DESCRIPTION
A doctor works in an office or a hospital. He or she treats illnesses and injuries.

F-20   DESCRIPTION
A dentist works in an office. He or she takes care of your teeth and gums.

DESCRIBING WORDS—SELECT
DIRECTIONS: Each exercise contains three words used in social studies followed by descriptions of two of the words. For each description, select the matching word and write it in the blank.

F-21
WORD CHOICES: country, map, photograph

Example: A drawing of all or part of the surface of the earth _____map_____

A. A picture taken by a camera _____photograph_____

F-22
WORD CHOICES: lake, river, ocean

A. A body of water completely surrounded by land _____lake_____

B. The body of salt water that covers a large part of the surface of the earth _____ocean_____

F-23
WORD CHOICES: continent, country, state

A. A nation made up of states _____country_____

B. A land mass made up of countries _____continent_____

DESCRIBING WORDS—SELECT
DIRECTIONS: Each exercise contains three words used in social studies followed by descriptions of two of the words. For each description, select the matching word and write it in the blank.

F-24
WORD CHOICES: blade, leaf, needle

A. The long, thin, pointed leaf of a pine tree _____needle_____

B. The broad leaf of a grass plant _____blade_____

F-25
WORD CHOICES: cloud, rainbow, star

A. A large, fluffy mass of water vapor in the sky _____cloud_____

B. A half circle of colors that sometimes appears in the sky. It is formed by the light of the sun passing through rain droplets. _____rainbow_____

F-26
WORD CHOICES: clock, thermometer, yardstick

A. A measuring device that is three feet long. It is divided into thirty-six parts. _____yardstick_____

B. A measuring device made of a glass tube containing a liquid. The liquid expands when heated and shows changes in temperature. _____thermometer_____

NAME THE ANIMAL—SUPPLY
DIRECTIONS: Each exercise contains a description of an animal. Read each description, then decide what is being described. Write the answer in the blank.

F-27
This large bird is raised to be eaten. It is often purchased for holiday celebrations. Many meat products are made from this bird. _____turkey_____

F-28
This large cat is a good hunter. It is tan or light brown with a large mane on its head. _____lion_____

F-29
This large fish lives in the ocean. The meat from this fish is often canned and used to make salad-type sandwiches. _____tuna_____

F-30
This beast of burden has two humps and can go days between drinks of water. _____camel_____

F-31
This insect builds hives and makes honey. _____bee_____

F-32
This reptile has two surfaces of hard shell. Its head and legs come out of the shell. _____turtle_____

NAME THE PLANT—SUPPLY
DIRECTIONS: Each exercise contains a description of a plant. Read each description, then decide what is being described. Write the answer in the blank.

F-33
This dark-green leafy vegetable is eaten cooked or served as a salad. _____spinach, turnip, or collard greens_____

F-34
This long yellow fruit is peeled before being eaten. It grows in bunches in warm countries. _____banana_____

F-35
This grain is grown on huge farms in the center of the United States. It is made into bread, baking flour, and many breakfast cereals. _____wheat, corn, or oats_____

F-36
This large tree has beautiful hard wood which is used to make furniture. Its seeds are called acorns. _____oak_____

F-37
This plant grows in the desert. It has many long, sharp points. _____cactus_____

F-38
This tree has soft wood which is used as lumber to build houses. Its seeds grow in a bunch called a "cone." Young trees of this kind are decorated at Christmas. _____pine_____

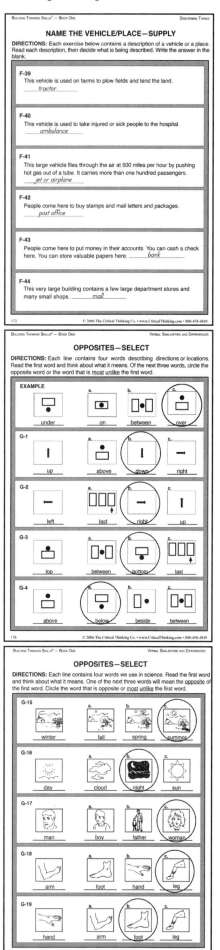

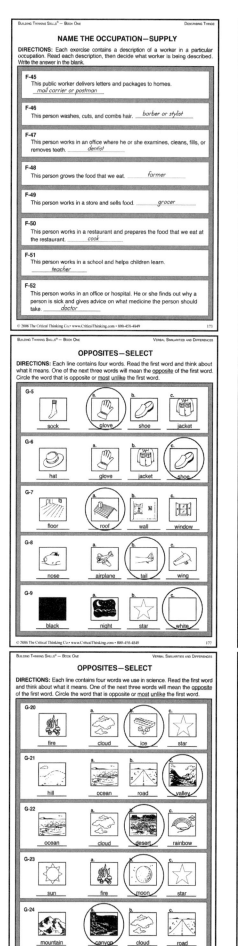

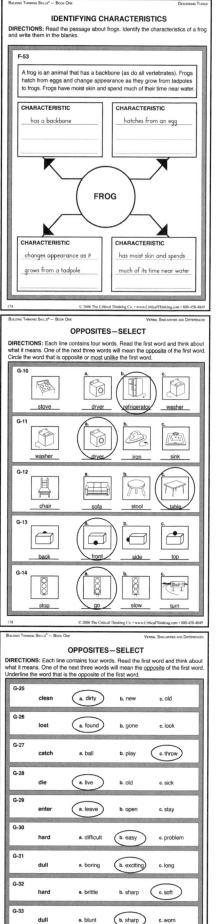

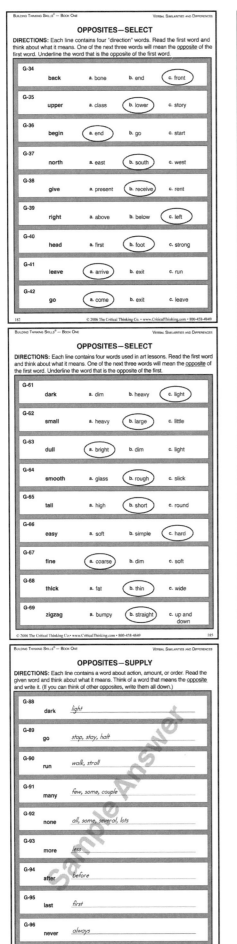

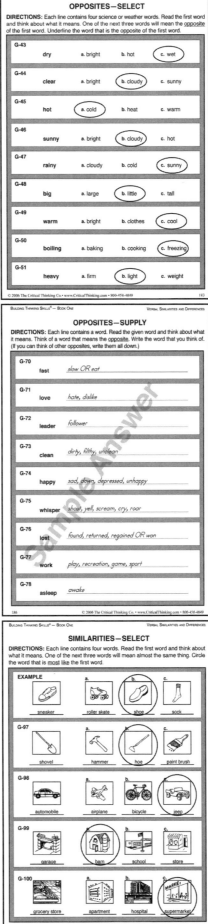

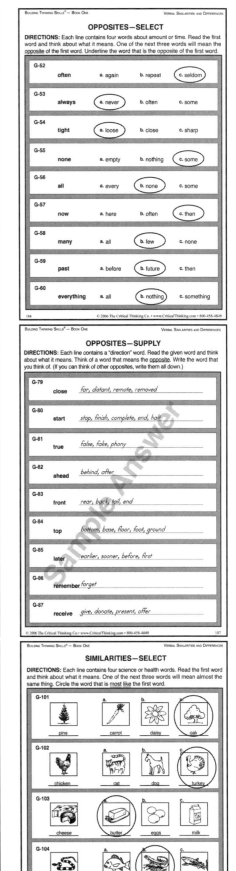

Top-left panel (page 182):

BUILDING THINKING SKILLS® — BOOK ONE   VERBAL SIMILARITIES AND DIFFERENCES

OPPOSITES—SELECT

DIRECTIONS: Each line contains four "direction" words. Read the first word and think about what it means. One of the next three words will mean the opposite of the first word. Underline the word that is the opposite of the first word.

G-34 back   a. bone   b. end   **c. front**
G-35 upper   a. class   **b. lower**   c. story
G-36 begin   **a. end**   b. go   c. start
G-37 north   a. east   **b. south**   c. west
G-38 give   a. present   **b. receive**   c. rent
G-39 right   a. above   b. below   **c. left**
G-40 head   a. first   **b. foot**   c. strong
G-41 leave   **a. arrive**   b. exit   c. run
G-42 go   **a. come**   b. exit   c. leave

182

Top-middle panel (page 183):

BUILDING THINKING SKILLS® — BOOK ONE   VERBAL SIMILARITIES AND DIFFERENCES

OPPOSITES—SELECT

DIRECTIONS: Each line contains four science or weather words. Read the first word and think about what it means. One of the next three words will mean the opposite of the first word. Underline the word that is the opposite of the first word.

G-43 dry   a. bright   b. hot   **c. wet**
G-44 clear   a. bright   **b. cloudy**   c. sunny
G-45 hot   **a. cold**   b. heat   c. warm
G-46 sunny   a. bright   **b. cloudy**   c. hot
G-47 rainy   a. cloudy   b. cold   **c. sunny**
G-48 big   a. large   **b. little**   c. tall
G-49 warm   a. bright   b. clothes   **c. cool**
G-50 boiling   a. baking   b. cooking   **c. freezing**
G-51 heavy   a. firm   **b. light**   c. weight

183

Top-right panel (page 184):

BUILDING THINKING SKILLS® — BOOK ONE   VERBAL SIMILARITIES AND DIFFERENCES

OPPOSITES—SELECT

DIRECTIONS: Each line contains four words about amount or time. Read the first word and think about what it means. One of the next three words will mean the opposite of the first word. Underline the word that is the opposite of the first word.

G-52 often   a. again   b. repeat   **c. seldom**
G-53 always   **a. never**   b. often   c. some
G-54 tight   **a. loose**   b. close   c. sharp
G-55 none   a. empty   b. nothing   **c. some**
G-56 all   a. every   **b. none**   c. some
G-57 now   a. here   b. often   **c. then**
G-58 many   a. all   **b. few**   c. none
G-59 past   a. before   **b. future**   c. then
G-60 everything   a. all   **b. nothing**   c. something

194

Middle-left panel (page 185):

BUILDING THINKING SKILLS® — BOOK ONE   VERBAL SIMILARITIES AND DIFFERENCES

OPPOSITES—SELECT

DIRECTIONS: Each line contains four words used in art lessons. Read the first word and think about what it means. One of the next three words will mean the opposite of the first word. Underline the word that is the opposite of the first.

G-61 dark   a. dim   b. heavy   **c. light**
G-62 small   a. heavy   **b. large**   c. little
G-63 dull   **a. bright**   b. dim   c. light
G-64 smooth   a. glass   **b. rough**   c. slick
G-65 tall   a. high   **b. short**   c. round
G-66 easy   a. soft   b. simple   **c. hard**
G-67 fine   **a. coarse**   b. dim   c. soft
G-68 thick   a. fat   **b. thin**   c. wide
G-69 zigzag   a. bumpy   **b. straight**   c. up and down

185

Middle-middle panel (page 186):

BUILDING THINKING SKILLS® — BOOK ONE   VERBAL SIMILARITIES AND DIFFERENCES

OPPOSITES—SUPPLY

DIRECTIONS: Each line contains a word. Read the given word and think about what it means. Think of a word that means the opposite. Write the word that you think of. (If you can think of other opposites, write them all down.)

G-70 fast   *slow OR eat*
G-71 love   *hate, dislike*
G-72 leader   *follower*
G-73 clean   *dirty, filthy, unclean*
G-74 happy   *sad, down, depressed, unhappy*
G-75 whisper   *shout, yell, scream, cry, roar*
G-76 lost   *found, returned, regained OR won*
G-77 work   *play, recreation, game, sport*
G-78 asleep   *awake*

186

Middle-right panel (page 187):

BUILDING THINKING SKILLS® — BOOK ONE   VERBAL SIMILARITIES AND DIFFERENCES

OPPOSITES—SUPPLY

DIRECTIONS: Each line contains a "direction" word. Read the given word and think about what it means. Think of a word that means the opposite. Write the word that you think of. (If you can think of other opposites, write them all down.)

G-79 close   *far, distant, remote, removed*
G-80 start   *stop, finish, complete, end, halt*
G-81 true   *false, fake, phony*
G-82 ahead   *behind, after*
G-83 front   *rear, back, tail, end*
G-84 top   *bottom, base, floor, foot, ground*
G-85 later   *earlier, sooner, before, first*
G-86 remember   *forget*
G-87 receive   *give, donate, present, offer*

187

Bottom-left panel (page 188):

BUILDING THINKING SKILLS® — BOOK ONE   VERBAL SIMILARITIES AND DIFFERENCES

OPPOSITES—SUPPLY

DIRECTIONS: Each line contains a word about action, amount, or order. Read the given word and think about what it means. Think of a word that means the opposite and write it. (If you can think of other opposites, write them all down.)

G-88 dark   *light*
G-89 go   *stop, stay, halt*
G-90 run   *walk, stroll*
G-91 many   *few, some, couple*
G-92 none   *all, some, several, lots*
G-93 more   *less*
G-94 after   *before*
G-95 last   *first*
G-96 never   *always*

188

Bottom-middle panel (page 189):

BUILDING THINKING SKILLS® — BOOK ONE   VERBAL SIMILARITIES AND DIFFERENCES

SIMILARITIES—SELECT

DIRECTIONS: Each line contains four words. Read the first word and think about what it means. One of the next three words will mean almost the same thing. Circle the word that is most like the first word.

EXAMPLE   sneaker   a. roller skate   **b. shoe**   c. sock
G-97   shovel   a. hammer   **b. hoe**   c. paint brush
G-98   automobile   a. airplane   b. bicycle   **c. jeep**
G-99   garage   **a. barn**   b. school   c. store
G-100   grocery store   a. apartment   b. hospital   **c. supermarket**

189

Bottom-right panel (page 190):

BUILDING THINKING SKILLS® — BOOK ONE   VERBAL SIMILARITIES AND DIFFERENCES

SIMILARITIES—SELECT

DIRECTIONS: Each line contains four science or health words. Read the first word and think about what it means. One of the next three words will mean almost the same thing. Circle the word that is most like the first word.

G-101   pine   a. carrot   b. daisy   **c. oak**
G-102   chicken   a. cat   b. dog   **c. turkey**
G-103   cheese   **a. butter**   b. eggs   c. milk
G-104   snake   a. fish   **b. lizard**   c. shark
G-105   pea   **a. bean**   b. carrot   c. potato

190

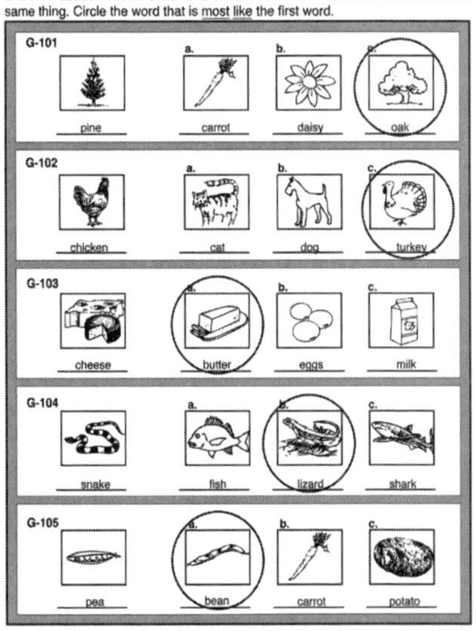

SIMILARITIES—SELECT

DIRECTIONS: Each line contains four words that tell what you do at school. Read the first word and think about what it means. One of the next three words will mean almost the same thing. Underline the word that is most like the first word.

G-106	listen	a. hear (circled)	b. speak	c. talk
G-107	talk	a. read	b. say (circled)	c. sing
G-108	draw	a. around	b. color (circled)	c. work
G-109	study	a. learn (circled)	b. lesson	c. talk
G-110	act	a. do (circled)	b. relax	c. rest
G-111	learn	a. discover (circled)	b. reply	c. show
G-112	ask	a. about	b. receive	c. question (circled)
G-113	answer	a. hear	b. reply (circled)	c. question
G-114	solve	a. ask	b. figure out (circled)	c. problem

SIMILARITIES—SELECT

DIRECTIONS: Each line contains four household words. Read the first word and think about what it means. One of the next three words will mean almost the same thing. Underline the word that is most like the first word.

G-115	newspaper	a. book	b. dictionary	c. magazine (circled)
G-116	cook	a. bake (circled)	b. dinner	c. soup
G-117	fix	a. build	b. repair (circled)	c. wreck
G-118	door	a. gate (circled)	b. roof	c. window
G-119	rug	a. carpet (circled)	b. floor	c. sweeper
G-120	curtains	a. drapes (circled)	b. door	c. window
G-121	clean	a. clothes	b. house	c. wash (circled)
G-122	meal	a. cook	b. dinner (circled)	c. vegetable
G-123	broom	a. sponge	b. handle	c. sweeper (circled)

SIMILARITIES—SELECT

DIRECTIONS: Each line contains four action words. Read the first word and think about what it means. One of the next three words will mean almost the same thing. Underline the word that is most like the first word.

G-124	pay	a. owe	b. spend (circled)	c. take
G-125	run	a. jog (circled)	b. sit	c. walk
G-126	look	a. hear	b. talk	c. watch (circled)
G-127	stay	a. go	b. leave	c. remain (circled)
G-128	call	a. say	b. shout (circled)	c. tell
G-129	take	a. carry (circled)	b. give	c. keep
G-130	throw	a. toss (circled)	b. catch	c. hit
G-131	build	a. fix	b. make (circled)	c. repair
G-132	hide	a. cover (circled)	b. seek	c. show

SIMILARITIES—SELECT

DIRECTIONS: Each line contains four words from science. Read the first word and think about what it means. One of the next three words will mean almost the same thing. Underline the word that is most like the first word.

G-133	sound	a. noise (circled)	b. quiet	c. silence
G-134	heat	a. light	b. stove	c. warmth (circled)
G-135	sun	a. beam	b. shine	c. star (circled)
G-136	rock	a. mountain	b. ocean	c. stone (circled)
G-137	fog	a. cloud (circled)	b. ice	c. snow
G-138	beak	a. bill (circled)	b. claw	c. wing
G-139	baby	a. brother	b. child (circled)	c. sister
G-140	earth	a. continent	b. country	c. world (circled)
G-141	map	a. country	b. drawing (circled)	c. photograph

SIMILARITIES—SUPPLY

DIRECTIONS: Each line contains a word used to describe something. Read the word and think about what it means. Think of a word or phrase that means almost the same and write it down. Write as many similar words as you can think of.

G-142	short	*not long, not tall, brief, rude, sudden*
G-143	big	*heavy, tall, large*
G-144	friendly	*helpful, nice, loving, caring*
G-145	heavy	*fat, stout, not light, massive, severe, forceful*
G-146	happy	*joyful, glad, pleased, satisfied, content*
G-147	good	*worthy, helpful, proper, right*
G-148	sweet	*pleasant, nice, sugary*
G-149	beautiful	*attractive, good-looking, handsome, pretty*
G-150	safe	*secure, unhurt, healthy, unharmed*

Sample Answer

SIMILARITIES—SUPPLY

DIRECTIONS: Each line contains an action word. Read the word and think about what it means. Think of a word or phrase that means almost the same and write it down. Write as many similar words as you can think of.

G-151	touch	*feel, handle, pet, pat*
G-152	see	*look, notice, watch, observe, view*
G-153	hear	*listen, find out, learn*
G-154	speak	*converse, talk, say, utter, lecture*
G-155	work	*job, occupation, employment, chore, effort*
G-156	study	*learn, examine, inspect, ponder, think about*
G-157	build	*assemble, construct, make, manufacture*
G-158	fix	*mend, repair, rebuild, overhaul*
G-159	destroy	*demolish, dismantle, ruin, wreck, tear down*

Sample Answer

SIMILARITIES—SUPPLY

DIRECTIONS: Each line contains a word used in instructions. Read the word and think about what it means. Think of a word or phrase that means almost the same and write it down. Write as many similar words as you can think of.

G-160	leave	*go, exit, quit, depart*
G-161	above	*aloft, higher, over, overhead*
G-162	enter	*admit, come in, enroll, join*
G-163	below	*beneath, under, underneath*
G-164	continue	*carry on, endure, last, persist, remain*
G-165	stop	*halt, end, close up, block, quit, cease*
G-166	choose	*elect, pick, select, take, want*
G-167	listen	*hear, learn, find out*
G-168	fasten	*adhere, attach, link, unite, join, affix*

Sample Answer

HOW ALIKE?—SELECT

DIRECTIONS: Each activity contains two pictures. Think about the ways these two things are alike. Circle the letters of the sentences that are true of both items.

EXAMPLE

bus   truck

a. Both are owned by schools and are used to carry children.
b. Both have large engines. (circled)
c. Both travel on roads. (circled)
d. Both are used to carry furniture.

G-169

candle   lamp

a. Both are electric.
b. Both are warm or hot to the touch. (circled)
c. Both burn out. (circled)
d. Both can give out light. (circled)

G-170

ear   eye

a. Both can get infected. (circled)
b. Both can close themselves.
c. Both can be used to learn. (circled)
d. Both sense either sound or light. (circled)

G-171

apple   tomato

a. Both are vegetables.
b. Both can be red when ripe. (circled)
c. Both grow on trees.
d. Both are part of a plant. (circled)

HOW ALIKE?—SELECT

DIRECTIONS: Each activity contains two pictures. Think about the ways these two things are alike. Circle the letters of the sentences that are true of both items.

G-172

stop sign   traffic light

a. Both always tell you to stop.
b. Both are electric.
c. Both can be red. (circled)
d. Both are used to give directions. (circled)

G-173

door   gate

a. Both can be locked. (circled)
b. Both can be made of wood. (circled)
c. Both can be opened. (circled)
d. Both lead into the house.

G-174

dryer   stove

a. Both are electric. (circled)
b. Both are used for cooking.
c. Both get hot when turned on. (circled)
d. Both are in the laundry room.

G-175

laptop computer   television

a. Both are electric. (circled)
b. Both can play games.
c. Both can play movies. (circled)
d. Both are in most automobiles.

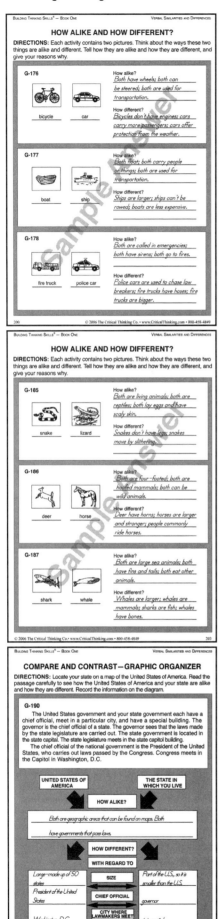

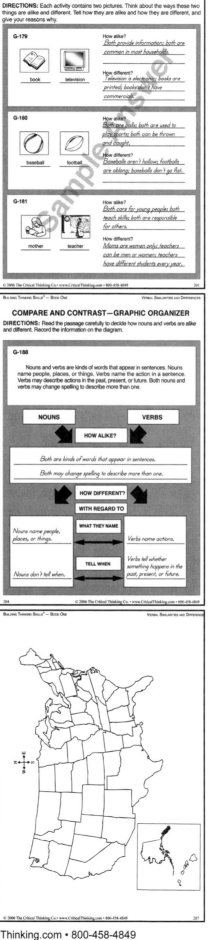

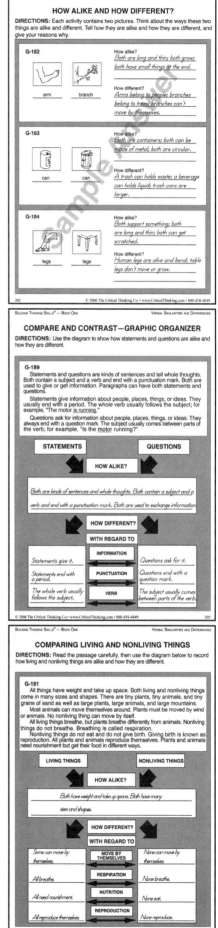

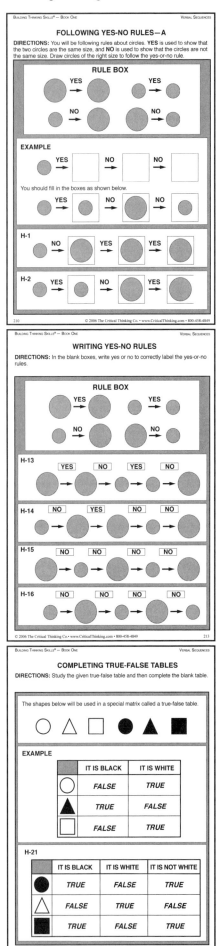

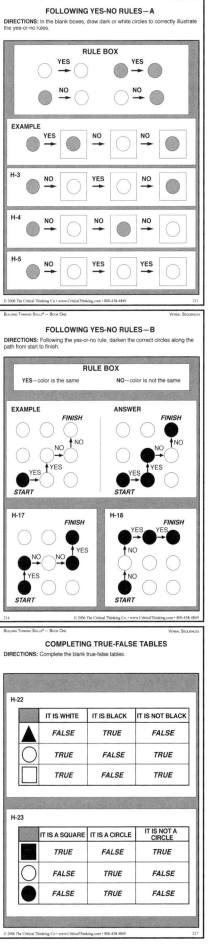

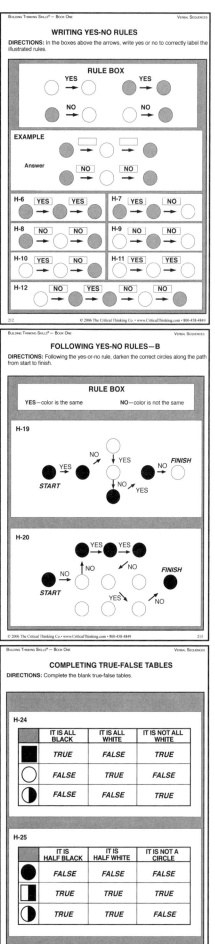

FINDING LOCATIONS ON MAPS

DIRECTIONS: Using the map, follow the directions or answer the question in each exercise.

TINY TOWN

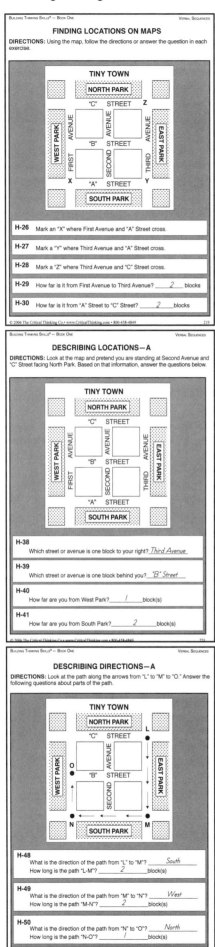

H-26 Mark an "X" where First Avenue and "A" Street cross.

H-27 Mark a "Y" where Third Avenue and "A" Street cross.

H-28 Mark a "Z" where Third Avenue and "C" Street cross.

H-29 How far is it from First Avenue to Third Avenue? __2__ blocks

H-30 How far is it from "A" Street to "C" Street? __2__ blocks

---

FINDING LOCATIONS ON MAPS

DIRECTIONS: Using the map, follow the directions or answer the question in each exercise.

TINY TOWN

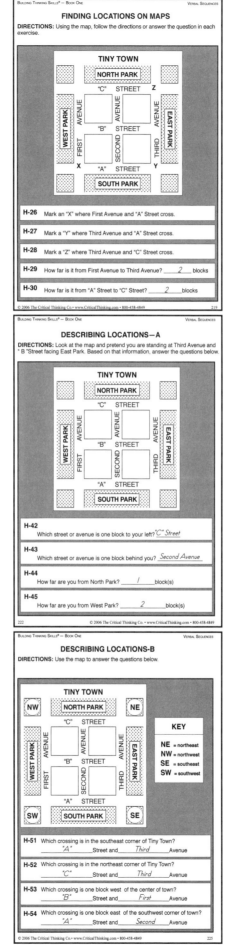

H-26 Mark an "X" where First Avenue and "A" Street cross.

H-27 Mark a "Y" where Third Avenue and "A" Street cross.

H-28 Mark a "Z" where Third Avenue and "C" Street cross.

H-29 How far is it from First Avenue to Third Avenue? __2__ blocks

H-30 How far is it from "A" Street to "C" Street? __2__ blocks

---

FINDING LOCATIONS ON MAPS

DIRECTIONS: Using the map, follow the directions or answer the question in each exercise.

TINY TOWN

H-31 Print a "P" where Second Avenue and "B" Street cross.

H-32 Print a "Q" where First Avenue and "C" Street cross.

H-33 Print an "R" where Third Avenue and "A" Street cross.

H-34 Which letter (P, Q, or R) is closest to East Park? _R_

H-35 Which letter (P, Q, or R) is at the center of town? _P_

H-36 Which letter (P, Q, or R) is in the northern part of town? _Q_

H-37 Which street ("A," "B," or "C") is the farthest south? _"A"_

DESCRIBING LOCATIONS—A

DIRECTIONS: Look at the map and pretend you are standing at Second Avenue and "C" Street facing North Park. Based on that information, answer the questions below.

TINY TOWN

H-38 Which street or avenue is one block to your right? _Third Avenue_

H-39 Which street or avenue is one block behind you? _"B" Street_

H-40 How far are you from West Park? _1_ block(s)

H-41 How far are you from South Park? _2_ block(s)

DESCRIBING LOCATIONS—A

DIRECTIONS: Look at the map and pretend you are standing at Third Avenue and "B" Street facing East Park. Based on that information, answer the questions below.

TINY TOWN

H-42 Which street or avenue is one block to your left? _"C" Street_

H-43 Which street or avenue is one block behind you? _Second Avenue_

H-44 How far are you from North Park? _1_ block(s)

H-45 How far are you from West Park? _2_ block(s)

DESCRIBING DIRECTIONS—A

DIRECTIONS: Look at the path along the arrows from "P" to "Q" to "R." Answer the following questions about parts of the path.

TINY TOWN

H-46 What is the direction of the path from "P" to "Q"? _North_
How many blocks long is the path from "P" to "Q"? _2 blocks_

H-47 What is the direction of the path from "Q" to "R"? _East_
How many blocks long is the path from "Q" to "R"? _1 block_

DESCRIBING DIRECTIONS—A

DIRECTIONS: Look at the path along the arrows from "L" to "M" to "O." Answer the following questions about parts of the path.

TINY TOWN

H-48 What is the direction of the path from "L" to "M"? _South_
How long is the path "L-M"? _2_ block(s)

H-49 What is the direction of the path from "M" to "N"? _West_
How long is the path "M-N"? _2_ block(s)

H-50 What is the direction of the path from "N" to "O"? _North_
How long is the path "N-O"? _1_ block(s)

DESCRIBING LOCATIONS-B

DIRECTIONS: Use the map to answer the questions below.

TINY TOWN

KEY
NE = northeast
NW = northwest
SE = southeast
SW = southwest

H-51 Which crossing is in the southeast corner of Tiny Town?
_"A"_ Street and _Third_ Avenue

H-52 Which crossing is in the northeast corner of Tiny Town?
_"C"_ Street and _Third_ Avenue

H-53 Which crossing is one block west of the center of town?
_"B"_ Street and _First_ Avenue

H-54 Which crossing is one block east of the southwest corner of town?
_"A"_ Street and _Second_ Avenue

DESCRIBING DIRECTIONS-B

DIRECTIONS: If you start at Second Avenue and "C" Street and travel two blocks south, you will be on the corner of Second Avenue and "A" Street (follow the arrow from START to FINISH). Answer the questions below.

TINY TOWN

H-55 If you start at First Avenue and "B" Street and travel two blocks east, where will you be?
Where _"B"_ Street meets _Third_ Avenue

H-56 If you start at the corner of Third Avenue and "A" Street and travel two blocks north, where will you be?
Where _"C"_ Street meets _Third_ Avenue

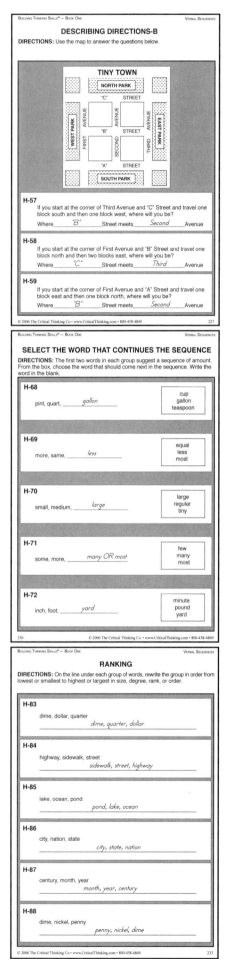

DESCRIBING DIRECTIONS-B

DIRECTIONS: Use the map to answer the questions below.

TINY TOWN

H-57
If you start at the corner of Third Avenue and "C" Street and travel one block south and then one block west, where will you be?
Where "B" Street meets Second Avenue

H-58
If you start at the corner of First Avenue and "B" Street and travel one block north and then two blocks east, where will you be?
Where "C" Street meets Third Avenue

H-59
If you start at the corner of First Avenue and "A" Street and travel one block east and then one block north, where will you be?
Where "B" Street meets Second Avenue

227

DESCRIBING DIRECTIONS—B

DIRECTIONS: Use the map to answer the questions below.

TINY TOWN

H-60
If you start at the corner of First Avenue and "C" Street and travel one block east and then two blocks south, where will you be?
Where "A" Street meets Second Avenue

H-61
If you start at the corner of Second Avenue and "B" Street and travel one block south and then one block west, where will you be?
Where "A" Street meets First Avenue

H-62
If you start at the corner of First Avenue and "A" Street and travel two blocks north and then one block east, where will you be?
Where "C" Street meets Second Avenue

228

SELECT THE WORD THAT CONTINUES THE SEQUENCE

DIRECTIONS: The first two words in each group suggest a time sequence. From the box, choose the word that should come next in the sequence. Write the word in the blank.

H-63
before, during, _after_

after
beside
whole

H-64
Monday, Tuesday, _Wednesday_

Saturday
Sunday
Wednesday

H-65
day, month, _year_

hour
week
year

H-66
first, second, _third_

beginning
last
third

H-67
Halloween, Thanksgiving, _Christmas_

April Fool's Day
Christmas
Labor Day

229

SELECT THE WORD THAT CONTINUES THE SEQUENCE

DIRECTIONS: The first two words in each group suggest a sequence of amount. From the box, choose the word that should come next in the sequence. Write the word in the blank.

H-68
pint, quart, _gallon_

cup
gallon
teaspoon

H-69
more, same, _less_

equal
less
most

H-70
small, medium, _large_

large
regular
tiny

H-71
some, more, _many OR most_

few
many
most

H-72
inch, foot, _yard_

minute
pound
yard

230

SELECT THE WORD THAT CONTINUES THE SEQUENCE

DIRECTIONS: The first two words in each group suggest a sequence of rank, degree, size, or order. From the box, choose the word that should come next in the sequence. Write the word in the blank.

H-73
above, beside, _below_

below
between
over

H-74
bad, worse, _worst_

better
less
worst

H-75
boy, teen, _man_

baby
child
man

H-76
enter, stay, _leave_

arrive
leave
remain

H-77
good, better, _best_

best
well
worst

231

RANKING

DIRECTIONS: On the line under each group of words, rewrite the group in order from lowest or smallest to highest or largest in size, degree, rank, or order.

EXAMPLE
all, none, some
none, some, all

H-78
afternoon, morning, night
morning, afternoon, night

H-79
always, never, sometimes
never, sometimes, always

H-80
giant, large, regular
regular, large, giant

H-81
many, more, most
many, more, most

H-82
first, last, middle
first, middle, last

232

RANKING

DIRECTIONS: On the line under each group of words, rewrite the group in order from lowest or smallest to highest or largest in size, degree, rank, or order.

H-83
dime, dollar, quarter
dime, quarter, dollar

H-84
highway, sidewalk, street
sidewalk, street, highway

H-85
lake, ocean, pond
pond, lake, ocean

H-86
city, nation, state
city, state, nation

H-87
century, month, year
month, year, century

H-88
dime, nickel, penny
penny, nickel, dime

233

RANKING

DIRECTIONS: On the line under each group of words, rewrite the group in order from lowest or smallest to highest or largest in size, degree, rank, or order.

H-89
body, head, tail
tail, body, head

H-90
rope, string, thread
thread, string, rope

H-91
game, inning, out
out, inning, game

H-92
continue, finish, start
start, continue, finish

H-93
book, page, word
word, page, book

H-94
baseball, basketball, Ping-Pong ball
Ping-Pong ball, baseball, basketball

234

SUPPLY A WORD THAT CONTINUES A SEQUENCE

DIRECTIONS: The first two words in each sequence suggest a degree, rank, size, or order. Think of a word that will continue the sequence and write it on the line. You may use a dictionary to get help.

H-95
second, minute, _hour_

H-96
ready, set, _go_

H-97
March, April, _May_

H-98
breakfast, lunch, _dinner_

H-99
inch, foot, _yard_

H-100
small, medium, _large_

H-101
beginning, middle, _end_

H-102
spring, summer, _fall_

H-103
penny, nickel, _dime_

Sample Answer

235

354

BUILDING THINKING SKILLS® — BOOK ONE   VERBAL SEQUENCES

SUPPLY A WORD THAT CONTINUES A SEQUENCE

DIRECTIONS: The first two words in each sequence suggest a degree, rank, size, or order. Think of a word that will continue the sequence and write it on the line. You may use a dictionary to get help.

H-104	ten, twenty, _____ *thirty*
H-105	yesterday, today, _____ *tomorrow*
H-106	second, third, _____ *fourth*
H-107	baby, girl, _____ *woman*
H-108	ounce, pound, _____ *ton*
H-109	go, going, _____ *gone*
H-110	white, gray, _____ *black*
H-111	cook, serve, _____ *eat*
H-112	one, three, _____ *five*

(Sample Answer watermark)

236   © 2006 The Critical Thinking Co.• www.CriticalThinking.com • 800-458-4849

BUILDING THINKING SKILLS® — BOOK ONE   VERBAL SEQUENCES

WARM-UP DEDUCTIVE REASONING

DIRECTIONS: The example below shows how to complete the exercises on the following pages, in which people are being compared. Given the clues in the sentences, you can determine who is the fastest swimmer (see the directions below).

EXAMPLE

Maria swims faster than Fred. Kim swims faster than Maria.
Who swims the fastest? _____

HOW TO FIGURE IT OUT

STEP1: Read the first clue and write the names, with the faster swimmer on top, in the space below.

Maria swims faster than Fred. Kim swims faster than Maria.

Maria
Fred

STEP2: Read the second clue and decide how Kim compares to the other two. Since Kim is faster than Maria, her name should be on top.

Maria swims faster than Fred. **Kim swims faster than Maria.**

Kim
Maria
Fred

Now you can answer that Kim swims the fastest(see below).

EXAMPLE

Maria swims faster than Fred. Kim swims faster than Maria.
Who swims the fastest? **Kim**

Kim
Maria
Fred

© 2006 The Critical Thinking Co.• www.CriticalThinking.com • 800-458-4849   237

BUILDING THINKING SKILLS® — BOOK ONE   VERBAL SEQUENCES

WARM-UP DEDUCTIVE REASONING

DIRECTIONS: In the sentences below, people are being compared according to some characteristic (weight, age, height, score, etc.). Read the sentences; in the space below the sentences, write the names in order, then answer the question.

H-113
Charlie is heavier than Bill. Bill is heavier than Albert.
Who is the heaviest? *Charlie*

Charlie
Bill
Albert

H-114
James is younger than Alice. Betty is younger than James.
Who is the youngest? *Betty*

Betty
James
Alice

H-115
Sally has more cats than Clare. Irene has more cats than Sally.
Who has the most cats? *Irene*

Irene
Sally
Clare

238   © 2006 The Critical Thinking Co.• www.CriticalThinking.com • 800-458-4849

BUILDING THINKING SKILLS® — BOOK ONE   VERBAL SEQUENCES

WARM-UP DEDUCTIVE REASONING

DIRECTIONS: In the sentences below, people are being compared according to some characteristic (weight, age, height, score, etc.). Read the sentences and fill in the blanks.

H-116
Doug runs faster than Ivan. Ivan runs faster than Lee.
List the runners in order from fastest to slowest.
Doug   *Ivan*   *Lee*

List the runners in order from slowest to fastest.
Lee   *Ivan*   *Doug*

H-117
John is older than Sam but younger than Lois.
List the people in order from oldest to youngest.
Lois   *John*   *Sam*

List the people in order from youngest to oldest.
Sam   *John*   *Lois*

H-118
David is taller than Fred. Fred is taller than George. George is taller than Harold.
Who is the tallest? *David*

© 2006 The Critical Thinking Co.• www.CriticalThinking.com • 800-458-4849   239

BUILDING THINKING SKILLS® — BOOK ONE   VERBAL SEQUENCES

WARM-UP DEDUCTIVE REASONING

DIRECTIONS: In the sentences below, people are being compared according to some characteristic (weight, age, height, score, etc.). Read the sentences and fill in the blanks.

H-119
Delores is shorter than Mary. June is shorter than Delores. Mary is shorter than Nancy.
Who is the shortest? *June*
Who is the tallest? *Nancy*

H-120
Gina caught fewer fish than Spiro. Nick caught fewer fish than Gina.
List the people in order from the one who caught the most fish to the one who caught the fewest fish.
Spiro   *Gina*   *Nick*

List the people in order from the one who caught the fewest fish to the one who caught the most fish.
Nick   *Gina*   *Spiro*

H-121
Pedro is older than Jose but younger than Manuel.
List the people in order from youngest to oldest.
Jose   *Pedro*   *Manuel*

240   © 2006 The Critical Thinking Co.• www.CriticalThinking.com • 800-458-4849

BUILDING THINKING SKILLS® — BOOK ONE   VERBAL SEQUENCES

WARM-UP DEDUCTIVE REASONING

DIRECTIONS: In the sentences below, people are being compared according to some characteristic (weight, age, height, score, etc.). Read the sentences and fill in the blanks.

H-122
Emil made more points in a basketball game than Carlos. Emil did not make as many points as Larry.
List the boys in order from high scorer to low scorer.
Larry   *Emil*   *Carlos*

List the boys in order from low scorer to high scorer.
Carlos   *Emil*   *Larry*

H-123
Pedro got more hits than Sol but fewer than Nina.
List the players in order from the one who made the most hits to the one who made the fewest hits.
Nina   *Pedro*   *Sol*

List the players in order from the one who made the fewest hits to the one who made the most hits.
Sol   *Pedro*   *Nina*

H-124
John is taller than Marna but shorter than Larry.
List the people in order from tallest to shortest.
Larry   *John*   *Marna*

List the people in order from shortest to tallest.
Marna   *John*   *Larry*

© 2006 The Critical Thinking Co.• www.CriticalThinking.com • 800-458-4849   241

BUILDING THINKING SKILLS® — BOOK ONE   VERBAL SEQUENCES

DEDUCTIVE REASONING

DIRECTIONS: The example below shows how to solve a Mind Benders® problem. Study it before going on to the next pages.

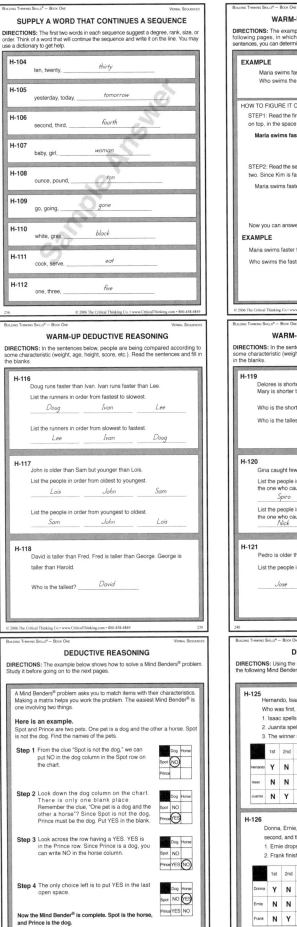

A Mind Benders® problem asks you to match items with their characteristics. Making a matrix helps you work the problem. The easiest Mind Bender® is one involving two things.

Here is an example.

Spot and Prince are two pets. One pet is a dog and the other a horse. Spot is not the dog. Find the names of the pets.

Step 1 From the clue "Spot is not the dog," we can put NO in the dog column in the Spot row on the chart.

Step 2 Look down the dog column on the chart. There is only one blank place. Remember the clue, "One pet is a dog and the other a horse"? Since Spot is not the dog, Prince must be the dog. Put YES in the blank.

Step 3 Look across the row having a YES. YES is in the Prince row. Since Prince is a dog, you can write NO in the horse column.

Step 4 The only choice left is to put YES in the last open space.

Now the Mind Bender® is complete. Spot is the horse, and Prince is the dog.

242   © 2006 The Critical Thinking Co.• www.CriticalThinking.com • 800-458-4849

BUILDING THINKING SKILLS® — BOOK ONE   VERBAL SEQUENCES

DEDUCTIVE REASONING

DIRECTIONS: Using the method given in the previous example, complete each of the following Mind Benders® problems.

H-125
Hernando, Isaac, and Juanita are in a spelling contest.
Who was first, second, and third in each contest.
1. Isaac spells three words correctly.
2. Juanita spells correctly one more word than Isaac.
3. The winner spells five words correctly.

	1st	2nd	3rd
Hernando	Y	N	N
Isaac	N	N	Y
Juanita	N	Y	N

Hernando was _____ *first*
Isaac was _____ *third*
Juanita was _____ *second*

H-126
Donna, Ernie, and Frank run a race. Who was first, second, and third in each contest.
1. Ernie drops out on the first lap.
2. Frank finishes behind Donna.

	1st	2nd	3rd
Donna	Y	N	N
Ernie	N	N	Y
Frank	N	Y	N

Donna was _____ *first*
Ernie was _____ *third*
Frank was _____ *second*

© 2006 The Critical Thinking Co.• www.CriticalThinking.com • 800-458-4849   243

BUILDING THINKING SKILLS® — BOOK ONE   VERBAL SEQUENCES

DEDUCTIVE REASONING

DIRECTIONS: Complete each of the following Mind Benders® problems.

H-127
Juan, Kyle, and Lori own bikes. The bikes are a one-speed, a three-speed, and a ten-speed.
Find out the owners of the three kinds of bikes.
1. Juan and Lori have bikes with more than one gear speed.
2. Lori's bike has the most gear speeds.

	1	3	10
Juan	N	Y	N
Kyle	Y	N	N
Lori	N	N	Y

The one-speed is owned by *Kyle*
The three-speed is owned by *Juan*
The ten-speed is owned by *Lori*

H-128
Three students—Green, Jones, and Perez—ride to school together. The students are in the second, third, and fourth grades.
Find out which student is in each grade.
1. Jones is in an odd-numbered grade.
2. Green is in a higher grade than Jones.

	Green	Jones	Perez
2	N	N	Y
3	N	Y	N
4	Y	N	N

Green is in the *fourth* grade.
Jones is in the *third* grade.
Perez is in the *second* grade.

244   © 2006 The Critical Thinking Co.• www.CriticalThinking.com • 800-458-4849

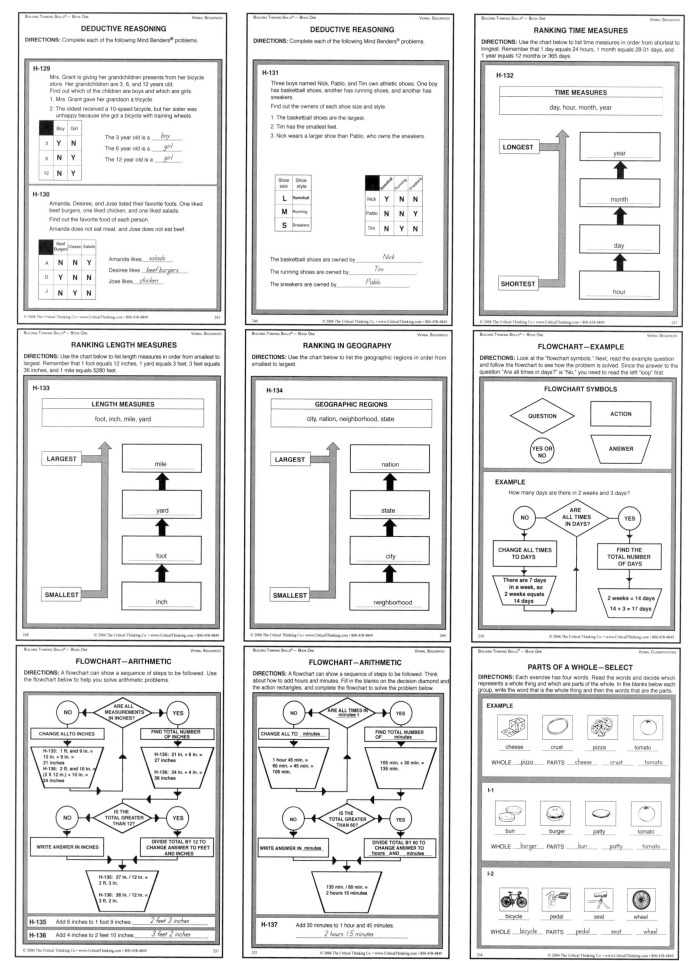

DEDUCTIVE REASONING

DIRECTIONS: Complete each of the following *Mind Benders®* problems.

H-129

Mrs. Grant is giving her grandchildren presents from her bicycle store. Her grandchildren are 3, 6, and 12 years old.
Find out which of the children are boys and which are girls.

1. Mrs. Grant gave her grandson a tricycle.

2. The oldest received a 10-speed bicycle, but her sister was unhappy because she got a bicycle with training wheels.

	Boy	Girl
3	Y	N
6	N	Y
12	N	Y

The 3 year old is a ___boy___

The 6 year old is a ___girl___

The 12 year old is a ___girl___

H-130

Amanda, Desiree, and Jose listed their favorite foots. One liked beef burgers, one liked chicken, and one liked salads.
Find out the favorite food of each person.

Amanda does not eat meat, and Jose does not eat beef.

	Beef Burgers	Chicken	Salads
A	N	N	Y
D	Y	N	N
J	N	Y	N

Amanda likes ___salads___

Desiree likes ___beef burgers___

Jose likes ___chicken___

DEDUCTIVE REASONING

DIRECTIONS: Complete each of the following *Mind Benders®* problems.

H-131

Three boys named Nick, Pablo, and Tim own athletic shoes. One boy has basketball shoes, another has running shoes, and another has sneakers.

Find out the owners of each shoe size and style.

1. The basketball shoes are the largest.

2. Tim has the smallest feet.

3. Nick wears a larger shoe than Pablo, who owns the sneakers.

Shoe size	Shoe style
L	Basketball
M	Running
S	Sneakers

	Basketball	Running	Sneakers
Nick	Y	N	N
Pablo	N	N	Y
Tim	N	Y	N

The basketball shoes are owned by ___Nick___

The running shoes are owned by ___Tim___

The sneakers are owned by ___Pablo___

RANKING TIME MEASURES

DIRECTIONS: Use the chart below to list time measures in order from shortest to longest. Remember that 1 day equals 24 hours, 1 month equals 28-31 days, and 1 year equals 12 months or 365 days.

H-132

TIME MEASURES

day, hour, month, year

LONGEST

year

month

day

SHORTEST

hour

RANKING LENGTH MEASURES

DIRECTIONS: Use the chart below to list length measures in order from smallest to largest. Remember that 1 foot equals 12 inches, 1 yard equals 3 feet, 3 feet equals 36 inches, and 1 mile equals 5280 feet.

H-133

LENGTH MEASURES

foot, inch, mile, yard

LARGEST

mile

yard

foot

SMALLEST

inch

RANKING IN GEOGRAPHY

DIRECTIONS: Use the chart below to list the geographic regions in order from smallest to largest.

H-134

GEOGRAPHIC REGIONS

city, nation, neighborhood, state

LARGEST

nation

state

city

SMALLEST

neighborhood

FLOWCHART—EXAMPLE

DIRECTIONS: Look at the "flowchart symbols." Next, read the example question and follow the flowchart to see how the problem is solved. Since the answer to the question "Are all times in days?" is "No," you need to read the left "loop" first.

FLOWCHART SYMBOLS

QUESTION

ACTION

YES OR NO

ANSWER

EXAMPLE

How many days are there in 2 weeks and 3 days?

NO ← ARE ALL TIMES IN DAYS? → YES

CHANGE ALL TIMES TO DAYS

FIND THE TOTAL NUMBER OF DAYS

There are 7 days in a week, so 2 weeks equals 14 days

2 weeks = 14 days
14 + 3 = 17 days

FLOWCHART—ARITHMETIC

DIRECTIONS: A flowchart can show a sequence of steps to be followed. Use the flowchart below to help you solve arithmetic problems.

NO ← ARE ALL MEASUREMENTS IN INCHES? → YES

CHANGE ALL TO INCHES

FIND TOTAL NUMBER OF INCHES

H-135: 1 ft. and 9 in. = 12 in. + 9 in. = 21 inches
H-136: 2 ft. and 10 in. = (2 X 12 in.) + 10 in. = 34 inches

H-135: 21 in. + 6 in. = 27 inches
H-136: 34 in. + 4 in. = 38 inches

NO ← IS THE TOTAL GREATER THAN 12? → YES

WRITE ANSWER IN INCHES

DIVIDE TOTAL BY 12 TO CHANGE ANSWER TO FEET AND INCHES

H-135: 27 in. / 12 in. = 2 ft. 3 in.
H-136: 38 in. / 12 in. = 3 ft. 2 in.

H-135 Add 6 inches to 1 foot 9 inches. ___2 feet 3 inches___

H-136 Add 4 inches to 2 feet 10 inches. ___3 feet 2 inches___

FLOWCHART—ARITHMETIC

DIRECTIONS: A flowchart can show a sequence of steps to be followed. Think about how to add hours and minutes. Fill in the blanks on the decision diamond and the action rectangles, and complete the flowchart to solve the problem below.

NO ← ARE ALL TIMES IN ___minutes___? → YES

CHANGE ALL TO ___minutes___

FIND TOTAL NUMBER OF ___minutes___

1 hour 45 min. = 60 min. + 45 min. = 105 min.

105 min. + 30 min. = 135 min.

NO ← IS THE TOTAL GREATER THAN 60? → YES

WRITE ANSWER IN ___minutes___

DIVIDE TOTAL BY 60 TO CHANGE ANSWER TO hours ___AND___ ___minutes___

135 min. / 60 min. = 2 hours 15 minutes

H-137 Add 30 minutes to 1 hour and 45 minutes. ___2 hours 15 minutes___

PARTS OF A WHOLE—SELECT

DIRECTIONS: Each exercise has four words. Read the words and decide which represents a whole thing and which are parts of the whole. In the blanks below each group, write the word that is the whole thing and then the words that are the parts.

EXAMPLE

cheese   crust   pizza   tomato

WHOLE ___pizza___ PARTS ___cheese___ ___crust___ ___tomato___

I-1

bun   burger   patty   tomato

WHOLE ___burger___ PARTS ___bun___ ___patty___ ___tomato___

I-2

bicycle   pedal   seat   wheel

WHOLE ___bicycle___ PARTS ___pedal___ ___seat___ ___wheel___

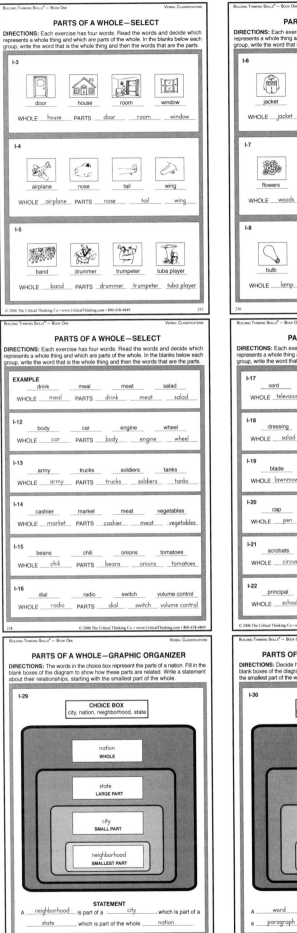
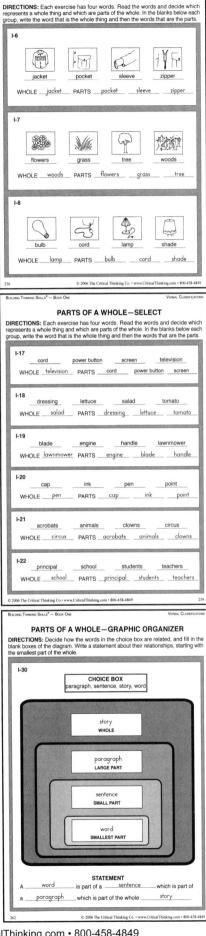

PARTS OF A WHOLE—SELECT

DIRECTIONS: Each exercise has four words. Read the words and decide which represents a whole thing and which are parts of the whole. In the blanks below each group, write the word that is the whole thing and then the words that are the parts.

I-3 door | house | room | window
WHOLE house PARTS door room window

I-4 airplane | nose | tail | wing
WHOLE airplane PARTS nose tail wing

I-5 band | drummer | trumpeter | tuba player
WHOLE band PARTS drummer trumpeter tuba player

I-6 jacket | pocket | sleeve | zipper
WHOLE jacket PARTS pocket sleeve zipper

I-7 flowers | grass | tree | woods
WHOLE woods PARTS flowers grass tree

I-8 bulb | cord | lamp | shade
WHOLE lamp PARTS bulb cord shade

I-9 arm | body | head | leg
WHOLE body PARTS arm head leg

I-10 branch | leaves | tree | trunk
WHOLE tree PARTS branch leaves trunk

I-11 bull | calf | cow | herd
WHOLE herd PARTS bull calf cow

PARTS OF A WHOLE—SELECT

EXAMPLE drink | meal | meat | salad
WHOLE meal PARTS drink meat salad

I-12 body | car | engine | wheel
WHOLE car PARTS body engine wheel

I-13 army | trucks | soldiers | tanks
WHOLE army PARTS trucks soldiers tanks

I-14 cashier | market | meat | vegetables
WHOLE market PARTS cashier meat vegetables

I-15 beans | chili | onions | tomatoes
WHOLE chili PARTS beans onions tomatoes

I-16 dial | radio | switch | volume control
WHOLE radio PARTS dial switch volume control

I-17 cord | power button | screen | television
WHOLE television PARTS cord power button screen

I-18 dressing | lettuce | salad | tomato
WHOLE salad PARTS dressing lettuce tomato

I-19 blade | engine | handle | lawnmower
WHOLE lawnmower PARTS engine blade handle

I-20 cap | ink | pen | point
WHOLE pen PARTS cap ink point

I-21 acrobats | animals | clowns | circus
WHOLE circus PARTS acrobats animals clowns

I-22 principal | school | students | teachers
WHOLE school PARTS principal students teachers

I-23 addition | arithmetic | numbers | subtraction
WHOLE arithmetic PARTS addition numbers subtraction

I-24 adjectives | language | nouns | verbs
WHOLE language PARTS adjectives nouns verbs

I-25 government | judge | president | senator
WHOLE government PARTS judge president senator

I-26 cover | book | pages | words
WHOLE book PARTS cover pages words

I-27 schools | houses | stores | city
WHOLE city PARTS houses stores schools

I-28 key | map | mountains | rivers
WHOLE map PARTS mountains key rivers

PARTS OF A WHOLE—GRAPHIC ORGANIZER

DIRECTIONS: The words in the choice box represent the parts of a nation. Fill in the blank boxes of the diagram to show how these parts are related. Write a statement about their relationships, starting with the smallest part of the whole.

I-29
CHOICE BOX: city, nation, neighborhood, state
- nation — WHOLE
- state — LARGE PART
- city — SMALL PART
- neighborhood — SMALLEST PART

STATEMENT
A neighborhood is part of a city, which is part of a state, which is part of the whole nation

PARTS OF A WHOLE—GRAPHIC ORGANIZER

DIRECTIONS: Decide how the words in the choice box are related, and fill in the blank boxes of the diagram. Write a statement about their relationships, starting with the smallest part of the whole.

I-30
CHOICE BOX: paragraph, sentence, story, word
- story — WHOLE
- paragraph — LARGE PART
- sentence — SMALL PART
- word — SMALLEST PART

STATEMENT
A word is part of a sentence, which is part of a paragraph, which is part of the whole story

CLASS AND MEMBERS—SELECT

DIRECTIONS: In each exercise are four words. Read the words and decide which represents a class to which the others belong. In the blanks below each group, write the word that represents the class and then the words that are its members.

EXAMPLE coin | dime | nickel | penny
CLASS coin MEMBERS dime nickel penny

I-31 clothing | coat | hat | pants
CLASS clothing MEMBERS coat hat pants

I-32 baseball | basketball | football | sport
CLASS sport MEMBERS baseball basketball football

I-33 blue | color | green | red
CLASS color MEMBERS blue green red

I-34 hammer | saw | screwdriver | tool
CLASS tool MEMBERS hammer saw screwdriver

I-35 arithmetic | reading | school subject | writing
CLASS school subject MEMBERS arithmetic reading writing

CLASS AND MEMBERS—SELECT

DIRECTIONS: Each exercise has four words. Read the words and decide which represents a class to which the others belong. In the blanks below each group, write the word that represents the class and then the words that are its members.

I-36
English   French   language   Spanish
CLASS _language_ MEMBERS _English_ _French_ _Spanish_

I-37
corn   grain   oats   wheat
CLASS _grain_ MEMBERS _corn_ _oats_ _wheat_

I-38
bass   fish   salmon   tuna
CLASS _fish_ MEMBERS _bass_ _salmon_ _tuna_

I-39
fruit   grain   plant   vegetable
CLASS _plant_ MEMBERS _fruit_ _grain_ _vegetable_

I-40
animal   bird   fish   reptile
CLASS _animal_ MEMBERS _bird_ _fish_ _reptile_

I-41
oak   palm   pine   tree
CLASS _tree_ MEMBERS _oak_ _palm_ _pine_

264

WHAT IS TRUE OF BOTH WORDS?—SELECT

DIRECTIONS: Decide what the following pairs of words have in common. Circle the letters of the characteristics that are true of both items.

EXAMPLE
ambulance   fire truck
a. is an emergency vehicle
b. carries sick people
c. has sirens
d. is used to fight fires

I-42
home   school
a. has an auditorium
b. has rooms
c. people learn there
d. people sleep there

I-43
post office   supermarket
a. people use scales there
b. people buy food there
c. people mail packages there
d. people work there

I-44
car   train
a. carries people
b. has an engine and wheels
c. is driven on the road
d. runs on a track

265

WHAT IS TRUE OF BOTH WORDS?—SELECT

DIRECTIONS: Decide what the following pairs of words have in common. Circle the letters of the characteristics that are true of both items.

I-45
chicken   turkey
a. flies well
b. is eaten
c. lays eggs
d. has a long neck

I-46
banana   pear
a. is a fruit
b. grows on trees
c. is a vegetable
d. can be yellow

I-47
cat   dog
a. barks
b. climbs trees
c. is furry
d. is a pet

I-48
lettuce   onion
a. can be used on sandwiches
b. has green leaves
c. makes your eyes water
d. is a vegetable

266

WHAT IS TRUE OF BOTH WORDS?—SELECT

DIRECTIONS: Decide what the following pairs of words have in common. Circle the letters of the characteristics that are true of both items.

I-49
clock   watch
a. fits on the wrist
b. is often round in shape
c. plugs into an electric socket
d. tells time

I-50
boat   duck
a. is an animal
b. grows on trees
c. can float
d. is a vehicle

I-51
moon   sun
a. always looks round
b. is in the sky
c. is round
d. shines only during the day

I-52
horse   motorcycle
a. is an animal
b. can carry one or two people
c. can move
d. is a vehicle

267

HOW ARE THESE WORDS ALIKE?—SELECT

DIRECTIONS: Decide what the words in each group have in common. Circle the letter of the one answer that best describes the class of the words.

I-53
door   gate   window
CLASS
a. entrance
b. front
c. opening

I-54
basket   box   can
CLASS
a. container
b. trash
c. waste

I-55
clown   play   puppet
CLASS
a. comedy
b. entertainment
c. television

I-56
baseball   basketball   football
CLASS
a. court sports
b. field sports
c. sports equipment

268

HOW ARE THESE WORDS ALIKE?—SELECT

DIRECTIONS: Decide what the words in each group have in common. Circle the letter of the one answer that best describes the class of the words.

I-57
dime   nickel   penny
CLASS
a. bills
b. checks
c. coins

I-58
scale   thermometer   yardstick
CLASS
a. length
b. measuring device
c. weight

I-59
circle   oval   rectangle
CLASS
a. curves
b. points
c. shapes

I-60
rectangle   square   triangle
CLASS
a. corners
b. lines
c. polygons

269

HOW ARE THESE WORDS ALIKE?—SELECT

DIRECTIONS: Decide what the words in each group have in common. Circle the letter of the one answer that best describes the class of the words.

I-61
airplane   glider   helicopter
CLASS
a. aircraft
b. kite
c. powered craft

I-62
helicopter   jeep   motorcycle
CLASS
a. aircraft
b. car
c. vehicle

I-63
dentist   doctor   nurse
CLASS
a. factory careers
b. health careers
c. teaching careers

I-64
firefighter   mail carrier   police officer
CLASS
a. health careers
b. service careers
c. teaching careers

270

HOW ARE THESE WORDS ALIKE?—SELECT

DIRECTIONS: Decide what the words in each group have in common. Circle the letter of the one answer that best describes the class of the words.

EXAMPLE
cake   cookie   pie
CLASS
a. dessert
b. dinner
c. fruit

Dinner is not the best answer; these foods are usually eaten after dinner. Fruit is not the answer, even though these foods can be made of fruit. Dessert is the best answer because it is a term which describes all three foods.

I-65
boxer   poodle   shepherd
CLASS
a. clothing
b. dog
c. job

I-66
button   snap   zipper
CLASS
a. fastener
b. hardware
c. tool

I-67
bed   desk   table
CLASS
a. chair
b. furniture
c. kitchen

I-68
curtains   drapes   shades
CLASS
a. floor covering
b. furniture covering
c. window covering

271

HOW ARE THESE WORDS ALIKE?—SELECT

DIRECTIONS: Decide what the words in each group have in common. Circle the letter of the one answer that best describes the class of the words.

I-69
letter   poem   song
CLASS
a. things people sing
b. things people speak
c. things people write

I-70
grow   increase   swell
CLASS
a. become higher
b. become larger
c. become lighter

I-71
baby   boy   girl
CLASS
a. children
b. mother
c. student

I-72
bush   flower   tree
CLASS
a. blossom
b. plant
c. wood

I-73
blue   rose   violet
CLASS
a. bird
b. color
c. flower

I-74
decrease   reduce   shrink
CLASS
a. become colder
b. become larger
c. become smaller

272

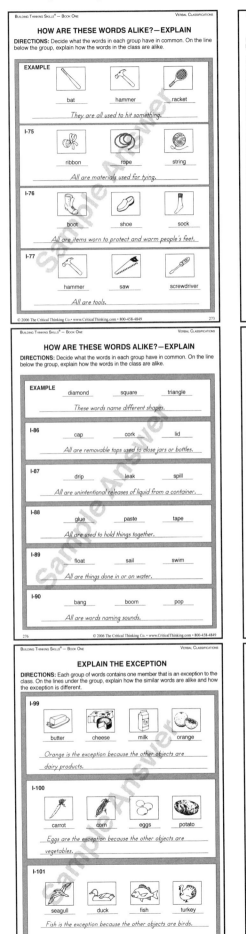

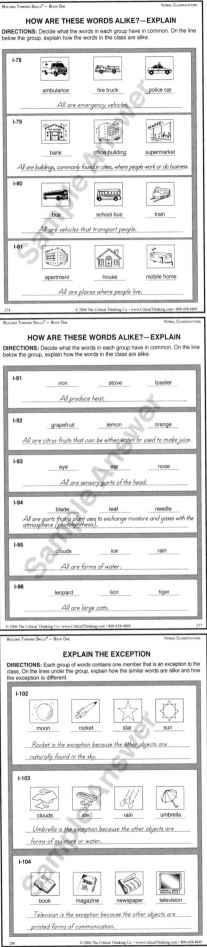

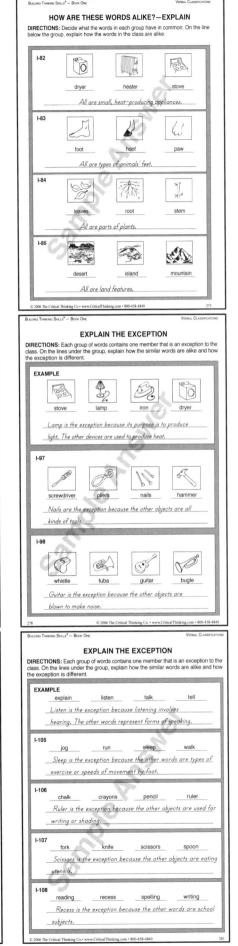

Page 273

BUILDING THINKING SKILLS® — BOOK ONE   VERBAL CLASSIFICATIONS

HOW ARE THESE WORDS ALIKE?—EXPLAIN

DIRECTIONS: Decide what the words in each group have in common. On the line below the group, explain how the words in the class are alike.

EXAMPLE
bat   hammer   racket
They are all used to hit something.

I-75
ribbon   rope   string
All are materials used for tying.

I-76
boot   shoe   sock
All are items worn to protect and warm people's feet.

I-77
hammer   saw   screwdriver
All are tools.

Page 274

HOW ARE THESE WORDS ALIKE?—EXPLAIN

DIRECTIONS: Decide what the words in each group have in common. On the line below the group, explain how the words in the class are alike.

I-78
ambulance   fire truck   police car
All are emergency vehicles.

I-79
bank   office building   supermarket
All are buildings, commonly found in cities, where people work or do business.

I-80
bus   school bus   train
All are vehicles that transport people.

I-81
apartment   house   mobile home
All are places where people live.

Page 275

HOW ARE THESE WORDS ALIKE?—EXPLAIN

DIRECTIONS: Decide what the words in each group have in common. On the line below the group, explain how the words in the class are alike.

I-82
dryer   heater   stove
All are small, heat-producing appliances.

I-83
foot   hoof   paw
All are types of animals' feet.

I-84
leaves   root   stem
All are parts of plants.

I-85
desert   island   mountain
All are land features.

Page 276

HOW ARE THESE WORDS ALIKE?—EXPLAIN

DIRECTIONS: Decide what the words in each group have in common. On the line below the group, explain how the words in the class are alike.

EXAMPLE
diamond   square   triangle
These words name different shapes.

I-86
cap   cork   lid
All are removable tops used to close jars or bottles.

I-87
drip   leak   spill
All are unintentional releases of liquid from a container.

I-88
glue   paste   tape
All are used to hold things together.

I-89
float   sail   swim
All are things done in or on water.

I-90
bang   boom   pop
All are words naming sounds.

Page 277

HOW ARE THESE WORDS ALIKE?—EXPLAIN

DIRECTIONS: Decide what the words in each group have in common. On the line below the group, explain how the words in the class are alike.

I-91
iron   stove   toaster
All produce heat.

I-92
grapefruit   lemon   orange
All are citrus fruits that can be either eaten or used to make juice.

I-93
eye   ear   nose
All are sensory parts of the head.

I-94
blade   leaf   needle
All are parts that a plant uses to exchange moisture and gases with the atmosphere (photosynthesis).

I-95
clouds   ice   rain
All are forms of water.

I-96
leopard   lion   tiger
All are large cats.

Page 278

EXPLAIN THE EXCEPTION

DIRECTIONS: Each group of words contains one member that is an exception to the class. On the lines under the group, explain how the similar words are alike and how the exception is different.

EXAMPLE
stove   lamp   iron   dryer
Lamp is the exception because its purpose is to produce light. The other devices are used to produce heat.

I-97
screwdriver   pliers   nails   hammer
Nails are the exception because the other objects are all kinds of tools.

I-98
whistle   tuba   guitar   bugle
Guitar is the exception because the other objects are blown to make noise.

Page 279

EXPLAIN THE EXCEPTION

DIRECTIONS: Each group of words contains one member that is an exception to the class. On the lines under the group, explain how the similar words are alike and how the exception is different.

I-99
butter   cheese   milk   orange
Orange is the exception because the other objects are dairy products.

I-100
carrot   corn   eggs   potato
Eggs are the exception because the other objects are vegetables.

I-101
seagull   duck   fish   turkey
Fish is the exception because the other objects are birds.

Page 280

EXPLAIN THE EXCEPTION

DIRECTIONS: Each group of words contains one member that is an exception to the class. On the lines under the group, explain how the similar words are alike and how the exception is different.

I-102
moon   rocket   star   sun
Rocket is the exception because the other objects are naturally found in the sky.

I-103
clouds   ice   rain   umbrella
Umbrella is the exception because the other objects are forms of moisture or water.

I-104
book   magazine   newspaper   television
Television is the exception because the other objects are printed forms of communication.

Page 281

EXPLAIN THE EXCEPTION

DIRECTIONS: Each group of words contains one member that is an exception to the class. On the lines under the group, explain how the similar words are alike and how the exception is different.

EXAMPLE
explain   listen   talk   tell
Listen is the exception because listening involves hearing. The other words represent forms of speaking.

I-105
jog   run   sleep   walk
Sleep is the exception because the other words are types of exercise or speeds of movement by foot.

I-106
chalk   crayons   pencil   ruler
Ruler is the exception because the other objects are used for writing or shading.

I-107
fork   knife   scissors   spoon
Scissors is the exception because the other objects are eating utensils.

I-108
reading   recess   spelling   writing
Recess is the exception because the other words are school subjects.

EXPLAIN THE EXCEPTION

DIRECTIONS: Each group of words contains one member that is an exception to the class. On the lines under the group, explain how the similar words are alike and how the exception is different.

I-109

color   draw   paint   write

Write is the exception because the other words are art processes.

I-110

few   many   none   some

None is the exception because the other words represent multiple members.

I-111

banana   grapefruit   lemon   orange

Banana is the exception because the other objects are citrus fruits.

I-112

bicycle   helicopter   jeep   motorcycle

Bicycle is the exception because the other objects are motorized vehicles.

I-113

chew   cook   drink   eat

Cook is the exception because the other words are methods of food consumption.

PICTURE DICTIONARY—SORTING INTO CLASSES

DIRECTIONS: Each picture is labeled with a place name. Sort the names into three groups by writing each place name in the appropriate column on the chart.

I-114

apartment, barber shop, farm, fire station, gas station, hospital, house, mobile home, police station, post office, restaurant, supermarket

PLACES WHERE PEOPLE

BUY THINGS	LIVE	GET SERVICES
gas station post office restaurant supermarket	apartment farm house mobile home	barber shop fire station gas station hospital police station post office supermarket

PICTURE DICTIONARY—SORTING INTO CLASSES

DIRECTIONS: Using the picture dictionary on the next two pages, sort the animals in on each chart below.

I-115

ANIMALS THAT
FLOAT/SWIM IN WATER

frog, jellyfish, snake (some), shark, whale

ANIMALS THAT
MOVE ON LAND

deer, duck, frog, kangaroo, lion, lizard, monkey, mouse, ostrich, snail, snake, spider, squirrel

PICTURE DICTIONARY—SORTING INTO CLASSES

DIRECTIONS: Use the words from the picture dictionary to fill in the charts on page 284.

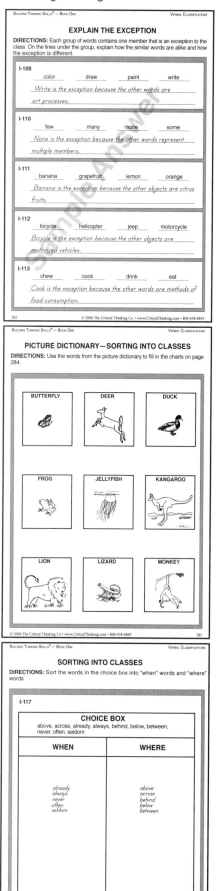

BUTTERFLY, DEER, DUCK, FROG, JELLYFISH, KANGAROO, LION, LIZARD, MONKEY

PICTURE DICTIONARY—SORTING INTO CLASSES

DIRECTIONS: Use the words from the picture dictionary to fill in the charts on page 284.

MOUSE, OSTRICH, OWL, SHARK, SNAIL, SNAKE, SPIDER, SQUIRREL, WHALE

SORTING INTO CLASSES

DIRECTIONS: Sort the words in the choice box into "happy" words and "sad" words.

I-116

CHOICE BOX
bright, cheerful, crying, glad, gloomy, grumpy, jolly, joyous, merry, upset

HAPPY WORDS	SAD WORDS
bright cheerful glad jolly joyous merry	crying gloomy grumpy upset

SORTING INTO CLASSES

DIRECTIONS: Sort the words in the choice box into "when" words and "where" words.

I-117

CHOICE BOX
above, across, already, always, behind, below, between, never, often, seldom

WHEN	WHERE
already always never often seldom	above across behind below between

PICTURE DICTIONARY—SORTING INTO CLASSES

DIRECTIONS: Use the words in the picture dictionary on page 290. Some words may be used more than once. Sort the words into the following four classes or groups.

I-118

MAKE MUSIC	ARE USED FOR INFORMATION	ARE USED FOR ENTERTAINMENT	WE RIDE ON
drum horn piano	letter newspaper laptop computer telephone television	baseball (bike) (boat) circus (horse) (jeep) (motorcycle) (piano) play puppet laptop computer (sled) (swing) television	airplane bike boat bus helicopter horse jeep motorcycle ship sled swing train

PICTURE DICTIONARY—SORTING INTO CLASSES

DIRECTIONS: Use the words from the picture dictionary to fill in the chart on page 289.

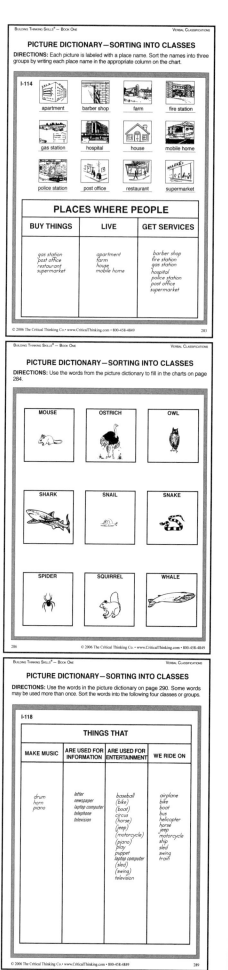

airplane, baseball, bike, boat, bus, circus, drum, helicopter, horn, horse, jeep, letter, motorcycle, newspaper, piano, play, puppet, radio, ship, sled, swing, telephone, television, train

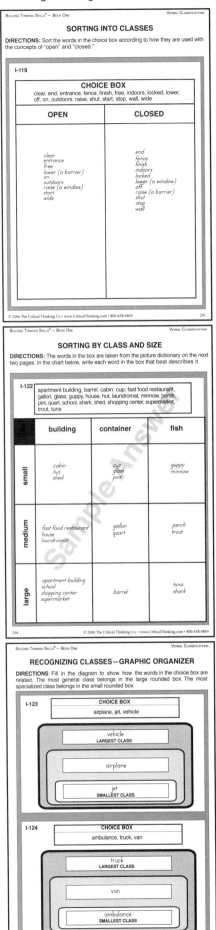

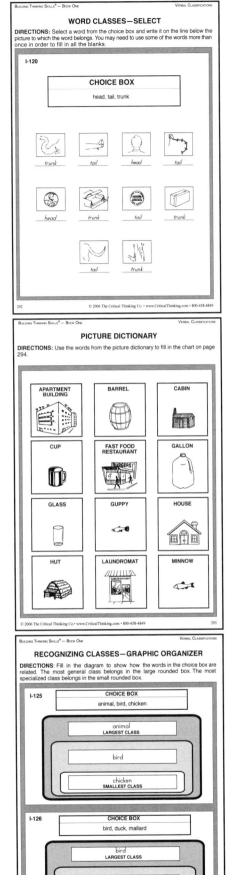

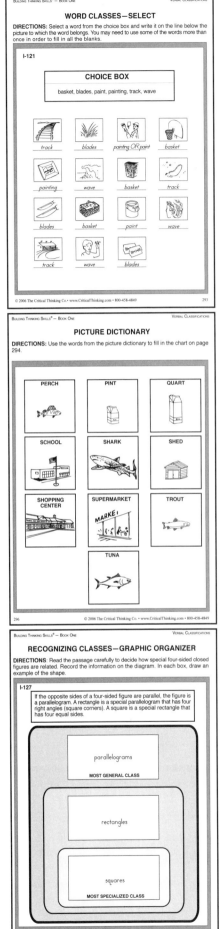

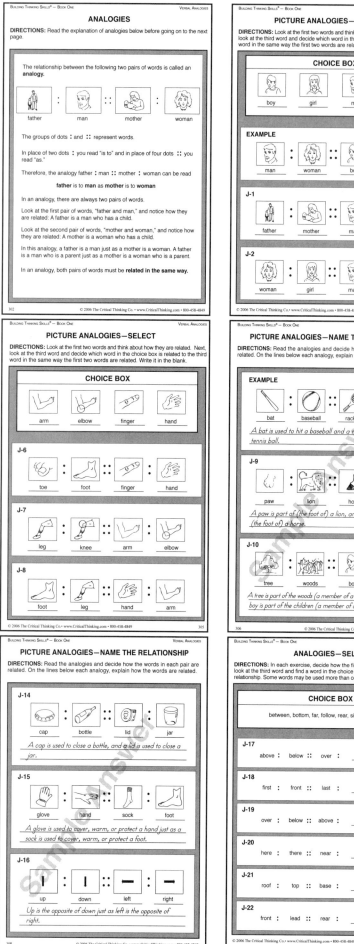

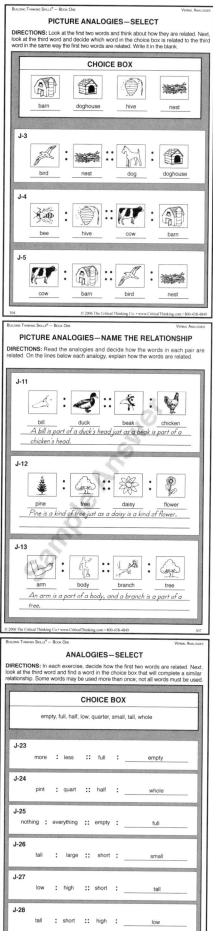

ANALOGIES—SELECT

BUILDING THINKING SKILLS® — BOOK ONE   VERBAL ANALOGIES

DIRECTIONS: In each exercise, decide how the first two words are related. Next, look at the third word and find a word in the choice box that will complete a similar relationship. Some words may be used more than once; not all words must be used.

CHOICE BOX

after, now, often, past, present, today, tomorrow, yesterday

J-29

today : present :: yesterday : _____ past _____

J-30

then : now :: past : _____ present _____

J-31

before : now :: yesterday : _____ today _____

J-32

today : yesterday :: present : _____ past _____

J-33

rarely : frequently :: seldom : _____ often _____

J-34

yesterday : before :: tomorrow : _____ after _____

ANALOGIES—SELECT

DIRECTIONS: In each exercise, decide how the first two words are related. Next, look at the third word and find a word in the choice box that will complete a similar relationship. Some words may be used more than once; not all words must be used.

CHOICE BOX

bird, cat, cow, deer, fish, horse, lion

J-35

puppy : dog :: colt : _____ horse _____

J-36

antlers : deer :: mane : _____ lion OR horse _____

J-37

meow : cat :: roar : _____ lion _____

J-38

swim : fish :: fly : _____ bird _____

J-39

fur : cat :: scales : _____ fish _____

J-40

mare : horse :: doe : _____ deer _____

ANALOGIES—SELECT

DIRECTIONS: In each exercise, decide how the first two words are related. Next, look at the third word and find a word in the choice box that will complete a similar relationship. Some words may be used more than once; not all words must be used.

CHOICE BOX

day, minute, month, week, year

J-41

minute : second :: hour : _____ minute _____

J-42

day : week :: week : _____ month OR year _____

J-43

hour : day :: month : _____ year _____

J-44

week : day :: month : _____ week OR day _____

J-45

century : year :: month : _____ day OR week _____

J-46

minute : hour :: second : _____ minute _____

ANALOGIES—SELECT

DIRECTIONS: In each exercise, decide how the first two words are related. Next, look at the third word and find a word in the choice box that will complete a similar relationship. Some words may be used more than once; not all words must be used.

CHOICE BOX

heat, light, odor, sound

J-47

eye : light :: ear : _____ sound _____

J-48

hear : sound :: feel : _____ heat _____

J-49

fire : heat :: speaker : _____ sound _____

J-50

lamp : light :: furnace : _____ heat _____

J-51

eye : light :: nose : _____ odor _____

J-52

hear : sound :: see : _____ light _____

ANALOGIES—SELECT

DIRECTIONS: In each exercise, decide how the first two words are related. Next, look at the third word and find a word in the choice box that will complete a similar relationship. Some words may be used more than once; not all words must be used.

CHOICE BOX

cup, gallon, pint, quart
(Note: 2 cups = 1 pint; 2 pints = 1 quart; 4 quarts = 1 gallon)

J-53

two pints : quart :: four quarts : _____ gallon _____

J-54

two quarts : gallon :: pint : _____ quart _____

J-55

gallon : quart :: half-gallon : _____ pint _____

J-56

pint : cup :: quart : _____ pint _____

J-57

gallon : quart :: quart : _____ cup _____

J-58

half-pint : cup :: two pints : _____ quart _____

ANALOGIES—SELECT

DIRECTIONS: In each exercise, decide how the first two words are related. Next, look at the third word and find a word in the list at right that will complete a similar relationship.

EXAMPLE

in : out :: down : _____ *up* _____

outside
over
under
up

J-59

read : book :: listen : _____ *radio* _____

magazine
newspaper
radio
picture

J-60

knife : cut :: hammer : _____ *pound* _____

handle
picture
pound
slice

J-61

silo : grain :: tank : _____ *water* _____

brick
metal
water
wood

ANALOGIES—SELECT

DIRECTIONS: In each exercise, decide how the first two words are related. Next, look at the third word and find a word in the list at right that will complete a similar relationship.

J-62

this : that :: these : _____ *those* _____

here
them
those
there

J-63

hot dog : sausage :: orange : _____ *fruit* _____

blossom
cherry
fruit
sandwich

J-64

read : poem :: sing : _____ *song* _____

song
talk
whisper
word

J-65

swim : water :: fly : _____ *air* _____

air
land
ocean
sea

ANALOGIES—SELECT

DIRECTIONS: In each exercise, decide how the first two words are related. Next, look at the third word and find a word in the list at right that will complete a similar relationship.

J-66

buy : sell :: take : _____ *give* _____

bought
give
have
save

J-67

here : there :: this : _____ *that* _____

that
them
these
those

J-68

come : go :: enter : _____ *leave* _____

bring
give
have
leave

J-69

car : garage :: tractor : _____ *barn* _____

barn
cow
field
plow

ANALOGIES—SELECT

DIRECTIONS: In each exercise, decide how the first two words are related. Next, look at the third word and find a word in the list at right that will complete a similar relationship.

J-70

nose : smell :: tongue : _____ *taste* _____

feel
see
taste
touch

J-71

mower : lawn :: saw : _____ *wood* _____

blade
handle
nail
wood

J-72

overpass : highway :: bridge : _____ *river* _____

cards
rail
river
train

J-73

breakfast : lunch :: lunch : _____ *supper* _____

eating
food
supper
vegetables

ANALOGIES—SUPPLY

DIRECTIONS: In each exercise, decide how the first two words are related. Next, look at the third word and pick a word from your memory that belongs in the blank. In this exercise, all the words have to do with things you wear.

J-74

shoe : sock :: jacket : *shirt OR blouse OR sweater*

J-75

button : shirt :: lace or string : *shoe OR boot OR sneaker*

J-76

bracelet : arm :: ring : *finger*

J-77

shoe : foot :: glove : *hand*

J-78

scarf : neck :: hat : *head*

J-79

pants : legs :: sweater : *arms*

ANALOGIES—SUPPLY

DIRECTIONS: In each exercise, decide how the first two words are related. Next, look at the third word and pick a word from your memory that belongs in the blank.

J-80

above : below :: ceiling : *floor*

J-81

outside : inside :: porch : *room*

J-82

door : wood :: window : *glass*

J-83

above : ceiling :: side : *walls*

J-84

shingles : roof :: rug : *floor*

J-85

chimney : roof :: window : *wall*

ANALOGIES—SUPPLY

DIRECTIONS: In each exercise, decide how the first two words are related. Next, look at the third word and pick a word from your memory that belongs in the blank.

J-86

cool : cold :: warm : *hot*

J-87

iron : heavy :: feathers : *light*

J-88

penny : coin :: dollar : *bill OR currency*

J-89

rabbit : fast :: turtle : *slow*

J-90

lid : eye :: shade : *window*

J-91

soldier : army :: sailor : *navy*

ANALOGIES—SUPPLY

DIRECTIONS: In each exercise, decide how the first two words are related. Next, look at the third word and pick a word from your memory that belongs in the blank.

J-92

tan : brown :: pink : *red*

J-93

handlebar : bicycle :: steering wheel : *car OR truck*

J-94

over : above :: under : *below*

J-95

front : first :: rear : *last*

J-96

sky : air :: lake : *water*

J-97

knife : slice :: scissors : *cut*

ANALOGIES—SUPPLY

DIRECTIONS: In each exercise, decide how the first two words are related. Next, look at the third word and pick a word from your memory that belongs in the blank.

J-98

red : stop :: green : *go*

J-99

fast : slow :: run : *walk*

J-100

side : wall :: bottom : *floor*

J-101

enter : come :: leave : *go*

J-102

cotton : soft :: steel : *hard*

J-103

bottle : cap :: pan : *lid*

ANALOGIES—SUPPLY

DIRECTIONS: In each exercise, decide how the first two words are related. Next, look at the third word and pick a word from your memory that belongs in the blank.

J-104

late : last :: early : *first*

J-105

last : first :: least : *most*

J-106

rain : spring :: snow : *winter*

J-107

book : read :: pencil : *write*

J-108

freeze : refrigerator :: boil : *stove*

J-109

boil : pot :: fry : *skillet OR pan*

ANALOGIES—SELECT THE RIGHT PAIR

DIRECTIONS: In each exercise, decide how the first two words are related. Next, look at the pairs of words in the list at right; find the pair with a similar relationship. Fill in the blanks to complete the analogy.

J-110

below : under ::

above : _over_

above : behind
above : over
between : over
beneath : over

J-111

dog : puppy ::

cat : _kitten_

calf : cow
cat : kitten
child : adult
colt : horse

J-112

now : then ::

present : _past_

give : take
here : there
present : past
this : that

J-113

true : false ::

right : _wrong_

lie : wrong
love : promise
right : answer
right : wrong

ANALOGIES—SELECT THE RIGHT PAIR

DIRECTIONS: In each exercise, decide how the first two words are related. Next, look at the pairs of words in the list at right; find the pair with a similar relationship. Fill in the blanks to complete the analogy.

J-114

up : down ::

over : _under_

below : under
beneath : under
over : under
over : upper

J-115

more : less ::

plus : _minus_

always : often
much : more
now : then
plus : minus

J-116

mother : child ::

parent : _baby_

brother : sister
girl : boy
parent : baby
son : mother

J-117

slow : fast ::

seldom : _often_

always : often
minus : less
much : more
seldom : often

Having finished this book, we recommend you consider *Building Thinking Skills*® Level 2 and these other award-winning products.

| Grade 2 | Grade 3 | Grade 4 | Grade 5 |

Mathematical Reasoning™ (PreK-Grade 5)

These books teach the mathematical concepts and skills students are expected to know per grade level. They also introduce several skills and concepts normally taught in the next grade level. *Mathematical Reasoning*™ helps students devise strategies to solve a wide variety of math problems. These books emphasize problem solving and computation to build the math reasoning skills necessary for success in higher level math and math assessments. All books are written to the standards of the National Council of Teachers of Mathematics. Beginning through Level F are complete curriculums for their grade levels.

These highly-effective activities take students far beyond drill-and-practice by using step-by-step, discussion-based problem solving to develop a conceptual bridge between computation and the reasoning required for upper-level math. Activities and units spiral slowly, allowing students to become comfortable with concepts but also challenging them to continue building their math skills.

AWARDS

CONTENTS	Gr. 2 Level C	Gr. 3 Level D	Gr. 4 Level E	Gr. 5 Level F
Action	x			
Addends	x	x	x	x
Addition	x	x	x	x
Age	x	x	x	x
Analyze Data	x	x	x	x
Angles		x	x	x
Area		x	x	x
Bar Graph	x	x	x	x
Calendar	x	x	x	x
Capacity	x	x	x	x
Characteristics			x	x
Circle Graphs	x	x	x	x
Coins	x	x	x	x
Congruence	x	x	x	x
Coordinates	x	x	x	x
Count	x	x	x	x
Data Analysis			x	x
Data Collection		x	x	x
Decimals		x	x	x
Division	x	x	x	x
Equations		x	x	x
Equivalence		x	x	x
Estimate	x	x	x	x
Expanded Notation	x	x		x
Fractions	x	x	x	x
Graphs	x	x	x	x
Inequalities	x	x	x	x
Language	x	x	x	x
Length	x	x	x	x
Manipulative	x			
Match	x	x	x	x
Mean			x	x
Median			x	x
Mode			x	
Money	x	x	x	x
Multiplication	x	x	x	x
Negative Numbers			x	x
Number Lines	x	x	x	x
Odd/Even	x	x	x	x
Order	x	x	x	x
Parallel		x	x	x
Patterns	x	x	x	x
Percent				x
Perimeter	x	x	x	x
Perpendicular	x		x	x
Place Value	x	x	x	x
Prediction	x	x	x	x
Prime/Composite			x	x
Probability	x	x	x	x
Properties			x	x
Real World Problems	x	x	x	x
Reflection/Translation/Reflection		x	x	x
Regrouping	x	x	x	x
Rounding	x	x	x	x
Rulers	x	x	x	x
Shapes	x	x	x	x
Subtraction	x	x	x	x
Survey	x	x	x	x
Symmetry	x	x	x	x
Tables	x	x	x	x
Temperature				x
Time	x	x	x	x
Variables	x	x	x	x
Volume				x
Weight	x	x	x	x
Whole Numbers	x	x	x	x
Word Problems		x	x	x

Grade 1

Grade 3

Language Smarts™ (Grades 1-3)

These books teach the language arts concepts and skills students are expected to know in each grade. They also introduce several skills and concepts normally taught in the next grade. These fun, mind-building books teach standards-based language arts and develop critical thinking skills. *Language Smarts™* can serve as a core curriculum for language arts or as a supplemental resource. Empower your child's mind as vocabulary, grammar, punctuation, reading, and writing skills improve.

Teaching and practicing language arts skills and concepts has never been easier! No lesson preparation needed! Each section introduces a specific topic, followed by appropriate practice and application activities. These engaging and colorful lessons develop critical thinking and language arts skills through a variety of activities and different genres.

Grade 2

CONTENTS	Gr. 1 Level B	Gr. 2 Level C	Gr. 3 Level D
Capitalization	x	x	x
Critical Thinking	x	x	x
Cause and Effect	x	x	x
Compare/Contrast	x	x	x
Deductive Reasoning	x	x	
Facts and Inferences	x	x	x
Imply/Infer			x
Inference			x
Opinion		x	x
Prediction	x	x	x
Adjectives		x	x
Adverbs		x	x
Antonyms	x	x	x
Articles	x	x	x
Conjunctions			x
Contractions	x	x	x
Friendly Letters		x	
Nouns	x	x	x
Prepositions			x
Pronouns	x	x	x
Sentences	x	x	x
Subject and Predicate	x	x	x
Subject-Verb Agreement	x	x	x
Synonyms	x	x	x
Verb Tenses	x	x	x
Grammar	x	x	x
Punctuation	x	x	x
Apostrophes	x	x	x
Colons			x
Commas	x	x	x
Exclamation Marks	x	x	x
Periods	x	x	x
Question Marks	x	x	x
Quotation Marks		x	x
Semicolons			x
Spelling	x	x	x
Alphabet	x		
Alphabetizing		x	x
Compound Words	x	x	x
Consonants	x	x	x
High Frequency Words	x	x	x
Prefixes, Suffixes, Roots		x	x
Silent E	x		x
Singular/Plural	x	x	x
Syllables	x		x
Letters	x		
Vowels	x	x	x
Word Families	x	x	x
Word Patterns	x		

CONTENTS (Cont.)	Gr. 1 Level B	Gr. 2 Level C	Gr. 3 Level D
Usage	x	x	x
Am, Is, and Are	x	x	
Categorizing	x	x	x
Comparing	x	x	x
Double Negatives	x		
Farther/Further			x
Good and Well			x
Homographs	x	x	x
Homophones	x	x	x
I, Me, and Myself	x	x	x
Less/Fewer			x
Metaphors			x
Ordering	x	x	x
Sequencing	x	x	x
Similes			x
Then/Than			x
Was and Were	x		
Writing Directions		x	
Writing	x	x	x
Characters	x	x	x
Comparing	x	x	x
Conflict		x	
Context Clues	x	x	x
Dewey Decimal System			x
Editing		x	x
Fiction and Nonfiction	x	x	x
Folktales		x	
Following Directions	x	x	
Number Word Expressions	x	x	x
Parts of a Book		x	
Plot			x
Poems	x	x	
Real and Make Believe		x	x
Reference Materials		x	x
Rhymes	x	x	
Riddles	x	x	
Setting	x	x	x
Story Maps			x
Table of Contents		x	x
Titles			x
Topic and Main Idea	x	x	x
Using a Dictionary		x	
Using a Glossary		x	
Using the Library			x
Writing a Research Paper			x

AWARDS

Grades 2-3

Grades 3-4

Grades 4-5

Editor in Chief® (Grades 2-12+)

These books improve students grammar, punctuation, spelling, capitalization, and attention to detail using a standards-based thinking approach rather than drill and practice. This effective method teaches students to carefully analyze and edit stories that contain errors in writing mechanics and story details.

Books or Software?

Choose one, the other, or both for maximum benefit (for example, A1 book and A2 software or vice versa). Whichever you choose, you can't go wrong!

Editor in Chief® Beginning 1 Sample Activity

Review Lessons 1-8

Read the paragraphs and correct the errors. Then write the contractions.

65. The Most Traveled Insect

Monarch butterflies travel every year from North america to get away from the cold winters. They fly 2,500 miles to Mexico, farther than any other insect Monarchs ate the milkweed plant. There's an toxin in the plant that the caterpillars eat to keep enemies like frogs, birds, mouses, and lizards far away.

①	Capitalization
①	Punctuation
①	An/A
①	Verb Tense
①	Singular/Plural

66. Lice-B-Gone

Lice are tiny insects that live in animal fur and human hair. When they nibble on a scalp, it itched. This does not feels very good. Lice they can be hard to get rid of. They like to share and will happily go to other scalps nearby. Several special shampoos is used to kill them.

①	Contraction
① ②	Verb Tense
①	Noun/Pronoun
①	Am/Is/Are

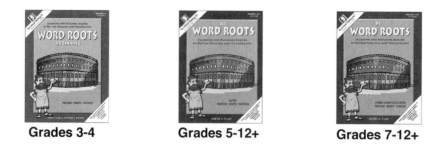

Grades 3-4   **Grades 5-12+**   **Grades 7-12+**

Word Roots (Grades 3-12+)

These books teach students the meanings of Latin and Greek prefixes, roots, and suffixes commonly used in English. Learning word elements dramatically improves spelling and the ability to decode unfamiliar words. *Word Roots* will add hundreds of words to your students' vocabulary and greater depth to their thinking and writing.

The books include a pretest/posttest, answers, and a dictionary of words derived from Latin or Latin/Greek roots. The software includes help and hints, automatic grading, and printable scores.

Books or Software?

Choose one or the other. Whichever you choose, you can't go wrong.

——————————— *Word Roots Beginning* **Sample Activity** ———————————

Lesson 1–Roots

Prefix	Meaning
peri-	around, surrounding

Root	Meaning
micro	small
scope	look at, examine
tele	distance, from afar

Plants are not the only things that grow from roots...so do words!

For example, let's start with the root, **scope**, meaning look at or examine. Other roots or word parts can be added to this root to grow new words.

Often, when a word ends with a root, an **e** or a **y** is added at the end, as in the words *telephone* and *euphony*. This added letter doesn't change the actual meaning of the word. It is used to complete the word.

Some roots can stand on their own as a word. An example of this is the root **meter**, which means measure. By adding beginnings (prefixes) or endings (suffixes) to roots, you form different words—with different meanings!

In the words on the following page, we have used the prefix **peri-** and the roots **micro**, **scope**, and **tele** to form words.

Lesson 1—Roots

Activity A
Draw a line from each word to the picture which shows its meaning.

periscope

microscope

telescope

Activity B
Underline the prefixes and circle the roots in the choice box below. Then write the correct word at the end of its matching definition.

> periscope   microscope   telescope

1. Attached to a submarine under water, this sticks up to look for other boats: _____

2. This helps see things that are far away, such as a bird high in a tree or the moon: _____

3. Even the hairs on a fly's leg can be seen closely with this: _____

Activity C
Some roots can go together to form new words.

    ROOT +   ROOT   +   SUFFIX   =   NEW WORD

Example

hydro*	+	**phob**	+	**-ia**	=	hydrophobia
(water)	+	(fear of)	+	(condition)	=	(fear of water)

> 💡 When animals have hydrophobia, better known as rabies, they have a terrifying fear of water.

| PreK-K | Grades 1-2 | Grades 3-6 | Grades 7-12+ |

Mind Benders® (PreK-12+)

These books our best-selling deductive thinking puzzles, develop the logic, reading comprehension, and mental organizational skills vital to achieving high grades and top test scores in all subjects. They're also great for developing real-life, problem-solving skills.

Your child will carefully analyze each *Mind Benders®* story and its clues, identifying logical associations between people, places, and things. The key is to start with the most obvious associations, then deduce less obvious associations until everything finally fits together.

Books and software both include step-by-step instructions and detailed answers. Levels spiral in difficulty within grade range. The software also includes many other features that allow your child to play and learn with little or no parent time required.

─────────────── *Mind Benders®* Book 3 Sample Activity ───────────────

Name the Animals

A cat, a small dog, a goat, and a horse are named Angel, Beauty, King, and Rover. Read the clues to find each animal's name.

1. King is smaller than both the dog and Rover.
2. The horse is younger than Angel.
3. Beauty is the oldest and is a good friend of the dog.

	Angel	Beauty	King	Rover
cat				
dog				
goat				
horse				